CAKES

& CAKE DECORATING, STEP-BY-STEP

CAKES

& CAKE DECORATING, STEP-BY-STEP

The complete practical guide to decorating with sugarpaste, icing
and frosting, with 200 beautiful cakes for every kind of occasion,
shown in over 1500 fabulous easy-to-follow colour photographs

Angela Nilsen, Sarah Maxwell & Janice Murfitt

LORENZ BOOKS

This edition published by Lorenz Books, an imprint of Anness Publishing Ltd
Hermes House, 88–89 Blackfriars Road, London SE1 8HA
tel. 020 7401 2077; fax 020 7633 9499

www.lorenzbooks.com; www.annesspublishing.com

If you like the images in this book and would like to investigate using them for publishing, promotions or advertising, please visit our
website www.practicalpictures.com for more information.

UK agent: The Manning Partnership Ltd; tel. 01225 478444;
fax 01225 478440; sales@manning-partnership.co.uk
UK distributor: Book Trade Services; tel. 0116 2759086;
fax 0116 2759090; uksales@booktradeservices.com;
exportsales@booktradeservices.com
North American agent/distributor: National Book Network;
tel. 301 459 3366; fax 301 429 5746; www.nbnbooks.com
Australian agent/distributor: Pan Macmillan Australia; tel. 1300
135 113; fax 1300 135 103; customer.service@macmillan.com.au
New Zealand agent/distributor: David Bateman Ltd; tel. (09) 415
7664; fax (09) 415 8892

Publisher: Joanna Lorenz
Project Editor: Felicity Forster
Recipes by: Catherine Atkinson, Carla Capalbo, Carole Clements,
Christine France, Sarah Gates, Carole Handslip, Patricia Lousada,
Sue Maggs, Sarah Maxwell, Janice Murfitt, Angela Nilsen, Louise
Pickford, Laura Washburn, Elizabeth Wolf-Cohen
Photographers: Karl Adamson, Edward Allwright, David
Armstrong, Steve Baxter, James Duncan, Amanda Heywood,
Tim Hill, Don Last
Editor: Beverley Jollands
Typesetter: Diane Pullen
Designer: Axis Design; Cover Designer: Jonathan Davison
Indexer: Dawn Butcher
Editorial Reader: Jan Cutler
Production Controller: Lee Sargent

ETHICAL TRADING POLICY

Because of our ongoing ecological investment programme, you, as
our customer, can have the pleasure and reassurance of knowing
that a tree is being cultivated on your behalf to naturally replace
the materials used to make the book you are holding. For further
information about this scheme, go to
www.annesspublishing.com/trees

Previously published as *Practical Encyclopedia
of Cakes & Cake Decorating*

Main front cover image shows Death by Chocolate –
for recipe, see page 268.

Notes

For all recipes, quantities are given in both metric and imperial
measures and, where appropriate, measures are also given in
standard cups and spoons. Follow one set, but not a mixture
because they are not interchangeable.
Standard spoon and cup measures are level. 1 tsp = 5ml,
1 tbsp = 15ml, 1 cup = 250ml/8fl oz
Australian standard tablespoons are 20ml. Australian readers
should use 3 tsp in place of 1 tbsp for measuring small quantities
of gelatine, flour, salt etc.
Medium (US large) eggs are used unless otherwise stated.

PUBLISHER'S NOTE

Although the advice and information in this book are believed to
be accurate and true at the time of going to press, neither the
authors nor the publisher can accept any legal responsibility or
liability for any errors or omissions that may be made.

Contents

Introduction

This book is not only an invaluable foundation course in cake-decorating techniques, but also a wonderful reference book for a host of tried-and-tested recipes for classic cake bases and icings, as well as inspirational cake projects, which you will use again and again.

Clearly structured, the decorating course leads you through all the different decorating techniques which can be applied to marzipan, sugarpaste, royal icing, chocolate and other icings. There are basic recipes for sponge cakes, Swiss rolls, Madeira cakes, fruit cakes and truffle cakes, with step-by-step instructions and photographs for piping, crimping, embossing, frills, plaques, colouring, run-outs, modelling, stencilling, flowers, as well as using purchased decorations such as sweet confections, ribbons and fresh flowers.

The wonderful decorated cakes featured in this book are a feast for the eye and palate. Follow the detailed illustrated step-by-step guides to perfect cake making and decorating to create a host of varied finishes, from the simple to the lavish.

Using this book

Within each recipe, three sets of equivalent measurements have been provided in the following order: metric, imperial and cups. Never mix the different measurements within a recipe. For best results, use eggs at room temperature. Sift flour from a fair height, to give it a chance to aerate and lighten.

No two ovens are alike. If possible, buy a reliable oven thermometer and test the temperature of your oven. Bake in the centre of the oven where the heat is more likely to be constant. For fan-assisted ovens, follow the manufacturer's guidelines. Good-quality cake tins will also improve results, as they conduct heat more efficiently.

There are some current health concerns about the use of raw egg in uncooked recipes. Home-made royal icing, marzipan and sugarpaste icing do include raw egg. An alternative recipe for royal icing, using pure albumen powder, has been provided in light of this. If you prefer to avoid raw egg, do buy ready-made marzipan and sugarpaste.

Follow these simple guidelines and baking success is yours.

$\mathcal{B}$asic Cake Recipes

$\mathcal{C}$akes are the highlight of many celebrations. What birthday would be complete without a cake with candles to blow out, or a wedding without a beautiful cake to cut? Some of the most traditional cake recipes provide the best bases for decorating. Recipes can be found in this chapter, and are used as bases for the decorated cakes later in the book. None of the cakes involve complicated techniques, and several are as simple as putting the ingredients into a bowl, and mixing them together.

Fruit cake is one of our most popular special occasion cakes. Among its advantages is that it keeps really well and in fact improves with storage, so it can be baked well ahead of time and decorated in easy stages. It also provides a wonderfully firm base for all sorts of elegant or novelty decorations. There are other ideas, too, for those who prefer a less rich tasting cake, such as the Madeira or a light fruit cake, as well as a quick-mix sponge for those last-minute, spontaneous celebrations.

Baking Equipment

A selection of basic equipment is needed for cake making. Here are a few of the more necessary items:

Scales For good, consistent results, ingredients for cake making require precise measuring. An accurate set of scales is therefore essential.

Bowls Various sizes of glass or china heatproof bowls with rounded sides make mixing easier and are useful when baking.

Measuring Jug Whether you are working in imperial, metric or cup measurements, a glass measuring jug is easy to read and means liquids are calculated accurately.

Measuring Spoons These are available in a standard size, making the measuring of small amounts more accurate.

Sieves These are used to aerate flour, making cakes lighter, and to remove lumps from icing sugar.

Electric Whisks These whisks are particularly useful for beating egg whites for Swiss rolls.

Balloon Whisks Useful for beating smaller amounts of either egg or cream mixtures.

Greaseproof Paper Used to line cake tins to prevent cakes from sticking.

Wooden and Metal Spoons Wooden spoons in various sizes are essential for beating mixtures together when not using an electric mixer, while metal spoons are necessary for folding in ingredients and for smoothing over mixtures to give a flat surface before baking.

Spatulas Because they are so pliable, plastic spatulas are particularly useful for scraping all the cake mixture from a bowl.

Cake Tins These are available in all shapes and sizes, and the thicker the metal the less likely the cake will be to overcook. Most cake icing specialists hire out cake tins, useful when very large or unusual shaped tins are required.

Oven Gloves Essential when removing anything hot from the oven. It is worth choosing a good quality, well lined pair of gloves.

Wire Racks Made from wire mesh, these are available in different sizes and shapes and allow cakes to 'breathe' as they cool.

Cake Boards Choose the shape and size to fit the cake. Thick boards are for large, heavy cakes, royal iced cakes and any other fruit cake coated in icing. The board should be 5 cm/2 inches larger than the size of the cake. Thinner boards are for small Madeira cakes and other lighter cakes covered with icings such as butter, glacé or fudge. These can be about 2.5 cm/1 inch larger than the cake size.

1 *glass mixing bowls*
2 *balloon whisk*
3 *large round cake tin*
4 *electric hand mixer*
5 *small round cake tin*
6 *scales*
7 *large square cake tin*
8 *measuring jug*
9 *measuring spoons*
10 *cake boards*
11 *pastry brush*
12 *pre-cut greaseproof paper tin liners*
13 *scissors*
14 *wooden mixing spoons*
15 *wire rack*
16 *sieve*
17 *oven gloves*
18 *plastic spatula*
19 *metal spoon*

LINING CAKE TINS

Greaseproof paper is normally used for lining cake tins. The paper lining prevents the cakes from sticking to the tins and makes them easier to turn out. Different cake recipes require slightly different techniques of lining, depending on the shape of the tin, the type of cake mixture, and how long the cake needs to cook. Quick-mix sponge cakes require only one layer of paper to line the base, for example, whereas rich fruit cakes that often bake for several hours if they are large in size need to be lined with a double layer of paper on the base and sides. This extra protection also helps cakes to cook evenly.

Lining a shallow round tin

This technique is used for a quick-mix sponge cake.

1 Put the tin on a piece of greaseproof paper and draw around the base of the tin. Cut out the circle just inside the marked line.

2 ▲ Lightly brush the inside of the tin with a little vegetable oil and position the paper circle in the base of the tin. Brush the paper with a little more vegetable oil.

Tip

Softened butter or margarine can be used as a greasing agent in place of vegetable oil, if wished.

Lining a Swiss roll tin

1 Put the tin on a piece of greaseproof paper and draw around the base. Increase the rectangle by 2.5 cm/1 inch on all sides. Cut out this rectangle and snip each corner diagonally down to the original rectangle.

2 ▲ Lightly brush the inside of the tin with a little vegetable oil and fit the paper into the tin, overlapping the corners slightly so that they fit neatly. Brush the paper with a little more vegetable oil.

Lining a deep round cake tin

This technique should be used for all rich or light fruit cakes and Madeira cakes. Use this method for a square tin, but cut out the sides separately.

1 Put the tin on a double thickness of greaseproof paper and draw around the base. Cut out just inside the line.

2 For the sides of the tin, cut out a double thickness strip of greaseproof paper that will wrap around the outside of the tin, allowing a slight overlap, and which is 2.5 cm/1 inch taller than the depth of the tin.

3 Fold over 2.5 cm/1 inch along the length of the side lining. Snip the paper along its length, inside the fold, at short intervals.

4 Brush the inside of the tin with vegetable oil. Slip the side lining into the tin so the snipped edge fits into the curve of the base and sits flat.

5 ▲ Position the base lining in the tin and brush the paper with a little more vegetable oil.

Testing cakes

• Always check the cake 5–10 minutes before the given cooking time is completed, just in case the oven is a little fast. It is always better to undercook a cake slightly, since the mixture continues to cook in the tin after removing it from the oven.
• Always test the cake immediately before removing it from the oven, just in case it is not ready at the advised time. This could be due to a slow oven.

• For all cakes, other than fruit cakes, test by pressing very lightly on the centre of the cake with the fingers; if it springs back, the cake is cooked. Otherwise your fingers will leave a slight depression, indicating the cake needs extra cooking time. Retest at 5-minute intervals.

• Fruit cakes are best tested using a warmed skewer inserted into the centre of the cake. If the skewer comes out clean, the cake is ready. Otherwise return the cake to the oven and retest at 10-minute intervals.

Storing cakes

Everyday cakes, sponges and meringues may be kept in an airtight container or simply wrapped in clear film or foil; this will ensure they keep moist and fresh with the exclusion of the air. Store the cakes in a cool, dry place for up to a week; meringues will store for up to a month. Avoid warm, moist conditions as this will encourage mould growth.

To store fruit cakes, leave the lining paper on the cakes. This seals on to the surface during cooking and keeps the cakes moist and fresh. Wrap the cakes in a double layer of foil and keep in a cool place. Never seal a fruit cake in an airtight container for long periods of time as this may encourage mould growth.

Rich, heavy fruit cakes keep well because of their high fruit content; although they are moist and full of flavour, they are at their best when they are first made. Such cakes do mature with keeping, but most should be consumed within three months. If you are going to keep a fruit cake for several months before marzipanning or icing it, pour over alcohol a little at a time at monthly intervals, turning the cake each time.

Light fruit cakes are stored in the same way as their rich cousins, but since they have less fruit in them, their keeping qualities are not so good. These cakes are at their best when first made, or eaten within a month of making.

For long term storage, fruit cakes are better frozen in their double wrapping and foil.

Once the cakes have been marzipanned and iced, they will keep longer. But iced cakes must be stored in cardboard boxes in a warm, dry atmosphere, to maintain them dust-free and in good condition. Damp and cold are the worst conditions, causing the icing to stain and colourings to run.

Freeze a decorated celebration cake in a cake box, ensuring the lid is sealed with tape. Take the cake out of its box and defrost it slowly in a cool, dry place. When the cake has thawed, transfer to a warm, dry place to ensure the icing dries completely. Wedding cakes which have been kept for a long time may need re-icing and decorating.

Calculating quantities and cutting cakes

To work out the number of servings from a round or square cake is extremely simple and the final total depends on whether you require just a small finger of cake or a more substantial slice.

Whether the cake is round or square, cut across the cake from edge to edge into about 2.5 cm/1 inch slices, thinner if desired. Cut each slice into 5 cm/ 2 inch pieces or thereabouts.

Using these guidelines, it should be easy to calculate the number of cake slices you can cut from any given size cake. A square cake is larger than a round cake of the same proportions and will yield more slices. On a round cake the slices become smaller at the curved edges, and the first and last slice of the cake is mainly marzipan and icing. Always keep this in mind when calculating the servings.

Example
According to the measurements above a 20 cm/8 inch square cake will yield about 40 slices and a 20 cm/8 inch round cake will yield about 35 slices.

Quick-mix Sponge Cake

Here's a no-fuss, foolproof all-in-one cake, where the ingredients are quickly mixed together. The following quantities and baking instructions are for a deep 20cm/8 inch round cake tin or a 20 cm/ 8 inch ring mould. For other quantities and tin sizes, follow the baking instructions given in the decorated cake recipes.

INGREDIENTS
115 g/4oz/1 cup self-raising flour
1 tsp baking powder
115 g/4 oz/½ cup soft margarine
115 g/4 oz/½ cup caster sugar
2 size 3 eggs

STORING AND FREEZING
The cake can be made up to two days in advance, wrapped in clear film or foil and stored in an airtight container. The cake can be frozen for up to three months.

FLAVOURINGS
The following amounts are for a 2-egg, single quantity cake, as above. Increase the amounts proportionally for larger cakes.
Chocolate *Fold 1 tbsp cocoa powder blended with 1 tbsp boiling water into the cake mixture.*
Citrus *Fold 2 tsp of finely grated lemon, orange or lime zest into the cake mixture.*

1 Preheat the oven to 160°C/325°F/ Gas 3. Grease the round cake tin, line the base with greaseproof paper and grease the paper, or grease and flour the ring mould.

2 ▲ Sift the flour and baking powder into a bowl. Add the margarine, sugar and eggs.

3 ▲ Beat with a wooden spoon for 2–3 minutes. The mixture should be pale in colour and slightly glossy.

4 Spoon the cake mixture into the prepared tin and then smooth the surface. Bake for 20–30 minutes. To test if cooked, press the cake lightly in the centre. If firm, the cake is done, if soft, cook for a little longer. Alternatively, insert a skewer into the centre of the cake. If it comes out clean the cake is ready. Turn out on to a wire rack, remove the lining paper and leave to cool completely.

This quick-mix sponge cake can be filled and simply decorated with icing for a special occasion.

Whisked Sponge Cake

This deliciously light-textured sponge can be used for making Swiss rolls, cakes or gâteaux. As it contains no fat it does not keep well, so it is best baked on the day of eating. The following quantities are for a 33 x 23 cm/13 x 9 inch Swiss roll tin or a 20 cm/8 inch round cake tin.

INGREDIENTS
4 size 3 eggs
115 g/4 oz/½ cup caster sugar
115 g/4 oz/1 cup plain flour

1 Preheat the oven to 180°C/350°F/ Gas 4. Grease the Swiss roll tin or round cake tin, line with greaseproof paper and grease the paper.

2 ▲ Whisk together the eggs and sugar in a heatproof bowl until thoroughly blended. Place the bowl over a saucepan of simmering water and whisk until thick and pale. Remove the bowl from the saucepan and continue whisking until the mixture is cool and leaves a thick trail when the beaters are lifted.

3 ▲ Sift the flour onto the surface and, using a metal spoon or plastic spatula, carefully fold the flour into the mixture until smooth.

4 ▲ Pour the cake mixture into the prepared tin and tilt to level. Bake in the centre of the oven for 12–15 minutes for the Swiss roll or 25–30 minutes for the round cake. To test if cooked, press lightly in the centre: if the cake springs back it is done.

5 Turn the Swiss roll out on to a piece of greaseproof paper sprinkled with caster sugar. Peel off the lining paper, fill as required and roll up. Leave the round cake in the tin for 5 minutes, then turn out onto a wire rack, peel off the lining paper and leave to cool completely.

Airy whisked sponge cake is the classic base for Swiss rolls; here incorporating a cream and raspberry filling.

$\mathscr{S}$wiss Roll

Swiss rolls are traditionally made without fat, so they don't keep as long as most other cakes. However, they have a deliciously light texture and provide the cook with the potential for all sorts of luscious fillings and tasty toppings.

INGREDIENTS
4 size 3 eggs, separated
115 g/4 oz/½ cup caster sugar
115 g/4 oz/1 cup plain flour
1 tsp baking powder

STORING AND FREEZING
Swiss rolls and other fat-free sponges do not keep well, so if possible bake on the day of eating. Otherwise, wrap in clear film or foil and store in an airtight container overnight or freeze for up to three months.

1 Preheat the oven to 180°C/350°F/ Gas 4. Grease a 33 × 23 cm/ 13 × 9 inch Swiss roll tin, line with greaseproof paper and grease the paper.

2 Whisk the egg whites in a clean, dry bowl until stiff. Beat in 2 tbsp of the sugar.

3 ▲ Place the egg yolks, remaining sugar and 1 tbsp water in a bowl and beat for about 2 minutes until the mixture is pale and leaves a thick trail when the beaters are lifted.

4 ▼ Carefully fold the beaten egg yolks into the egg white mixture with a metal spoon.

5 Sift together the flour and baking powder. Carefully fold the flour mixture into the egg mixture with a metal spoon.

6 ▲ Pour the cake mixture into the prepared tin and then smooth the surface, being careful not to press out any air.

7 Bake in the centre of the oven for 12–15 minutes. To test if cooked, press lightly in the centre. If the cake springs back it is done. It will also start to come away from the edges of the tin.

8 Turn the cake out on to a piece of greaseproof paper lightly sprinkled with caster sugar. Peel off the lining paper and cut off any crisp edges of the cake with a sharp knife. Spread with jam, if wished, and roll up, using the greaseproof paper as a guide. Leave to cool on a wire rack.

Vary the flavour of a traditional Swiss roll by adding a little grated orange, lime or lemon rind to the basic mixture.

Truffle Cake Mix

This is a no-cook recipe, using leftover pieces of sponge cake or plain shop-bought sponge to make a moist, rich cake mixture, which is used in several of the novelty cakes.

INGREDIENTS
175 g/6 oz plain sponge cake pieces
175 g/6 oz/2 cups ground almonds
75g/3 oz/scant ⅓ cup dark brown muscovado sugar
1 tsp ground mixed spice
pinch of ground cinnamon
finely grated zest of 1 orange
3 tbsp freshly squeezed orange juice
5 tbsp clear honey

STORING AND FREEZING
The mixture can be made up to two days in advance, wrapped in clear film and stored in an airtight container. Not suitable for freezing.

1 Place the sponge cake pieces into the bowl of a food processor or blender and process for a few seconds to form fine crumbs.

2 Place the cake crumbs, ground almonds, sugar, spices, orange zest, orange juice and honey in a large mixing bowl. Stir well to combine into a thick, smooth mixture.

3 ▲ Use the mixture as directed in the novelty cake recipes. The truffle mixture can be made and moulded into any simple shape, such as a log or round balls. The moulded mixture can be covered with marzipan or sugarpaste icing.

Tip
Dampen your hands slightly before handling the truffle mixture, as it is very sticky.

Here the truffle mixture has been rolled into a log shape to form the sausage in this sweet-tasting novelty Hot Dog cake.

$\mathcal{M}$adeira Cake

*This fine-textured cake makes a good base for decorating and is therefore a useful
alternative to fruit cake, although it will not keep as long. It provides a firmer,
longer-lasting base than a Victoria sponge, and can be covered with butter icing,
fudge frosting, a thin layer of marzipan or sugarpaste icing. For the ingredients,
decide what size and shape of cake you wish to make and
then follow the chart shown opposite.*

STORING AND FREEZING
*The cake can be made up to a week
in advance, wrapped in clear film
or foil and stored in an airtight
container. The cake can be frozen
for up to three months.*

*Madeira cake provides a firmer base
for icing than a Victoria sponge. It
can be covered with a thin layer of
sugarpaste, as here, or marzipan,
and is a great alternative for anyone
who does not like fruit cake.*

1 Preheat the oven to 160°C/325°F/
Gas 3. Grease a deep cake tin, line
the base and sides with a double
thickness of greaseproof paper and
grease the paper.

2 ▲ Sift together the flour and baking
powder into a mixing bowl. Add the
margarine, sugar, eggs and lemon juice.

3 ▲ Stir the ingredients together with
a wooden spoon until they are all
well combined.

4 ▲ Beat the mixture for about
2 minutes until smooth and glossy.

5 Spoon the mixture into the
prepared tin and smooth the top.
Bake in the centre of the oven, following
the chart opposite as a guide for baking
times. If the cake browns too quickly,
cover the top loosely with foil. To test if
baked, press lightly in the centre. If the
cake springs back it is done.
Alternatively, test by inserting a skewer
into the centre of the cake. If it comes
out clean the cake is done. Leave the
cake to cool in the tin for 5 minutes and
then turn out on to a wire rack. Remove
the lining paper and leave to cool.

MADEIRA CAKE CHART

Cake tin sizes	18 cm/7 in round	20 cm/8 in round	23 cm/9 in round	25 cm/10 in round	30 cm/12 in round
	15 cm/6 in square	18 cm/7 in square	20 cm/8 in square	23 cm/9 in square	28 cm/11 in square
Plain flour	225 g/ 8 oz/ 2 cups	350 g/ 12 oz/ 3 cups	450 g/ 1 lb/ 4 cups	500 g/ 1 lb 2 oz/ 4½ cups	625g/ 1½ lb/ 6 cups
Baking powder	1½ tsp	2 tsp	2½ tsp	1 tbsp	4 tsp
Soft margarine	175 g/ 6 oz/ ¾ cup	250 g/ 9 oz/ 1¼ cups	350 g/ 12 oz/ 1½ cups	400 g/ 14 oz/ 1¾ cups	550g/ 1 lb 3 oz 2¼ cups
Caster Sugar	175 g/ 6 oz/ ¾ cup	250 g/ 9 oz/ 1¼ cups	350 g/ 12 oz/ 1½ cups	400 g/ 14 oz/ 1¾ cups	550g/ 1 lb 3 oz/ 2½ cups
Eggs, size 3, beaten	3	4	6	7	10
Lemon juice	1 tbsp	1½ tbsp	2 tbsp	2½ tbsp	4 tbsp
Approx. baking time	1¼–1½ hours	1½–1¾ hours	1¾–2 hours	1¾–2 hours	2¼–2¼ hours

A traditional Madeira cake peaks and cracks slightly on the top. For a flat surface on which to ice, simply level the top with a sharp knife.

Rich Fruit Cake

This is the traditional cake mixture for many cakes made for special occasions such as weddings, Christmas, anniversaries and christenings. Make the cake a few weeks before icing, keep it well wrapped and stored in an airtight container and it should mature beautifully. Because of all its rich ingredients, this fruit cake will keep moist and fresh for several months. Follow the ingredients guide in the chart opposite for the size of cake you wish to make.

STORING

When the cake is cold, wrap in a double thickness of greaseproof paper or foil. Store in an airtight container in a cool dry place where it will keep for several months. During storage, the cake can be unwrapped and the bottom brushed with brandy (about half the amount used in the recipe). Re-wrap before storing again. As the cake keeps so well, there is no need to freeze.

A long-lasting cake which is full of rich flavours.

1 Preheat the oven to 140°C/275°F Gas 1. Grease a deep cake tin, line the base and sides with a double thickness of greaseproof paper and grease the paper.

2 ▲ Place all the ingredients in a large mixing bowl.

3 ▲ Stir to combine, then beat throughly with a wooden spoon for 3–6 minutes (depending on size), until well mixed.

4 ▲ Spoon the mixture into the prepared tin and smooth the surface with the back of a wet metal spoon. Make a slight impression in the centre to help prevent the cake from doming.

5 Bake in the centre of the oven. Use the chart opposite as a guide for timing the cake you are baking. Test the cake about 30 minutes before the end of the baking time. If the cake browns too quickly, cover the top loosely with foil. To test if baked, press lightly in the centre. If the cake feels firm and when a skewer inserted in the centre comes out clean, it is done. Test again at intervals if necessary.

6 Leave the cake to cool in the tin. When completely cool, turn out of the tin. The lining paper can be left on to help keep the cake moist.

RICH FRUIT CAKE CHART

Cake tin sizes	15 cm/6 in round	18 cm/7 in round	20 cm/8 in round	23 cm/9 in round	25 cm/10 in round	28 cm/11 in round	30 cm/12 in round	33 cm/13 in round
	13 cm/5 in square	15 cm/6 in square	18 cm/7 in square	20 cm/8 in square	23 cm/9 in square	25 cm/10 in square	28 cm/11 in square	30 cm/12 in square
Currants	200 g/ 7 oz/ 1¼ cups	275 g/ 10 oz/ 1¾ cups	375 g/ 13 oz/ 2¼ cups	450 g/ 1 lb/ 3 cups	575 g/ 1¼ lb/ 3½ cups	675 g/ 1½ lb/ 4½ cups	800 g/ 1¾ lb/ 5 ¼ cups	900 g/ 2 lb/ 6 cups
Sultanas	115 g/ 4 oz/ ²/₃ cup	200 g/ 7 oz/ 1 cup	250 g/ 9 oz/ 1½ cups	300 g/ 11 oz/ 1¾ cups	375 g/ 13 oz/ 2 cups	450 g/ 1 lb/ 2½ cups	550 g/ 1 lb 3 oz/ 3 cups	625 g/ 1 lb 6 oz/ 3½ cups
Raisins	65 g/ 2½ oz/ ⅓ cup	115 g/ 4 oz/ ²/₃ cup	150 g/ 5 oz/ ¾ cup	175 g/ 6 oz/ 1 cup	200 g/ 7 oz/ 1 cup	225 g/ 8 oz/ 1¼ cups	250 g/ 9 oz/ 1½ cups	275 g/ 10 oz/ 1½ cups
Glacé cherries, halved	40 g/ 1½ oz/ ¼ cup	65 g/ 2½ oz/ ⅓ cup	90 g/ 3½ oz/ ½ cup	115 g/ 4 oz/ ½ cup	150 g/ 5 oz/ ²/₃ cup	175 g/ 6 oz/ ¾ cup	200 g/ 7 oz/ 1 cup	225 g/ 8 oz/ 1¼ cups
Almonds, chopped	40 g/ 1½ oz/ ⅓ cup	65 g/ 2½ oz/ ½ cup	90 g/ 3½ oz/ ¾ cup	115 g/ 4 oz/ 1 cup	150 g/ 5 oz/ 1¼ cups	175 g/ 6 oz/ 1½ cups	200 g/ 7 oz/ 1²/₃ cups	225 g/ 8 oz/ 2 cups
Mixed peel	40 g/ 1½ oz/ ¼ cup	65 g/ 2½ oz/ ½ cup	65 g/ 2½ oz/ ½ cup	90 g/ 3½ oz/ ²/₃ cup	115 g/ 4 oz/ ¾ cup	150 g/ 5 oz/ 1 cup	175 g/ 6 oz/ 1 cup	200 g/ 7 oz/ 1⅓ cups
Lemon, grated rind	½	1	1	2	2	2	3	3
Brandy	1½ tbsp	2 tbsp	2½ tbsp	3 tbsp	3½ tbsp	4 tbsp	4½ tbsp	5 tbsp
Plain flour	150 g/ 5 oz/ 1⅓ cups	200 g/ 7 oz/ 1¾ cups	250 g/ 9 oz/ 2 cups	300 g/ 11 oz/ 2¾ cups	400 g/ 14 oz/ 3½ cups	450 g/ 1 lb/ 4 cups	550 g/ 1 lb 3 oz/ 4½ cups	625 g/ 1 lb 6 oz/ 5½ cups
Ground mixed spice	1 tsp	1 tsp	1¼ tsp	1½ tsp	1½ tsp	2 tsp	2½ tsp	1 tbsp
Ground nutmeg	¼ tsp	½ tsp	½ tsp	1 tsp	1 tsp	1 tsp	1½ tsp	2 tsp
Ground almonds	40 g/ 1½ oz/ ½ cup	50 g/ 2 oz/ ²/₃ cup	65 g/ 2½ oz/ ¾ cup	75 g/ 3 oz/ 1 cup	90 g/ 3½ oz/ 1¼ cups	115 g/ 4 oz/ 1⅓ cups	130 g/ 4½ oz/ 1½ cups	150 g/ 5 oz/ 1²/₃ cups
Soft margarine or butter	115 g/ 4 oz/ ½ cup	150 g/ 5 oz/ ²/₃ cup	200 g/ 7 oz/ scant 1 cup	250 g/ 9 oz/ scant 1¼ cups	300 g/ 11 oz/ scant 1½ cups	375 g/ 13 oz/ scant 1¾ cups	425 g/ 15 oz/ scant 2 cups	500 g/ 1 lb 2 oz/ 2¼ cups
Soft brown sugar	130 g/ 4½ oz/ ²/₃ cup	175 g/ 6 oz/ ¾ cup	225 g/ 8 oz/ 1 cup	275 g/ 10 oz/ 1⅓ cups	350 g/ 12 oz/ 1½ cups	400 g/ 14 oz/ scant 2 cups	450 g/ 1 lb/ 2 cups	500 g/ 1 lb 2 oz/ 2¼ cups
Black treacle or molasses	1 tbsp	1 tbsp	1 tbsp	1½ tbsp	2 tbsp	2 tbsp	2 tbsp	2½ tbsp
Eggs, size 3, beaten	3	4	5	6	7	8	9	10
Approx. baking time	2¼–2½ hours	2½–2¾ hours	3–3½ hours	3¼–3¾ hours	3¼–4¼ hours	4–4½ hours	4½–5¼ hours	5¼–5¾ hours

*L*ight Fruit Cake

For those who prefer a lighter fruit cake, here is a less rich version, still ideal for marzipanning and covering with sugarpaste or royal icing. Follow the ingredients guide in the chart opposite according to the size of cake you wish to make.

STORING AND FREEZING
When the cake is cold, wrap well in greaseproof paper, clear film or foil. It will keep for several weeks, stored in an airtight container. As the cake keeps so well, there is no need to freeze, but, if wished, freeze for up to three months.

1 Preheat the oven to 150°C/300°F/ Gas 2. Grease a deep cake tin, line the sides and base with a double thickness of greaseproof paper and grease the paper.

2 ▲ Measure and prepare all the ingredients, then place them all together in a large mixing bowl.

3 ▲ Stir to combine, then beat thoroughly with a wooden spoon for 3–4 minutes, depending on the size, until well mixed.

4 ▲ Spoon the mixture into the prepared tin and smooth the surface with the back of a wet metal spoon. Make a slight impression in the centre to help prevent the cake from doming.

5 Bake in the centre of the oven. Use the chart opposite as a guide according to the size of cake you are baking. Test the cake about 15 minutes before the end of the baking time. If the cake browns too quickly, cover the top loosely with foil. To test if baked, press lightly in the centre. If the cake feels firm, and when a skewer inserted in the centre comes out clean, it is done. Test again at intervals if necessary.

6 Leave the cake to cool in the tin. When completely cool, turn out of the tin. The lining paper can be left on to help keep the cake moist.

Round, square, ring or heart-shaped – the shape of this light fruit cake can be varied to suit the occasion.

LIGHT FRUIT CAKE CHART

Cake tin sizes	15 cm/6 in round	18 cm/7 in round	20 cm/8 in round	23 cm/9 in round
	13 cm/5 in square	15 cm/6 in square	18 cm/7 in square	20 cm/8 in square
Soft margarine or butter	115 g/ 4 oz/ ½ cup	175 g/ 6 oz/ ¾ cup	225 g/ 8 oz/ 1 cup	275 g/ 10 oz/ 1⅓ cups
Caster sugar	115 g/ 4 oz/ ½ cup	175 g/ 6 oz/ ¾ cup	225 g/ 8 oz/ 1 cup	275 g/ 10 oz/ 1⅓ cups
Orange, grated rind	½	½	1	1
Eggs, size 3, beaten	3	4	5	6
Plain flour	165 g 5½ oz/ 1½ cups	200 g/ 7 oz/ 1¾ cups	300 g/ 11 oz/ 2¾ cups	400 g/ 14 oz/ 3½ cups
Baking powder	¼ tsp	½ tsp	½ tsp	1 tsp
Ground mixed spice	1 tsp	1½ tsp	2 tsp	2½ tsp
Currants	50 g/ 2 oz/ ⅓ cup	115 g/ 4 oz/ ⅔ cup	175 g/ 6 oz/ 1 cup	225 g/ 8 oz/ 1½ cups
Sultanas	50 g/ 2 oz/ ⅓ cup	115 g/ 4 oz/ ⅔ cup	175 g/ 6 oz/ 1 cup	225 g/ 8 oz/ 1⅓ cups
Raisins	50 g/ 2 oz/ ⅓ cup	115 g/ 4 oz/ ⅔ cup	175 g/ 6 oz/ 1 cup	225 g/ 8 oz/ 1⅓ cups
Dried apricots, chopped	25 g/ 1 oz/ 7	50 g/ 2 oz/ 14	50 g/ 2 oz/ 14	75 g/ 3 oz/ 21
Mixed cut peel	50 g/ 2 oz/ scant ½ cup	75 g/ 3 oz/ good ½ cup	115 g/ 4 oz/ ¾ cup	150 g/ 5 oz/ 1 cup
Approx. baking time	2¼– 2½ hours	2½– 2¾ hours	2¾– 3¼ hours	3¼– 3¾ hours

$\mathcal{B}$asic Icing Recipes

Cakes can take on many guises, and nothing enhances their appearance more for that extra special occasion than a little icing. This chapter offers a range of simple classic icing recipes to suit the type of cake you have made and which can be adapted according to the occasion. Ideas range from quick-mix icings, such as butter icing and satin chocolate icing, which may be instantly poured, spread, swirled or piped on to sponge and Madeira cakes or Swiss rolls, to the more regal icings, such as royal icing and sugarpaste icing. These are ideal for covering and decorating fruit cakes intended for more formal occasions, such as anniversaries, christenings and weddings.

The icings in this section are all fairly traditional. However, if you want to substitute any of them with a favourite icing recipe when decorating, make sure that it suits the cake on which you are working.

Decorating Equipment

With a few simple tools, it is possible to create the most stunning of cake decorations. Thick swirls of butter icing formed with a palette knife, or stark white icing sugar dusted over a contrastingly dark chocolate icing, instantly provide an impressive effect. As your skills develop, however, you will probably want to invest in some specialized pieces of icing equipment, such as those listed here.

Icing Turntable This is one of the most expensive but useful items for either the novice or more advanced cake decorator. Because it revolves, it is particularly handy for piping, or for icing the sides of a round cake with royal icing.
Straight-edge Ruler Choose one made of stainless steel so that it will not bend as you pull it across a layer of royal icing, to give a smooth, flat surface to a cake.
Plastic Scrapers These can have straight or serrated edges for giving a smooth or patterned surface to the sides or tops of cakes coated with royal, butter or fudge icing.
Small Rolling Pin Made in a handy size for rolling out small amounts of marzipan or sugarpaste icing for decorations.

Nozzles There are numerous shapes and sizes to choose from, but it is best to start off with some of the basic shapes. Small straight-sided nozzles fit home-made greaseproof paper piping bags. Larger ones are more suitable for the commercially-made material bags when piping large amounts of icing.
Nozzle Brush A small wire brush which makes the job of cleaning out nozzles a lot easier.
Flower Nail Used as a support when piping flowers.
Crimping Tools These are available with different end-shapes which produce varied patterns and offer a quick way of giving a professional finish to a cake.
Paintbrushes Brushes for painting designs on to cakes, adding highlights to flowers or modelled shapes, or for making run-outs are available at cake icing specialists, stationers or art supply shops.
Florist's Wire, Tape and Stamens All available from cake icing specialists, the wire, available in different gauges, is handy for wiring small sugarpaste flowers together to form floral sprays. The tape is used to neaten the stems, and the stamens, available in many colours, form the centres of the flowers.

Papers There are several papers used in cake decorating. Greaseproof paper is used for making piping bags and for drying sugar-frosted flowers and fruits, while baking parchment is used for spreading melted chocolate and for icing run-outs.

Cutters Small cocktail cutters are useful for making cut-out shapes from chocolate, sugarpaste and marzipan. Blossom cutters, available in different shapes and sizes, are good for making small flowers, while a special frill cutter can be used to cut out quick-and-easy frills.

1 food colourings
2 greaseproof paper and baking parchment
3 piping nozzles
4 fabric piping bag
5 nozzle brush
6 paintbrushes
7 icing turntable
8 florist's wire
9 stamens
10 florist's tape
11 straight-edge ruler
12 cake pillars

13 cake pillar supports
14 crimping tools
15 food colouring pens
16 flower nail
17 frill cutter
18 textured rolling pin
19 foam pad
20 shaped cutters
21 modelling tool
22 plunger cutters
23 dual blossom cutter
24 cocktail cutters
25 plain and serrated side scrapers

*M*arzipan

With its smooth, pliable texture, marzipan has been popular for centuries in cake making, especially for large cakes such as wedding and christening cakes. It is also excellent for making a variety of cake decorations. The following recipe is sufficient to cover the top and sides of an 18 cm/7 inch round or a 15 cm/6 inch square cake. Make half the amount if only the top is to be covered.

2 ▲ Add the lemon juice, almond essence and enough beaten egg to mix to a soft but firm dough. Gather together with your fingers to form a ball.

3 ▲ Knead the marzipan on a work surface lightly dusted with sifted icing sugar until smooth.

INGREDIENTS
Makes 450 g/1 lb
225 g/8 oz/2¼ cups ground almonds
115 g/4 oz/1 cup icing sugar, sifted
115 g/4 oz/½ cup caster sugar
1 tsp lemon juice
2 drops almond essence
1 size 4 egg, beaten

STORING
The marzipan will keep for up to four days, wrapped in clear film in an airtight container, and stored in the refrigerator.

1 ▲ Put the ground almonds, icing and caster sugars into a bowl and mix together.

Using Marzipan
Marzipan is applied to the sides and top of a cake, particularly rich fruit cakes, to prevent moisture seeping through the cake and to provide a smooth under-coat for the top covering of royal icing or sugarpaste icing.

Once the marzipan has been applied, leave it to dry for a day or two before applying the icing. For a richer taste you can mix up your own marzipan. However, if you have any concerns about using raw eggs in uncooked recipes, especially in light of current health warnings, do buy ready-made marzipan. It is very good quality, does not contain raw egg and is available in two colours, white and yellow. White is the best choice if you want to add your own colours and create different moulded shapes.

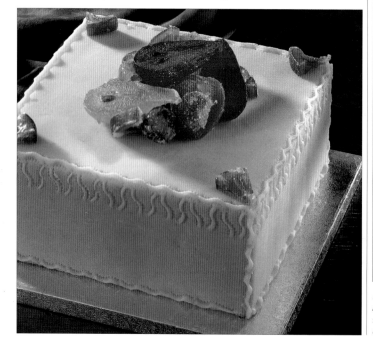

Marzipan can be used as an attractive cake coating in its own right as well as providing a base for other icings.

Sugarpaste Icing

Sugarpaste icing has opened up a whole new concept in cake decorating. It is wonderfully pliable, easy to make and use, and can be coloured, moulded and shaped in the most imaginative fashion. Though quick to make at home, shop-bought sugarpaste, also known as easy-roll or ready-to-roll icing, is very good quality and handy to use. This recipe makes sufficient to cover the top and sides of an 18 cm/7 inch round or a 15 cm/6 inch square cake.

INGREDIENTS
Makes 350 g/12 oz
1 size 3 egg white
1 tbsp liquid glucose, warmed
350 g/12 oz/3 cups icing sugar,
sifted

STORING
The icing will keep for up to a week, wrapped in clear film or a plastic bag and stored in the refrigerator. Bring to room temperature before using. If a thin crust forms, trim off before using or it will make the icing lumpy. Also, if the icing dries out or hardens, knead in a little boiled water to make it smooth and pliable again.

3 Knead the mixture with your fingers until it forms a ball.

4 ▲ Knead the sugarpaste on a work surface lightly dusted with sifted icing sugar for several minutes until smooth, soft and pliable. If the icing is too soft, knead in some more sifted icing sugar until it is firm and pliable.

Tip

Ready-made shop-bought sugarpaste does not contain raw egg, so do use if you prefer to avoid uncooked egg in recipes in light of current health warnings.

Tinted or left pure white, sugarpaste icing can be used to cover cakes, and moulded to make decorations to suit any shape of cake.

1 Put the egg white and glucose in a bowl. Stir together with a wooden spoon to break up the egg white.

2 ▲ Add the icing sugar and mix together with a palette knife or knife, using a chopping action, until well blended and the icing begins to bind together.

Royal Icing

Royal icing has gained a regal position in the world of icing. Any special occasion cake which demands a classical, professional finish uses this smooth, satin-like icing. The following recipe makes sufficient to cover the top and sides of an 18 cm/7 inch round or a 15 cm/6 inch square cake.

INGREDIENTS
Makes 675 g/1½ lb
3 size 3 egg whites
about 675 g/1½ lb/6 cups icing sugar, sifted
1½ tsp glycerine
few drops lemon juice
colouring (optional)

STORING
Royal icing will keep for up to three days in an airtight container, stored in the refrigerator. Stir the icing well before using.

Tips

• Always sift the icing sugar before using, to get rid of any lumps.
• Never add more than the stated amount of glycerine. Too much will make the icing crumbly and too fragile to use.
• A little lemon juice is added to prevent the icing from discolouring, but too much will make the icing become hard.

1 ▲ Put the egg whites in a bowl and stir lightly with a wooden spoon to break them up.

2 ▲ Add the icing sugar gradually in small quantities, beating well with a wooden spoon between each addition. Add sufficient icing sugar to make a smooth, white, shiny icing with the consistency of very stiff meringue. It should be thin enough to spread, but thick enough to hold its shape.

3 ▲ Beat in the glycerine, lemon juice and food colouring, if using.

4 It is best to let the icing sit for about 1 hour before using. Cover the surface with a piece of damp clear film or a lid so the icing does not dry out. Before using, stir the icing to burst any air bubbles. Even when working with royal icing, always keep it covered.

Royal Icing Using Pure Albumen Powder

If you are concerned about current health warnings advising against the use of raw eggs in uncooked recipes, try the following recipe.

INGREDIENTS
Makes 450 g/1 lb
450 g/1 lb/4 cups icing sugar, sifted
6 tbsp water
12.5g/½ oz/7 tsp pure albumen powder

STORING
This royal icing will keep for up to a week in an airtight container, stored in a cool place.

1 Mix the pure albumen powder with the water. Leave to stand for 15 minutes, then stir until the powder dissolves.

2 Sieve the albumen solution into a mixing bowl. Add half the icing sugar and beat until smooth. Add the remaining sugar and beat again for 12–14 minutes or until smooth.

3 Adjust the consistency as needed, adding a little more icing sugar for a stiffer icing or a little water for a thinner one. If storing, transfer to an airtight container, cover the surface of the royal icing with clear film and then close the lid.

ICING CONSISTENCIES

For flat icing

▲ The recipes on the opposite page are for a consistency of icing suitable for flat icing a rich fruit cake covered in marzipan. When the spoon is lifted out of the icing, it should form a sharp point, with a slight curve at the end, known as a 'soft peak'.

For peaking

▲ Make the royal icing as before, but to a stiffer consistency so that when the spoon is lifted out of the bowl the icing stands in straight peaks.

For piping

For piping purposes, the icing needs to be slightly stiffer than for peaked icing so that it forms a fine, sharp peak when the spoon is lifted out. This allows the icing to flow easily for piping, at the same time enabling it to keep its definition.

For run-outs

For elegant and more elaborate cakes, you may want to pipe outlines of shapes and then fill these in with different coloured icing. These are known as run-outs. For the outlines, you need to make the icing to a piping consistency, while for the insides you need a slightly thinner icing with a consistency of thick cream, so that with a little help it will flow within the shapes. Ideally the icing should hold its shape and be slightly rounded after filling the outlines.

The right consistency

If you need to change the consistency of your icing, add a little sifted icing sugar to make it stiffer, or beat in a little egg white for a thinner icing. Be sure to do this carefully, as a little of one or the other will change the consistency fairly quickly.

A traditional look for a classic royal icing. This square rich fruit cake has been marzipanned and then flat iced with three, ultra-smooth layers of royal icing. It is simply, but elegantly, decorated with piped borders, a crisp, white ribbon and fresh roses.

$\mathcal{B}$utter Icing

The creamy, rich flavour and silky smoothness of butter icing are popular with both children and adults. The icing can be varied in colour and flavour and makes a decorative filling and coating for sponge and Madeira cakes or Swiss rolls. Simply swirled, or more elaborately piped, butter icing gives a delicious and attractive finish. The following quantity makes enough to fill and coat the sides and top of a 20 cm/8 inch sponge cake.

INGREDIENTS
Makes 350 g/12 oz
75 g/3 oz/6 tbsp butter, softened,
or soft margarine
225 g/8 oz/2 cups icing sugar, sifted
1 tsp vanilla essence
2–3 tsp milk

STORING
The icing will keep for up to three days, in an airtight container stored in the refrigerator.

1 ▲ Put the butter or margarine, icing sugar, vanilla essence and 1 tsp of the milk in a bowl.

2 ▲ Beat with a wooden spoon or an electric mixer, adding sufficient extra milk to give a light, smooth and fluffy consistency.

FLAVOURINGS
The following amounts are for a single quantity of icing. Increase or decrease the amounts proportionally as needed.
Chocolate *Blend 1 tbsp cocoa powder with 1 tbsp hot water. Allow to cool before beating into the icing.*
Coffee *Blend 2 tsp instant coffee powder or granules with 1 tbsp boiling water. Allow to cool before beating into the icing.*
Lemon, orange or lime *Substitute the vanilla essence and milk for lemon, orange or lime juice and 2 tsp of finely grated citrus zest. Omit the zest if using the icing for piping. Lightly colour the icing with the appropriate shade of food colouring, if wished.*

Generous swirls of butter icing give a mouth-watering effect to a cake.

Crème au Beurre

This icing takes a little more time to make, but it is well worth it. The rich, smooth, light texture makes it suitable for spreading, filling or piping on to special cakes and gâteaux. Use it as soon as it is made for best results, or keep it at room temperature for a few hours. Do not reheat or it will curdle. The following amount will fill and decorate the top and sides of a 20 cm/8 inch round cake.

INGREDIENTS
Makes 350 g/12 oz
60 ml/4 tbsp water
75 g/3 oz/6 tbsp caster sugar
2 size 3 egg yolks
150 g/5 oz/⅔ cup butter, softened

FLAVOURINGS
The following amounts are for a single quantity of icing. Increase or decrease the amounts proportionally as needed.
Orange, lemon or lime *Replace the water with orange, lemon or lime juice and 10 ml/2 tsp finely grated orange, lemon or lime zest.*
Chocolate *Add 50 g/2 oz plain chocolate, melted.*
Coffee *Blend 10 ml/2 tsp instant coffee powder or granules with 15 ml/1 tbsp boiling water. Cool before folding into the icing.*

1 Place the water in a small saucepan, bring to boil, remove the saucepan from the heat and stir in the sugar. Heat gently until the sugar has completely dissolved. Remove the spoon.

2 ▲ Boil rapidly until the mixture becomes syrupy. To test, remove the pan from the heat and place a little syrup on the back of a dry teaspoon. Press a second teaspoon on to the syrup and gently pull apart. The syrup should form a fine thread. If not, return the saucepan to the heat.

3 ▲ Whisk the egg yolks together in a bowl. Continue whisking while slowly adding the sugar syrup in a steady stream. Whisk until the mixture becomes thick, pale and cool, and leaves a trail on the surface when the beaters are lifted.

4 ▲ Beat the butter in a separate bowl until light and fluffy. Add the egg mixture gradually, beating well after each addition, until thick and fluffy. Fold in the chosen flavouring, using a spatula, until evenly blended.

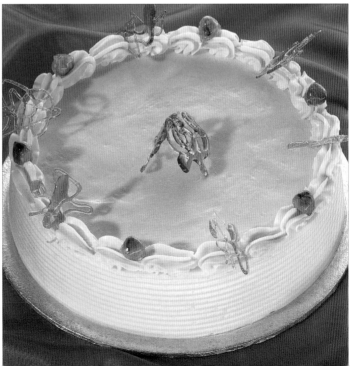

American Frosting

A light marshmallow icing which crisps on the outside when left to dry, this versatile frosting may be swirled or peaked into a soft coating. It looks perfect as a snowy landscape for your Christmas cake. The following amount is sufficient to cover a 20 cm/8 inch round cake.

INGREDIENTS
Makes 350 g/12 oz
1 size 3 egg white
30 ml/2 tbsp water
15 ml/1 tbsp golden syrup
5 ml/1 tsp cream of tartar
175 g/6 oz/1½ cups icing sugar,
sifted

American frosting makes a light, fluffy yet crisp topping, its soft white contrasting well with chocolate caraque.

1 ▲ Place the egg white, water, golden syrup and cream of tartar in a heatproof bowl. Whisk together until thoroughly blended.

2 ▲ Stir the icing sugar into the mixture and place the bowl over a saucepan of simmering water. Whisk until the mixture becomes thick and white and holds soft peaks.

3 Remove the bowl from the saucepan and continue to whisk the frosting until cool and thick, and the mixture stands up in soft peaks.

4 ▲ Use immediately to fill or cover the cake. Once iced, the cake can be decorated in any way you like, such as with chocolate curls, as shown here.

*G*lacé Icing

*This icing can be made in just a few minutes
and can be varied by adding a few drops of food colouring or
flavouring. The following quantity makes enough to cover the top
and decorate a 20 cm/8 inch round sponge cake.*

INGREDIENTS
Makes 225 g/8 oz
225 g/8 oz/2 cups icing sugar
2–3 tbsp warm water or fruit juice
food colouring, optional

STORING
*Not suitable for storing. The icing
must be used immediately after
making.*

1 ▲ Sift the icing sugar into a mixing
bowl to get rid of any lumps.

2 ▲ Using a wooden spoon, gradually
stir in enough water to make an
icing with the consistency of thick
cream. Beat until the icing is smooth. It
should be thick enough to coat the back
of the spoon. If it is too runny, beat in a
little more sifted icing sugar.

3 To colour the icing, beat in a few
drops of food colouring. Use the
icing immediately for coating or piping.

*Drizzled or spread, glacé icing can
quickly turn a plain cake into
something special.*

$\mathcal{B}$utterscotch Frosting

This is a richly flavoured frosting, using brown sugar and black treacle. It is useful for coating any sponge cake to impart a smooth or swirled finish.

INGREDIENTS
Makes 450 g/1 lb
75 g/3 oz/6 tbsp butter
45 ml/3 tbsp milk
25 g/1 oz/2 tbsp soft light brown
sugar
15 ml/1 tbsp black treacle
350 g/12 oz cups icing sugar, sifted

Butterscotch frosting is deliciously caramel-flavoured and an unusual alternative for coating a cake.

FLAVOURINGS
The following amounts are for a single quantity of icing. Increase or decrease the amounts proportionally as needed.
Orange, lemon or lime *Replace the treacle with golden syrup and add 10 ml/2 tsp of finely grated orange, lemon or lime zest.*
Chocolate *Sift 15 ml/1 tbsp cocoa powder with the icing sugar.*
Coffee *Replace the treacle with 15 ml/1 tbsp instant coffee powder or granules.*

1 ▲ Place the butter, milk, sugar and treacle in a heatproof bowl over a saucepan of simmering water. Stir occasionally, using a wooden spoon, until the butter and sugar have melted.

2 ▲ Remove the bowl from the saucepan. Stir in the icing sugar, then beat until smooth and glossy.

3 ▲ Pour immediately over the cake for a smooth finish, or allow to cool for a thicker spreading consistency.

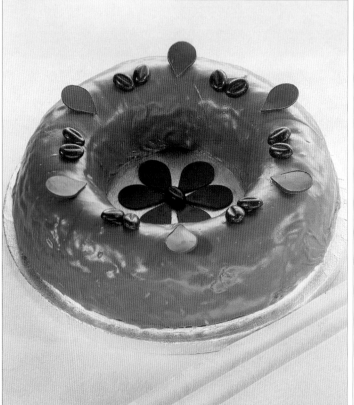

Fudge Frosting

A rich, darkly delicious frosting, this can transform a simple sponge cake into
one worthy of a very special occasion. Spread fudge frosting smoothly over the cake or swirl it.
Or be even more elaborate with a little piping - it is very versatile. The following amount
will fill and coat the top and sides of a 20 cm/8 inch or 23 cm/9 inch round sponge cake.

INGREDIENTS
Makes 350 g/12 oz
50 g/2 oz plain chocolate
225 g/8 oz/2 cups icing sugar, sifted
50 g/2 oz/4 tbsp butter or margarine
3 tbsp milk or single cream
1 tsp vanilla essence

STORING
Not suitable for storing. The icing
must be used immediately after
making.

1 ▲ Break or chop the chocolate into small pieces. Put the chocolate, icing sugar, butter, milk and vanilla essence in a heavy-based saucepan.

2 ▲ Stir over a very low heat until the chocolate and butter or margarine melt. Remove from the heat and stir until evenly blended.

3 ▲ Beat the icing frequently as it cools until it thickens sufficiently to use for spreading or piping. Use immediately and work quickly once it has reached the right consistency.

Thick glossy swirls of fudge icing
almost make a decoration in
themselves on this cake.

*S*atin Chocolate Icing

Shiny as satin and smooth as silk, this dark chocolate icing can be poured over a sponge cake. A few fresh flowers, pieces of fresh fruit, simple chocolate shapes or white chocolate piping add the finishing touch. Use this recipe to cover a 20 cm/8 inch square or a 23 cm/9 inch round quick-mix sponge or Madeira cake.

INGREDIENTS
Makes 225 g/8 oz
175 g/6 oz plain chocolate
150 ml/¼ pint/⅔ cup single cream
½ tsp instant coffee powder

STORING
Not suitable for storing. The icing must be used immediately after making.

*T*ip

Before using the icing, place the cake on a wire rack positioned over a baking sheet or a piece of grease-proof paper. This will avoid unnecessary mess.

2 ▲ Stir over a very low heat until the chocolate melts and the mixture is smooth and evenly blended.

3 Remove from the heat and immediately pour the icing over the cake, letting it slowly run down the sides to coat it completely. Spread the icing with a palette knife as necessary, working quickly before the icing has time to thicken.

Satin chocolate icing brings a real touch of sophistication to the most humble of cakes.

1 ▲ Break or chop the chocolate into small pieces. Put the chocolate, cream and coffee in a small heavy-based saucepan. Place the cake to be iced on a wire rack.

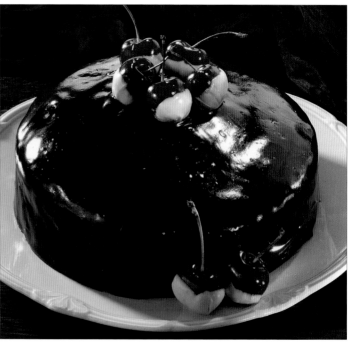

Meringue Frosting

A lightly whisked meringue cooked over hot water and combined with softly beaten butter, this icing may be varied with the suggested flavourings, and should be used directly it is made. The following amount will fill and coat the top and sides of a 20 cm/8 inch sponge cake.

INGREDIENTS
Makes 350 g/12 oz
2 size 3 egg whites
115 g/4 oz/1 cup icing sugar, sifted
150 g/5 oz/⅔ cup butter, softened

FLAVOURINGS
The following amounts are for a single quantity of icing. Increase or decrease the amounts proportionally as needed.
Orange, lemon or lime Fold in 10 ml/ 2 tsp finely grated orange, lemon or lime zest.
Chocolate Fold in 50 g/2 oz plain chocolate, melted.
Coffee Blend 10 ml/2 tsp instant coffee powder or granules with 1 tbsp boiling water. Allow to cool before folding into the icing.

1 Whisk the egg whites in a clean, ovenproof bowl, add the icing sugar and gently whisk to mix well.

2 Place the bowl over a saucepan of simmering water and whisk until thick and white. Remove the bowl from the saucepan, continue to whisk until it is cool and the meringue stands up in soft peaks.

3 ▲ Beat the butter in a separate bowl until light and fluffy. Add the meringue gradually, beating well after each addition, until thick and fluffy. Fold in the chosen flavouring, using a spatula, until evenly blended.
Use immediately for coating, filling and piping cakes.

Meringue frosting creates a fluffy coating for cakes that can be spread or peaked to create a variety of effects.

Petal Paste

Petal paste is used only for making cake decorations. It is exceptionally strong and can be moulded into very fine flowers or cut into individual sugar pieces which dry very quickly. Liquid glucose and gum tragacanth are available from chemist's or cake-icing specialists. Petal paste can also be bought in a powdered form ready to mix. This is very convenient for small quantities but can be rather expensive if using large amounts.

INGREDIENTS
Makes 575 g/1¼ lb
10 ml/2 tsp powdered gelatine
25 ml/5 tsp cold water
10 ml/2 tsp liquid glucose
10 ml/2 tsp white vegetable fat
450 g/1 lb/4 cups icing sugar, sifted
5 ml/1 tsp gum tragacanth
1 size 3 egg white

1 ▲ Place the gelatine, water, liquid glucose and white vegetable fat in a heatproof bowl over a saucepan of hot water until melted, stirring occasionally. Remove the bowl from the heat.

2 ▲ Sift the icing sugar and gum tragacanth into a bowl. Make a well in the centre and add the egg white and gelatine mixture. Mix together with a wooden spoon to form a soft paste.

4 ▲ Place in a polythene bag or wrap in clear film and seal well to exclude all the air. Leave for 2 hours before use, then re-knead and use small pieces at a time, leaving the remaining petal paste well sealed.

3 ▲ Knead on a surface dusted with icing sugar until smooth, white and free from cracks.

Petal paste can be used to make tiny flowers for a special celebratory or formal birthday cake.

Covering Cakes

Covering cakes with icing – whether marzipan, royal or sugarpaste – not only provides a wonderful surface for decorating but also helps to keep the cake moist. The icings need to be applied with care to ensure that the finish is beautifully smooth. Always plan ahead; it will take several days to marzipan and royal ice a cake, allowing for the drying out times.

Marzipanning a Cake for Sugarpaste Icing

Marzipan can be applied as an icing in its own right, but is mainly used as a base for sugarpaste or royal icing. Unlike a cake covered in royal icing which traditionally has sharp, well defined corners, a cake covered in sugarpaste has much smoother lines with rounded corners and edges. There are therefore two different techniques depending on how you wish to ice the cake.

1 If the cake is not absolutely flat, fill any hollows or build up the top edge (if it is lower than the top of the cake) with a little marzipan. Brush the top of the cake with a little warmed and sieved apricot jam.

2 ▲ Lightly dust a work surface with icing sugar. Knead the marzipan into a smooth ball. Roll out to a 5 mm/¼ inch thickness and large enough to cover the top and sides of the cake, allowing about an extra 7.5 cm/3 inches all around for trimming. Make sure the marzipan does not stick to the work surface and moves freely.

3 ▲ Lift the marzipan using your hands, or place it over a rolling pin to support it, and position over the top of the cake. Drape the marzipan over the cake to cover it evenly.

4 ▲ Smooth the top with the palm of your hand to eliminate any air bubbles. Then carefully lift up the edges of the marzipan and let them fall against the sides of the cake, being careful not to stretch the marzipan. Ensure the marzipanned sides are flat and there are no creases – all the excess marzipan should fall on to the work surface. Use the palms of your hands to smooth the sides and eliminate air bubbles.

5 ▲ With a sharp knife, trim the excess marzipan, cutting it flush with the base of the cake.

6 ▲ With your hands, work in a circular motion over the surface of the marzipan to give it a smooth finish. Spread a little royal icing over the middle of a cake board and place the cake in the centre to secure. Lay a piece of greaseproof paper over the top to protect the surface, then leave for at least 12 hours to dry before covering with icing.

Marzipanning a Round Cake for Royal Icing

1 ▲ If the cake is not absolutely flat, fill any hollows or build up the top edge (if it is lower than the top of the cake) with a little marzipan.

2 Brush the top of the cake with warmed and sieved apricot jam.

3 Lightly dust a work surface with icing sugar. Using one-third of the marzipan, knead it into a ball. Roll out to a round 5 mm/¼ inch thickness and 1 cm/½ inch larger than the top of the cake. Make sure that the marzipan does not stick to the work surface and moves freely.

4 ▲ Invert the top of the cake on to the marzipan. Trim the marzipan almost to the edge of the cake. With a small metal palette knife, press the marzipan inwards so it is flush with the edge of the cake.

▶ The method for marzipanning a square cake for royal icing is the same as for a round one, except for the sides. Measure the length and height of the sides with string and roll out the marzipan in four separate pieces, using the string measurements as a guide.

5 Carefully turn the cake the right way up. Check the sides of the cake. If there are any holes, fill them with marzipan to make a flat surface. Brush the sides with apricot jam.

6 Knead the remaining marzipan and any trimmings (making sure there are no cake crumbs on the work surface) to form a ball. For the sides of the cake, measure the circumference with a piece of string, and the height of the sides with another piece.

7 ▲ Roll out a strip of marzipan to the same thickness as the top, matching the length and width to the measured string. Hold the cake on its side, being careful to touch the marzipanned top as lightly as possible. Roll the cake along the marzipan strip, pressing the marzipan into position to cover the sides. Trim if necessary to fit.

8 ▲ Smooth the joins together with a palette knife. Spread a little royal icing into the middle of a cake board and place the cake in the centre to secure. Lay a piece of greaseproof paper very loosely over the top to protect the surface, then leave for at least 24 hours to dry before covering with icing.

Tip

When buying marzipan, it is best to choose the white kind for covering a cake, as the bright yellow marzipan may discolour pale coloured sugarpaste or royal icing.

Covering a Round Cake with Royal Icing

A cake which is coated with royal icing is always covered with marzipan first. The marzipan should be applied one to two days before the royal icing so it has time to dry out slightly, giving a firm surface on which to work. The royal icing is then built up in two or three layers, each one being allowed to dry out before covering with the next. The final coat should be perfectly flat and smooth, with no air bubbles.

Tip

It is difficult to calculate the exact amount of icing required, but if you work with 450 g/1 lb/⅔ quantity batches, it should always be fresh. While working, keep the royal icing in a bowl and cover with a clean, damp cloth or clear film so it does not dry out.

1 The icing should be of 'soft peak' consistency. Put about 2 tbsp of icing in the centre of the marzipanned cake (the amount will depend on the size of cake you are icing).

2 ▲ Using a small palette knife, spread the icing over the top of the cake, working back and forth with the flat of the knife to eliminate any air bubbles. Keep working the icing in this way until the top of the cake is completely covered. Trim any icing that extends over the edge of the cake with the palette knife.

3 ▲ Position a straight-edge ruler on the top edge of the cake furthest away from you. Slowly and smoothly pull the ruler across the surface of the icing, holding it at a slight angle. Do this without stopping to prevent ridges forming. You may need several attempts to get a smooth layer, in which case simply re-spread the top of the cake with icing and try again.

4 ▲ Trim any excess icing from the top edges of the cake with the palette knife to give a straight, neat edge. Leave the icing to dry for several hours, or overnight, in a dry place before continuing.

5 ▲ Place the cake on a turntable. To cover the sides, spread some icing on to the side of the cake with a palette knife. Rock the knife back and forth as you spread the icing to eliminate air bubbles. Rotate the turntable as you work your way around the cake.

6 ▲ Using a plain side-scraper, hold it firmly in one hand against the side of the cake at a slight angle. Turn the turntable round in a continuous motion and in one direction with the other hand, while pulling the scraper smoothly in the opposite direction to give a smooth surface to the iced sides. When you have completed the full turn, carefully lift off the scraper to leave a neat join. Trim off any excess icing from the top edge and the cake board.

7 Leave the cake to dry, uncovered, then apply the icing in the same way to give the cake two or three more coats of icing. For a really smooth final layer, use a slightly softer consistency of icing.

Covering a Square Cake Rough Icing a Cake

The method is essentially the same as for icing a round cake.

1 Cover the top with icing as for the round cake. Leave to dry.

2 ▲ Cover the sides as for the round cake, but work on one side at a time and allow the icing to dry out before continuing with the next side. You will not need a turntable. Simply pull the scraper firmly and smoothly across each side in a single movement, repeating if necessary, for a really smooth finish.

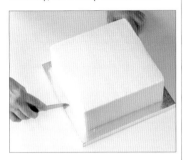

3 ▲ Trim off any excess icing from the cake board with a knife.

4 Leave the cake to dry, uncovered, then apply the icing in the same way to give the cake two or three more coats of icing. For a really smooth final layer, use a slightly softer consistency.

This colourful Christmas Tree cake shows an interesting version of peaked, or rough, icing. The fruit cake is first covered with coloured marzipan and left to dry for 12 hours, then royal icing is peaked around the lower half of the sides. The decorations are also made of coloured marzipan.

Peaking the icing to give it a rough appearance, like that of snow, is a much quicker and simpler way of applying royal icing to a cake. It is also much quicker to apply as you only need one covering of icing.

1 ▲ Spread the icing evenly over the cake, bringing the icing right to the edges so the cake is completely covered.

2 ▲ Starting at the bottom of the cake, press the flat side of a palette knife into the icing, then pull away sharply to form a peak. Repeat until the whole cake is covered with peaks. Alternatively, flat ice the top of the cake and rough ice the sides - or vice versa.

Covering with Sugarpaste Icing

Sugarpaste icing is a quick, professional way to cover a cake. Although fruit cakes are usually covered with marzipan first, this is not necessary if you are using a sponge base. The sugarpaste can be applied in one coating, unlike royal icing which requires several coats for a really smooth finish. Keep the icing white or knead in a little food colouring to tint. Ready-made sugarpaste is extremely good quality and is available in various colours for fast and professional results.

1 Carefully brush a little water or sherry over the marzipanned surface to help the icing stick to the marzipan. (If you miss a patch, unsightly air bubbles may form.)

2 ▲ Lightly dust a work surface with icing sugar. Roll out the sugarpaste to a 5 mm/¼ inch thickness and large enough to cover the top and sides of the cake plus a little extra for trimming. Make sure the icing does not stick to the surface and moves freely.

3 ▲ Lift the sugarpaste using your hands, or place it over a rolling pin to support it, and position over the top of the cake. Drape the sugarpaste over the cake to cover it evenly.

4 ▲ Dust your hands with a little cornflour. Smooth the top and sides of the cake with your hands, working from top to bottom, to eliminate any air bubbles.

5 ▲ With a sharp knife, trim off the excess sugarpaste, cutting flush with the base of the cake.

6 Spread a little royal icing into the middle of a cake board and place the cake in the centre to secure.

Tip
To avoid damaging the surface of the cake while you move it, slide the cake to the edge of the work surface and support it underneath with your hand. Lift it and place on the cake board.

Covering Awkward Shapes

Although most shapes of cake can be covered smoothly with one piece of sugarpaste icing, there are some which need to be covered in sections. A cake baked in a ring mould is one such. The top and outer side of the cake is covered with two identical pieces of sugarpaste, and the inner side with a third piece.

1 ▲ Measure half of the outer circumference of the cake with a piece of string, then measure the side and rounded top with another piece of string.

2 ▲ Take three-quarters of the sugarpaste icing and cut in half. Keep the remaining icing well wrapped until needed. Brush the marzipan lightly with water. Roll out each half of the icing into a rectangle, matching the string measurements. Cover the top and side of the cake in two halves.

3 Measure the circumference and the height of the inner side with two pieces of string. Roll out the reserved sugarpaste icing into a rectangle matching the string measurements, and use to cover the inside of the ring. Trim the sugarpaste to fit and press the joins together securely.

FOOD COLOURINGS & TINTS

Food colourings and tints for cake making are available today in almost as large a range as those found on an artist's palette. This has opened up endless possibilities for the cake decorator to create the most imaginative and colourful designs. Liquid colours are only suitable for marzipan and sugarpaste icing if a few drops are required to tint the icing a very pale shade. If used in large amounts they will soften the icings too much. So for vibrant, stronger colours, as well as for subtle sparkling tints, use pastes or powders, available from cake icing specialists. When choosing colours for icings, ensure that they are harmonious, and complement your design.

Colouring icings

How you apply the colour to an icing depends on whether it is in liquid form, a paste or powder. While working with the colourings it is best to stand them on a plate or washable board so they do not mark your work surface. When using cocktail sticks for transferring the colour to the icing, select a fresh stick for each colour so the colours do not become mixed.

2 ▲ To colour firmer icings, such as sugarpaste and marzipan, use paste colourings. Dip a cocktail stick into the colouring and streak it on to the surface of a ball of the icing.

4 ▲ To create subtle tints in specific areas, brush powdered colourings on to the surface of the icing.

1 ▲ Add liquid colour to the icing a few drops at a time until the required shade is reached. Stir into softer icings, such as butter, royal or glacé.

3 ▲ Knead thoroughly until the colour is evenly worked in and there is no streaking. Add sparingly at first, remembering that the colour becomes more intense as the icing stands, then leave for about 10 minutes to see if it is the shade you need.

A cake decorator's palette – a vivid array of food colourings to help bring out the artist in you.

$\mathcal{D}$ecorating with Royal Icing

Of all the icings, royal icing is probably the most complex and hardest to work with. But once the techniques are mastered, it provides a classic backdrop for both traditional as well as more contemporary cake designs. Traditionally it is used for decorating white wedding and Christmas cakes, but as colour is being introduced more and more into cake decorating, royal icing can now be used in many imaginative ways. This chapter demonstrates how to introduce a modern look using a wide variety of classic techniques.

Making and Using Piping Bags

A piping bag is an essential tool when working with royal icing. You can buy piping bags made of washable fabric and icing syringes, which are ideal for the beginner or for piping butter icing in bold designs. However, for more intricate piping, particularly if using several icing colours and nozzles, home-made greaseproof paper or baking parchment piping bags are more practical and flexible to handle. Make up several ahead of time, following the instructions given here, then fit them with straight-sided nozzles. Do not use nozzles with ridges as they do not have such a tight fit in the bag. To prevent the icing drying out when working with several bags, cover the nozzle ends with a damp cloth when not in use.

2 ▶ With the point of the triangle facing away from you, hold the triangle with your thumb in the middle of the longest edge. Take the left corner and bring it over to meet the point of the triangle, as shown.

3 ▼ Hold in position and bring the remaining corner round and back over to meet the other two points, forming a cone shape. Holding all the points together, position them to make the cone tight and the point of it sharp, as shown.

1 ▲ Cut out a 25 cm/10 inch square of greaseproof paper or baking parchment. Fold it in half diagonally to make a triangle.

4 ▲ With the cone open, turn the points neatly inside the top edge, creasing firmly down. Secure the cone with a staple.

5 For using with a nozzle, cut off the pointed end of the bag and position the nozzle so it fits snugly into the point. Half-fill the bag with icing and fold over the top to seal. To use without a nozzle, add the icing, seal, then cut a small straight piece off the end of the bag to pipe lines.

6 For ease and control, it is important to hold the bag in a relaxed position. You may find it easier to hold it with one or both hands. For one hand, hold the bag between your middle and index fingers and push out the icing with your thumb.

7 ▲ If using both hands, simply wrap the other hand around the bag in the same manner, so both thumbs can push the icing out.

8 ▲ To pipe, hold the bag so the nozzle is directly over the area you want to pipe on. The bag will be held straight or at an angle, depending on the shape you are piping. Gently press down with your thumb on the top of the bag to release the icing, and lift your thumb to stop the flow of icing. Use a small palette knife to cut off any excess icing from the tip of the nozzle as you lift the bag from each piped shape, to keep the shapes neat.

Royal icing is the perfect icing for piping. This cake shows how you can achieve pretty effects with shells, stars, lines and beads. Piped roses in full bloom complement the colour chosen for the top of the cake, and the petal tips have been highlighted with food colouring. Carry the design on to the cake board for a classic celebratory cake.

Piping Shapes

Royal icing gives cakes a professional finish, and is often used in decorating to give a formal and ornate character to a cake. However, simple piping skills can easily be achieved given a little practice. This section shows you how, with just a few piping nozzles, you can enhance the look of your cakes. Remember that the icing must be of the correct consistency – not too firm or it will be difficult to squeeze out of the piping bag, and not too soft or the piping will not hold its shape. Small nozzles are used for the delicate designs made with royal icing. Larger ones are more suitable for butter icing and frostings.

PIPING TWISTED ROPES AND LEAVES

For the ropes, fit nozzles Nos 43 or 44, or a writing nozzle, into a greaseproof paper piping bag and half-fill with icing. Hold the bag at a slight angle and pipe in a continuous line with even pressure, twisting the bag as you pipe. For leaves, you can use a No 18 petal nozzle or simply cut off the point of the bag in the shape of an arrow. Place the tip of the bag on the cake, holding the bag at a slight angle. Pipe out the icing, then pull away quickly to make the tapering end of a leaf.

Twisted ropes and leaves

Stars, swirls and scrolls

PIPING STARS

For a simple star shape, choose a star-shaped nozzle in a size to suit your design. Hold the piping bag upright directly over the area to be iced. Gently squeeze the bag to release the icing and to form a star. Pull off quickly and sharply, keeping the bag straight, to give a neat point to the star.

PIPING SWIRLS

Choose a star-shaped nozzle in a size to suit your design. Hold the piping bag directly over the area to be iced. Pipe a swirl in a circular movement, then pull off quickly and sharply, keeping the bag straight to leave a neat point.

PIPING SCROLLS

Choose star or rope nozzles in a size to suit your design. Hold the piping bag at a slight angle and place the tip of the nozzle on the cake. Pipe the icing lightly upwards and outwards, then come down in a circular movement, tailing off the icing so the end rests on the cake to make a scroll. The action is a little like piping a large 'comma'. For a reverse scroll, repeat as before, but pipe in the opposite direction, going inwards to reverse the shape. A scroll border can be particularly effective if you alternate two colours of icing.

PIPING CORNELLI

Cornelli is a fun technique which can be carried out in one or more colours. It is a little like doodling. Use writing nozzles Nos 1 or 2 and pipe a continuous flow of icing, squiggling the lines in the shape of W's and M's.

PIPING SIMPLE EMBROIDERY

Piped embroidery is very fine work, requiring writing nozzles Nos 0 or 1. Keep the design simple and work in one or several colours. Pipe little circles, lines and dots to make a delicate pattern for your cake. Look at textile embroidery designs for some ideas.

Cornelli and simple embroidery

PIPING DOTS OR BEADS

Use writing nozzles Nos 1, 2 or 3. Hold the piping bag directly over the area you wish to pipe. Press out the icing so it forms a bead, then release the pressure on the bag and take it off gently to one side. The smaller size nozzle will make simple dots. Neither dots nor beads should end in a sharp point. If this happens, lightly press any sharp points back into the bead with a small damp brush, or try making the icing a little softer.

PIPING SHELLS

Use star nozzles Nos 5 or 8. Rest the tip of the nozzle on the cake and pipe out a little icing to secure it to the surface. Gently squeeze out the icing while lifting the bag slightly up and then down, ending with the nozzle back on the surface of the cake. Pull off to release the icing. Repeat, allowing the beginning of the next shell to touch the end of the first one and continue in this way until you have completed a continuous line of shells.

PIPING LINES

Use a writing nozzle, remembering that the smaller the hole, the finer the line. Hold the bag at an angle, rest the nozzle on the cake and pipe out a little icing to secure it to the surface. Pipe the icing, lifting the bag slightly as you work, so it is just above the surface of the cake. Continue to pipe, allowing the line of piping to fall in a straight line. Do not pull or the line will break. At the end of the line, release the pressure, rest the nozzle on the surface of the cake and pull off to break the icing. The line can be varied by curving or looping it.

PIPING TRELLISES

To pipe trellises, use the same technique as above to pipe a set of parallel lines. Then overpipe a set in the opposite direction for squares, or horizontally across the lines for diamonds. You can also get different effects by using different widths of writing nozzles.

PIPING ZIGZAGS

Use a No 2 or 3 writing nozzle and pipe either one continuous zigzag, or stop and start at the end of each point to make them sharper.

Dots and beads

Lines, trellises and zigzags

Shells

Piped Sugar Pieces

These little piped sugar pieces are very fragile and have the appearance of fine lace. They must be made ahead of time, and left to dry. The sugar pieces need to be handled carefully, and it is a good idea to make plenty in case of breakages.

1 ▲ On a piece of greaseproof paper, draw your chosen design several times with pencil. The designs should be kept fairly small.

Shapely forms – delicate piped sugar pieces can be made in all kinds of designs and colours and attached to the sides, tops or edges of cakes with a dab of royal icing.

2 ▲ Tape the paper to the work surface or a flat board and secure a piece of greaseproof paper or baking parchment over the top. Tape the paper down at the corners with masking tape.

3 ▲ Fit a piping bag with a No 1 writing nozzle. Half-fill with royal icing, and fold over the top to seal. Pipe over each design, carefully following the pencilled lines with a continuous thread of icing. Repeat, piping as many pieces as you need plus a few extra in case of any breakages.

4 Leave to dry for at least two hours. Remove from the paper by carefully turning it back and lifting off each piece with a palette knife. When dry, store in a box between layers of tissue paper.

Simple Piped Flowers

To make these pretty piped flowers, you will need a petal nozzle – either small, medium or large depending on how big you want the flowers to be – a paper piping bag, a cocktail stick and a flower nail. Make the flowers ahead of time and, when dry, store in a box between layers of tissue paper.

ROSE

1 For a tightly formed rose, make a fairly firm icing. Colour the icing, or leave it white. Fit the petal nozzle into a paper piping bag, half-fill with royal icing and fold over the top to seal.

2 Hold the piping bag so the wider end of the nozzle is pointing into what will be the base of the flower, and hold a cocktail stick in the other hand. Pipe a small cone shape around the tip of a cocktail stick. Pipe a petal half way around the cone, lifting it so it is at an angle and curling outwards, not flat, and turning the cocktail stick at the same time.

3 ▲ Repeat with more petals so they overlap each other slightly. The last petals can lie flatter and be more open. Remove the rose from the cocktail stick by threading the stick through a large hole on a grater. The rose will rest on the grater. Leave until dry and firm.

PANSY

1 Colour the icing. Fit the petal nozzle into a paper piping bag, half-fill with royal icing and fold over the top to seal. Cut out a small square of greaseproof paper and secure to the flower nail with a little icing.

2 ▲ Holding the nozzle flat, pipe the petal shape in a curve, turning the flower nail at the same time. Pipe five petals in all. Pipe beads of yellow icing in the centre with a small writing nozzle, or use stamens.

3 Remove the paper from the flower nail, but leave the pansy on the paper until it is dry and firm. Coloured details can be added by painting with food colouring, or using food colouring pens, once the flower has dried. Lift the pansy from the paper by carefully slipping a palette knife underneath the base of the flower.

COLOURED SUMMER FLOWERS

1 Colour the icing. Make up the flowers in a variety of shades for a colourful arrangement. Fit the petal nozzle into a paper piping bag, half-fill with royal icing and fold over the top to seal. Cut out a small square of greaseproof paper and secure to the flower nail with a little icing.

2 ▲ Pipe five flat petals in a circle so they slightly overlap each other. Pipe beads of yellow icing in the centre of each flower or sprinkle with hundreds and thousands. Leave to dry and add coloured details as for the pansy.

Bouquet of iced blossoms, including roses, pansies and bright summer flowers – arrangements of piped flowers make colourful cake decorations.

Run-outs

Designs for run-outs can be as complicated or as simple as you like. It is best to start off with a fairly solid shape for your first attempt, as these decorations can be quite fragile to handle. Always make a few more run-outs than you think you will need in case of breakages.

1 Make up the royal icings to the correct consistencies: a stiffer one for the outline, and a softer one for filling in (see the basic recipe for Royal Icing). Leave the icing to stand, preferably overnight, to allow any air bubbles to come to the surface. Stir the icing before using. On a piece of greaseproof paper, draw your chosen design several times.

2 ▲ Tape the paper to the work surface or a flat board and lay a piece of baking parchment over the top. Tape the paper down at the corners with masking tape.

3 ▲ Fit a paper piping bag with a No 1 writing nozzle, and half-fill with the stiffer icing for piping the outline. Carefully pipe over the outline of your design with a continuous thread of icing.

4 ▲ Add the softer icing for filling in into a second paper piping bag. Cut the pointed end off the bag in a straight line. Do not make it too big, or the icing will flow out too quickly. Pipe the icing into the outlines to fill, working from the outline into the centre, being careful not to touch the outline or it may break. To prevent air bubbles forming, keep the end of the bag in the icing. The icing should look overfilled and rounded, as it will shrink slightly as it dries.

5 ▲ You now need to work quickly while the icing is still soft. Move a paintbrush carefully through the icing to fill in any gaps and to ensure it goes right to the edge of the outline, keeping the icing smooth. If any air bubbles do appear, smooth them out with the brush or burst with a pin.

6 ▲ Leave the run-outs on the paper to dry; the drying time will vary depending on their size, but leave for at least one day and preferably longer. When completely dry, remove by carefully slipping a palette knife under the shapes and easing them off the paper. Decorative details can then be piped on to the dried run-outs. Allow these to dry before using or storing.

7 Store the run-outs in a box between layers of greaseproof paper.

When royal icing is presented in bright colours it takes on a lively new look. The hearts and brilliant butterflies are made using the run-out technique. The wings are made separately, then joined with a line of piping to form the body of each butterfly. This also secures them to the cake. Piped sugar pieces, scroll borders and polka dots complete the design.

Decorating with Sugarpaste Icing

As a covering, sugarpaste icing gives a softer look to a cake than royal icing. It is much quicker to work with, requiring only one rolled out layer. This is then placed in position so it curves itself over the edges of the cake. Because it is so pliable, sugarpaste can also be used for a wide range of decorative effects. When making sugarpaste decorations, always wrap any icing you are not using immediately in clear film to stop it drying out.

Marbling

As an alternative to covering a cake in a single colour, sugarpaste icing can be marbled for a multi-coloured effect. Use several colours and keep them quite vibrant, or use one or two delicate tones. Marbled sugarpaste icing can also be used to make effective moulded flowers and other modelled decorations.

1 ▲ Form the sugarpaste icing into a smooth roll or ball. Dip the end of a cocktail stick into the food colouring and dab a few drops on to the icing. Repeat with more colours if wished.

2 ▲ Knead the sugarpaste icing just a few times. The colouring should look very patchy.

3 ▲ On a work surface lightly sprinkled with icing sugar, roll out the sugarpaste icing to reveal the marbled effect.

4 ▲ Alternatively, for a very bold interweaving of colours, use the following technique. Divide the sugarpaste icing into three or four equal portions, depending on how many colours you want to use. Colour them with food colouring. Divide each colour into four or five portions and roll out with your hands into sausage shapes. If you like, you could even put two colours together to make an instant marbled sausage. Place the different-coloured sausages side-by-side on the work surface.

5 ▲ Twist the colours together and knead for several seconds until the strips of colour are fused together but retain their individual colours.

6 ▲ Roll out the marbled icing on a work surface lightly dusted with icing sugar.

Crimping

Crimping tools are similar to large tweezers with patterned ends and are available in a good variety of styles. Crimping is a very quick and efficient way of giving decorative edges and borders to sugarpaste-coated cakes – the effect is similar to the embroidery technique of smocking. For a simple finish to the crimped cake, top with a small posy of edible flowers, a ribbon, or other bought decorations.

3 ▲ Slowly release the crimper so as not to tear the icing. Repeat the pattern, either touching the last one or spacing them evenly apart. The pattern can be varied by using different crimping tools.

1 ▲ Cover the cake with sugarpaste icing. For crimping, the icing must still be soft, so do not allow it to dry out before decorating. Dip the crimping tool in a little cornflour.

2 ▼ Position the crimping tool on the cake in the place you wish to start the design and squeeze the teeth together to make the pattern.

4 ▲ The same technique can be used to crimp decorative designs down the sides of a cake. If applying sugarpaste frills to a cake, crimp the edges for a neat and pretty finish.

Embossing

Special embossing tools can be purchased from cake icing specialists, but you can also use any other patterned items such as cookie stamps, cutters or icing nozzles.

1 ▲ Cover the cake with sugarpaste icing. For embossing, the icing must still be soft, so do not allow it to dry out. Brush a little cornflour on to the embossing tool and press firmly on to the soft icing. Repeat, brushing with cornflour each time.

2 ▲ To add colour, brush a little powdered food colouring on to the embossing tool instead of the cornflour and press on to the icing as before. Highlights can also be added with food colouring pens, as shown.

3 ▲ Textured rolling pins are also available from cake icing specialists. Cover the cake with sugarpaste icing as before and smooth over with your hand. Roll over the surface of the icing with the textured rolling pin. This rolling pin gives a basketweave effect.

Modelling

Sugarpaste is wonderfully adaptable, and can be used to model almost any shape you can think of. Choose small objects, such as flowers, fruits, vegetables, animals, or whatever is going to suit your cake. Using this technique, every cake you make will be unique. Remember to dust the work surface lightly with icing sugar before you start, to prevent sticking. Leave the modelled shapes to dry on greaseproof paper, before applying to the cake.

SMART TEDDY BEAR

▲ Mould each part of the bear's body separately in cream-coloured sugarpaste icing. Roll out the waistcoat to fit the body and cut out the bow tie in purple icing. Mould the buttons and eyes in black icing. Attach the head to the body with a little water, pressing together to secure. Brush the body lightly with water and wrap the waistcoat round, folding back the top two corners. Attach the arms, legs and ears with a little water, pressing to secure, then bend into shape. Attach the bow tie, buttons and eyes with a little water, then paint on any details such as nose and mouth with brown food colouring.

FROSTY SNOWMAN

▲ Mould the snowman's body, head and arms in white sugarpaste icing. Roll out the scarf in red icing, cutting the ends with a sharp knife to represent the tassels. Shape two small balls of blue icing for the eyes, one of red for the nose and two of black for buttons. Using black icing, shape the hat in two pieces, as shown. Attach the head to the body with a little water, then the arms, pressing lightly to secure. Attach the scarf, eyes, nose, buttons and hat in the same way.

HUNGRY RABBIT

▼ Mould the rabbit's body and head, legs, tail and ears in light brown sugarpaste icing. Shape two small balls of blue icing for the eyes. Attach the tail, legs and ears to the rabbit's body with a little water, pressing lightly to secure. Paint the nose and details on the eyes with brown food colouring. For the carrots, shape long ovals out of orange icing, tapering at one end, then make markings on them with the back of a knife. Attach small pieces of green icing on to the ends.

CAT ON A MAT

▲ Mould and shape the cat's body, head, legs, tail and ears in grey marbled sugarpaste icing. Shape two small ovals in black for the eyes and a small pink ball for the nose. Roll out a piece of green icing for the mat. Attach the head to the body with a little water, then the legs, tail, ears, eyes and nose, pressing lightly to secure and bending into shape where necessary. Press four short lengths of florist's wire into the head to represent whiskers (these must be removed before serving the cake). Paint the mouth with black food colouring and place the cat on the mat.

Let your imagination run riot when it comes to using sugarpaste icing. All the inhabitants of this water-lily pond are moulded or cut out of sugarpaste. The water lilies are formed with a small petal-shaped cocktail cutter, then bent into shape. The lily pads are formed with a small round cutter, and then snipped with a knife to make them more lifelike. A blossom cutter creates the flowers on the grassy bank, and the irises, bulrushes, frog and goldfish are modelled by hand.

Cut-out Shapes

Using a variety of shaped cutters, sugarpaste icing can be stamped out to make all kinds of colourful shapes for decorating cakes.

1 Colour the sugarpaste icing to the desired shade, then roll out evenly on a work surface lightly dusted with icing sugar.

2 ▲ Dip the ends of the cutter in icing sugar and cut out the shapes. Leave to dry flat on greaseproof paper, then attach the shapes to the cake with a little royal icing.

The sky's the limit – use cutters or make your own templates for creating a variety of cut-out images.

Cut-out Borders

Borders on the cutting edge – cut-out shapes can also be positioned around the edge of a cake to add a decorative border. Make the borders in bold or delicate designs so that they fit the character of the cake.

1 ▲ Roll out the sugarpaste icing thinly and cut out with a medium-sized cutter – a round, fluted biscuit cutter has been used here. Leave whole or cut in half, depending on the shape.

2 ▲ Use smaller cutters to cut out inside shapes for a filigree effect, or make up your own shapes and use templates cut out of card.

3 Leave the shapes to dry flat on greaseproof paper, then attach them around the top edges of the cake with a little royal icing.

Plunger Blossoms

A special plunger blossom cutter, available in different sizes, is used to make these dainty flowers. The cutter contains a plunger for ejecting the delicate shapes once they have been cut out.

1 ▲ Roll out the icing thinly on a work surface lightly dusted with icing sugar. Dip the cutter in cornflour and cut out the flower shapes.

2 ▲ The flower should remain on the end of the cutter. To remove the flower, hold the cutter on a foam pad and depress the plunger. As it goes into the foam it will bend the flower into shape and release it.

3 The flowers can be simply finished with a little bead of royal icing piped into the centre when they are dry, or you can make a spray of flowers using florist's wire and stamens.

4 ▲ To make a spray, push a pin through the centre of each flower. Leave the flowers to dry on the foam.

5 ▲ When dry, pipe a little royal icing on to a stamen and thread it through the hole. This will hold it in position. Repeat with all the flowers.

6 ▲ When the individual flowers are completely dry, twist a piece of florist's wire on to the end of each stamen. Group the flowers and twist the wires together to make a spray.

This pretty Teddy Bear Christening cake is simply decorated with a modelled bear and delicate plunger blossoms.

Frills

Sugarpaste frills give a particularly elaborate finish to a cake and are especially appropriate for decorating wedding, christening and anniversary cakes. Try layering two different coloured frills together for a very special occasion.

1 ▲ Roll out the sugarpaste icing thinly on a work surface lightly dusted with icing sugar. Use a special frill cutter to cut out the rings for the frills. One ring will make one large or two smaller frills.

2 ▲ Position the end of a wooden cocktail stick over about 5 mm/ ¼ inch of the outer edge of the ring. Roll the stick back and forth firmly around the edge with your finger. The edge will become thinner and start to frill. Continue in this way until the ring is completely frilled.

3 ▲ Using a sharp knife, cut through the ring once to open it up. Gently ease it open. For shorter frills, cut the ring in half to make two frills.

4 ▲ Cut out a template the size of the opened frill and hold against the side of a covered cake. Mark with a pin to show where to attach the frill, and repeat all around the cake.

5 ▲ To attach the frill, either pipe a line of royal icing on to the cake or brush a line of water. Carefully secure the frill on to the line of royal icing or water. Overlay with a second frill in the same or a different coloured icing if wished. Repeat around the cake. The top edge of each frill can be decorated with piping or with a crimping tool.

Tip

If you do not have a special frill cutter you can use individual pastry cutters instead. Use a 7.5–10 cm/ 3–4 inch plain or fluted cutter to cut out the outer circle and a 4–5 cm/ 1½–2 inch plain cutter to cut out the inner circle.

Design Variations

1 ▲ Looped frills look very pretty attached to the cake 'upside-down' as shown here. They are made and attached in the same way as described for looped frills, except that you need to cut out a larger hole from the middle of the ring to make the frills thinner. They will drape more effectively this way.

2 ▲ Frills look equally attractive applied diagonally to the cake sides at regular intervals. They are made and attached to the cake in exactly the same way as described for looped frills, although each ring will probably be large enough to make two frills.

Plaques

A plaque can simply be a plain cut-out shape, or it can be more decorative with, for example, a frilled edge and delicate piping work. Use a plaque as a focal point on a cake to dedicate it to someone special, for weddings, christenings, anniversaries and birthdays, or as a base on which to paint a picture with food colourings.

1 ▲ For a plain plaque, roll out the sugarpaste thinly on a work surface lightly dusted with icing sugar. Dip a cutter (round, oval, heart-shaped or fluted) in a little cornflour. Cut out the shape and leave it to dry flat on greaseproof paper.

2 ▲ Using royal or glacé icing, pipe on a decoration or name. Alternatively, write or draw on the plaque with a food colouring pen, or with food colourings and a fine paintbrush.

3 ▲ For a frilled plaque, cut out the shape as described above. While the icing is still soft, position the end of a wooden cocktail stick over about 5 mm/¼ inch of the outer edge of the plaque. Roll the stick back and forth firmly around the edge with your finger. The edge will become thinner and start to frill. Continue until the edge of the plaque is completely frilled.

Endlessly versatile, sugarpaste icing can be embossed, crimped, cut out and marbled, techniques which are all displayed on this unusual diamond-shaped cake. Small cutters have been used for the embossed pattern on the sides, and different crimping tools for the designs at the corners. 'Paprika' food colouring has been used for the sugarpaste covering for a contemporary terracotta shade, and the trimmings have been marbled with a little blue icing both for the unusual cut-out edging and the star decorations.

ecorating with Marzipan

Marzipan can be a decorative icing in its own right, or it can provide a firm undercoat for a royal icing or sugarpaste icing covering. It is extremely pliable, and the white variety in particular takes colour well.

Marzipan can be moulded and shaped, crimped and embossed, and cut out or modelled into all kinds of animal shapes, figures, flowers, fruits, and even edible Christmas decorations, to name just a few possibilities.

Embossing

A 'pattern in relief' can be created on cakes by using special embossing tools, or any piece of kitchen equipment that will leave a patterned indentation on the marzipan. To make the embossed picture more interesting, paint on highlights with food colouring.

1 Cover the cake with marzipan, then emboss straight away before the icing dries. Dust the embossing tool with a little cornflour, press firmly into the marzipan, then lift off carefully to reveal the pattern. Alternatively, for a coloured design, brush a little powdered food colouring on to the embossing tool instead of the cornflour and press on to the marzipan as before.

2 ▼ Paint on coloured highlights with food colouring, if you wish.

Very simple versions of crimping and embossing have been applied to the marzipan top of this Simnel cake. The edges are crimped – or fluted – with the fingers and the top is embossed using the back of the fork.

Crimping

As with sugarpaste icing, marzipan can be crimped to give simple, pretty edgings and patterns to cakes.

1 Cover a cake with marzipan, but do not allow to dry out. To prevent the crimping tool from sticking, dip it in a little cornflour.

2 Place the crimping tool on the edge of the cake where it is to be decorated and then squeeze the teeth together to make the design. Slowly release the crimping tool, being careful not to let it open quickly or it will tear the marzipan.

3 ▲ Re-position the crimper and repeat to complete the design. You can decorate both the top and base edges of the cake, or the whole side of the cake, if you wish. The crimping tool can also be used to make a pattern on top of the cake.

Marzipan Cut-outs

Small flower and other shaped cutters can be purchased from cake icing specialists for cutting out marzipan shapes. Aspic, cocktail or biscuit cutters can also be used. Once you have cut out the basic shapes, you can decorate them with different coloured marzipan trims, small sweets or piping. Here are some ideas for cut-out marzipan flowers.

COLOURFUL BLOSSOMS

▲ Colour the marzipan to the desired shades. Roll out evenly on a work surface lightly dusted with icing sugar. Dip the ends of a leaf cutter or a small round cutter in icing sugar, and cut out five petals for each flower. Overlap the petals in a circle, securing with a little water. Shape small balls of yellow or orange marzipan and place one in the centre of each flower.

FRILLY BLOSSOMS AND LEAVES

▲ Colour and roll out the marzipan as for the Colourful Blossoms. For each flower, cut out two circles using two fluted cutters, one slightly smaller than the other. (The sizes will depend on the size of flower you are making.) To frill the edges, position the end of a wooden cocktail stick over 3 mm/⅛ inch of the outer edge of each circle. Roll the stick firmly back and forth around the edges with your finger so the edges become thinner and begin to frill. Continue until the circles are completely frilled.

Place the smaller frill on top of the larger, and lightly press together to secure. Take a small ball of the deeper shade of marzipan and press through a fine sieve. Cut off the marzipan which has been pushed through the sieve and place in the centre of the flower.

Cut out leaves from green marzipan with a leaf cutter. Bend the leaves slightly to make them look more life-like. Larger leaves can be left to bend over the handle of a wooden spoon until firm.

VIOLETS

▲ Colour the marzipan purple and roll out as for the Colourful Blossoms. Cut out each flower with a four-petal cocktail cutter. With a little yellow marzipan, shape small balls and then position in the centre of each flower.

Creative cut-outs – marzipan can be used in unusual ways to make imaginative shapes and borders.

Modelling

Marzipan is a wonderful icing to use for modelling. Work with either coloured marzipan, or use white and highlight it with colour after shaping. If colouring your own marzipan, tint it to the required shade, then paint on extra tones and details when the model is assembled to make the objects more life-like. Here are just a few suggestions for shaping fruits and vegetables.

RED-HOT CHILLI PEPPERS

▲ Colour equal portions of marzipan red and green. Mould the chilli shapes, tapering them to a point towards the ends. Shape the stems from green marzipan and attach to the chillies, pressing together lightly to secure.

BUNCH OF GRAPES

▲ Colour the marzipan purple. Shape a cone for the main body of the grape bunch, then mould small individual balls for the grapes. Mould the stem, using a little brown marzipan. Arrange the grapes until the cone is completely covered. Use a little water if necessary to make them stick and press lightly to secure. Make a small indentation in the top of the cone and press in the stem to secure.

RIPE BANANAS

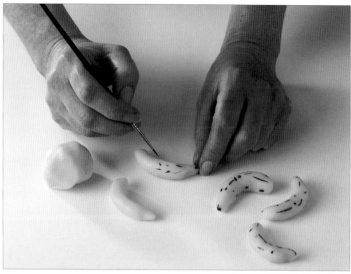

▲ Colour the marzipan yellow or use yellow marzipan. Mould and bend small pieces of the icing into the shapes of bananas. Paint on highlights with brown food colouring.

ROSY APPLES

▲ Colour the marzipan green for the apples and brown for the stems. Shape the green marzipan into rounds and make an indent at one end with a modelling tool. Shape small pieces of brown icing for the stems. Paint a rosy bloom on the apples with red food colouring and press the stems into the indents.

More familiar as an undercoat for a cake, marzipan should not be neglected as a decoration in itself. It takes colour well, and when used to coat this light fruit ring cake, it should certainly not be covered up. Marzipan's plasticity also makes it ideal for moulding flowers, such as this colourful collection of roses, and for twisting into ropes to make a colourful edging.

Plaiting and Weaving

Use these techniques with marzipan to make colourful edgings and decorations for cakes.

CANDY-STRIPE ROPE

1 Take two pieces of different coloured marzipan. On a work surface lightly dusted with icing sugar, roll out two or three ropes of even length and width with your fingers.

2 ▲ Pinch the ends together at the top, then twist into a rope. Pinch the other ends to seal neatly.

PLAIT

1 Take three pieces of different coloured marzipan. On a work surface lightly dusted with icing sugar, roll out three ropes of even length and width with your fingers.

2 ▲ Pinch the ends together at the top, then plait the ropes neatly and pinch the other ends to seal neatly.

MARZIPAN TWIST

1 Colour the marzipan (working with one or two colours). On a work surface lightly dusted with icing sugar, roll out each piece of marzipan to a 5 mm/¼ inch thickness, then cut each piece into 1 cm/½ inch wide strips.

2 ▲ Take two different coloured strips and pinch the ends together at the top. Twist the strips together, joining on more strips with water, if needed.

BASKET-WEAVE

1 ▲ On a work surface lightly dusted with icing sugar, roll out a piece of marzipan (or work with two colours and roll out each one separately) to a 5 mm/¼ inch thickness. Cut into 5 mm/ ¼ inch wide strips.

2 ◄ Arrange the strips, evenly spaced, in parallel lines, then weave the strips in and out. Alternate the colours if using two, as shown. This decoration looks stunning on top of a cake. The edges can be trimmed to fit the shape of the cake.

Marzipan Roses

Not only do these roses smell sweet, they taste good too. Though they may look difficult to make, marzipan roses are quite simple to mould. For a formally decorated cake, shape the roses in a variety of colours and sizes, then arrange flamboyantly on top.

1 ▲ Take a small ball of coloured marzipan and form it into a cone shape. This forms the central core which supports the petals.

2 ▲ To make each petal, take a small piece of marzipan about the size of a large pea, and work it with your fingers to a petal shape which is slightly thicker at the base. If the marzipan sticks, dust your fingers in icing sugar or cornflour.

3 ▲ Wrap the petal around the cone as shown. Press the petal to the cone to secure. Bend the ends of the petal back slightly, to curl.

4 ▲ Mould the next petal in the same way and attach as before, so it just overlaps the first one. Curl the ends back slightly. Repeat with several more petals, making them slightly bigger until you have the size of rose you want. Overlap each petal and curl the ends back as before. Make sure all the petals are securely attached, then cut off the base of the cone. This provides a flat surface so the rose will stand on the cake.

5 For rosebuds, make just a few smaller petals and do not curl the ends back.

6 To add more detail to the rose, paint tints on to the petals using a paintbrush and food colouring. Leave to stand on greaseproof paper until firm.

Blooming roses – moulded roses can add glamour to any cake.

ecorating with Butter Icing

Butter icing is very quick to make up and is easy to use for quick and simple decorations. It can be used to sandwich cakes together, or to coat the top and sides with a thick, creamy layer of icing. To make your butter-iced cakes a little more individual, texture the icing on the tops or sides – or both if you wish. To finish, you can pipe the icing in swirls.

Cake Sides

For decorating cake sides, all you need is a plain or serrated scraper, depending on whether you want a smooth or a textured finish to the icing. If you have an icing turntable, it will make icing cake sides a much simpler task, but it is not essential.

Here a chocolate-flavoured and green-coloured butter icing have been realistically swirled to imitate tree bark and leaves in this delightful novelty cake idea.

1 ▲ Secure the cake to a cake board with a little icing. Cover the top and sides of the cake with icing and put it on an icing turntable. Using a plain or serrated scraper, hold it with one hand firmly against the side of the cake at a slight angle.

2 ▲ Turn the turntable round in a steady continuous motion and in one direction with the other hand, while pulling the scraper smoothly in the opposite direction to give a smooth or serrated surface to the iced sides. When you have completed the full turn, stop the turntable and carefully lift off the scraper to leave a neat join. Trim off any excess icing from the top edge and the cake board.

Cake Tops

More intricate patterns can be made on the tops of cakes with a few simple tools. Use a small palette knife, a plain or serrated scraper or a fork to give a silky smooth finish to the cake, or to make a variety of patterned ridges or some deep, generous swirls.

SWIRLS

1 ▲ Spread the icing smoothly over the top of the cake, then work over the icing with the tip of a palette knife from side to side to create a series of swirled grooves.

2 For a more formal appearance, draw the tip of a palette knife through the swirled grooves in evenly spaced lines.

RIDGED SPIRAL

1 Spread the icing smoothly over the top of the cake, then place the cake on a turntable.

2 ▲ Hold a serrated scraper at a slight angle, pointing it towards the centre of the cake. Rotate the cake with your other hand, while moving the scraper sideways to make undulations and a ridged spiral pattern.

FEATHERED SPIRAL

1 Spread the icing smoothly over the top of the cake and place the cake on a turntable. Rotate the turntable slowly, drawing the flat tip of a palette knife in a continuous curved line, starting from the edge of the cake and working in a spiral into the centre.

2 ▲ Pull out lines with the tip of the knife, radiating out from a central point to the edge of the cake.

RIDGED SQUARES

1 Spread the icing smoothly over the top of the cake. Pull a fork across the cake four or five times, depending on the size of the cake, to produce groupings of evenly spaced lines.

2 ▲ Pull the fork across the cake four or five times as before, but at right angles to the first lines, to give a series of large squares.

DIAMONDS

1 Spread the icing smoothly over the top of the cake. Then lightly dredge with cocoa powder, if using white or lightly tinted butter icing, or icing sugar if using chocolate icing.

2 ▲ Draw a series of lines with the flat side of a knife to expose the butter icing and to make a diamond pattern over the top.

Piping with Butter Icing

The butter icing needs to be of the correct consistency for piping. To check, dip a palette knife and then lift out – the icing should form a sharp point. If too stiff, the icing will be difficult to pipe, if too soft, it will not hold its shape. Add a little extra milk or fruit juice if the consistency is too stiff, or more icing sugar if it is too thin.

DRAMATIC TOUCHES
Piping butter icing in bold, swirling designs with large nozzles can produce dramatic effects.

1 ▲ Cover the top of the cake with a smooth, thin layer of butter icing and smooth the sides with a plain scraper. Using a No 13 plain piping nozzle fitted in a material piping bag, pipe large overlapping spirals to cover the top of the cake. For each spiral, start in the centre and work outwards, until they are the required size.

2 ▼ Pipe large beads of icing around the edges of the cake, using a large writing nozzle. Lightly sprinkle the spirals with either a little sifted cocoa or icing sugar, depending on the colour of the butter icing.

DAINTY DESIGNS
For a more delicate effect, use small nozzles to pipe shapes such as dots and beads, stars or scrolls, as demonstrated for royal icing.

1 Cover the top of the cake with a smooth, thin layer of butter icing. Make a ridged pattern with a serrated scraper around the sides of the cake and a swirled spiral with a palette knife over the top.

2 Using a writing nozzle fitted in a paper piping bag, pipe loops and beads of icing in a contrasting colour.

3 ▲ Pipe beads of icing at the ends of each loop in the same colour as used to cover the cake.

BASKET-WEAVE DESIGN
Butter icing can be piped very effectively with a ribbon nozzle to make a basket-weave design. You can use different colours for the vertical and horizontal lines.

1 Fit a ribbon nozzle into a paper piping bag. Add the icing and fold over the top of the bag to secure. Pipe a vertical line the length of the area you wish to cover with basket weave.

2 Pipe 2 cm/³⁄₄ inch horizontal lines over the vertical line (slightly longer each side than the width of the vertical line) at 1 cm/½ inch intervals.

3 ▲ Pipe another vertical line so that it just covers one end of all the horizontal lines.

4 ▲ Fill in the spaces between the horizontal lines with an alternating row of horizontal lines to make the basket-weave design. Repeat until the area you wish to cover is completed.

Few can resist the glossy smoothness of butter icing. If you add flavouring and food colouring, the colour of the icing should reflect the taste, as with this tangy lemon-iced cake. Use a serrated scraper to create ridges in the icing on the sides and a palette knife to make the swirled and feathered effect on the top of the cake. Finish off with generous swirls of piped white butter icing.

Decorating with Glacé Icing

Using white and coloured glacé icing, simple but effective patterns can be created for decorating sponges, Madeira cakes or Swiss rolls. To vary the ideas shown here using one colour of icing, make up two colours of icing and pipe them alternately. Glacé icing sets quickly but needs to be very soft to create the following designs, so make a batch just before you want to decorate the cake and work quickly before it hardens.

Cobweb, Feather and Fan Icing

Cobweb, feather and fan effects are created using the same basic technique. For the cobweb, the coloured lines are piped in circles. For the fan, the colour is applied in straight lines and the skewer is pulled across in radiating lines. For feather icing the skewer is pulled at right angles through them.

COBWEB ICING

1 Make the glacé icing, colour a portion and put in a paper piping bag, as for feather icing. Coat the top of the cake evenly with the remaining white icing.

2 ▲ Work quickly before the icing has a chance to set. Pipe evenly spaced circles on top of the icing, starting from the centre of the cake and moving towards the edge.

3 ▲ Using a skewer, pull it in straight lines from the edge of the cake to the centre so that it is evenly divided into four sections.

4 ▲ Working from the centre of the cake to the edge, pull the skewer between the four lines to divide the cake evenly into eight. Leave to set.

For an effective Spider's web cake, use the cobweb icing technique. First cover the cake with yellow glacé icing. Pipe a continuous spiral of black glacé icing, then draw a skewer down from the top at regular intervals.

FEATHER ICING

1 Make the glacé icing (see Basic Icing Recipes). Put 2 tbsp of the icing in a small bowl and colour with a little food colouring.

2 Fit a paper piping bag with a No 2 writing nozzle, then spoon in the coloured icing and fold over the top of the bag to secure.

3 ▼ Coat the top of the cake evenly with the remaining white icing. Working quickly so the icing does not set, pipe the coloured icing in straight lines across the cake. You may find it easier to work from the centre outwards when doing this.

4 ▲ Using a skewer, pull it at right angles through the coloured lines in one direction, leaving an even spacing between the lines.

5 ▲ Working in the space between the lines, pull the skewer in the opposite direction, to give a feather pattern. Leave to set.

FAN ICING

1 Make the glacé icing, colour a portion and put in a paper piping bag. Ice the top of the cake as for the Feather and Cobweb techniques.

2 Working quickly so the icing does not set, pipe the coloured icing in evenly spaced straight lines across the cake. You may find it easier to work from the centre outwards.

3 ▲ Using a skewer, pull it through the coloured lines, starting from a point at one edge of the cake and radiating the lines out from it.

4 ▲ Working in the space between the lines, pull the skewer through the piped lines in the opposite direction to give a fan pattern. Leave to set.

Squiggle Icing

Here a random patterning of icing, similar to cornelli (see Decorating with Royal Icing), is lightly feathered or marbled. The technique is shown here using white icing on a chocolate-tinted background, but would be equally effective using one or two colours on a white icing background.

1 Make the glacé icing. Put 2 tbsp of the icing into a paper piping bag fitted with a No 2 writing nozzle, and colour the rest with cocoa mixed with a little water. Coat the top of the cake evenly with the chocolate icing.

2 ▲ Working quickly before the icing has a chance to set, pipe haphazard squiggles all over the top of the cake in a continuous line.

3 ▼ Using a cocktail stick, pull it through the lines in short, swirling movements and in different directions, to create a random feathered effect.

Marbling Flowers and Leaves

The feathering technique can also be used to give a marbled effect to piped decorations. The technique has been used here for a pretty flower and leaf design. The method is also effective for holly leaves, with the lines being pulled outwards to create the spiky points on the leaves.

1 Make the glacé icing, colour a small portion green and a portion red and put each in a paper piping bag fitted with a No 2 writing nozzle. Coat the top of the cake evenly with the remaining white icing.

2 ▲ Working quickly before the icing sets, pipe a floral design on to the cake, piping circles for flowers in the red icing, and ovals for leaves in the green icing.

3 ▲ To marble the flowers, pull a skewer through the lines from the outer edge almost to the middle. The number of petals will be determined by the number of lines you pull. Do the same for the leaves.

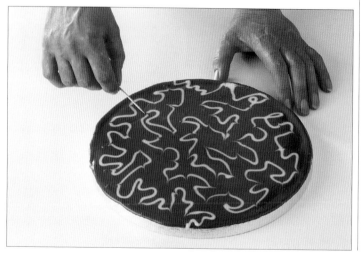

Tip

If the top of the cake is not perfectly flat for piping on, simply turn the cake upside down and use the flat base as the top.

Piping with Glacé Icing

All kinds of imaginative designs can be created, using the following method, to decorate the tops and edges of cakes.

This cake is covered with white glacé icing and the side is then coated with green-tinted desiccated coconut. The bold, exotic flowers are piped in red and green glacé icing and then marbled with a small cocktail stick, before the white or coloured icings have time to set, for a delicate finish.

1 Make the glacé icing, reserving a few tablespoons for piping. Coat the top of the cake evenly with the remaining icing (either white or coloured) and leave to set.

2 Divide the reserved icing into two equal portions and colour each in contrasting but complementary shades. Spoon the icings into two separate paper piping bags, each fitted with a No 2 writing nozzle. Use one colour to pipe geometric shapes or other simple designs over the icing.

3 ▲ Pipe a border around the edge of the cake with the other colour.

ecorating with Chocolate

Nothing adds a luxurious touch to a cake quite like chocolate, whether it is poured over to form a glossy icing, or piped, shaved, dipped or curled. There are several types of chocolate to choose from, and all should be used with care. Couverture is the best and used for professional chocolate work, but it is expensive and requires particularly careful handling. For the following techniques, good-quality baking or eating chocolate is suitable. Chocolate-flavoured cake covering is easy to use but is inferior both in taste and texture.

Chocolate decorations can look particularly interesting if different kinds of chocolate – dark, milk and white – are used in combination. White chocolate can be coloured, but make sure you use powdered food colouring for this as liquid colourings will thicken it. Store chocolate decorations in the refrigerator in a plastic container between layers of greaseproof paper until ready to use. Also, handle the decorations as little as possible with your fingers, as they will leave dull marks on the shiny surface of the chocolate.

Melting

For most of the decorations described in this section, the chocolate must be melted first.

1 ▼ Break the chocolate into small pieces and place in a bowl set over a pan of hot water. Do not allow the bowl to touch the water and do not let the water boil; the chocolate will spoil if overheated. Melt the chocolate slowly and stir occasionally. Be careful not to let water or steam near the chocolate or it will become too thick.

2 ▲ When the chocolate is completely melted, remove the pan from the heat and stir.

Coating Cakes

1 ▲ Stand the cake on a wire rack. It is a good idea to place a sheet of greaseproof paper or a baking sheet underneath the rack to catch any chocolate drips. Pour the chocolate icing over the cake quickly, in one smooth motion, to coat the top and sides.

2 Use a palette knife to smooth the chocolate over the sides, if necessary. Allow the chocolate to set, then coat with another layer, if wished.

Piping with Chocolate

Chocolate can be piped directly on to a cake, or it can be piped on to baking parchment to make run-outs, small outlined shapes or irregular designs. After melting the chocolate, allow it to cool slightly so it just coats the back of a spoon. If it still flows freely it will be too runny to hold its shape when piped. When it is the right consistency, you then need to work fast as the chocolate will set quickly.

Chocolate Outlines

Pipe the chocolate in small, delicate shapes to use as elegant decorations on cakes. Or pipe random squiggles and loosely drizzle a contrasting chocolate over the top.

1 Melt 115 g/4 oz chocolate and allow to cool slightly. Tape a piece of baking parchment to a baking sheet or flat board.

2 ▼ Fill a paper piping bag with the chocolate. Cut a small piece off the pointed end of the bag in a straight line. Pipe your chosen shape in a continuous line, and repeat or vary. Leave to set in a cool place, then carefully lift off the paper with a palette knife.

Piping on to Cakes

This looks effective on top of a cake iced with coffee glacé icing.

1 Melt 50 g/2 oz each of white and dark chocolate in separate bowls and allow to cool slightly. Place the chocolates in separate paper piping bags. Cut a small piece off the pointed end of each bag in a straight line.

2 ▲ Hold each piping bag in turn above the surface of the cake and pipe the chocolates all over. Here, the chocolates have been piped in overlapping semi-circles of different sizes. Try your own designs, too.

Chocolate Lace Curls

Make lots of these curly shapes and store them in a cool place ready for using as cake decorations. Try piping the lines in contrasting colours of chocolate to vary the effect.

1 ▲ Melt 115 g/4 oz chocolate and allow to cool slightly. Cover a rolling pin with baking parchment and attach it with tape. Fill a paper piping bag with the chocolate and cut a small piece off the pointed end in a straight line.

2 ▲ Pipe lines of chocolate backwards and forwards over the baking parchment, as shown.

3 ▲ Leave the chocolate lace curls to set in a cool place, then carefully peel off the paper.

Marbling Chocolate — Chocolate Run-Outs

Here, dark chocolate is swirled over a white glacé-iced cake for a stunningly simple effect. Before melting the chocolate, make the icing, then work very quickly while both the chocolate and the icing are still soft.

1 Melt 50 g/2 oz of dark chocolate. Coat the top of the cake evenly with white glacé icing.

2 ▲ Spoon the chocolate into a paper piping bag, cut a small piece off the pointed end in a straight line and then quickly pipe the chocolate in large, loose loops.

3 ▼ Pull a cocktail stick through the chocolate in short, swirling movements and in different directions, to create a random marbled effect.

The same basic method used for making royal icing run-outs is used here with chocolate. Try piping the outline in one colour of chocolate and filling in the middle with another.

1 ▲ Tape a piece of greaseproof paper to a baking sheet or flat board. Draw around a shaped biscuit cutter on to the paper, or trace or draw a shape of your choice freehand. Repeat the design several times.

2 Secure a piece of baking parchment over the top of the pencilled design. Tape it down securely at the corners with masking tape.

3 ▲ Fill two paper piping bags with melted chocolate. Cut a small piece off the pointed end of one of the bags in a straight line and pipe over the outline of your design in a continuous thread.

4 ▲ Cut the end off the other bag, slightly wider than before, and pipe the chocolate to fill in the outline so it looks slightly rounded. Leave to set in a cool place, then carefully lift off the paper with a palette knife.

Chocolate icing and decorating techniques are demonstrated in all their glory on this sumptuous chocolate gâteau. The cake is covered with fudge frosting. A neat ring of cocoa is then dusted around the edge, using a round stencil to protect the centre of the cake. The cake is decorated with mottled white and plain chocolate leaves. Chocolate curls adorn the top, and haphazardly piped white chocolate shapes, loosely overpiped with dark chocolate, complete the ultimate chocoholic extravaganza.

Chocolate Leaves

Chocolate Cut-Outs

Chocolate leaves are made by coating real leaves with dark, white or milk chocolate or any combination of the three. Choose small freshly-picked leaves with simple shapes and well-defined veins, such as rose leaves. Leave a short stem on the leaves so you have something to hold.

You can make abstract shapes, or circles, squares and diamonds, by cutting them out freehand with a sharp knife. Alternatively, use a large biscuit cutter or ruler as a guide, or cut out the shapes with small biscuit or cocktail cutters. These shapes look equally attractive whether evenly positioned around the sides of the cake, spaced apart or overlapping each other, or simply arranged haphazardly.

1 ▲ Wash and dry the leaves well on kitchen paper. Melt 115 g/4 oz chocolate. Using a paintbrush, brush the underside of each leaf with chocolate. Take care not to go over the edge of the leaf or the chocolate will be difficult to peel off.

1 ▲ Cover a baking sheet with baking parchment and tape down at each corner. Melt 115 g/4 oz dark, milk or white chocolate. Pour the chocolate on to the baking parchment.

3 ▲ Press the cutter firmly through the chocolate and lift off the paper with a palette knife. Try not to touch the surface of the chocolate or you will leave marks on it.

2 ▲ Using different chocolates for a mottled effect, brush the leaves in the same way, partly with plain or milk and partly with white chocolate.

3 Place the leaves chocolate-side up on baking parchment. Leave to set.

2 ▲ Spread the chocolate evenly with a palette knife. Allow to stand until the surface is firm enough to cut, but not so hard that it will break. It should no longer feel sticky when touched with your finger.

4 ▲ The finished shapes can be left plain or piped with a contrasting chocolate if you wish.

5 ▲ Abstract shapes can be cut with a knife freehand. They look particularly effective pressed on to the sides of a butter iced cake.

4 ▲ Carefully peel the leaf from the chocolate, handling the chocolate as little as possible. If the chocolate seems too thin, re-coat with more melted chocolate. Leave to set.

Chocolate-dipped Fruit and Nuts

Use small, fresh fruit such as strawberries, grapes and kumquats for dipping, and whole nuts such as almonds, cashews, brazils or macadamias. Make sure that the fruit and nuts are at room temperature, or the chocolate will set too quickly.

1 Line a baking sheet with baking parchment. Wash the fruit and dry well on kitchen paper. Hold the fruit by its stem, then dip into the chocolate. You can either coat the piece of fruit completely, or just dip half of it, leaving the line of chocolate straight or at a slight angle. Remove the fruit, shake it gently and let any excess chocolate fall back into the bowl. Place on baking parchment and leave to set.

2 ▲ For nuts, place a nut on the end of a long kitchen fork or dipping fork. Lower into the chocolate and coat completely. Lift out of the chocolate and shake off any excess, then leave to set as for fruit. To coat just half of the nut, hold it between your fingers and dip part way into the chocolate.

3 For a two-tone effect, melt dark and white chocolate in separate bowls. Dip the fruit or nuts into one colour to coat completely, then, when set, half-dip into the other colour.

Chocolate Curls

1 Melt 115 g/4 oz chocolate. Pour the chocolate on to a firm, smooth surface such as a marble, wood or plastic laminate, set on a slightly damp cloth to prevent slipping. Spread the chocolate evenly over the surface with a large palette knife.

2 ▲ Leave the chocolate to cool slightly. It should feel just set, but not hard. Hold a large sharp knife at a 45° angle to the chocolate and push it along the chocolate in short sawing movements from right to left and left to right to make curls.

3 ▲ Remove the curls by sliding the point of the knife underneath each one and lifting off. Leave until firm.

Chocolate Shavings

The quickest way to turn chocolate into a decoration is simply to grate or shave it. The chocolate should be at room temperature for this.

1 ▲ For fine shavings, grate the chocolate on the coarse side of a grater. For coarser shavings, peel off curls with a vegetable peeler.

This sophisticated heart-shaped cake is a wonderful idea for Valentine's Day or to celebrate an engagement. It is completely covered with rich, dark chocolate curls.

COLOUR EFFECTS

*If you think of the surface of a cake as an artist's canvas, it opens up
all sorts of decorating ideas using painting and drawing techniques.
This is made possible by the wide range of colours available in the form
of food colourings and food colouring pens.*

Using Stencils

Cards with stencil patterns on them can be found at cake icing specialists or at stationers, or you can make your own stencils out of thin card.

1 Coat the cake with sugarpaste, royal or marzipan icing and leave to dry.

2 ▲ Lay the stencil over the surface of the cake. Dip a dry, clean paintbrush into powdered food colouring and dab into the stencil. Lift off the stencil to reveal the design. You could also fill in the colour with a food colouring pen.

Flicking

Use one colour or several. This is almost a decoration in itself.

1 Cover the cake with sugarpaste, royal or marzipan icing and leave to dry. Place the cake on a fairly large sheet of greaseproof paper to protect the work surface.

2 ▲ Water down the food colouring, and then load up the end of the paintbrush with the colour. Position the brush over the area you wish to colour, then flick your wrist in the direction of the cake, so the colour falls on to it in small beads.

Linework

Food colouring pens are a quick way to add simple line designs to the tops and sides of cakes. Use a ruler to achieve straight lines, and a pair of compasses for large curved lines.

1 Cover the cake and leave to dry. Royal icing gives the firmest surface for the pens. Work out the design.

2 ▲ For small circles, curves or semi-circles, draw around the edge of a plain round cutter.

3 ▼ Add details to the design with small dots.

Painting and Drawing

Food colourings can be used like water-colours and food colouring pens like crayons or felt-tip pens on iced cakes. Let the icing dry before applying the design. Before working on the cake, you might find it easier to practise on a spare piece of icing. When painting different colours next to each other, allow the first colour to dry before applying the second to prevent colours running into each other – unless that is the effect you wish to achieve.

1 ▲ Dilute food colourings with a little water or use straight from the bottle. A small plastic palette is useful for mixing the colours. Work out the design and either paint it straight on to the cake, or draw it out first with a food colouring pen.

2 ▲ Food colouring pens look like felt-tip pens, but are filled with edible food colourings. They are a speedy way to add lively highlights to designs. They can also be used to colour in patterned borders, to draw personalized pictures or to write messages on cakes.

3 ▶ Look to the great artists, such as Matisse and Picasso, for inspiration, either for a painting style or theme.

Stippling

This is normally used as a background decoration, so it is best to keep the colours delicate. Try blending two soft shades together.

1 Cover the cake with sugarpaste, royal or marzipan icing and leave until the icing is dry.

2 ▲ Water down the food colouring and apply with a dry, clean piece of sponge or kitchen paper, by dabbing it on to the surface of the cake.

Powdered Tints

These can be brushed on dry, either with a paintbrush for detail, or with a clean, dry piece of sponge when you wish to cover larger areas.

1 Cover the cake with sugarpaste, royal or marzipan icing and leave until the icing is dry.

2 ▲ Draw on the design with different coloured food colouring pens, and then brush in the colours with powdered tints.

Using Bought Decorations

When you want to put a cake together in a hurry for a last-minute celebration, or even if you do not have much time to spend on decorating cakes, remember there are all kinds of easy-to-use edible items and ready-to-use decorations that can be found in supermarkets, health food shops, and in confectionery and specialist cake icing shops.

Edible Decorations

Here are just some of the delicious edible decorations which can be used for quick-and-easy cake decorating. Keep a few of these in your cupboard, ready for an impromptu celebration cake.

Sweets Choose small, colourful, simple shapes such as jelly babies, jelly beans, coloured chocolate beans, chocolate buttons, liquorice allsorts, chocolate-coated espresso beans, yogurt-coated nuts and raisins, small moulded chocolate shapes or sugared almonds. These are just a few of the sweets which, used with imagination and flair, turn a cake into something special.
Jellied Shapes Packaged jellied orange and lemon slices are also useful, either whole or cut into wedges, as are jelly diamonds, available in several colours.
Nuts Use these chopped or whole, plain or toasted, for decorating the tops and to coat the sides of cakes.
Glacé and Crystallized Fruits Glacé cherries and angelica are probably the most familiar of these popular quick cake decorations, but there are many other tasty varieties to choose from, such as pineapple and ginger – even diced papaya. Depending on their size, the fruits can be halved, sliced, chopped or cut into shapes ready for arranging on the cake.
Coconut Desiccated coconut is another useful cake decoration, particularly as it can also be tinted with a few drops of food colouring to give an attractive coating for the sides of a cake. Other more unusual kinds of coconut are also available; such as coconut threads, coconut chips and coconut slices. All can be used raw or toasted.

Marzipan Fruits and Sugar Flowers Both can be bought ready-made if you do not wish to shape your own.
Citrus Fruits Fresh lemon, lime and orange zest can be transformed into attractive cake decorations. Cut off thin, curly strips of rind with a sharp knife or zester. Alternatively, use tiny aspic cutters to cut out shapes from the rinds, but be careful not to include the white pith. The shapes can be grouped together or linked to form a border around the cake.

MAKING PATTERNS WITH EDIBLE DECORATIONS

1 ▲ Arrange jelly diamonds and jellied orange slices on a square or round cake to form a pretty stylized design such as the one shown.

2 ▲ This jazzy design is ideal for a child's cake. It is made from whole and halved coloured chocolate beans.

3 ▲ Sugared almonds, flaked toasted almonds and silver balls add life to any cake iced in pastel shades, and are ideal for Easter.

Decorative edibles help to make cake decorating fun as well as easy.

Sweet Flowers

Stencilling

Edible decorations can be used in different combinations to make attractive floral designs for cakes.

For this technique you can use icing sugar, cocoa or even finely ground nuts to create the stencilling effect.

It's time to have fun. Load up a paintbrush with orange food colouring and then flick it over a sugarpaste-iced cake. Cut out bears with the icing and paint on their features. Line up jelly teddy bears, jelly beans and other colourful sweets, paint a bright design on the iced board and you have a cake that is surprisingly easy to decorate.

1 ▲ Use jelly diamonds for the petals and leaves, slices of dolly mixtures for the centres and strips of angelica for the stems.

1 ▲ For a quick stencilled pattern, lay a patterned doiley on the cake and sift icing sugar over the top. Lift off the doiley to reveal the pattern. The centre can be cut out of the doiley to create another stencilled area. For maximum contrast, use icing sugar on a chocolate cake and cocoa on a plain cake.

2 ▲ Arrange halved coloured chocolate beans, cut-side down, to form a flower. Use different colours, with a silver ball for the centre.

2 ▼ Another stencilling method is to lay strips of paper over the cake, either in straight lines, diagonally or in a lattice pattern. Use fairly thick paper so it lies flat. For more dramatic effects, cut out strips of paper in wavy, zigzag or other geometric patterns.

3 ▲ Dip blanched whole almonds in melted chocolate to form the petals of a flower, then arrange with a chocolate button or chocolate bean for the centre.

Ribbon Decorations

Stripy ones, dotty ones, sparkly ones, wide and pencil-thin ones – ribbons are a lovely way to add height, colour and a special celebratory look to a cake. They can be wrapped around the cake, using varying widths and colours for different effects, made into simple shapes, or threaded into the icing. Tiny coloured bows can be purchased from cake icing specialists, or you can make your own decorations as suggested here.

RIBBON LOOPS

These look pretty if one or several loops are attached to florist's wire, or if alternating colours are looped together.

1 Use thin ribbon, about 5 mm/¼ inch wide. Make two or three small loops of ribbon.

2 ▲ Using a piece of florist's wire, twist it around the ends of the ribbon to secure the loops together. Trim the ends of the ribbon. The wire will form a stem for the loops, so cut it to the required length and use it to put the loops in position on the cake. The loops must be removed from the cake before serving.

RIBBON CURLS

▲ Use a thin piece of gift wrapping ribbon, about 5 mm/¼ inch wide, and cut into the chosen lengths. Run the blade of a pair of scissors or a sharp knife down the length of the ribbons to make them curl.

MULTIPLE CURLS

▲ Use a thick piece of gift wrapping ribbon, about 2 cm/¾ inch wide, and cut into the chosen lengths. Tear the ribbon into four or five thin strips, almost to the end. Run the blade of a pair of scissors or a sharp knife down the length of each strip to curl.

OVALS

▲ Hold both ends of a thin piece of ribbon. With your left hand bring the end up and twist it over to cross and form an oval with two straight ends hanging down. Where the ribbon crosses, secure with a little royal icing. Cut the ends diagonally to neaten.

RIBBON DESIGNS

▲ Use combinations of colours and widths of ribbons and bows to create special patterns on the tops and sides of cakes. Secure with a little royal icing.

A riot of ribbons – let the colours or patterns of ribbon you choose complement the shade and design of the cake without dominating it.

RIBBON INSERTION

This technique looks much more difficult than it actually is. A cake covered with sugarpaste icing provides the best surface for this decoration. Leave the icing to dry until it is soft underneath and just firm on the top.

1 ▲ Work out your design for the number and size of slits, and whether the design is to be straight or curved. Draw the design on a piece of greaseproof paper.

2 ▲ Cut pieces of ribbon which are fractionally longer than the size of each slit.

3 ▲ Secure the template to the cake with pins. Cut through the drawn lines to make the slits in the icing using a scalpel. Remove the template.

4 ▲ With the aid of a pointed tool, insert one end of the ribbon into the first slit and the other end into the second slit.

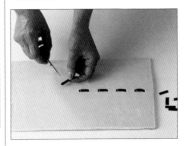

5 ▲ Leave a space and repeat, filling all the slits with the pieces of ribbon in the same way.

Sugar-frosting Flowers and Fruit

Something as simple as a spray of fresh sugar-frosted flowers or a grouping of small fruits is often all that is needed to decorate a cake. When frosting flowers choose ones that are edible, such as pansies, primroses, violets, roses, freesias, tiny daffodils or nasturtiums.

FLOWERS

Sugar-frosted flowers keep surprisingly well, and you may want to make the most of springtime primroses and violets to liven up cakes later in the year. Once the flowers are dry, store them in a single layer between sheets of tissue paper in a small box. Keep the box in a cool, dry place.

1 ▲ Lightly beat an egg white in a small bowl, and sprinkle some caster sugar on to a plate. Dry the flower on kitchen paper. If possible, leave some stem attached. Evenly brush both sides of the petals with the egg white.

2 ▲ Holding the flower by its stem over a plate lined with kitchen paper, sprinkle it evenly with the sugar, then shake off any excess.

Frosty florals – whole flowers or individual petals can be frosted in the same way.

3 ▲ Place on a flat board or wire rack covered with kitchen paper and leave to dry in a warm place.

FRUITS

When frosting fruits, choose really fresh ones which are small and firm such as kumquats, cherries, grapes or strawberries. Frosted fruits will only keep as long as the fruits themselves stay fresh. Place on a lined tray and keep in the refrigerator. Eat within two days.

1 Wash the fruit and pat dry on kitchen paper.

2 ▲ Lightly beat an egg white in a small bowl, and sprinkle some caster sugar on to a plate. Hold the fruit by the stem if possible and evenly brush all over with the egg white.

Sometimes the simplest cakes can be the most elegant. The stark white background of sugarpaste icing is all that is needed to show off a sweeping spray of frosted flowers, an interlocking design of ribbons and a few ribbon curls and bows.

3 ▲ Holding the fruit over a plate lined with kitchen paper, sprinkle it evenly with the sugar, then shake off any excess.

4 Place on a flat board or wire rack covered with kitchen paper and leave to dry in a warm place.

Frosty fruits – make a pile of these luscious fruits for a stunning centrepiece on a cake.

lassic Cakes

This chapter features new takes on the perennial
favourites that form an essential part of every good
cake-maker's repertoire. Ranging from the
ever-popular apple crumble to the sheer luxury of
a Black Forest Gâteau, this is the ultimate collection
of family favourites that will continue to entice
generation after generation.

Simple Chocolate Cake

An easy, everyday chocolate cake which can be simply filled with chocolate butter icing, or pepped up with a rich chocolate ganache for a special occasion.

INGREDIENTS
Serves 6–8
115 g/4 oz plain chocolate
3 tbsp milk
150 g/5 oz/⅔ cup butter or margarine, softened
150 g/5 oz/¾ cup light muscovado sugar
3 size 3 eggs
200 g/7 oz/1¼ cups self-raising flour
1 tbsp cocoa powder

For the Filling
350 g/12 oz/1 quantity chocolate-flavour Butter Icing

To Decorate
icing sugar and cocoa powder, for dusting

1 Preheat the oven to 180°C/350°F/ Gas 4. Grease two 18 cm/7 inch round sandwich cake tins and line the base of each with baking parchment. Melt the chocolate with the milk in a heatproof bowl set over a pan of simmering water.

2 ▲ Cream the butter or margarine with the sugar in a mixing bowl until pale and fluffy. Add the eggs one at a time, beating well after each addition. Stir in the chocolate mixture and mix until thoroughly combined.

3 ▲ Sift the flour and cocoa over the mixture and fold in with a metal spoon until evenly mixed. Divide the mixture between the prepared tins, smooth level and bake for 35–40 minutes or until well risen and springy to the touch. Turn out on to wire racks, peel off the lining paper and leave to cool.

4 ▲ Sandwich the cake layers together with the butter icing. Dust with a mixture of icing sugar and cocoa just before serving.

Tip

For a richer finish, make a double quantity of butter icing and spread or pipe over the top of the cake as well as using for the filling.

Spiced Apple Cake

*Grated apple and chopped dates give this cake a natural sweetness – omit 25 g/
1 oz/2 tbsp of the sugar if the fruit is very sweet.*

2 ▲ Mix the sugar with the pear and apple spread in a small bowl. Gradually stir in the apple juice. Add to the dry ingredients with the eggs, oil and apples. Mix thoroughly.

3 ▲ Spoon the mixture into the tin, sprinkle with the walnuts and bake for 60–65 minutes or until a skewer inserted into the centre of the cake comes out clean. Transfer to a wire rack, peel off the lining paper and leave to cool.

1 ▲ Preheat the oven to 180°C/350°F/ Gas 4. Grease a deep 20 cm/8 inch round cake tin, line the base with greaseproof paper and grease the paper. Sift the flour, baking powder and cinnamon into a mixing bowl, then mix in the dates and make a well in the centre.

Tip

It is not necessary to peel the apples – the skin adds extra fibre and softens on cooking.

Black Forest Gâteau

*A perfect gâteau for a special occasion tea party, or for serving
as a sumptuous dessert at a dinner party.*

INGREDIENTS
Serves 10–12
5 size 3 eggs
175 g/6 oz/³⁄₄ cup caster sugar
50 g/2 oz/¹⁄₂ cup plain flour, sifted
*50 g/2 oz/¹⁄₂ cup cocoa powder,
sifted*
75 g/3 oz/6 tbsp butter, melted

For the Filling
5–6 tbsp Kirsch
*575 ml/1 pint/2¹⁄₂ cups double
cream*
*1 x 425 g/15 oz can black cherries,
drained, stoned and chopped*

To Decorate
225 g/8 oz plain chocolate
*15–20 fresh cherries, preferably
with stems*
sifted icing sugar (optional)

1 Preheat the oven to 180°C/350°F/
Gas 4. Grease two deep 20 cm/8
inch round cake tins, line the bases with
greaseproof paper and grease the paper.

2 ▲ Place the eggs and sugar in a
large mixing bowl and beat with an
electric mixer for about 10 minutes or
until the mixture is thick and pale.

3 Sift together the flour and cocoa
powder, then sift again into the
whisked mixture. Fold in very gently,
then slowly trickle in the melted butter
and continue to fold in gently.

4 Divide the mixture between the tins
and smooth the surfaces. Bake in
the centre of the oven for about 30
minutes, or until springy to the touch.
Leave in the tin for about 5 minutes,
then turn out on to a wire rack, peel off
the lining paper and leave to cool.

5 ▲ Cut each cake in half horizontally
and lay on a work surface. Sprinkle
the four layers with the Kirsch.

6 ▲ In a large bowl, whip the cream
until it holds soft peaks. Transfer
two-thirds of the cream to another bowl
and stir in the chopped cherries. Place a
layer of cake on a serving plate or cake
board and spread over one-third of the
filling. Top with another layer of cake
and continue layering, finishing with a
layer of cake.

7 Use the remaining whipped cream
to cover the top and sides of the
gâteau, spreading it evenly with a knife.

8 To decorate the gâteau, melt the
chocolate in a bowl over a pan of
hot water, or in a double boiler. Spread
the chocolate out on to a plastic
chopping board and allow to set.

9 ▲ Using a long sharp knife, scrape
along the surface of the melted
chocolate to make thin shavings and use
these to cover the sides of the cake and
to decorate the top. Finish by arranging
the cherries on top of the gâteau. Dust
with sifted icing sugar, if wished.

Tip

If liked, the cherries can be coated
or half-coated in chocolate before
arranging on the cake. To do this,
reserve 2–3 tbsp of the melted
chocolate and dip the cherries into
it. Allow the dipped cherries to set
on greaseproof paper.

*M*ocha-hazelnut Battenberg

The traditional Battenberg cake originated in Germany when the Prince of Battenberg married Queen Victoria's daughter, Beatrice. This recipe is a variation of the original theme.

INGREDIENTS
Serves 6–8
115 g/4 oz/½ cup butter, softened
115 g/4 oz/½ cup caster sugar
2 size 3 eggs
115 g/4 oz/1 cup self-raising flour, sifted
50 g/2 oz/½ cup ground hazelnuts
2 tsp coffee essence
1 tbsp cocoa powder

To Finish
7 tbsp apricot jam, warmed and sieved
225 g/8 oz yellow marzipan
50 g/2 oz/½ cup ground hazelnuts
sifted icing sugar, for rolling out
ground hazelnuts, to decorate

1 Preheat the oven to 180°C/350°F/ Gas 4. Grease an 18 cm/7 inch square cake tin, line the base with greaseproof paper and grease the paper.

2 ▲ Place the butter and sugar in a bowl and beat until fluffy. Gradually beat in the eggs, then fold in the flour. Transfer mixture to another bowl.

3 ▲ Stir the ground hazelnuts into one half of the cake mixture and the coffee essence and cocoa powder into the other half.

4 ▲ Prepare a strip of foil to fit the width and height of the cake tin, then place the mocha-flavoured cake mixture in one half of the tin. Position the strip of foil down the centre, then spoon the hazelnut-flavoured cake mixture into the other half of the tin. Smooth the surface of both mixtures.

5 Bake for 30–35 minutes or until a skewer inserted into the centre of both halves comes out clean. Leave the cakes to cool in the tin for about 5 minutes, then turn out on to a wire rack, peel off the lining paper and leave to cool completely.

6 ▲ Separate the cakes and cut each one in half lengthways. Take one portion of the mocha-flavoured cake and brush along one long side with a little apricot jam. Sandwich this surface with a portion of the hazelnut-flavoured cake. Brush the top of the cakes with apricot jam and position the other portion of mocha-flavoured cake on top of the hazelnut base. Brush along the inner long side with apricot jam and sandwich with the final portion of hazelnut-flavoured cake. Set aside.

7 Knead the marzipan on the work surface to soften, then knead in the ground hazelnuts until evenly blended. On the work surface lightly dusted with icing sugar, roll out the marzipan into a rectangle large enough to wrap around the cake, excluding the ends.

8 Brush the long sides of the cake with apricot jam, then lay the cake on top of the marzipan. Wrap the marzipan around the cake, sealing the edge neatly. Place the cake on a serving plate, seal-side down, and pinch the edges of the marzipan to give an attractive finish. Score the top surface with a knife and sprinkle with ground hazelnuts.

Apple Crumble Cake

*In the autumn use windfall apples. Served
warm with thick cream or custard this cake doubles as a dessert.*

INGREDIENTS
Serves 8–10
For the Topping
75 g/3 oz/ ¾ cup self-raising flour
½ tsp ground cinnamon
40 g/1½ oz/3 tbsp butter
25 g/1 oz/2 tbsp caster sugar

For the Base
50 g/2 oz/4 tbsp butter, softened
75 g/3 oz/6 tbsp caster sugar
1 size 3 egg, beaten
115 g/4 oz/1 cup self-raising
flour, sifted
2 cooking apples, peeled, cored
and sliced
50 g/2 oz/ ⅓ cup sultanas

To Decorate
1 red dessert apple, cored, thinly
sliced and tossed in lemon juice
2 tbsp caster sugar, sifted 1
pinch of ground cinnamon

1 Preheat the oven 180°C/350°F/
Gas 4. Grease a deep 18 cm/7 inch
springform tin, line the base with
greaseproof paper and grease the paper.

2 ▲ To make the topping, sift the
flour and cinnamon into a mixing
bowl. Rub the butter into the flour until
it resembles breadcrumbs, then stir in
the sugar. Set aside.

3 ▲ To make the base, put the butter,
sugar, egg and flour into a bowl
and beat for 1–2 minutes until smooth.
Spoon into the prepared tin.

4 ▲ Mix together the apple slices and
sultanas and spread them evenly
over the top. Sprinkle with the topping.

5 Bake in the centre of the oven for
about 1 hour. Cool in the tin for 10
minutes before turning out on to a wire
rack and peeling off the lining paper.
Serve warm or cool, decorated with
slices of red dessert apple and caster
sugar and cinnamon sprinkled over.

*M*arbled Spice Cake

This cake is baked in a fluted ring-shaped tin called a kugelhupf, or gugelhupf, mould from Germany and Austria to give it a pretty shape.

INGREDIENTS
Serves 8–10
75 g/3 oz/6 tbsp butter, softened
115 g/4 oz/½ cup caster sugar
2 size 3 eggs, lightly beaten
few drops of vanilla essence
130 g/4½ oz plain flour
1½ tsp baking powder
3 tbsp milk
3 tbsp black treacle
1 tsp ground mixed spice
½ tsp ground ginger
175 g/6 oz/1⅛ cups icing sugar,
sifted, to decorate

2 Cream the butter and sugar together in a bowl until light and fluffy. Beat in the egg and vanilla essence.

3 ▲ Sift together the flour and baking powder, then fold into the mixture, alternating with the milk, until evenly combined.

4 Spoon about one-third of the mixture into a small bowl and stir in the treacle and spices.

1 Preheat the oven to 180°C/350°F/ Gas 4. Grease and flour a 900 g/2 lb kugelhupf mould or ring-shaped cake tin.

5 ▲ Drop alternating spoonfuls of the light and dark mixtures into the tin. Run a knife or skewer through them to give a marbled effect.

6 ▲ Bake in the centre of the oven for about 50 minutes or until a skewer inserted into the centre comes out clean. Leave in the tin for 10 minutes before turning out on to a wire rack to cool.

7 ▲ To decorate, stir enough warm water into the icing sugar to make a smooth icing. Spoon quickly over the cake. Allow to set before serving.

*T*ip
If you do not have a kugelhupf mould or a ring-shaped cake tin, use a 20 cm/8 inch round cake tin.

*B*est-ever Chocolate Cake

This classic layered cake is a crowd-pleaser whatever the occasion. Three extra-chocolatey layers of sponge are sandwiched together with an irresistible chocolate icing. It looks magnificent left unadorned, but could be embellished with chocolate curls, leaves or other decorations.

INGREDIENTS
Serves 12–14
115 g/4 oz/½ cup unsalted butter
115 g/4 oz/1 cup plain flour
50 g/2 oz/½ cup unsweetened
cocoa powder
5 ml/1 tsp baking powder
1 ml/⅛ tsp salt
6 eggs
200 g/7 oz/1 cup sugar
10 ml/2 tsp vanilla extract

For the Icing
8 × 25 g/1 oz squares plain
chocolate, chopped
75 g/3 oz/6 tbsp unsalted butter
3 eggs, separated
250 ml/8 fl oz/1 cup whipping
cream
40 g/1½ oz/3 tbsp sugar

1 Preheat the oven to 180°C/350°F/
Gas 4. Line three 20 x 4 cm/8 x
1½ inch round cake tins with wax
paper and grease.

2 ▲ Dust evenly with flour and
spread with a brush. Set aside.

3 ▲ Melt the butter over low heat.
With a spoon, skim off any foam
that rises to the surface. Set aside.

4 ▲ Sift the flour, cocoa, baking
powder and salt together three
times and set aside.

5 Place the eggs and sugar in a large
heatproof bowl set over a pan of
hot water. With an electric mixer, beat
until the mixture doubles in volume
and is thick enough to leave a ribbon
trail when the beaters are lifted, about
10 minutes. Add the vanilla.

6 ▲ Sift over the dry ingredients in
three batches, folding in carefully
after each addition. Fold in the butter.

7 Divide the batter between the tins
and bake until the cakes pull away
from the sides of the tin, about 25
minutes. Transfer to a rack.

8 For the icing, melt the chopped
chocolate in the top of a double
boiler, or in a heatproof bowl set over
hot water.

9 ▲ Off the heat, stir in the butter
and egg yolks. Return to low heat
and stir until thick. Remove from the
heat and set aside. Whip the cream
until firm; set aside. In another bowl,
beat the egg whites until stiff. Add the
sugar and beat until glossy.

10 Fold the cream into the chocolate mixture, then carefully fold in the egg whites. Refrigerate for 20 minutes to thicken the icing.

11 ▶ Sandwich the cake layers with icing, stacking them carefully. Spread the remaining icing evenly over the top and sides of the cake.

Tip

For a simpler icing, combine 250ml/8 fl oz/1 cup whipping cream with 230 g/ 8 oz finely chopped plain chocolate in a saucepan. Stir over low heat until the chocolate has melted. Cool and whisk to spreading consistency.

*A*ngel Food Cake

This is a true American classic. Although similar to a whisked sponge cake, it differs in that it contains no egg yolks. This results in a delicate snowy white texture. The cream of tartar helps to stiffen the egg whites, and the addition of the sugar forms a light meringue mixture. The cake is baked in a non-stick ungreased tube tin. This enables the mixture to cling to the sides of the tin as it rises. The traditional whipped frosting is a basic Italian meringue mixture, which has a hot sugar syrup whisked into it.

INGREDIENTS
Serves 20
65 g/2½ oz/5 tbsp plain flour
15 ml/1 tbsp cornflour
225 g/8 oz/1 cup caster sugar
10 size 3 egg whites
5 ml/1 tsp cream of tartar
7.5 ml/1 tsp vanilla essence

For the Frosting
115 g/4 oz/½ cup caster sugar
60 ml/4 tbsp water
2 size 3 egg whites
10 ml/2 tsp golden syrup
2.5 ml/½ tsp vanilla essence

To Decorate
15 g/2 tsp each desiccated coconut,
chopped pistachio nuts and
chopped candied orange peel
gold and silver dragées

1 Preheat the oven to 180°C/350°F/Gas 4. Sift the flour, cornflour and 50 g/2 oz/ ¼ cup of the sugar together three times.

2 ▲ Whisk 10 of the egg whites with the cream of tartar until stiff, and gradually whisk in the remaining sugar, a tablespoon at a time, until the mixture is thick and glossy.

3 ▲ Fold in the sifted flours and sugar and vanilla essence until combined, and transfer to a 25 cm/ 10 inch non-stick ring mould. Bake for 35–40 minutes until risen and golden. Remove from the oven, invert the cake in its tin, and leave to cool. To make the frosting, heat the sugar and water in a small pan until the sugar dissolves. Increase the heat and boil until the temperature reaches 115°C/240°F on a sugar thermometer (or the thread stage).

4 ▲ As soon as the mixture boils, whisk the egg whites until very stiff and dry. Pour the syrup, in a steady stream, into the centre of the egg whites, whisking continually, until thick and glossy. Beat in the golden syrup and vanilla essence and continue beating for 5 minutes until the frosting is cooled.

5 ▲ Carefully remove the cooled cake from its tin, place on a turntable and coat with the frosting, using a palette knife to make a swirling pattern and peak effect.

6 ▲ To decorate, sprinkle over the coconut, pistachios and orange peel, and decorate with gold and silver dragées.

Savarin with Fresh Berries

This classic French yeast cake is soaked with a rum syrup and glazed, then served with fresh cream and a mixture of fresh berries. Choose your favourite fruits in season.

INGREDIENTS
Serves 8
15 ml/1 tbsp dried yeast
40 ml/2½ tbsp caster sugar
90 ml/6 tbsp tepid milk
225 g/8 oz/2 cups strong plain flour
pinch of salt
4 size 3 eggs, beaten
115 g/4 oz/½ cup butter, softened

For the Syrup
120 ml/4 fl oz/½ cup clear honey
60 ml/4 tbsp water
30 ml/2 tbsp lemon juice
30 ml/2 tbsp dark rum or Grand
Marnier

To Decorate
45 ml/3 tbsp apricot jam, warmed
and sieved
150 ml/¼ pint/⅔ cup double cream
115 g/4 oz/¼ lb summer fruits
lemon balm leaves

1 Grease and flour a 1.5 litre/
2½ pint/6¼ cup capacity ring mould.
Blend the yeast, 7.5 ml/1½ tsp sugar,
milk and 15 ml/1 tbsp flour together.
Cover and leave in a warm place for
15 minutes, until frothy.

2 ▲ Sift the remaining flour and salt
into a bowl and stir in the
remaining sugar. Make a well in the
centre and beat in the yeast mixture,
eggs and butter, until glossy.

3 Heat the oven to 200°C/400°F/
Gas 6. Transfer the batter to the
prepared tin, cover and leave in a warm
place for 30 minutes, or until the batter
almost reaches the top of the tin. Bake
for 35 minutes until risen and golden.
Remove from the oven, cool in the tin
for 5 minutes before turning out on to
a wire rack. Prick the cake all over with
a skewer.

4 ▲ To make the syrup, heat the
honey, water and lemon juice
together and boil for 3 minutes, until
thick and syrupy. Remove from the
heat. Stir in the rum or Grand Marnier
and spoon over the cooling cake. Leave
to cool completely.

5 ▲ Heat the apricot jam until it just
boils, remove from the heat and
brush over the cooled cake.

6 ▲ Whip the cream until thick and
transfer to a piping bag. Pipe swirls
all around the top of the cake and
decorate with the fruits and lemon
balm leaves.

Dundee Cake

This is the perfect fruit cake for those who prefer a lighter style than the traditional sticky fruit cake. It has a wonderful fruit and nut flavour and a light, slightly crumbly texture.

INGREDIENTS
Serves 16–20
175 g/6 oz/³/₄ cup butter
175 g/6 oz/³/₄ cup soft light
brown sugar
3 size 3 eggs
225 g/8 oz/2 cups plain flour
10 ml/2 tsp baking powder
5 ml/1 tsp ground cinnamon
2.5 ml/½ tsp ground cloves
1.5 ml/¼ tsp ground nutmeg
225 g/8 oz/1⅓ cups sultanas
175 g/6 oz/1 cup raisins
175 g/6 oz/³/₄ cup glacé
cherries, halved
115 g/4 oz/³/₄ cup chopped
mixed peel
50 g/2 oz/½ cup blanched
almonds, chopped
grated zest of 1 lemon
30 ml/2 tbsp brandy

To Decorate
75–130 g/3–4 oz/⅔ cup whole
blanched almonds

1 Preheat the oven to 180°C/350°F/ Gas 4. Grease a deep 20 cm/8 inch round cake tin, line the base and sides with greaseproof paper and grease the paper.

2 Cream the butter and sugar together until pale and light. Add the eggs, one at a time, beating well after each addition.

3 ▲ Sift the flour, baking powder and spices together and fold into the creamed mixture alternately with the remaining ingredients, until all the ingredients are evenly incorporated.

4 ▲ Spoon into the prepared tin and smooth the surface, making a small dip in the centre. Begin decorating the top of the cake with almonds.

5 ▲ Continue decorating the cake by pressing almonds in decreasing circles over the entire surface. Bake for 2–2¼ hours until a skewer, inserted in the centre, comes out clean.

6 Remove the cake from the oven, leave to cool in the tin for 30 minutes, and transfer to a wire rack to cool completely.

Carrot Cake

So easy to make, this is a wonderfully moist and tasty cake, enriched with grated carrots and vegetable oil – a classic 'all-in-one' cake. The chopped nuts impart an even fuller flavour. Although often served with a simple dusting of icing sugar, the cream cheese icing and marzipan carrots make the cake a little more special.

INGREDIENTS
Serves 8
225 g/8 oz/1 cup caster sugar
3 size 3 eggs
200 ml/7 fl oz/1 scant cup vegetable oil
grated zest and juice of 1 orange
225 g/8 oz/2 cups self-raising wholemeal flour
5 ml/1 tsp ground cinnamon
2.5 ml/½ tsp ground nutmeg
2.5 ml/½ tsp salt
350 g/12 oz/3–4 carrots, finely grated and squeezed dry
115 g/4 oz/1 cup walnuts, ground

For the Filling
225 g/8 oz/1 cup cream cheese
30 ml/2 tbsp clear honey
15 ml/1 tbsp orange juice

To Decorate
50 g/2 oz marzipan
orange food colouring
angelica
2 walnut halves (optional)

1 Preheat the oven to 180°C/350°F/ Gas 4. Grease a 20 cm/8 inch round cake tin, line the base with greaseproof paper and grease the paper.

2 Beat the sugar, eggs, oil, orange zest and juice together until light and frothy. Sift in the flour, spices and salt and beat for a further minute. Stir in the carrots and nuts and spoon the mixture into the prepared tin.

3 Bake for 1½–1¾ hours until risen and a skewer inserted into the centre of the cake comes out clean.

4 ▲ To make the icing, beat the cheese, honey and 15 ml/1 tbsp orange juice together until smooth. Chill for 30 minutes to firm up.

5 ▲ Tint the marzipan with the food colouring to resemble the colour of carrots.

6 Break off small pieces and roll between your palms to form small carrot shapes.

7 ▲ Using a small knife, press marks around the sides and stick a small piece of angelica in the top of each one to resemble the stalk.

8 ▲ Spread the icing over the top of the cooled cake. Arrange the carrots, in a bunch, in the centre of the cake and decorate with the walnut halves, if using.

Panforte

*This rich, spicy nougat-type cake is a speciality of Siena in Italy, where
it is traditionally baked at Christmas. It is a combination of chopped candied
peel and nuts, which are mixed with a sugar syrup before baking.
It will keep well for several weeks in an airtight container.
Keep to hand over the Christmas season to serve with morning coffee.*

INGREDIENTS
Serves 8
275 g/10 oz/2 cups mixed candied
exotic peel, to include: papaya,
pineapple, orange, lemon and citron
115 g/4 oz/³⁄₄ cup unblanched
almonds
50 g/2 oz/¹⁄₂ cup walnut halves
50 g/2 oz/¹⁄₂ cup plain flour
5 ml/1 tsp ground cinnamon
1.5 ml/¹⁄₄ tsp each nutmeg, cloves
and coriander
175 g/6 oz/³⁄₄ cup caster sugar
60 ml/4 tbsp water

To Decorate
icing sugar

1 Preheat the oven to 180°C/350°F/
Gas 4. Grease a 20 cm/8 inch round
loose-bottom cake tin and line the base
with a sheet of rice paper.

2 Combine the mixed candied peel
and nuts in a bowl. Sift in the flour
and spices and mix well.

3 Heat the sugar and water in a small
pan, until the sugar dissolves.
Increase the heat and boil until the
mixture reaches 115°C/240°F on a
sugar thermometer, or until it reaches
the thread stage.

4 ▲ Remove from the heat and pour
on to the fruit mixture, stirring with
a wooden spoon until well coated.
Transfer to the prepared tin, pressing
the mixture firmly into the sides with a
metal spoon.

5 ▲ Bake for 25–30 minutes, until
the mixture is bubbling all over.
Remove from the oven and leave in the
tin to cool for 5 minutes.

6 ▲ With a lightly-oiled palette knife,
work around the edges of the cake
to loosen and remove the side of the
tin, leaving the base in place. Leave to
cool completely.

7 ▲ Remove from the base and
decorate with a generous dusting of
icing sugar.

Cassata Siciliana

This is a chilled cake from Sicily, where it is traditional to cover the cake with a layer of almond paste and to decorate the top with an exotic selection of glacé fruits.

INGREDIENTS
Serves 12
*1 quantity Whisked Sponge Cake
baked in a 23 cm/9 inch round tin
100 ml/3½ fl oz/scant ½ cup Marsala*

For the Filling
*350 g/12 oz/1½ cups ricotta cheese
30 ml/2 tbsp clear honey
1.5 ml/¼ tsp vanilla essence
grated zest and juice of ½ lemon
115 g/4 oz/¾ cup mixed candied peel,
finely chopped
75 g/3 oz/½ cup plain chocolate chips*

For the Icing
*175 g/6 oz/1½ cups ground almonds
75 g/3 oz/6 tbsp caster sugar
75 g/3 oz/¾ cup icing sugar, sifted
1 size 3 egg white, lightly whisked
5 ml/1 tsp lemon juice
2 drops almond essence
green food colouring
45 ml/3 tbsp apricot jam, warmed
and sieved*

To Decorate
225 g/8 oz mixed glacé fruits

1 Line a 20 cm/8 inch round spring form tin with clear film.

2 ▲ Cut the cake into three layers. Trim one to fit into the base of the tin. Cut the second into strips to line the sides. Brush with a little Marsala.

3 ▲ To make the filling, beat the ricotta, honey, 15 ml/1 tbsp Marsala, vanilla essence, lemon zest and juice together until very smooth. Chop the sponge trimmings and stir into the cheese mixture, with the peel and chocolate chips. Spoon into the sponge cake case, pressing the mixture into the sides.

4 ▲ Smooth the surface and trim the reserved layer of sponge cake to fit tightly over the filling. Pour over the remaining Marsala and cover with clear film. Place a weight on top of the cake and chill for several hours, until firm.

5 Meanwhile, make the icing. Combine the almonds, caster sugar and icing sugar together. Make a well in the centre and work in the egg white, lemon juice and almond essence to form a soft pliable paste. Add a few drops of food colouring and knead on a clean surface, dusted with a little icing sugar, until smooth and evenly coloured. Wrap the icing and keep cool until required.

6 ▲ Remove the cake from the refrigerator and turn out of the tin. Remove the clear film and brush the cake with warmed apricot jam. Roll out the almond paste to a circle a little larger than the cake, and use to cover, pressing gently to the top and sides. Smooth over the icing with a palette knife or small rolling pin. Transfer to a cakeboard.

7 ▲Make an attractive arrangement of mixed glacé fruits in the centre of the cake.

$\mathcal{K}$ulich

This Russian yeast cake is known under other names throughout Eastern Europe, where it is traditionally made at Easter time. This delicious spiced cake is baked in special moulds which can be purchased at some speciality shops, but for convenience the recipe has been converted for use in either clay flower pots or coffee tins. The cake is best eaten on the day it is made.

INGREDIENTS
Makes 2 cakes
15 ml/1 tbsp dried yeast
90 ml/6 tbsp tepid milk
75 g/3 oz/6 tbsp caster sugar
500 g/1 lb 2 oz/4½ cups plain flour
pinch of saffron strands
30 ml/2 tbsp dark rum
2.5 ml/½ tsp ground cardamom
2.5 ml/½ tsp ground cumin
50 g/2 oz/4 tbsp butter
2 size 3 eggs plus 2 egg yolks
½ vanilla pod, finely chopped
25 g/2 tbsp each: chopped mixed
candied peel, chopped crystallized
ginger, chopped almonds and
currants

To Decorate
75 g/3 oz/¾ cup icing sugar, sifted
7.5–10 ml/1½–2 tsp warm water
1 drop almond essence
blanched almonds
mixed candied peel
2 candles

1 Blend the yeast, milk, 25 g/1 oz/
2 tbsp sugar and 50 g/2 oz/½ cup
flour together, until smooth. Leave in a
warm place for 15 minutes, until
frothy. Soak the saffron in the rum for
15 minutes.

2 ▲ Sift the remaining flour and
spices into a bowl and rub in the
butter. Stir in the remaining sugar, make
a well in the centre and work in the
frothed yeast mixture, the saffron liquid
and remaining ingredients to form a
fine dough.

3 ▲ Knead on a lightly floured
surface for 5 minutes until smooth
and pliable. Place in an oiled bowl,
cover and leave to rise in a warm place
for 1–1½ hours, until doubled in size.

4 ▲ Preheat the oven to 190°/375°F/
Gas 5. Grease two 15 cm/6 inch
clay flower pots or two 500 g/1¼ lb
coffee tins. Line the bases with
greaseproof paper and flour the sides.

5 ▲ Knock back the dough. Divide in
two and form each lump into a
round. Press into the prepared pots,
cover and leave in a warm place for a
further 30 minutes, until the dough
comes two-thirds of the way up the
sides. Bake for 35 minutes if using the
coffee tins or 50 minutes if using the
clay pots. Test with a skewer and
remove from the oven. Turn out on to a
wire rack and leave to cool.

6 Blend the icing sugar, water and
almond essence together until
smooth, to form a thick glacé icing.
Drizzle over the top of each cake and
decorate with the nuts, peel and candles.

Baked Cheesecake with Fresh Fruits

A rich, creamy, American-style cheesecake, baked on a sweet biscuit base. It is topped with a selection of exotic fresh fruit; vary the decoration to suit the season.

INGREDIENTS
Serves 12
175 g/6 oz digestive biscuits,
crushed
50 g/2 oz/4 tbsp butter, melted
450 g/1 lb curd cheese
150 ml/¼ pint/⅔ cup sour cream
115 g/4 oz/½ cup caster sugar
3 size 3 eggs, separated
grated zest of 1 lemon
30 ml/2 tbsp Marsala
2.5 ml/½ tsp almond essence
50 g/2 oz/½ cup ground almonds
50 g/2 oz/⅓ cup sultanas

To Decorate
450 g/1 lb prepared mixed fruits
(figs, cherries, peaches, strawberries,
hulled, halved and stoned, as
necessary)

1 ▲ Preheat the oven to 180°C/350°F/ Gas 4. Grease the sides of a 25 cm/ 10 inch round springform tin and line with baking parchment.

2 ▲ Mix the crushed biscuits with the butter until well combined and press into the base of the prepared tin. Smooth the surface with a metal spoon and chill for 20 minutes.

3 ▲ Meanwhile prepare the cake mixture. Beat the cheese, cream, sugar, egg yolks, lemon zest, Marsala and almond essence together until smooth and creamy.

4 ▲ Whisk the egg whites until stiff and fold into the creamed mixture with the remaining ingredients until evenly combined. Pour over the chilled biscuit base and bake for 45 minutes, until risen and just set in the centre.

5 Remove from the oven and leave in the tin in a warm, draught-free place, until completely cold. Carefully remove the tin and peel away the lining paper.

6 ▲ Chill the cheesecake for at least an hour before decorating with the prepared fruits, just before serving.

Chilled Grape Cheesecake

An attractive and unusual topping decorates this classic chilled cheesecake. Use green grapes and white grape juice if wished, for an equally attractive cheesecake.

INGREDIENTS
Serves 12
175 g/6 oz gingernuts, crushed
50 g/2 oz/4 tbsp butter, melted
350 g/12 oz/1½ cups cream cheese
200 g/7 oz/scant 1 cup
fromage frais
90 ml/6 tbsp clear honey
2 size 3 eggs, separated
5 ml/1 tsp grated lemon zest
15 ml/1 tbsp lemon juice
60 ml/4 tbsp Muscat de Beaumes de
Venise (or other sweet white
dessert wine)
15 ml/1 tbsp powdered gelatine

For the Topping
115 g/4 oz red or green seedless
grapes, halved
small piece of angelica
30 ml/2 tbsp Muscat de Beaumes de
Venise (or other sweet white
dessert wine)
7.5 ml/1½ tsp powdered gelatine
300 ml/½ pint/1¼ cups red or white
grape juice

1 Grease the sides of a 23 cm/9 inch round springform tin and line with baking parchment.

2 Mix the crushed gingernuts with the butter until well combined. Press into the base of the prepared tin. Smooth the surface with a metal spoon and chill for 20 minutes.

3 To prepare the cake mixture, beat together the cheese, fromage frais, honey, egg yolks, lemon zest and juice, until smooth and creamy.

4 ▲ Heat the wine and gelatine together in a small pan, over a low heat, until the gelatine dissolves. Remove from the heat, stir in a little of the creamed mixture, and pour back into the remaining creamed mixture, stirring until combined.

5 Whisk the egg whites until stiff and fold into the creamed mixture, until evenly incorporated. Pour over the chilled biscuit base and return to the refrigerator to set.

6 ▲ When the cheesecake is just setting, arrange the grapes over the top, in the shape of a bunch of grapes, and make a stalk from the angelica. Chill until completely set.

7 To complete the topping, heat the wine and gelatine together as before, until dissolved. Pour in the grape juice and leave to get cold.

8 ▲ Using a small paintbrush, carefully dampen the edges of the lined tin, directly above the set level of the cheesecake.

9 ▲ Carefully pour over the cooled grape juice to cover the grapes. Chill again until set.

10 ▲ Just before serving, remove the tin and carefully peel away the lining paper, using a palette knife to help the process.

Sticky Gingerbread Loaf

Moist and sticky, this classic gingerbread loaf is made even more delicious with a tart lemon glacé icing drizzled over the top. The icing is simple, but looks extremely effective.

INGREDIENTS
Makes 1 loaf
175 g/6 oz/1½ cups plain flour
10 ml/2 tsp ground ginger
2.5 ml/½ tsp ground mixed spice
2.5 ml/½ tsp bicarbonate of soda
30 ml/2 tbsp black treacle
30 ml/2 tbsp golden syrup
75 g/3 oz/½ cup soft dark
brown sugar
75 g/3 oz/6 tbsp butter
1 size 3 egg
15 ml/1 tbsp milk
15 ml/1 tbsp orange juice
2 pieces of stem ginger, finely
chopped
50 g/2 oz/⅓ cup sultanas
5 no-soak dried apricots,
finely chopped

For the Icing
45 ml/3 tbsp icing sugar
10 ml/2 tsp lemon juice

1 Preheat the oven to 160°C/325°F/
Gas 3. Grease a 900 g/2 lb loaf tin,
line with greaseproof paper and grease
the paper. Sift the plain flour, mixed
spices and bicarbonate of soda into
a bowl.

2 ▲ Place the black treacle, syrup,
sugar and butter in a pan and heat
gently until the butter has melted.

3 ▲ In a separate bowl, beat the egg,
milk and orange juice together. Add
the syrup mixture, egg mixture,
chopped stem ginger, sultanas and
apricots to the dry ingredients and stir
to combine thoroughly.

4 ▲ Spoon into the prepared tin and
level with the back of a metal
spoon. Bake in the centre of the oven
for about 50 minutes, or until the
gingerbread is well risen, firm when
touched gently in the centre and cooked
through.

5 ▲ Leave the loaf to cool in the tin,
then turn out on to a wire rack.
Mix the icing sugar with the lemon
juice in a bowl and beat until smooth.
Drizzle the icing back and forth over
the top of the gingerbread, leave to set,
then cut into thick slices to serve.

$\mathcal{I}$rish Whiskey Cake

This moist rich fruit cake is drizzled with whiskey as soon as it comes out of the oven.

INGREDIENTS
Serves 12
115 g/4 oz/½ cup glacé cherries
*175 g/6 oz/1 cup dark muscovado
sugar*
115 g/4 oz/⅔ cup sultanas
115 g/4 oz/⅔ cup raisins
115 g/4 oz/⅔ cup currants
300 m l/½ pint/1¼ cups cold tea
*300 g/11 oz/2¼ cups self-raising
flour, sifted*
1 size 3 egg
45 ml/3 tbsp Irish whiskey

1 ▲ Mix the cherries, sugar, dried fruit and tea in a large bowl. Leave to soak overnight until all the tea has been absorbed by the fruit. If time is short, use hot tea and soak the fruit for just 2 hours.

2 ▲ Preheat the oven to 180°C/350°F/ Gas 4. Grease a 900 g/2 lb loaf tin, line with greaseproof paper and grease the paper. Add the flour, then the egg to the fruit mixture and beat thoroughly.

3 ▲ Pour the mixture into the prepared tin and bake for 1½ hours or until a skewer inserted into the centre of the cake comes out clean.

4 ▲ Prick the top of the cake with a skewer and drizzle over the whiskey while the cake is still hot. Allow to stand for about 5 minutes, then remove from the tin and cool on a wire rack.

Banana-lemon Layer Cake

Banana loaf is a favourite teabread: here is its more sophisticated cousin. This moist banana and walnut cake is deliciously complemented by a tangy lemon butter icing.

INGREDIENTS
Serves 8–10
250 g/9 oz/2 cups plain flour
7.5 ml/1½ tsp baking powder
2.5 ml/½ tsp salt
115 g/4 oz/½ cup butter, softened
225 g/8 oz/1 cup granulated sugar
75 g/3 oz/½ cup soft light brown sugar
2 size 3 eggs
2.5 ml/½ tsp grated lemon zest
2 very ripe bananas, mashed
5 ml/1 tsp vanilla essence
60 ml/4 tbsp milk
75 g/3 oz/¾ cup chopped walnuts
pared lemon zest, to decorate

For the Icing
115 g/4 oz/½ cup butter, softened
500 g/1¼ lb/5 cups icing sugar
5 ml/1 tsp grated lemon zest
45–75 ml/3–5 tbsp lemon juice

1 Preheat the oven to 180°C/350°F/ Gas 4. Grease two 23 cm/9 inch round cake tins, line the bases with greaseproof paper and grease the paper. Sift the flour with the baking powder and salt.

2 ▲ Cream the butter with the sugars until light and fluffy. Beat in the eggs, then stir in the grated lemon zest.

3 ▲ In a small bowl mix the mashed bananas with the vanilla essence and milk. Add the banana mixture and the dry ingredients to the butter mixture alternately in two or three batches and stir until just blended. Fold in the nuts.

4 Divide the mixture between the cake tins. Bake for 30–35 minutes, let stand for 5 minutes, then turn out on to a wire rack.

5 Make the icing. Cream the butter until smooth, then gradually beat in the icing sugar. Stir in the lemon zest and enough juice to make a spreadable consistency.

6 ▲ Put one of the cake layers on a serving plate. Cover with about one-third of the icing. Top with the second cake layer. Spread the remaining icing evenly over the cake and decorate with the pared lemon zest.

Genoese Cake with Fruit and Cream

Genoese is a classic sponge which can be used as the base for both simple and elaborate creations. In this version a little butter is added to make a moister cake. You could simply dust it with icing sugar, or layer it with seasonal fruits.

INGREDIENTS
Serves 6
115 g/4 oz/1 cup plain flour
pinch of salt
4 size 3 eggs, at room temperature
115 g/4 oz/½ cup caster sugar
2.5 ml/½ tsp vanilla essence
50 g/2 oz/4 tbsp butter, melted or
clarified and cooled

For the Filling
450 g/1 lb fresh strawberries
30–60 ml/2–4 tbsp caster sugar
475 ml/16 fl oz/2 cups whipping cream
5 ml/1 tsp vanilla essence

1 Preheat the oven to 180°C/350°F/ Gas 4. Lightly butter a 23 cm/9 inch springform tin or deep cake tin. Line the base with baking parchment and dust lightly with flour. Sift the flour and salt together twice.

2 ▲ Half-fill a medium saucepan with hot water and set over a low heat (do not allow the water to boil). Break the eggs into a heatproof bowl which just fits over the pan without touching the water. Using an electric mixer, beat the eggs, gradually adding the sugar, for 8–10 minutes until the mixture is very thick and pale and leaves a ribbon trail. Remove the bowl from the pan, add the vanilla essence and continue beating until cool.

3 ▲ Fold in the flour mixture in three batches, using a balloon whisk or metal spoon. Before the third addition of flour, stir a large spoonful of the cake mixture into the melted or clarified butter, then fold the butter mixture into the remaining mixture with the last addition of flour. Work quickly, but gently, so the mixture does not deflate. Pour into the prepared tin, smoothing the top so the sides are slightly higher than the centre.

4 ▲ Bake for 25–30 minutes until the top of the cake springs back when touched and the edge begins to shrink away from the side of the tin. Place the cake in its tin on a wire rack to cool for 5–10 minutes, then invert the cake on to the rack and leave to cool completely. Peel off the lining paper.

5 ▲ To make the filling, slice the strawberries, place in a bowl, sprinkle with 15–30 ml/1–2 tbsp of the sugar and set aside. Beat the cream with enough of the remaining sugar to sweeten it to your taste. Beat in the vanilla essence until the cream holds soft peaks: do not overbeat.

6 ▲ To assemble the cake, split the sponge in half horizontally, using a serrated knife. Place the top, cut side up, on a serving plate. Spread with a third of the cream and cover with a layer of sliced strawberries. Place the bottom half of the cake, cut side down, on top of the filling and press lightly. Spread the remaining cream over the top and sides of the cake. Chill and serve with the remaining strawberries.

Peach Swiss Roll

A feather-light sponge enclosing peach jam, this would be delicious at tea-time. It needs to be baked on the day you are going to serve it.

INGREDIENTS
Serves 6–8
3 size 3 eggs
115 g/4 oz/½ cup caster sugar, plus extra for dusting
75 g/3 oz/¾ cup plain flour, sifted
90 ml/6 tbsp peach jam
icing sugar, for dusting (optional)

1 ▲ Preheat the oven to 200°C/400°F/ Gas 6. Grease a 30 x 20 cm/12 x 8 inch Swiss roll tin and line with baking parchment. Combine the eggs and sugar in a bowl. Beat with a hand-held electric whisk until the mixture is thick and pale and leaves a trail on the surface when the beaters are lifted.

2 ▲ Carefully fold in the flour with a large metal spoon, then add 15 ml/ 1 tbsp boiling water in the same way.

3 ▲ Spoon into the prepared tin, spread evenly to the edge and bake for about 10–12 minutes until the cake springs back when lightly pressed in the centre.

4 ▲ Spread a sheet of greaseproof paper on a flat surface, sprinkle it with caster sugar, then invert the cake on top. Peel off the lining paper.

5 ▲ Neatly trim the edges of the cake. Make a neat cut two-thirds of the way through the cake, about 1cm/ ½ in from the short edge nearest you.

6 ▲ Spread the cake with the peach jam and roll up quickly from the partially cut end. Hold in position for a minute, making sure the join is underneath. Cool on a wire rack. Dust with icing sugar before serving or decorate with Glacé Icing (see Tip).

Tip

To decorate the Swiss roll, put 115 g/4 oz Glacé Icing in a piping bag fitted with a small writing nozzle and pipe lines over the top of the cake.

Queen of Sheba Cake

This rich chocolate and almond cake is so moist it needs no filling. It is wonderful for entertaining as it can be made in advance and stored, well wrapped, in the fridge for up to three days.

INGREDIENTS
Serves 8–10
90 g/3½ oz/⅔ cup whole blanched
almonds, lightly toasted
115 g/4 oz/½ cup caster sugar
40 g/1½ oz/¼ cup plain flour
115 g/4 oz/½ cup unsalted
butter, softened
150 g/5 oz plain chocolate, melted
3 eggs, separated
30 ml/2 tbsp almond liqueur
(optional)

For the Chocolate Glaze
175 ml/6 fl oz/¾ cup whipping
cream
225 g/8 oz plain chocolate, chopped
25 g/1 oz/2 tbsp unsalted butter
30 ml/2 tbsp almond
liqueur (optional)
chopped toasted almonds,
to decorate

3 ▲ In a medium bowl, beat the butter with an electric mixer until creamy, then add half of the remaining sugar and beat for about 1–2 minutes until very light and creamy. Gradually beat in the melted chocolate until well blended, then add the egg yolks one at a time, beating well after each addition, and beat in the liqueur, if using.

5 Bake for 30–35 minutes until the edges are puffed but the centre is still soft and wobbly (a skewer inserted about 5 cm/2 inches from the edge should come out clean). Transfer the cake in its tin to a wire rack to cool for about 15 minutes, then remove the sides of the cake tin and leave to cool completely. Invert the cake on to a 20 cm/8 inch cake board and remove the base of the tin and the paper.

6 To make the chocolate glaze, bring the cream to the boil in a saucepan. Remove from the heat and add the chocolate. Stir gently until the chocolate has melted and is smooth, then beat in the butter and liqueur, if using. Cool for about 20–30 minutes until slightly thickened, stirring the mixture occasionally.

1 ▲ Preheat the oven to 180°C/350°F/ Gas 4. Lightly butter a 20–23 cm/ 8–9 inch springform tin or deep loose-based cake tin. Line the base with non-stick baking paper and dust the tin lightly with flour.

2 In the bowl of a food processor fitted with the metal blade, process the almonds and 30 ml/2 tbsp of the sugar until very fine. Transfer to a bowl and sift over the flour. Stir to mix, then set aside.

4 ▲ In another bowl, beat the egg whites until soft peaks form. Add the remaining sugar and beat until the whites are stiff and glossy, but not dry. Fold a quarter of the whites into the chocolate mixture to lighten it, then alternately fold in the almond mixture and the remaining whites in three batches. Spoon the mixture into the prepared tin and spread evenly. Tap the tin gently to release any air bubbles.

7 ▲ Place the cake on a wire rack over a baking sheet and pour over the warm chocolate glaze to cover the top completely. Using a palette knife, smooth the glaze around the sides of the cake. Spoon a little of the glaze into a piping bag fitted with a writing nozzle and use to write the name, if you like. Leave to stand for 5 minutes to set slightly, then carefully press the nuts on to the sides of the cake. Using two long palette knives, transfer the cake to a serving plate and chill until ready to serve.

Sachertorte

One of the world's finest – and most famous – cakes, Sachertorte is a dark and delectable chocolate cake. Serve in tiny slices for afternoon tea.

INGREDIENTS
Serves 8–10
50g/2 oz plain chocolate
50 g/2 oz dark chocolate
75 g/3 oz/6 tbsp butter, softened
115 g/4 oz/½ cup granulated sugar
4 size 3 eggs, separated, plus 1 egg white
1.5 ml/¼ tsp salt
65 g/2½ oz/½ cup plain flour

For the Topping
75 g/3 oz/5 tbsp apricot jam
250 ml/8 fl oz/1 cup water plus 15 ml/1 tbsp extra
15 g/½ oz/1 tbsp butter
175 g/6 oz dark chocolate
175 g/6 oz/¾ cup granulated sugar
ready-made chocolate icing (optional)

1 ▲ Preheat the oven to 160°C/325°F/ Gas 3. Grease a 23 cm/9 inch round cake tin. Line the tin with greaseproof paper and grease the paper. Melt both chocolates in the top of a double boiler, or in a heatproof bowl set over hot water. Set aside.

2 ▲ Cream the butter and sugar until fluffy. Stir in the chocolate, then beat in the egg yolks, one at a time.

3 ▲ In a grease-free bowl, beat the egg whites with the salt until stiff. Fold a dollop of whites into the chocolate mixture to lighten it. Fold in the remaining whites in three batches, alternating with the sifted flour.

4 ▲ Pour into the tin and bake for about 45 minutes, until a skewer inserted into the centre of the cake comes out clean. Cool on a wire rack.

5 ▲ Make the topping. Melt the jam with 15 ml/1 tbsp of the water over a low heat, then strain for a smooth consistency. In the top of a double boiler or in a heatproof bowl set over hot water, melt the butter and the chocolate together.

6 ▲ In a heavy saucepan, dissolve the sugar in the remaining water over a low heat. Raise the heat and boil until the mixture reaches 110°C/230°F on a sugar thermometer. Immediately plunge the bottom of the pan into cold water and leave for 1 minute. Pour into the chocolate mixture and stir to blend. Let the icing cool for a few minutes. Meanwhile, brush the warm jam over the cake. Starting in the centre, pour over the chocolate icing and work outward in a circular movement. Tilt the rack to spread; only use a spatula for the sides of the cake. Leave to set overnight. If wished, decorate with chocolate icing.

Mississippi Mud Cake

There are many versions of this cake, but all of them are based on a dark cocoa-based chocolate cake, which is meant to be reminiscent of the cocoa-black shores of the Mississippi River.

INGREDIENTS
Serves 8–10
cocoa powder for dusting
275 g/10 oz/2½ cups plain flour
5 ml/1 tsp baking powder
150 g/5 oz cooking chocolate
225 g/8 oz/1 cup butter
300 ml/½ pint/1¼ cups strong coffee
or espresso
pinch of salt
400 g/14 oz/2 cups granulated sugar
60 ml/4 tbsp bourbon or whisky
2 size 3 eggs, lightly beaten
10 ml/2 tsp vanilla essence
130 g/4½ oz/2 cups sweetened
desiccated coconut

For the Filling
250 ml/8 fl oz/1 cup evaporated
milk
115 g/4 oz/½ cup (packed) light
brown sugar
115 g/4 oz/½ cup butter
75 g/3 oz plain chocolate
3 size 3 egg yolks, lightly beaten
5 ml/1 tsp vanilla essence
225 g/8 oz/2 cups pecans, chopped
65 g/2½ oz/1 cup miniature
marshmallows

For the Topping
350 ml/12 fl oz/1½ cups whipping
or double cream
5 ml/1 tsp vanilla essence

To Decorate
fresh coconut

1 ▲ Preheat the oven to 180°C/350°F/ Gas 4. Grease two 23 cm/9 inch cake tins, and dust bottoms and sides with cocoa. In a bowl sift the flour and baking powder. In a saucepan over low heat, melt the chocolate, butter, coffee, salt and sugar, stirring occasionally until the mixture is smooth and the sugar has dissolved. Stir in the bourbon or whisky. Pour the chocolate mixture into a bowl and cool slightly. With an electric mixer on medium speed, beat in the eggs and vanilla, decrease the speed and beat in the flour; stir in the coconut. Pour into the prepared tins.

2 ▲ Bake for 25–30 minutes until a skewer inserted in the centre comes out with just a few crumbs attached; do not overbake or the cake will be too dry. Leave to cool on a wire rack for 10 minutes. Remove the cakes from the tins and place on a wire rack to cool completely.

3 ▲ For the filling, combine the evaporated milk, sugar, butter, chocolate, egg yolks and vanilla in a large heavy-based saucepan. Cook over medium heat, stirring frequently for 8–10 minutes until the chocolate is melted and smooth and the mixture is thick enough to coat the back of a wooden spoon; do not boil or the mixture will curdle. Remove from the heat and stir in the nuts and marshmallows, stirring until melted. Refrigerate until thick enough to spread, stirring occasionally to prevent a skin forming.

4 ▲ Assemble the cake. With a serrated knife, slice both cake layers in half crosswise, making four layers. Spread each of the bottom cake layers with half the chocolate nut filling and cover each bottom half with its respective top layer.

6 Using a heavy hammer and nail, puncture the eyes of a fresh coconut. Drain off the liquid and reserve if wished. Place the coconut in a strong plastic bag and hit the shell very hard with the hammer to crack the coconut open.

5 ▲ In a medium bowl, whip the cream and the vanilla until firm peaks form. Place one filled cake layer on a serving plate and spread with half the whipped cream. Top with the second filled cake layer and spread with the remaining cream, swirling it to form an attractive pattern.

Tip

If fresh coconut is unavailable, you can decorate the cake with unsweetened desiccated coconut.

7 ▲ With a strong blunt-bladed knife, separate the flesh from the shell; it will break into medium-sized pieces. Rinse the pieces under cold running water and store in cold water. With a swivel-bladed peeler, draw the blade along the curved edge of a coconut piece to make thin wide curls with a brown edge. Use these to decorate the top of the cake.

Strawberry Gâteau

It is hard to believe that this delicious gâteau is low in fat, but the sponge base contains no fat and the filling is made of low-fat soft cheese and fromage frais. Enjoy it with a clear conscience.

INGREDIENTS
Serves 6
2 size 3 eggs
75 g/3 oz/6 tbsp caster sugar
grated zest of ½ orange
50 g/2 oz/½ cup plain flour

For the Filling
275 g/10 oz/1¼ cups low-fat
soft cheese
grated zest of ½ orange
30 ml/2 tbsp caster sugar
60 ml/4 tbsp low-fat fromage frais
25 g/1 oz/¼ cup chopped
almonds, toasted

To Decorate
225 g/8 oz strawberries, halved
strawberry leaves
icing sugar

1 Preheat the oven to 190°C/375°F/
Gas 5. Grease a 30 x 20 cm/12 x
8 inch Swiss roll tin and line with
baking parchment.

2 ▲ In a bowl, whisk the eggs, sugar
and orange zest together for about
2 minutes until the mixture is pale and
leaves a thick trail when the beaters
are lifted.

3 ▲ Fold in the flour with a metal
spoon, being careful not to knock
out any air. Turn into the prepared tin.
Bake for 15–20 minutes, or until the
cake springs back when lightly pressed.
Turn the cake on to a wire rack,
remove the lining paper and leave to
cool completely.

4 ▲ Meanwhile make the filling. In a
bowl, mix the soft cheese with the
orange rind, sugar and fromage frais
until smooth. Divide between two
bowls. Chop half the strawberry halves
and add to one bowl of filling.

5 ▲ Cut the sponge widthways into
three equal pieces and sandwich
them together with the strawberry
filling. Spread two-thirds of the plain
filling over the sides of the cake and
press on the toasted almonds.

6 ▲ Spread the rest of the filling over
the top of the cake and decorate
with the remaining strawberry halves
and strawberry leaves. Dust with icing
sugar and transfer to a serving plate.

Tip

Use other soft fruits in season, such
as currants, raspberries, blackberries
or blueberries, or try a mixture of
different berries.

Kugelhopf

Guaranteed to rise to the occasion, this fruit-and-nut bread looks as good as it tastes.

INGREDIENTS
Makes 1 loaf
115 g/4 oz/²/₃ cup raisins
15 ml/1 tbsp kirsch or brandy
15 ml/1 tbsp dried yeast
60 ml/4 tbsp lukewarm water
115 g/4 oz/½ cup butter
115 g/4 oz/½ cup caster sugar
3 size 3 eggs
grated zest of 1 lemon
5 ml/1 tsp salt
2.5 ml/½ tsp vanilla essence
350 g/12 oz/3 cups flour
120 ml/4 fl oz/½ cup milk
25 g/1 oz/¼ cup slivered almonds
50 g/2 oz/½ cup blanched almonds,
chopped
icing sugar, for dusting

1 ▲ In a bowl, combine the raisins and kirsch or brandy. Set aside. Combine the yeast and water, stir and leave for 5 minutes until frothy.

2 With an electric mixer, cream the butter and sugar until thick and fluffy. Beat in the eggs, one at a time. Add the lemon zest, salt and vanilla essence. Stir in the yeast mixture.

3 ▲ Add the flour, alternating with the milk, until the mixture is well blended. Cover and leave to rise in a warm place until doubled in volume, about 2 hours.

4 ▲ Grease a 2.4 litre/4 pint/10 cup kugelhopf tin, then sprinkle the slivered almonds evenly over the bottom of the tin.

5 Work the raisins and blanched almonds into the dough, then spoon into the tin. Cover with a plastic bag and leave to rise in a warm place for about 1 hour until the dough almost reaches the top of the tin. Preheat the oven to 180°C/350°F/Gas 4.

6 Bake for 45 minutes, or until golden brown. If the top browns too quickly, cover it with foil. Allow to cool in the tin for 15 minutes, then turn out on to a rack. Dust the top lightly with icing sugar before serving.

Fruit and Nut Cake

This fruit cake is made without saturated fat, yet retains the rich, familiar flavour of traditional fruit cakes. It improves with keeping.

INGREDIENTS
Serves 12–14

175 g/6 oz/1½ cups self-raising
wholemeal flour
175 g/6 oz/1½ cups self-raising
white flour
10 ml/2 tsp mixed spice
15 ml/1 tbsp apple and apricot spread
45 ml/3 tbsp clear honey
15 ml/1 tbsp molasses or black treacle
90 ml/6 tbsp sunflower oil
175 ml/6 fl oz/¾ cup orange juice
2 size 3 eggs, beaten
675 g/1½ lb/4 cups luxury mixed
dried fruit
45 ml/3 tbsp split almonds
50 g/2 oz/¼ cup glacé cherries, halved

3 ▲ Put the apple and apricot spread in a small bowl. Gradually stir in the honey and molasses or treacle. Add to the dry ingredients with the oil, orange juice, eggs and mixed fruit. Mix together thoroughly.

4 ▲ Turn the mixture into the prepared tin and smooth the surface. Arrange the almonds and cherries in a pattern over the top. Stand the tin on newspaper and bake for 2 hours or until a skewer inserted into the centre of the cake comes out clean. Leave on a wire rack until cold, then lift out of the tin and remove the paper.

1 ▲ Preheat the oven to 160°C/325°F/ Gas 3. Grease a deep 20 cm/8 inch cake tin. Line with greaseproof paper and grease the paper. Secure a band of brown paper around the outside.

2 ▲ Sift the flours into a mixing bowl with the mixed spice and make a well in the centre.

Teatime Treats

Here, you will find a tempting array of cakes to enjoy with afternoon tea or morning coffee. Featuring popular classics from around the world, from light sponges, chocolate brownies and Swiss rolls to delicious meringues, this chapter includes indulgent cakes for all tastes.

Chestnut Cake

An Italian speciality, this is definitely a cake to mark an occasion. Rich, moist and heavy, it can be made up to a week in advance and kept, undecorated, wrapped and stored in an airtight container. Allow the cake to come to room temperature before serving.

INGREDIENTS
Serves 8–10
150 g/5 oz/1¼ cups plain flour
pinch of salt
225 g/8 oz/1 cup butter, softened
150 g/5 oz/¾ cup caster sugar
439 g/15½ oz can chestnut purée
9 size 3 eggs, separated
7 tbsp dark rum
300 ml/½ pint/1¼ cups double cream

To Decorate
marrons glacés, chopped
icing sugar, sifted

1 Preheat the oven to 180°C/350°F/ Gas 4. Grease a 21 cm/8½ inch springform cake tin, line the base with greaseproof paper and grease the paper.

2 Sift together the flour and salt, and set aside. Place the butter and three-quarters of the sugar in a bowl and beat until fluffy.

3 ▲ Fold in two-thirds of the chestnut purée, alternating with the egg yolks, and beat. Fold in the flour and salt.

4 ▲ Whisk the egg whites in a clean, dry bowl until stiff. Beat a little of the egg whites into the chestnut mixture, until evenly blended, then fold in the remainder.

5 ▲ Transfer the cake mixture to the prepared tin and smooth the surface. Bake in the centre of the oven for about 1¼ hours, or until a skewer inserted into the centre of the cake comes out clean.

6 Place the cake, still in the tin, on a wire rack. Using a skewer, pierce holes evenly all over the cake. Sprinkle 4 tbsp of the rum over the top, then allow the cake to cool completely.

7 ▲ Remove the cake from the tin, peel off the lining paper and cut horizontally into two layers. Place the bottom layer on a serving plate. Whisk the cream in a mixing bowl with the remaining rum, sugar and chestnut purée until thick and smooth.

8 To assemble the cake, spread two-thirds of the chestnut cream mixture over the bottom layer and place the other layer on top. Spread some of the remaining chestnut cream over the top and sides of the cake, then fill a greaseproof paper piping bag, fitted with a star nozzle, with the rest of the chestnut mixture. Pipe big swirls around the outside edge of the cake. Decorate with the marrons glacés and sifted icing sugar.

Tip

In order to have the most control over a piping bag, it is important to hold it in a relaxed position. You may find it easier to hold it with one or both hands.

Crunchy-topped Madeira Cakes

Traditionally served with a glass of Madeira wine in Victorian England, this light sponge still makes a perfect tea-time treat.

INGREDIENTS
Serves 8–10
200 g/7 oz/14 tbsp butter, softened
finely grated zest of 1 lemon
150 g/5 oz/³/₄ cup caster sugar
3 size 3 eggs
75 g/3 oz/³/₄ cup plain flour, sifted
150 g/5 oz/1¹/₄ cups self-raising
flour, sifted

For the Topping
3 tbsp clear honey
115 g/4 oz/³/₄ cup plus 2 tbsp
chopped mixed peel
50 g/2 oz/¹/₂ cup flaked almonds

1 Preheat the oven to 180°C/350°F/ Gas 4. Grease a 450 g/1 lb loaf tin, line the base and sides with greaseproof paper and grease the paper.

2 ▲ Place the butter, lemon zest and sugar in a mixing bowl and beat until light and fluffy. Beat in the eggs, one at a time, until evenly blended.

3 ▲ Sift together the flours, then stir into the egg mixture. Transfer the cake mixture to the prepared tin and smooth the surface.

4 ▲ Bake in the centre of the oven for 45–50 minutes or until a skewer inserted into the centre of the cake comes out clean. Leave the cake in the tin for about 5 minutes. Turn out on to a wire rack, peel off the lining paper and leave to cool completely.

5 ▲ To make the topping, place the honey, chopped mixed peel and almonds in a small saucepan and heat gently until the honey melts. Remove from the heat and stir briefly to coat the peel and almonds, then spread over the top of the cake. Allow to cool completely before serving.

Banana Coconut Cake

*Slightly over-ripe bananas are best for
this perfect coffee morning cake.*

INGREDIENTS
Serves 8–10
75 g/3 oz/1½ cups desiccated
coconut
115 g/4 oz/½ cup butter, softened
115 g/4 oz/½ cup caster sugar
2 size 3 eggs
115 g/4 oz/1 cup self-raising flour
50 g/2 oz/½ cup plain flour
1 tsp bicarbonate of soda
100 ml/4 fl oz/½ cup milk
2 large bananas, peeled and mashed

For the Topping
25 g/1 oz/2 tbsp butter
2 tbsp clear honey
115 g/4 oz/2 cups shredded coconut

1 Preheat the oven to 190°C/375°F/
Gas 5. Grease a deep 18 cm/7 inch
square cake tin, line the base and sides
with greaseproof paper and then grease
the paper.

2 ▲ Spread the desiccated coconut
out on a baking sheet and place
under a hot grill for about 5 minutes,
stirring and turning the coconut until
evenly toasted.

3 Place the butter and sugar in a
mixing bowl and beat until they are
smooth and creamy. Beat in the eggs,
one at a time.

4 Sift together the flours and
bicarbonate of soda, then sift half
of this mixture into the butter and egg
mixture and stir to mix.

5 Mix together the milk and mashed
banana in a small bowl, then add
half to the egg mixture. Beat well to
combine, then add the remaining flour
and toasted coconut together with the
remaining banana mixture. Stir to mix,
then transfer to the prepared cake tin
and smooth the surface.

6 Bake in the centre of the oven for
about 1 hour, or until a skewer
inserted into the centre of the cake
comes out clean. Leave the cake in the
tin for about 5 minutes, then turn out
on to a wire rack, peel off the lining
paper and leave to cool completely.

7 To make the topping, place the
butter and honey in a small
saucepan and heat gently until melted.
Stir in the shredded coconut and cook,
stirring constantly, for about 5 minutes
or until lightly browned. Remove from
the heat and allow to cool slightly.

8 ▲ Spoon the topping over the top of
the cake and allow to cool
completely before serving.

Almond and Apricot Cake

Although canned apricots can be used in this recipe, nothing quite. beats using the fresh fruit in season. Choose sweet-smelling, ripe fruit for this delicious cake.

INGREDIENTS
Serves 6–8
4–5 tbsp fine dry white
breadcrumbs
225 g/8 oz/1 cup butter, softened
225 g/8 oz/1 cup caster sugar
4 size 3 eggs
175 g/6 oz/1½ cups self-raising
flour
1–2 tbsp milk
115 g/4 oz/1⅓ cups ground
almonds
few drops of almond essence
450 g/1 lb fresh apricots, stoned
and halved
sifted caster sugar, to decorate

3 ▲ Place the butter and sugar in a mixing bowl and beat with an electric mixer until light and fluffy. Beat in the eggs, one at a time, then fold in the flour, milk, ground almonds and almond essence.

4 ▲ Spoon half of the cake mixture into the prepared tin and smooth the surface. Arrange half of the apricots over the top, then spoon over the remaining cake mixture. Finish with the other half of the apricots. Bake the cake in the centre of the oven for 30–35 minutes, or until a skewer inserted into the centre of the cake comes out clean.

5 Turn the cake out on to a wire rack, peel off the lining paper and sprinkle over the sifted caster sugar. Serve warm or leave to cool.

1 Preheat the oven to 180°C/350°F/ Gas 4. Grease a 23 cm/9 inch round cake tin, line the base with greaseproof paper and grease the paper.

2 ▲ Sprinkle the breadcrumbs into the prepared cake tin and tap them around the tin to coat the base and sides evenly.

Upside-down Pear & Ginger Cakes

A light spicy sponge topped with glossy baked fruit and ginger. This is also good served warm for pudding.

INGREDIENTS
Serves 6–8

1 x 900 g/2 lb can pear halves, drained
8 tbsp finely chopped stem ginger
8 tbsp ginger syrup from the jar
175 g/6 oz/1½ cups self-raising flour
½ tsp baking powder
1 tsp ground ginger
175 g/6 oz/¾ cup soft light brown sugar
175 g/6 oz/¾ cup butter, softened
3 size 3 eggs, lightly beaten

4 ▲ Carefully spoon the mixture into the tin and smooth the surface.

5 ▲ Bake in the centre of the oven for about 50 minutes, or until a skewer inserted in the centre of the cake comes out clean. Leave the cake to cool in the tin for about 5 minutes. Turn out on to a wire rack, peel off the lining paper and leave to cool completely. Add the reserved chopped ginger to the pear halves and drizzle over the remaining ginger syrup.

1 Preheat the oven to 180°C/350°F/ Gas 4. Grease a deep 20 cm/8 inch round cake tin, line the base with greaseproof paper and grease the paper.

2 ▲ Fill the hollow in each pear with half the chopped ginger. Arrange the pear halves, flat sides down, over the base of the cake tin, then spoon half the ginger syrup over the top.

3 Sift the flour, baking powder and ground ginger into a mixing bowl. Stir in the soft brown sugar and butter, then add the eggs and beat together for 1–2 minutes until level and creamy.

One-stage Victoria Sandwich

Originally made in an oblong shape, today's Victoria sandwich is made using a variety of different flavourings and decorations, and is baked and cut into all sorts of shapes and sizes. Use this basic recipe to suit the occasion.

INGREDIENTS
Serves 6–8
175 g/6 oz/1½ cups self-raising flour
pinch of salt
175 g/6 oz/¾ cup butter, softened
175 g/6 oz/¾ cup caster sugar
3 size 3 eggs

To Finish
4–6 tbsp raspberry jam
caster sugar or icing sugar

3 ▲ Place one of the cakes on a serving plate and spread with the raspberry jam. Place the other cake on top, then dredge with caster or icing sugar, to serve.

Variation
Makes 8–10 iced fancies

1 ▲ Place the cake mixture in a greased and lined 23 × 33 cm/9 × 13 inch Swiss roll tin and smooth the surface. Bake in the centre of the oven for 25–30 minutes, or until a skewer inserted into the centre of the cake comes out clean. Turn out on to a wire rack, peel off the lining paper and leave to cool completely.

2 ▲ Cut the cake into individual sized shapes, such as fingers, diamonds, squares or small rounds, using a knife or biscuit cutters. Using one quantity of Butter Icing, cover with decorative piping. You can flavour or colour the butter icing by substituting orange or lemon juice for the milk and/or adding a few drops of food colouring.

3 For alternative decorations, you could try a selection of the following: glacé cherries, angelica, jellied fruits, grated chocolate, chopped or whole nuts, or choose one of your own ideas.

Tip

To make the decorative stencilled pattern with icing sugar shown here, cut out star shapes from paper. Lay the paper stars over the top of the cake and then dredge with icing sugar. Remove the paper shapes carefully to reveal the stencilled pattern. You could also use a paper doily as a stencil.

1 Preheat the oven to 180°C/375°F/ Gas 4. Grease two deep 18 cm/7 inch round cake tins, line the bases with greaseproof paper and grease the paper.

2 ▲ Place all the ingredients in a mixing bowl and whisk together using an electric hand whisk. Divide the mixture between the prepared tins and smooth the surfaces. Bake in the centre of the oven for 25–30 minutes, or until a skewer inserted into the centre of the cakes comes out clean. Turn out on to a wire rack, peel off the lining paper and leave to cool completely.

Carrot and Almond Cake

Made with grated carrots and ground almonds, this unusual
fat-free sponge makes a delicious afternoon treat.

INGREDIENTS
Serves 8–10
5 size 3 eggs, separated
finely grated zest of 1 lemon
300 g/10 oz/1¹/₃ cups caster sugar
350 g/12 oz/5–6 carrots, peeled and
finely grated
225 g/8 oz/1¹/₄ cups ground almonds
115 g/4 oz/1 cup self-raising flour,
sifted
sifted icing sugar, to decorate
marzipan carrots, to decorate
(optional)

Tip

To make the marzipan carrots, knead a little orange food colouring into 115 g/4 oz marzipan until evenly blended. On a work surface lightly dusted with icing sugar, divide the marzipan into even-sized pieces, about the size of small walnuts. Mould into carrot shapes and press horizontal lines along each carrot with a knife blade. Press a tiny stick of angelica into the end of each piece to resemble the carrot top. Position the marzipan carrots on the cake, to decorate.

1 Preheat the oven to 190°C/375°F/ Gas 5. Grease a deep 20 cm/8 inch round cake tin, line the base with greaseproof paper and grease the paper.

2 ▲ Place the egg yolks, lemon zest and sugar in a bowl. Beat with an electric mixer for about 5 minutes, until the mixture is thick and pale.

3 ▲ Mix in the grated carrot, ground almonds and flour and stir until evenly combined.

4 In a clean, dry bowl, whisk the egg whites until stiff. Using a large metal spoon or rubber spatula, mix a little of the whisked egg whites into the carrot mixture, then fold in the rest.

5 ▲ Spoon the mixture into the prepared cake tin and bake in the centre of the oven for about 1¹/₄ hours, or until a skewer inserted into the centre of the cake comes out clean. Leave the cake in the tin for about 5 minutes, then turn out on to a wire rack, peel off the lining paper and leave to cool completely.

6 ▲ Decorate with sifted icing sugar and marzipan carrots.

Flourless Fruit Cake

A really easy recipe which everyone will enjoy. Children can have fun crushing the cornflakes and helping you to beat the ingredients together.

INGREDIENTS
Serves 12–15
1 x 450 g/1 lb jar mincemeat
350 g/12 oz/2 cups dried mixed fruit
115 g/4 oz/1 cup no-soak dried
apricots, chopped
115 g/4 oz/1 cup no-soak dried figs,
chopped
115 g/4 oz/¹/₂ cup glacé cherries,
halved
115 g/4 oz/1 cup walnut pieces
225 g/8 oz/8–10 cups cornflakes,
crushed
4 size 3 eggs, lightly beaten
1 x 410 g/14¹/₂ oz can evaporated
milk
1 tsp ground mixed spice
1 tsp baking powder
mixed glacé fruits, chopped, to
decorate

1 Preheat the oven to 150°C/300°F/ Gas 2. Grease a 25 cm/10 inch round cake tin, line the base and sides with a double thickness of greaseproof paper and grease the paper.

2 Put all the ingredients into a large mixing bowl. Beat together well.

3 ▲ Turn into the prepared tin and smooth the surface with the back of a spoon.

4 ▲ Bake in the centre of the oven for about 1³/₄ hours, or until a skewer inserted in the centre of the cake comes out clean. Allow the cake to cool in the tin for 10 minutes, then turn out on to a wire rack, peel off the lining paper and leave to cool completely. Decorate with the chopped glacé fruits.

Tip

This cake may be iced and marzipanned to make a Christmas or birthday cake. A useful recipe for anyone who needs to avoid eating wheat flour.

Vegan Chocolate Gâteau

It isn't often that vegans can indulge in a slice of chocolate cake and this one tastes so delicious, they'll all be back for more!

Ingredients
Serves 8–10
300 g/10 oz/2½ cups self-raising
wholemeal flour
50 g/2 oz/⅓ cup cocoa powder
3 tsp baking powder
250 g/9 oz/1¼ cups caster sugar
few drops of vanilla essence
9 tbsp sunflower oil
350 ml/12 fl oz/1½ cups water
sifted cocoa powder, to decorate
25 g/1 oz/¼ cup chopped nuts, to
decorate

For the Chocolate Fudge
50 g/2 oz/¼ cup vegan (soya)
margarine
3 tbsp water
250 g/9 oz/2⅓ cups icing sugar
2 tbsp cocoa powder
1 – 2 tbsp hot water

1 Preheat the oven to 170°C/325°F/ Gas 3. Grease a deep 20 cm/8 inch round cake tin, line the base and sides with greaseproof paper and grease the paper.

2 Sift the flour, cocoa powder and baking powder into a large mixing bowl. Add the caster sugar and vanilla essence, then gradually beat in the sunflower oil and water to make a smooth batter.

3 Pour the cake mixture into the prepared tin and smooth the surface with the back of a spoon.

4 ▲ Bake in the centre of the oven for about 45 minutes or until a skewer inserted into the centre of the cake comes out clean. Leave in the tin for about 5 minutes, then turn out on to a wire rack, peel off the lining paper and leave to cool. Cut the cake in half.

5 ▲ To make the chocolate fudge, place the margarine and water in a pan and heat gently until the margarine has melted. Remove from the heat and add the sifted icing sugar and cocoa powder, beating until smooth and shiny. Allow to cool until firm enough to spread and pipe.

6 ▲ Place the bottom layer of cake on a serving plate and spread over two-thirds of the chocolate fudge mixture. Top with the other layer of cake. Fit a piping bag with a star nozzle, fill with the remaining chocolate fudge and pipe stars over the cake. Sprinkle with cocoa powder and chopped nuts.

Autumn Passionettes

Perfect for a tea party or packed lunch, this passion cake mixture can also be made as one big cake to serve for a celebration or as a dessert.

INGREDIENTS
Makes 24

150 g/5 oz/³/₄ cup butter, melted
200 g/7 oz/⁷/₈ cup soft light
brown sugar
115 g/4 oz/1 cup carrots, peeled and
finely grated
50 g/2 oz/1 cup dessert apples,
peeled and finely grated
pinch of salt
1–2 tsp ground mixed spice
2 size 3 eggs
200 g/7 oz/1³/₄ cups self-raising
flour
2 tsp baking powder
115 g/4 oz/1 cup shelled walnuts,
finely chopped

For the Topping

175 g/6 oz/³/₄ cup full-fat soft cheese
4–5 tbsp single cream
50 g/2 oz/¹/₂ cup icing sugar, sifted
25 g/1 oz/¹/₄ cup shelled walnuts,
halved
2 tsp cocoa powder, sifted

1 Preheat the oven to 180°C/350°F/
Gas 4. Arrange 24 fairy cake paper
cases in bun tins and put to one side.

2 ▲ Place the butter, sugar, carrots,
apples, salt, mixed spice and eggs in a
mixing bowl and beat well to combine.

3 ▲ Sift together the flour and baking
powder into a small bowl, then sift
again into the mixing bowl. Add the
chopped walnuts and fold in until
evenly blended.

4 ▲ Fill the paper cases half-full with
the cake mixture, then bake for
20–25 minutes, or until a skewer
inserted into the centres of the cakes
comes out clean.

5 Leave the cakes in the tins for about
5 minutes, before transferring them
to a wire rack to cool completely.

6 ▲ To make the topping, place the
full-fat soft cheese in a mixing bowl
and beat in the cream and icing sugar
until smooth. Put a dollop of the
topping in the centre of each cake, then
decorate with the walnuts. Dust with
sifted cocoa powder and allow the icing
to set before serving.

Tip

To make one big cake, which will
serve 6–8, grease a 20 cm/8 inch
fluted American bundt cake tin and
line the base with greaseproof
paper. Grease the paper. Place all
of the cake mixture in the tin and
bake for about 1¹/₄ hours, or until a
skewer inserted into the centre of
the cake comes out clean. Leave the
cake in the tin for about 5 minutes.
Turn out on to a wire rack, peel off
the lining paper and leave to cool
completely. Decorate with the topping mixture, walnuts and sifted
cocoa powder.

utumn Passionettes

Perfect for a tea party or packed lunch, this passion cake mixture can also be made as one big cake to serve for a celebration or as a dessert.

INGREDIENTS
Makes 24
150 g/5 oz/³/₄ cup butter, melted
200 g/7 oz/⁷/₈ cup soft light brown sugar
115 g/4 oz/1 cup carrots, peeled and finely grated
50 g/2 oz/1 cup dessert apples, peeled and finely grated
pinch of salt
1–2 tsp ground mixed spice
2 size 3 eggs
200 g/7 oz/1³/₄ cups self-raising flour
2 tsp baking powder
115 g/4 oz/1 cup shelled walnuts, finely chopped

For the Topping
175 g/6 oz/³/₄ cup full-fat soft cheese
4–5 tbsp single cream
50 g/2 oz/¹/₂ cup icing sugar, sifted
25 g/1 oz/¹/₄ cup shelled walnuts, halved
2 tsp cocoa powder, sifted

1 Preheat the oven to 180°C/350°F/ Gas 4. Arrange 24 fairy cake paper cases in bun tins and put to one side.

2 ▲ Place the butter, sugar, carrots, apples, salt, mixed spice and eggs in a mixing bowl and beat well to combine.

3 ▲ Sift together the flour and baking powder into a small bowl, then sift again into the mixing bowl. Add the chopped walnuts and fold in until evenly blended.

4 ▲ Fill the paper cases half-full with the cake mixture, then bake for 20–25 minutes, or until a skewer inserted into the centres of the cakes comes out clean.

5 Leave the cakes in the tins for about 5 minutes, before transferring them to a wire rack to cool completely.

6 ▲ To make the topping, place the full-fat soft cheese in a mixing bowl and beat in the cream and icing sugar until smooth. Put a dollop of the topping in the centre of each cake, then decorate with the walnuts. Dust with sifted cocoa powder and allow the icing to set before serving.

ip

To make one big cake, which will serve 6–8, grease a 20 cm/8 inch fluted American bundt cake tin and line the base with greaseproof paper. Grease the paper. Place all of the cake mixture in the tin and bake for about 1¹/₄ hours, or until a skewer inserted into the centre of the cake comes out clean. Leave the cake in the tin for about 5 minutes. Turn out on to a wire rack, peel off the lining paper and leave to cool completely. Decorate with the topping mixture, walnuts and sifted cocoa powder.

utumn Cake

*Greengages, plums or stoned semi-dried prunes
are delicious in this recipe.*

INGREDIENTS
Serves 6–8
*115 g/4 oz/½ cup butter, softened
150 g/5 oz/¾ cup caster sugar
3 size 3 eggs, beaten
75 g/3 oz/1 cup ground hazelnuts
150 g/5 oz/1¼ cup shelled pecan
nuts, chopped
50 g/2 oz/½ cup plain flour
1 tsp baking powder
½ tsp salt
675 g/1½ lb stoned plums,
greengages or semi-dried prunes
4 tbsp lime marmalade
1 tbsp lime juice
2 tbsp blanched almonds, chopped,
to decorate*

4 ▲ Bake in the centre of the oven for 45–50 minutes or until a skewer inserted into the centre of the cake comes out clean.

5 ▲ Remove from the oven and carefully arrange the fruit on top. Return to the oven and bake for a further 10–15 minutes until the fruit has softened. Transfer to a wire rack to cool completely then remove the cake from the tin.

6 Place the marmalade and lime juice in a small saucepan and warm gently. Brush over the fruit, then sprinkle with the almonds. Allow to set, then chill before serving.

1 Preheat the oven to 180°C/350°F/ Gas 4. Grease a 23 cm/9 inch round, fluted tart tin.

2 ▲ Place the butter and sugar in a mixing bowl and beat with an electric mixer until light and fluffy. Gradually beat in the eggs, alternating with the ground hazelnuts, until evenly combined.

3 Stir in the pecan nuts, then sift in the flour, baking powder and salt. Fold in until evenly combined, then transfer the mixture to the prepared tin.

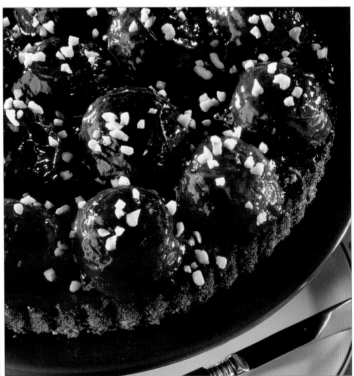

Chocolate Mint-filled Cupcakes

For extra mint flavour, chop 8 thin mint cream-filled after dinner mints and fold into the cake batter before filling paper liners. Omit the cream filling if you wish.

INGREDIENTS
Makes 12
225 g/8 oz/2 cups plain flour
5 ml/1 tsp bicarbonate of soda
pinch of salt
50 g/2 oz/½ cup unsweetened cocoa
150 g/5 oz/⅔ cup unsalted butter,
softened
300 g/11 oz/1½ cups caster sugar
3 eggs
5 ml/1 tsp peppermint essence
250 ml/8 fl oz/1 cup milk

For the Mint Cream Filling
300 ml/10 fl oz/1¼ cups double or
whipping cream
5 ml/1 tsp peppermint essence

For the Chocolate Mint Glaze
175 g/6 oz plain chocolate
115 g/4 oz/½ cup unsalted butter
5 ml/1 tsp peppermint essence

1 ▲ Preheat the oven to 180°C/350°F/ Gas 4. Line a 12-cup 6.5 cm/2½ inch baking tray with paper cases. Into a bowl, sift together the flour, bicarbonate of soda, salt and cocoa. In a large mixing bowl with an electric mixer, beat the butter and sugar until light and creamy, about 3–5 minutes. Add the eggs one at a time, beating well after each addition; beat in the peppermint essence. On low speed, beat in the flour-cocoa mixture alternately with the milk, until just blended. Spoon into paper cases.

2 Bake for 12–15 minutes until a cake tester inserted into the centre comes out clean; do not overbake. Immediately remove the cupcakes to a wire rack to cool completely. When cool, remove paper cases.

3 Prepare the filling. In a small bowl, whip the cream and peppermint essence with an electric mixer until stiff peaks form. Spoon into a small icing bag fitted with a small plain tip. Push the tip into the bottom of a cupcake and squeeze gently, releasing about 15 ml/1 tbsp of cream into the centre. Repeat with the remaining cupcakes.

4 ▲ Prepare the glaze. In a saucepan over low heat, melt the chocolate and butter, stirring until smooth. Remove from the heat and stir in the peppermint essence. Cool, then spread on top of each cupcake.

Gooseberry Cake

*This cake is delicious served warm
with fresh whipped cream.*

INGREDIENTS
Serves 6–8
115 g/4 oz/¹/₂ cup butter
165 g/5¹/₂ oz/1¹/₃ cups self-raising
flour
1 tsp baking powder
2 size 3 eggs, beaten
115 g/4 oz/¹/₂ cup caster sugar
1–2 tsp rose water
pinch of freshly grated nutmeg
1 x 115 g/4 oz jar gooseberries in
syrup, drained, juice reserved
caster sugar, to decorate
whipped cream, to serve

4 ▲ Mix in 1–2 tbsp of the reserved
gooseberry juice, then pour half of
the batter mixture into the prepared tin.
Scatter over the gooseberries. Pour over
the remaining batter mixture, evenly
covering the gooseberries.

5 Bake in the centre of the oven for
about 45 minutes, or until a skewer
inserted into the centre of the cake
comes out clean.

6 ▲ Leave in the cake tin for about 5
minutes, then turn out on to a wire
rack, remove the lining paper and allow
to cool for a further 5 minutes. Dredge
with caster sugar and serve immediately
with whipped cream, or leave the cake
to cool completely before decorating
and serving.

1 Preheat the oven to 180°C/350°F/
Gas 4. Grease an 18 cm/7 inch
square cake tin, line the base and sides
with greaseproof paper and then grease
the paper.

2 Place the butter in a medium
saucepan and melt over a gentle
heat. Remove the pan from the heat,
transfer the melted butter to a mixing
bowl and allow to cool.

3 ▲ Sift together the flour and
baking powder and add to the
melted butter. Beat in the eggs, one at a
time, the sugar, rose water and grated
nutmeg, to make a smooth batter.

Lemon and Apricot Cake

This more-ish cake is topped with a crunchy layer of flaked almonds and pistachio nuts, and is soaked in a tangy lemon syrup after baking to keep it really moist.

INGREDIENTS
Serves 10–12
175 g/6 oz/³/₄ cup butter, softened
175 g/6 oz/1¹/₂ cups self-raising
flour, sifted
¹/₂ tsp baking powder
175 g/6 oz/³/₄ cup caster sugar
3 size 3 eggs, lightly beaten
finely grated zest of 1 lemon
175 g/6 oz/1¹/₂ cups no-soak dried
apricots, finely chopped
75 g/3 oz/1 cup ground almonds
40 g/1¹/₂ oz/¹/₃ cup pistachio nuts,
chopped
50 g/2 oz/¹/₃ cup flaked almonds
15 g/¹/₂ oz/2 tbsp whole pistachio
nuts

For the Syrup
freshly squeezed juice of 1 lemon
3 tbsp caster sugar

3 ▲ Spoon the mixture into the prepared tin and smooth the surface. Sprinkle with the flaked almonds and the whole pistachio nuts. Bake in the centre of the oven for about 1¹/₄ hours, or until a skewer inserted into the centre of the cake comes out clean. Check the cake after about 45 minutes and cover with a piece of foil when the top is nicely brown. Leave the cake to cool in the tin.

4 ▲ To make the lemon syrup, put the lemon juice and caster sugar into a small saucepan and heat gently, stirring until the sugar has dissolved.

5 ▲ Spoon the syrup over the cake. When the cake is completely cooled, turn it carefully out of the tin and peel off the lining paper.

1 Preheat the oven to 180°C/350°F/ Mark 4. Grease a 900 g/2 lb loaf tin, line the base and sides with greaseproof paper and grease the paper.

2 Place the butter together with the sifted flour and baking powder into a mixing bowl, then add the sugar, eggs and lemon zest. Beat for 1–2 minutes until smooth and glossy, and then stir in the apricots, ground almonds and the chopped pistachio nuts.

Vegan Chocolate Gâteau

It isn't often that vegans can indulge in a slice of chocolate cake and this one tastes so delicious, they'll all be back for more!

INGREDIENTS
Serves 8–10
300 g/10 oz/2¹/₂ cups self-raising wholemeal flour
50 g/2 oz/¹/₃ cup cocoa powder
3 tsp baking powder
250 g/9 oz/1¹/₄ cups caster sugar
few drops of vanilla essence
9 tbsp sunflower oil
350 ml/12 fl oz/1¹/₂ cups water
sifted cocoa powder, to decorate
25 g/1 oz/¹/₄ cup chopped nuts, to decorate

For the Chocolate Fudge
50 g/2 oz/¹/₄ cup vegan (soya) margarine
3 tbsp water
250 g/9 oz/2¹/₃ cups icing sugar
2 tbsp cocoa powder
1 – 2 tbsp hot water

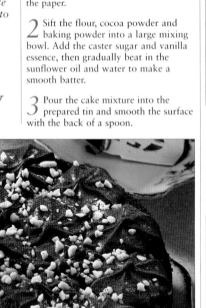

1 Preheat the oven to 170°C/325°F/ Gas 3. Grease a deep 20 cm/8 inch round cake tin, line the base and sides with greaseproof paper and grease the paper.

2 Sift the flour, cocoa powder and baking powder into a large mixing bowl. Add the caster sugar and vanilla essence, then gradually beat in the sunflower oil and water to make a smooth batter.

3 Pour the cake mixture into the prepared tin and smooth the surface with the back of a spoon.

4 ▲ Bake in the centre of the oven for about 45 minutes or until a skewer inserted into the centre of the cake comes out clean. Leave in the tin for about 5 minutes, then turn out on to a wire rack, peel off the lining paper and leave to cool. Cut the cake in half.

5 ▲ To make the chocolate fudge, place the margarine and water in a pan and heat gently until the margarine has melted. Remove from the heat and add the sifted icing sugar and cocoa powder, beating until smooth and shiny. Allow to cool until firm enough to spread and pipe.

6 ▲ Place the bottom layer of cake on a serving plate and spread over two-thirds of the chocolate fudge mixture. Top with the other layer of cake. Fit a piping bag with a star nozzle, fill with the remaining chocolate fudge and pipe stars over the cake. Sprinkle with cocoa powder and chopped nuts.

$\mathcal{A}$lmond and Raspberry Swiss Roll

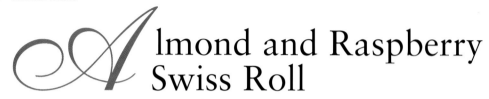

A light and airy whisked sponge cake is rolled up with a delicious fresh cream and raspberry filling, making this a classic Swiss roll.

INGREDIENTS
Serves 8
1 quantity Whisked Sponge Cake
mixture, replacing 25 g/1 oz/2 tbsp
plain flour with 25 g/1 oz/2 tbsp
ground almonds
a little caster sugar
225 ml/8 fl oz/1 cup double cream
250 g/8 oz fresh raspberries

To Decorate
caster sugar
reserved raspberries
16 flaked almonds, toasted

1 Preheat the oven to 200°C/400°F/
Gas 6. Grease a 33 x 23 cm/13 x 9
inch Swiss roll tin and line with baking
parchment.

2 Make the whisked sponge mixture,
spoon into the prepared tin and
bake for 10–12 minutes, until risen and
springy to the touch.

3 ▲ Lay a sheet of greaseproof paper
on a flat surface and sprinkle with
caster sugar. Turn out the cake on to
the sheet, and leave to cool with the tin
in place. Remove the tin and peel away
the lining paper.

4 ▲ Reserve a little cream for
decoration, and whip the rest until
it holds its shape. Fold in all but eight
raspberries and spread the mixture over
the cooled cake, leaving a narrow
border around the edge.

5 ▲ Carefully roll the cake up from a
narrow end to form a Swiss roll.
Sprinkle liberally with caster sugar.

6 ▲ Whip the remaining cream until
it just holds its shape, and spoon
the cream along the centre of the cake.
Decorate with the reserved raspberries
and toasted flaked almonds.

Fudgy Glazed Chocolate Brownies

For a simpler brownie, omit the fudge glaze and dust with icing sugar or cocoa instead.

INGREDIENTS
Serves 18–10
250 g/9 oz dark or plain chocolate,
chopped
25 g/1 oz cooking chocolate,
chopped
115 g/4 oz/½ cup unsalted butter,
cut into pieces
90 g/3½ oz/½ cup (packed) light
brown sugar
50 g/2 oz/¼ cup granulated sugar
2 eggs
15 ml/1 tbsp vanilla essence
65 g/2½ oz/½ cup plain flour
115 g/4 oz/1 cup pecans or walnuts,
toasted and chopped
150 g/5 oz fine quality white
chocolate, chopped into 5 mm/
¼ inch pieces
pecan halves to decorate (optional)

For the Fudgy Chocolate Glaze
175 g/6 oz plain or dark chocolate,
chopped
50 g/2 oz/4 tbsp unsalted butter, cut
into pieces
30 ml/2 tbsp corn or golden syrup
10 ml/2 tsp vanilla essence
5 ml/1 tsp instant coffee powder

1 ▲ Preheat the oven to 180°C/350°F/
Gas 4. Invert a 20 cm/8 inch square
baking tin and mould a piece of foil over
the bottom. Turn the tin over and line
with moulded foil. Lightly grease the foil.

2 ▲ In a medium saucepan over a low
heat, melt the dark chocolate and
butter until smooth, stirring frequently.
Remove the pan from the heat.

3 Stir in the sugars and continue
stirring for 2 more minutes, until
the sugar has dissolved. Beat in the eggs
and vanilla and stir in the flour just
until blended. Stir in the pecans and
white chocolate. Pour the batter into
the prepared tin.

4 ▲ Bake the brownies for 20–25
minutes until a cake tester inserted
5 cm/2 inches from the centre comes
out with just a few crumbs attached (do
not overbake). Place the tin on a wire
rack to cool for 30 minutes. Using the
foil to lift, remove the brownies from
the tin and cool on the rack for at least
2 hours.

5 ▲ Prepare the glaze. In a medium
saucepan over medium heat, melt
the chocolate, butter, syrup, vanilla and
coffee powder until smooth, stirring
frequently. Remove from the heat.
Refrigerate for 1 hour or until
thickened and spreadable.

6 ▲ Invert the brownies on to the
wire rack, and remove the foil from
the bottom. Turn top side up. Using a
metal palette knife, spread a thick layer
of fudgy glaze over the top of the
brownies just to the edges. Refrigerate
for 1 hour until set. Cut into squares or
'fingers'. If you wish, top each with a
pecan half.

Hazelnut Chocolate Meringue Torte with Pears

Do not assemble this torte more than 3–4 hours before serving, as the pears may give off liquid and soften the cream too much.

INGREDIENTS
Serves 8–10
150 g/5 oz/¾ cup granulated sugar
1 vanilla bean, split
450 ml/¾ pint/scant 2 cups water
4 ripe pears, peeled, halved and cored
30 ml/2 tbsp pear- or hazelnut-flavour liqueur
185 g/6½ oz/1¼ cups hazelnuts, toasted
6 egg whites
pinch of salt
350 g/12 oz/3 cups icing sugar
5 ml/1 tsp vanilla essence
50 g/2 oz plain chocolate, melted

For the Chocolate Cream
275 g/10 oz fine quality dark or plain chocolate, chopped
450 ml/¾ pint/scant 2 cups whipping cream
65 ml/2 fl oz/¼ cup pear- or hazelnut-flavour liqueur

1 In a saucepan large enough to hold the pears in a single layer, combine the sugar, vanilla bean and water. Over high heat, bring to the boil, stirring until the sugar dissolves. Reduce the heat to medium. Lower the pears into the syrup. Cover the pears and simmer gently for 12–15 minutes until tender. Remove the pan from the heat and allow the pears to cool in their poaching liquid. Carefully remove the pears from the liquid and drain. Place on a large flat plate lined with layers of kitchen paper. Sprinkle each pear half with the liqueur. Cover and refrigerate overnight.

2 ▲ Preheat the oven to 180°C/ 350°F/Gas 4. With a pencil, draw a 23 cm/9 inch circle in the centre of each of two sheets of non-stick baking paper or well-greased foil. Turn the sheets of paper over on to two baking sheets (so pencil marks are underneath) or slide foil on the baking sheets. In a food processor fitted with a metal blade, process the toasted hazelnuts until medium-fine crumbs form.

3 In a large bowl with an electric mixer on medium, beat the egg whites until frothy. Add salt and beat on high speed until soft peaks form. Reduce the mixer speed and gradually add the sugar, beating well after each addition until all the sugar is added and the egg whites are stiff and glossy; this takes 12–15 minutes.

4 Gently fold in the nuts and vanilla and spoon meringue on to baking sheets, spreading into 23 cm/9 inch circles, smoothing the top and sides. Bake for 1 hour until the tops are dry and firm. Turn off the oven and allow to cool in the oven 2–3 hours or until completely dry. Prepare the chocolate cream. Place the chocolate in a small bowl over a pan of simmering water, and turn off the heat. Stir the chocolate until melted and smooth. Cool the chocolate to room temperature.

5 ▲ In a bowl with an electric mixer, beat the cream to soft peaks. Quickly fold the cream into the melted chocolate; fold in the liqueur. Spoon about one third of the chocolate cream into an icing bag fitted with a star tip. Set aside. To assemble, with a sharp knife, thinly slice each pear in half lengthwise. Place one meringue layer on a serving plate. Spread with half the chocolate cream and arrange half the sliced pears evenly over the cream. Pipe a border of rosettes around the edge.

6 ▲ Top with the second meringue layer and spread with the remaining chocolate cream. Arrange the remaining pear slices over the chocolate cream. Pipe a border of rosettes around the edge. Spoon the melted chocolate into a small paper cone and drizzle the chocolate over the pears. Refrigerate for at least 1 hour before serving.

Pear and Cardamom Spice Cake

Fresh pear and cardamom – a classic combination of flavours – are used together in this moist fruit and nut cake to provide a delicious, mouth-watering teatime treat.

INGREDIENTS
Serves 8–12
115 g/4 oz/½ cup butter
115 g/4 oz/½ cup caster sugar
2 size 3 eggs, lightly beaten
225 g/8 oz/2 cups plain flour
15 ml/1 tbsp baking powder
30 ml/2 tbsp milk
crushed seeds from 2 cardamom pods
50 g/2 oz/½ cup walnuts, chopped
15 ml/1 tbsp poppy seeds
500 g/1¼ lb dessert pears, peeled, cored and thinly sliced

To Decorate
3 walnut halves
reserved pear slices
45 ml/3 tbsp clear honey

1 Preheat the oven to 180°C/350°F/ Gas 4. Grease a 20 cm/8 inch round loose-bottom cake tin and line the base with greaseproof paper.

2 Cream the butter and sugar together until pale and light. Gradually beat in the eggs, a little at a time, until incorporated. Sift the flour and baking powder together, and fold in with the milk.

3 ▲ Stir in the cardamom, chopped nuts and poppy seeds. Reserve one-third of the pear slices, and chop the rest. Fold the chopped pears into the creamed mixture.

4 ▲ Transfer to the prepared tin. Smooth the surface, making a small dip in the centre.

5 ▲ Place the three walnut halves in the centre of the cake mixture, and fan the reserved pear slices around the walnuts, covering the cake mixture. Bake for 1¼–1½ hours, or until a skewer inserted in the centre of the cake comes out clean.

6 ▲ Remove the cake from the oven. Cool in the tin for 20 minutes, then turn out on to a wire rack, brush with the clear honey and leave to cool completely.

Spiced Honey Nut Cake

A combination of ground pistachio nuts and breadcrumbs replaces the flour in this recipe, resulting in a light, moist sponge cake. Soaking the cooled cake is typical of many Middle Eastern cakes, and the combination of pistachio, lemon and cinnamon is mouth-watering.

INGREDIENTS
Serves 8
115 g/4 oz/½ cup caster sugar
4 size 3 eggs, separated
grated zest and juice of 1 lemon
130 g/4½ oz/1¼ cups ground
pistachio nuts
50 g/2 oz/½ cup dried breadcrumbs
1 lemon
90 ml/6 tbsp clear honey
1 cinnamon stick
15 ml/1 tbsp brandy

To Decorate
shredded lemon zest
cinnamon sticks

1 Preheat the oven to 180°C/350°F/ Gas 4. Grease a 20 cm/8 inch square cake tin and line the base with greaseproof paper. Grease the paper.

2 Beat the sugar, egg yolks, lemon zest and juice together until pale and creamy. Fold in 115 g/4 oz/1 cup of the ground pistachio nuts and all the breadcrumbs.

3 ▲ Whisk the egg whites until stiff and fold into the creamed mixture. Spoon into the prepared tin and bake for 45 minutes, until risen and springy to the touch. Remove from the oven, cool in the tin for 10 minutes, then turn on to a wire rack to cool completely.

4 ▲ Meanwhile, to make the syrup, peel the lemon and cut the zest into very thin strips. Squeeze the juice into a small pan and add the honey and cinnamon stick. Bring to the boil, add the shredded rind, and simmer fast for 1 minute. Cool the syrup slightly and stir in the brandy.

5 ▲ Place the cold cake on a serving plate, prick all over with a skewer and pour over the cooled syrup, lemon shreds and cinnamon sticks.

6 ▲ Sprinkle the reserved ground pistachio nuts in an even layer over the top of the cake.

*S*t Clements Marbled Crown

A tangy orange-and-lemon marbled cake is transformed into a spectacular centrepiece by the pretty arrangement of fresh flowers in the centre of the ring. The icing is decorated with crystallized fruits, dragées and sugared almonds, creating a dramatic jewelled effect.

INGREDIENTS
Serves 8
175 g/6 oz/¾ cup butter
75 g/3 oz/½ cup soft light brown
sugar
3 size 3 eggs, separated
grated zest and juice of 1 orange
165 g/5½ oz/1½ cups self-raising
flour
75 g/3 oz/6 tbsp caster sugar
grated zest and juice of 1 lemon
15 g/½ oz/2 tbsp ground almonds

For the Topping
350 ml/12 fl oz/1½ cups double
cream
15 ml/1 tbsp Grand Marnier

To Decorate
16 crystallized orange and lemon
slices
silver dragées
8 gold sugared almonds
fresh flowers

1 Preheat the oven to 180°C/350°F/
Gas 4. Grease and flour a 900 ml/
1½ pint/3¾ cup ring mould.

2 Cream half the butter and the soft
brown sugar together until pale and
light. Gradually beat in the egg yolks,
orange zest and juice until incorporated,
and fold in 75 g/3 oz/¼ cup of the flour.

3 Cream the remaining butter and
caster sugar together, stir in the
lemon zest and juice and fold in the
remaining flour and ground almonds.
Whisk the egg whites until stiff, and
fold in.

4 ▲ Spoon the two mixtures
alternately into the prepared tin.

5 ▲ Using a skewer or small spoon,
swirl through the mixture, to create
a marbled effect. Bake for 45–50
minutes, until risen and a skewer
inserted into the cake comes out clean.
Cool in the tin for 10 minutes, then
turn out on to a wire rack and leave
to cool completely.

6 ▲ Whip the cream and Grand
Marnier together until lightly
thickened. Spread over the cooled cake
and swirl a pattern over the cream.

7 ▲ Decorate the ring with the
crystallized fruits, dragées and
almonds to resemble a jewelled crown.
Arrange a few pretty fresh flowers in
the centre.

Caramel Frosted Gingerbread

This is an unusual gingerbread, made with all golden syrup rather than a mixture of syrup and treacle. This gives a lighter mixture – and the addition of desiccated coconut adds a wonderful flavour and texture to the cake. Serve slices of this cake with a warm drink for a light and tasty teatime treat.

INGREDIENTS
Makes 18–20
300 g/11 oz/1½ cups soft light brown sugar
225 g/8 oz/1 cup butter
275 ml/9 fl oz/1¼ cups golden syrup
90 ml/6 tbsp stem ginger syrup
350 g/12 oz/3 cups self-raising flour
115 g/4 oz/2 cups desiccated coconut
25 g/1 oz/2 tbsp chopped stem ginger
5 ml/1 tsp ground ginger
2.5 ml/½ tsp bicarbonate of soda
300 ml/½ pint/1¼ cups milk
1 size 3 egg, lightly beaten

To Decorate
50 g/2 oz/1 cup desiccated coconut

1 Preheat the oven to 180°C/350°F/ Gas 4. Grease a deep 25 x 20 cm/ 10 x 8 inch rectangular cake tin, line with greaseproof paper and grease the paper.

2 ▲ Heat 225 g/8 oz/1 cup of the sugar, 175 g/6 oz/¾ cup butter, the golden syrup and 60 ml/4 tbsp stem ginger syrup together gently, until melted. Combine the flour, coconut, stem ginger, ground ginger and bicarbonate of soda in a large bowl. Gradually beat in the melted syrup mixture, milk and egg, and continue beating for 1 minute.

3 Pour into the prepared tin and bake for 1½ hours, or until a skewer inserted in the centre comes out clean. Remove from the oven, cool in the tin for 10 minutes then turn out on to a wire rack to cool completely.

4 ▲ Melt the remaining sugar, butter and stem ginger syrup together. Increase the heat and boil for 1 minute. Remove from the heat and allow the bubbling to stop. Pour over the cooled cake in one smooth motion, letting a little drizzle over the edges.

5 ▲ Immediately sprinkle over the coconut, mark into 18–20 fingers with a sharp knife and leave in a cool place until the caramel icing has set. Cut along the marked lines into fingers.

Fig, Banana and Brazil Nut Teabread

Mashed bananas are a classic ingredient in teabreads. Combined here with dried figs and brazil nuts, they make an exceptionally moist and flavoursome cake, perfect for a mid-afternoon pick-me-up or with morning coffee.

INGREDIENTS
Serves 8–12
225 g/8 oz/2 cups plain flour
10 ml/2 tsp baking powder
5 ml/1 tsp ground mixed spice
115 g/4 oz/½ cup butter, diced
115 g/4 oz/½ cup soft light brown sugar
2 size 3 eggs, lightly beaten
30 ml/2 tbsp milk
30 ml/2 tbsp dark rum
2 medium bananas, peeled and mashed
115 g/4 oz/⅔ cup dried figs, chopped
50 g/2 oz/½ cup brazil nuts, chopped

To Decorate
8 whole brazil nuts
4 whole dried figs, halved
30 ml/2 tbsp apricot jam
5 ml/1 tsp dark rum

1 Preheat the oven to 180°C/350°F/ Gas 4. Grease a 900 g/2 lb loaf tin, line the base with greaseproof paper and grease the paper.

2 Sift the flour, baking powder and mixed spice into a bowl. Rub in the butter until the mixture resembles fine breadcrumbs. Stir in the sugar.

3 ▲ Make a well in the centre and work in the eggs, milk and rum until combined. Stir in the remaining ingredients and spoon in to the prepared tin.

4 ▲ Press the whole brazil nuts and halved figs gently into the mixture, to form an attractive pattern. Bake for 1¼ hours or until a skewer inserted in the centre comes out clean. Remove from the oven, cool in the tin for 10 minutes then turn out on to a wire rack.

5 ▲ Heat the jam and rum together in a small pan. Increase the heat and boil for 1 minute. Remove from the heat and pass through a fine sieve. Cool the glaze slightly and brush over the cake while still warm. Leave to cool completely and then store in an airtight container.

Tip
This cake is at its best if stored for 3–4 days in an airtight container before eating.

Chocolate Banana Cake

This chocolate cake is delicious yet low in fat, thanks to the addition of ripe bananas which result in a moist cake with a good depth of flavour.

INGREDIENTS
Serves 8
225 g/8 oz/2 cups self-raising flour
45 ml/3 tbsp cocoa powder
115 g/4 oz/½ cup light muscovado
sugar
30 ml/2 tbsp malt extract
30 ml/2 tbsp golden syrup
2 size 3 eggs
60 ml/4 tbsp milk
60 ml/4 tbsp sunflower oil
2 large ripe bananas

For the Icing
225 g/8 oz/2 cups icing sugar, sifted
35 ml/7 tsp cocoa powder, sifted
15–30 ml/1–2 tbsp warm water

1 ▲ Preheat the oven to 160°C/325°F/ Gas 3. Grease a deep 20 cm/8 inch round cake tin, line the base with greaseproof paper and grease the paper.

2 ▲ Sift the flour into a mixing bowl with the cocoa powder. Add the sugar and mix together well.

3 ▲ Make a well in the centre and add the malt extract, golden syrup, eggs, milk and oil. Mash the bananas thoroughly and stir them into the mixture until thoroughly combined.

4 ▲ Pour the cake mixture into the prepared tin and bake for 1–1¼ hours or until the centre of the cake springs back when lightly pressed.

5 ▲ Remove the cake from the tin and leave on a wire rack until completely cool.

6 ▲ Reserve 50 g/2 oz/½ cup icing sugar and 5 ml/1 tsp cocoa powder. Make a darker icing by beating the remaining sugar and cocoa powder with enough of the warm water to make a thick icing. Pour it over the top of the cake and spread evenly to the edges. Make a thinner, lighter icing by mixing the remaining icing sugar and cocoa powder with a few drops of water. Drizzle or pipe this icing across the top of the cake to decorate.

Tip

This cake also makes a delicious dessert if heated in the microwave. The icing melts to a puddle of sauce. Serve a slice topped with a large dollop of fromage frais for a really special treat.

Chocolate and Orange Angel Cake

This light-as-air sponge is a variation on the classic American angel food cake, made without fat or egg yolks. The dark chocolate cake contrasts dramatically with the sparkling white frosting.

INGREDIENTS
Serves 10
25 g/1 oz/¼ cup plain flour
15 g/½ oz/2 tbsp cocoa powder
15 g/½ oz/2 tbsp cornflour
pinch of salt
5 size 3 egg whites
2.5 ml/½ tsp cream of tartar
115 g/4 oz/½ cup caster sugar

For the Frosting
200 g/7 oz/scant 1 cup caster sugar
1 size 3 egg white

To Decorate
blanched and shredded zest of 1 orange

1 Preheat the oven to 180°C/350°F/ Gas 4. Sift the flour, cocoa powder, cornflour and salt together three times. Beat the egg whites in a large bowl until foamy. Add the cream of tartar, then whisk until soft peaks form.

2 ▲ Add the caster sugar to the egg whites a spoonful at a time, whisking after each addition. Sift a third of the flour and cocoa mixture over the meringue and gently fold in. Repeat, sifting and folding in the flour and cocoa mixture two more times.

3 ▲ Spoon the mixture into a non-stick 20 cm/8 inch ring mould and level the top. Bake in the oven for 35 minutes or until springy when lightly pressed. Invert on to a wire rack and leave to cool in the tin. Carefully ease out of the tin.

4 ▲ To make the frosting, put the sugar in a pan with 5 tbsp cold water. Stir over a low heat until dissolved. Boil until the syrup reaches a temperature of 115°C/240°F on a sugar thermometer, or the thread stage. Remove from the heat.

5 ▲ Meanwhile, as soon as the syrup boils, whisk the egg white until stiff and dry. Add the syrup in a thin stream, whisking all the time. Continue to whisk until the mixture is very thick and glossy.

6 ▲ Spread the icing over the top and sides of the cooled cake. Sprinkle the orange zest over the top of the cake to decorate.

Tip

Make sure you do not over-beat the egg whites for the cake mixture. They should not be stiff but should form soft peaks, so that the air bubbles can expand further during cooking and help the cake to rise.

Decorated Cupcakes

These little cakes are perfect for children's parties, with their appealing, colourful decorations.

INGREDIENTS
Makes 16
*115 g/4 oz/½ cup butter, at
room temperature
200 g/7 oz/1 cup granulated sugar
2 eggs, at room temperature
215 g/7½ oz/1½ cups plain flour
1.5 ml/¼ tsp salt
7.5 ml/1½ tsp baking powder
115 g/4 fl oz/½ cup plus 115 ml/
1 tbsp milk
5 ml/1 tsp vanilla extract*

For the Icing and Decorations
*2 large egg whites
400 g/14 oz/3½ cups sifted icing sugar
1–2 drops glycerine
juice of 1 lemon
food colourings
coloured sprinkles, for decorating
glacé lemon and orange slices,
for decorating*

1 Preheat the oven to 190°C/375°F/
Gas 5.

2 ▲ Fill 16 muffin cups with fluted
paper baking liners, or grease.

3 With an electric mixer, cream the
butter and sugar until light and
fluffy. Add the eggs, one at a time,
beating well after each addition. Sift
together the flour, salt and baking
powder. Stir into the butter mixture,
alternating with the milk. Stir in the
vanilla extract.

4 ▲ Fill the cups half-full and bake
until the tops spring back when
touched lightly, about 20 minutes. Let
the cupcakes stand in the pan for
5 minutes, then unmould and transfer
to a rack to cool completely.

5 For the meringue icing, beat the
egg whites until stiff but not dry.
Gradually add the icing sugar, glycerine
and lemon juice, and continue beating
for 1 minute. The consistency should
be spreadable. If necessary, thin with a
little water or add some more sifted
icing sugar.

6 ▲ Divide the icing between several
bowls and tint with food
colourings. Spread different coloured
icings over the cooled cupcakes.

7 ▲ Decorate the cupcakes any way
you wish, such as with different
coloured sprinkles.

8 ▲ Other decorations include glacé
orange and lemon slices. Cut into
small pieces and arrange on top of the
cupcakes. Alternatively, use other
suitable sweets.

9 ▲ To decorate with coloured icings,
fill paper piping bags with different
coloured icings. Pipe on faces, or make
other designs.

Nectarine Amaretto Cake

Make this delicious cake for afternoon tea or serve it as a dessert with a dollop of fromage frais.

INGREDIENTS
Serves 8
3 size 3 eggs, separated
175 g/6 oz/¾ cup caster sugar
grated zest and juice of 1 lemon
50 g/2 oz/⅓ cup semolina
40 g/1½ oz/½ cup ground almonds
25 g/1 oz/¼ cup plain flour

For the Syrup
75 g/3 oz/6 tbsp caster sugar
90 ml/6 tbsp water
30 ml/2 tbsp Amaretto liqueur

To Decorate
2 nectarines or peaches, halved
45 ml/3 tbsp apricot jam
15 ml/1 tbsp water

3 ▲ Whisk the egg whites in a grease-free bowl until fairly stiff. Using a metal spoon, stir a generous spoonful of the whites into the semolina mixture to lighten it, then fold in the remaining egg whites. Spoon the mixture into the prepared cake tin.

4 ▲ Bake for 30–35 minutes until the centre of the cake springs back when lightly pressed. Remove the cake from the oven and carefully loosen around the edge of the cake with a palette knife. Prick the top with a skewer and leave to cool slightly in the tin.

5 ▲ Meanwhile, make the syrup. Heat the sugar and water in a small pan, stirring until dissolved, then boil without stirring for 2 minutes. Add the Amaretto liqueur and drizzle slowly over the cake.

6 ▲ Remove the cake from the tin and put it on a serving plate. Slice the nectarines or peaches and arrange them over the top. Heat the jam and water together in a small pan. Remove from the heat and pass through a sieve. Cool the glaze slightly and brush over the cake.

1 ▲ Preheat the oven to 180°C/350°F/Gas 4. Grease a 20 cm/8 inch round loose-bottom cake tin. Whisk the egg yolks, caster sugar, lemon zest and juice in a bowl until thick, pale and creamy.

2 ▲ Fold in the semolina, almonds and flour until smooth.

Tip

Use drained canned mandarin orange segments for the topping, if preferred, and use an orange-flavoured liqueur instead of the Amaretto.

Cinnamon Apple Gâteau

A spiced Genoese sponge sandwiched with a mouthwatering filling of apples and soft cheese makes a lovely cake for an autumn tea-party.

INGREDIENTS
Serves 8
3 size 3 eggs
115 g/4 oz/½ cup caster sugar
75 g/3 oz/¼ cup plain flour
5 ml/1 tsp ground cinnamon

For the Filling and Topping
4 large eating apples
60 ml/4 tbsp clear honey
30 ml/2 tbsp water
75 g/3 oz/½ cup sultanas
2.5 ml/½ tsp ground cinnamon
350 g/12 oz/1½ cups low fat soft cheese
60 ml/4 tbsp fromage frais
10 ml/2 tsp lemon juice
30 ml/2 tbsp apricot jam
mint sprigs, to decorate

1 ▲ Preheat the oven to 190°C/375°F/ Gas 5. Grease a 23 cm/9 inch sandwich cake tin, line with greaseproof paper and grease the paper. Place the eggs and caster sugar in a bowl and beat with an electric mixer for about 10 minutes or until thick and pale.

2 Sift the flour and cinnamon over the egg mixture and carefully fold in with a large spoon. Pour into the prepared tin and bake for 25–30 minutes or until the cake springs back when lightly pressed. Slide a palette knife between the cake and the tin to loosen the edge, then turn the cake on to a wire rack to cool.

3 ▲ To make the filling, peel, core and slice three of the apples and put them in a saucepan. Add 30 ml/2 tbsp of the honey and 15 ml/1 tbsp of the water. Cover and cook over a gentle heat for about 10 minutes until the apples have softened. Add the sultanas and cinnamon, stir well, replace the lid and leave to cool.

4 ▲ Put the soft cheese in a bowl with the remaining honey, the fromage frais and half the lemon juice. Beat until the mixture is smooth.

5 ▲ Halve the cake horizontally, place the bottom half on a board and drizzle over any liquid from the apples. Spread with two-thirds of the cheese mixture, then top with the apple filling. Fit the top of the cake in place.

6 ▲ Swirl the remaining cheese mixture over the top of the sponge. Core and slice the remaining apple, sprinkle with lemon juice and arrange around the edge. Heat the jam and 15 ml/1 tbsp of the water together in a small pan and pass through a sieve. Cool the glaze slightly, then brush over the apples. Decorate with mint sprigs.

Coffee Almond Flower Gâteau

*There are all kinds of reasons for making a cake for someone -
sometimes it may be simply to say 'thank you'.*

INGREDIENTS
Serves 8–10
1 quantity Quick-Mix Sponge
Cake mix
25 g/1 oz/¼ cup nuts, such as
almonds or walnuts, finely chopped
1½ x quantity coffee-flavour
Butter Icing
75 g/3oz/3 squares plain chocolate
20 blanched almonds
4 chocolate-coated espresso beans

MATERIALS AND EQUIPMENT
2 x 18 cm/7 inch round cake tins
serrated scraper
2 greaseproof paper piping bags
No 2 writing nozzle

1 Preheat the oven to 160°C/325°F/
Gas 3. Grease the cake tins, line the
bases with greaseproof paper and grease
the paper. Fold the nuts into the cake
mixture. Divide the mixture evenly
between the tins and smooth the
surfaces. Bake in the centre of the oven
for about 20 minutes or until firm to
the touch. Turn out on to a wire rack,
peel off the lining paper and leave to
cool completely.

2 Place one of the cakes on a piece of
greaseproof paper on a turntable.
Use the butter icing to sandwich the
cakes together and to ice the top and
side. Coat the top by spreading the icing
smoothly with a palette knife. Coat the
side with a serrated scraper. Reserve
two spoonfuls of icing for piping.

3 ▲ Melt the chocolate in a heatproof
bowl over a pan of hot water.
Remove from the heat, then dip half of
each almond into the chocolate at a
slight angle. Shake off any excess
chocolate and leave the almonds to dry
on baking parchment. Return the
chocolate to the pan of hot water (off
the heat) so it does not set. Remove
and allow to cool slightly before using
for piping.

4 Arrange the almonds on top of the
cake to represent flowers.

5 ▲ Place a chocolate-coated espresso
bean in the centre of each almond
flower. Spoon the remaining melted
chocolate into a greaseproof paper
piping bag. Cut a small piece off the
end in a straight line. Pipe the chocolate
in wavy lines over the top of the cake
and in small beads around the top edge.

6 Transfer the cake to a cake stand or
serving plate. Work quickly so the
chocolate in the piping bag does not
become too firm to pipe. Place the
reserved butter icing in a fresh piping
bag fitted with the No 2 writing nozzle.
Pipe beads of icing all around the
bottom of the cake, then top with small
beads of chocolate, allowing the
chocolate to drizzle on to the stand.

ummer Strawberry Shortcake

A summer-time treat. Serve with a cool glass of pink sparkling wine for a truly refreshing dessert.

INGREDIENTS
Serves 6–8
*225 g/8 oz/2 cups plain flour
1 tbsp baking powder
½ tsp salt
50 g/2 oz/4 tbsp caster sugar
50 g/2 oz/4 tbsp butter, softened
150 ml/¼ pint/⅔ cup milk
300 ml/½ pint/1¼ cups double cream
450 g/1 lb fresh strawberries, halved and hulled*

1 Preheat the oven to 220°C/425°F/ Gas 7. Grease a baking sheet, line the base with greaseproof paper and grease the paper.

2 ▲ Sift the flour, baking powder and salt together into a large mixing bowl. Stir in the sugar, cut in the butter and toss into the flour mixture until it resembles coarse breadcrumbs. Stir in just enough milk to make a soft dough.

3 ▲ Turn out the dough on to a lightly floured work surface and pat, using your fingers, into a 30 × 15 cm/12 × 6 inch rectangle. Using a template, cut out two 15 cm/6 inch rounds, indent one of the rounds dividing it into eight equal portions, and place them on the baking sheet.

4 ▲ Bake in the centre of the oven for 10–15 minutes or until slightly risen and golden. Leave the shortcake on the baking sheet for about 5 minutes, then transfer to a wire rack, peel off the lining paper and leave to cool completely.

5 Place the cream in a mixing bowl and whip with an electric mixer until it holds soft peaks. Place the unmarked shortcake on a serving plate and spread or pipe with half of the cream. Top with two-thirds of the strawberries, then the other shortcake. Use the remaining cream and strawberries to decorate the top layer. Chill for at least 30 minutes before serving.

Spiced Passion Cake

If you can't resist the lure of a slice of iced cake, you'll love this moist, spiced sponge with its delicious creamy topping.

INGREDIENTS
Serves 10
1 medium carrot
1 medium courgette
3 size 3 eggs separated
115 g/4 oz/½ cup soft light brown sugar
30 ml/2 tbsp ground almonds
finely grated zest of 1 orange
115 g/4 oz/1 cup self-raising wholemeal flour
5 ml/1 tsp ground cinnamon

For the Topping
175 g/6 oz/¾ cup low-fat soft cheese
5 ml/1 tsp clear honey

To Decorate
sugarpaste carrots and courgettes

1 ▲ Preheat the oven to 180°C/350°F/ Gas 4. Line an 18 cm/7 inch square tin with baking parchment. Coarsely grate the carrot and courgette.

2 Put the egg yolks, sugar, ground almonds and orange zest into a bowl and whisk until very thick and light.

3 ▲ Sift the flour and cinnamon together and fold into the mixture with the grated vegetables. Add any bran left from the flour in the sieve.

4 ▲ Whisk the egg whites until stiff and carefully fold them in, half at a time. Spoon into the prepared tin. Bake in the oven for 1 hour, covering the top with foil after 40 minutes.

5 ▲ Leave to cool in the tin for about 5 minutes, then turn out on to a wire rack and carefully remove the lining paper.

6 ▲ For the topping, beat together the cheese and honey and spread over the cake. Decorate with sugar paste carrots and courgettes.

Banana Gingerbread Slices

Bananas make this spicy bake delightfully moist. The flavour develops on keeping, so store the gingerbread for a few days before cutting into slices, if possible.

INGREDIENTS
Makes 20 slices
275 g/10 oz/2½ cups plain flour
5 ml/1 tsp bicarbonate of soda
20 ml/4 tsp ground ginger
10 ml/2 tsp mixed spice
115 g/4 oz/½ cup soft light
brown sugar
60 ml/4 tbsp sunflower oil
30 ml/2 tbsp black treacle
30 ml/2 tbsp malt extract
2 size 3 eggs
60 ml/4 tbsp orange juice
3 ripe bananas
115 g/4 oz/⅔ cup raisins or sultanas

1 ▲ Preheat the oven to 180°C/350°F/ Gas 4. Lightly grease a 28 x 18 cm/ 11 x 7 inch shallow baking tin, line with greaseproof paper and grease the paper.

2 ▲ Sift the flour, bicarbonate of soda and spices into a bowl. Sieve in the sugar and some of the flour mixture.

3 ▲ Make a well in the centre of the dry ingredients and add the oil, treacle, malt extract, eggs and orange juice. Mix thoroughly.

4 ▲ Mash the bananas on a plate. Add the raisins or sultanas to the gingerbread mixture, then mix in the mashed bananas.

5 ▲ Pour the mixture into the prepared baking tin. Bake for about 35–40 minutes or until the centre of the gingerbread springs back when lightly pressed with your finger.

6 ▲ Leave the gingerbread in the tin to cool for 5 minutes, then turn out on to a wire rack to cool completely. Transfer to a board and cut into 20 slices to serve.

Tip

If your brown sugar is lumpy, mix it with a little flour and it will be easier to sift.

Banana and Apricot Chelsea Buns

Traditional favourites are given a new twist with a delectable fruit filling.

INGREDIENTS
Makes 9
90 ml/6 tbsp warm milk
5 ml/1 tsp dried yeast
pinch of sugar
225 g/8 oz/2 cups strong plain flour
10 ml/2 tsp mixed spice
2.5 ml/½ tsp salt
25 g/1 oz/2 tbsp butter
50 g/2 oz/¼ cup caster sugar
1 size 3 egg

For the Filling
1 large ripe banana
175 g/6 oz/1 cup no-soak
dried apricots
30 ml/2 tbsp light muscovado sugar

For the Glaze
30 ml/2 tbsp caster sugar
30 ml/2 tbsp water

1 ▲ Grease an 18 cm/7 inch square cake tin. Put the warm milk in a jug. Sprinkle the yeast on top. Add a pinch of sugar to help activate the yeast, mix well and leave for 30 minutes.

2 ▲ Sift the flour, spice and salt into a mixing bowl. Rub in the butter, then stir in the sugar. Make a central well, pour in the yeast mixture and the egg. Gradually mix in the flour to make a soft dough, adding extra milk if the mixture is too dry.

3 ▲ Turn the dough out on to a floured surface and knead for 5 minutes until smooth and elastic. Return to the clean bowl, cover with a damp dish towel and leave in a warm place to rise for about 2 hours until doubled in bulk.

4 ▲ Meanwhile prepare the filling. Mash the banana in a bowl. Using kitchen scissors, snip the apricots, then stir them into the mashed banana with the sugar.

5 ▲ Knead the risen dough on a floured surface for 2 minutes, then roll out to a 30 x 23 cm/12 x 9 inch rectangle. Spread the banana and apricot filling over the dough and roll up lengthways like a Swiss roll, with the join underneath.

6 ▲ Cut the roll into 9 pieces and place, cut side down, in the prepared tin. Cover and leave to rise in a warm place for about 30 minutes. Preheat the oven to 200°C/400°F/Gas 6.

7 ▲ Bake the buns for 20–25 minutes until golden brown and cooked in the centre. Meanwhile make the glaze. Mix the caster sugar and water in a small saucepan. Heat, stirring, until dissolved, then boil for 2 minutes. Brush the glaze over the buns while still hot, then remove the buns from the tin and leave them to cool on a wire rack.

Chocolate and Banana Brownies

Nuts traditionally give brownies their chewy texture. Here oat bran is used instead, creating a moist, moreish, yet healthy alternative.

INGREDIENTS
Makes 9
75 ml/5 tbsp cocoa powder
15 ml/1 tbsp caster sugar
75 ml/5 tbsp milk
3 large bananas, mashed
215 g/7½ oz/1 cup soft light
brown sugar
5 ml/1 tsp vanilla essence
5 size 3 egg whites
75 g/3 oz/¾ cup self-raising flour
75 g/3 oz/¾ cup oat bran
15 ml/1 tbsp icing sugar, for dusting

1 ▲ Preheat the oven to 180°C/ 350°F/Gas 4. Line a 20 cm/8 inch square tin with baking parchment.

2 ▲ Blend the cocoa powder and caster sugar with the milk. Add the bananas, soft brown sugar and vanilla.

3 ▲ Lightly beat the egg whites with a fork. Add the chocolate mixture and continue to beat well. Sift the flour over the mixture and fold in with the oat bran. Pour into the prepared tin.

4 ▲ Cook for 40 minutes or until firm. When completely cool, cut into squares and lightly dust with icing sugar before serving.

White Chocolate Brownies with Milk Chocolate Macadamia Topping

White chocolate makes a light-coloured mixture for these brownies, which are dotted with dark chocolate chips and finished with a sensational topping of chunky macadamia nuts.

INGREDIENTS
Serves 12

150 g/5 oz/1¼ cups plain flour
2.5 ml/½ tsp baking powder
pinch of salt
175 g/6 oz fine quality white chocolate, chopped
90 g/3½ oz/scant ½ cup caster sugar
115 g/4 oz/½ cup butter, cut into pieces
2 size 3 eggs, lightly beaten
5 ml/1 tsp vanilla essence
175 g/6 oz plain chocolate chips or plain chocolate, chopped

For the Topping
200 g/7 oz milk chocolate, chopped
210 g/7½ oz/1 cup unsalted macadamia nuts, chopped

1 Preheat the oven to 180°C/350°F/ Gas 4. Grease a 23 cm/9 inch springform tin. Sift together the flour, baking powder and salt and set aside.

2 ▲ In a medium saucepan over medium heat, melt the white chocolate, sugar and butter until smooth, stirring frequently. Cool slightly, then beat in the eggs and vanilla. Stir in the flour until well blended. Stir in the chocolate chips or chopped chocolate. Spread evenly in the prepared tin, smoothing the top.

3 ▲ Bake for 20–25 minutes until a skewer inserted 5 cm/2 inches from the side of the tin comes out clean; do not over-bake. Remove from the oven to a heatproof surface. Immediately sprinkle the chopped milk chocolate evenly over the surface (avoid touching the side of tin) and return to the oven for 1 minute.

4 ▲ Remove from the oven and gently spread the softened chocolate evenly over the top. Sprinkle with the macadamia nuts and gently press into the chocolate. Cool on a wire rack for 30 minutes, then refrigerate for 1 hour. Run a sharp knife around the tin to loosen; then unclip the springform tin side and carefully remove. Cut into thin wedges.

Marbled Chocolate Peanut Butter Cake

This cake cannot be tested with a skewer because the peanut butter remains soft in the centre.
Rely on the fingertip method: the cake should spring back when touched after 50–60 minutes.

INGREDIENTS
Serves 12–14
115 g/4 oz cooking chocolate, chopped
225 g/8 oz/1 cup butter, softened
225 g/8 oz/1 cup smooth or crunchy peanut butter
200 g/7 oz/1 cup granulated sugar
200 g/7 oz/1 cup (packed) light brown sugar
5 size 3 eggs
275 g/10 oz/2½ cups plain flour
10 ml/2 tsp baking powder
2.5 ml/½ tsp salt
120 ml/4 fl oz/½ cup milk
50 g/2 oz/⅓ cup chocolate chips

For the Chocolate Peanut Butter Glaze
25 g/1 oz/2 tbsp butter, cut up
25 g/1 oz/2 tbsp smooth peanut butter
45 ml/3 tbsp golden syrup
5 ml/1 tsp vanilla essence
175 g/6 oz plain chocolate, broken into pieces
15 ml/1 tbsp water

1 ▲ Preheat the oven to 180°C/350°F/ Gas 4. Generously grease and flour a 25 cm/10 inch ring mould. In the top of a double boiler over low heat, melt the chocolate.

2 ▲ Place the butter, peanut butter and sugars in a large bowl and beat with an electric mixer until light and creamy, about 3–5 minutes, scraping the side of the bowl occasionally. Add the eggs one at a time, beating well after each addition.

3 In a medium bowl, stir together the flour, baking powder and salt. Add to the butter mixture alternately with the milk until just blended.

4 ▲ Pour half the batter into another bowl. Stir the melted chocolate into one half of the batter until well blended. Stir the chocolate chips into the other half of the batter.

5 ▲ Using a large spoon, drop alternate spoonfuls of chocolate batter and peanut butter batter into the prepared tin. Using a knife, pull through the batters to create a swirled marbled effect; do not let the knife touch the side or bottom of the tin and do not over-mix. Bake the cake for 50–60 minutes until the top springs back when lightly pressed. Cool in the tin on a wire rack for 10 minutes, then turn out on to the rack and leave to cool completely.

6 ▲ To prepare the glaze, combine all the ingredients in a small pan. Melt over a low heat, stirring until well blended and smooth. Cool slightly. When slightly thickened, drizzle the glaze over the cake, allowing it to run down the side.

✒️pecial Occasions

*Special occasions deserve equally special cakes.
For inspired ideas for weddings, christenings, birthdays
and anniversaries, this chapter provides a tempting
selection. Featuring intricate designs that use a variety of
different techniques, these recipes range from chocolate
extravaganzas to iced masterpieces that will ensure you
have a cake that will truly match the occasion.*

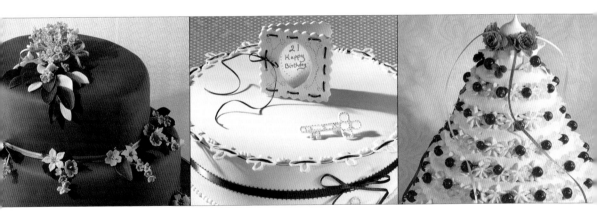

Teddy Bear Christening Cake

To personalise the cake, make a simple plaque for the top and pipe or write the name of the new baby with a food colouring pen.

INGREDIENTS
Serves 30
20 cm/8 inch square Light
Fruit Cake
3 tbsp apricot jam, warmed and
sieved
900 g/2 lb marzipan
800 g/1¾ lb/2⅓ x quantity
Sugarpaste Icing
peach, yellow, blue and brown
food colourings
115 g/4oz/⅙ quantity Royal Icing

MATERIALS AND EQUIPMENT
25 cm/10 inch square cake board
crimping tool
blossom cutter or plunger
foam pad
7.5 cm/3 inch round cutter
frill cutter
wooden cocktail stick
peach ribbon
small blue ribbon bow

1 Brush the cake with the apricot jam. Roll out the marzipan on a work surface lightly dusted with icing sugar, then use to cover the cake. Leave to dry for 12 hours.

2 Colour 500 g/1¼ lb of the sugarpaste icing peach. Roll out the icing. Brush the marzipan with a little water and cover the cake with the icing.

3 ▲ Position the cake on the cake board. Using a crimping tool dipped in cornflour, crimp the top and bottom edges of the cake.

4 Divide the remaining sugarpaste into three portions. Leave one-third white and colour one-third yellow. Cut the remaining third in half and colour one portion peach and the other blue.

5 ▲ To make the flowers, roll out the peach and blue sugarpaste thinly on a work surface lightly dusted with icing sugar. Dip the end of the blossom cutter or a plunger in cornflour and cut out small and larger flowers. Place a small ball of peach icing in the centre of the blue flowers; and a small ball of blue icing in the centre of the peach flowers. Secure with water, if necessary. Leave the flowers to dry on a foam pad for several hours or overnight. Gather together the blue icing trimmings and set aside, wrapped in clear film.

6 ▲ Make the teddy bear with the yellow icing. Shape the head, body, arms and ears of the bear and press together with a little water to secure. Make the button for the chest out of a little blue icing. Paint on highlights, such as eyes, nose and mouth, with brown food colouring. Leave the bear to dry on a piece of greaseproof paper for several hours or overnight.

7 To make the blanket, roll out the blue icing and cut out a circle with the 7.5 cm/3 inch round cutter. Slice off a small piece, about 1 cm/½ inch, to give a straight line for the top. Set aside. Roll out the white icing thinly and, using the frill cutter, cut out a ring. Put the end of the wooden cocktail stick over about 5 mm/¼ inch of the outer edge of the ring. Roll the stick around the edge firmly back and forth with your finger so the edge becomes thinner and begins to frill. Continue until the ring is completely frilled. Using a sharp knife, cut through the ring once to open it up. Gently ease it open.

8 ▲ Brush the edge of the blue blanket with water and secure the white frill on to the edge.

9 Decorate the cake with the ribbon. Position the bear on top and lay the blanket over it, securing with a little water or royal icing. Secure the flowers with a little royal icing and then the bow to the bear's neck in the same way.

Daisy Christening Cake

A ring of moulded daisies sets off this pretty pink christening cake. It can be made in easy stages, giving time for the various icings to dry before adding the next layer.

INGREDIENTS
Serves 20–25
20 cm/8 inch round Rich Fruit Cake
3 tbsp apricot jam, warmed and sieved
675 g/1½ lb marzipan
900 g/2 lb/1⅓ x quantity Royal Icing
115 g/4 oz/⅓ quantity Sugarpaste Icing
pink and yellow food colourings

MATERIALS AND EQUIPMENT
25 cm/10 inch round cake board
5 cm/2 inch fluted cutter
wooden cocktail stick
2 greaseproof paper piping bags
No 42 nozzle
pink and white ribbon

1 Brush the cake with the apricot jam. Roll out the marzipan on a work surface lightly dusted with icing sugar and use to cover the cake. Leave to dry for 12 hours.

2 Secure the cake to the cake board with a little of the icing. Colour three-quarters of the icing pink. Flat ice the cake with three or four layers of smooth icing, using the white icing for the top and the pink for the sides. Allow each layer to dry overnight before applying the next. Set aside a little of both icings in airtight containers, to decorate the cake.

3 Meanwhile, make the daisies. You will need about 28. For each daisy cut off a small piece of sugarpaste icing. Dust your fingers with a little cornflour to prevent sticking.

4 ▲ Shape the icing with your fingers to look like a golf tee, with a stem and a thin, flat, round top.

5 ▲ Using scissors, make small cuts all the way around the edge of the daisy. Carefully curl the cut edges slightly in different directions. Place the daisies on a sheet of greaseproof paper to dry.

6 ▲ When dry, trim the stems and paint the edges with pink and the centres with yellow food colouring.

7 ▲ To make the plaque, roll out the remaining sugarpaste icing on a work surface lightly dusted with icing sugar and cut out a circle with the fluted cutter. Position the end of a wooden cocktail stick over 5 mm/¼ inch of the outer edge of the circle. Roll the stick firmly back and forth around the edge with your finger until the edge becomes thinner and begins to frill. Continue until the edge of the plaque is completely frilled. Place on a sheet of greaseproof paper to dry, then paint the name in the centre of the plaque and the edges with pink food colouring.

8 ▲ Fit a paper piping bag with the nozzle and pipe a twisted rope around the top and bottom edges of the cake with the remaining white royal icing. Wash the nozzle, fit it in a fresh paper piping bag and pipe a row of stars around the top of the cake with the remaining pink icing.

9 Secure the plaque to the centre of the cake with a little royal icing. Arrange the daisies on the cake, also securing with the icing, and decorate with the ribbons.

Frills and Flowers Christening Cake

This pretty cake, decorated with flowers and frills, is perfect for a baby girl's christening, and would be ideal for a little girl's birthday cake, too.

INGREDIENTS
Serves 50
20 cm/8 inch round Rich Fruit Cake
30 ml/2 tbsp apricot jam, warmed and sieved
800 g/1¾ lb marzipan
1.2 kg/2½ lb/3⅓ x quantity Sugarpaste Icing
pink and red food colourings
115 g/4 oz/⅛ quantity Royal Icing

MATERIALS AND EQUIPMENT
23 cm/9 inch round silver cake board
deep pink ribbon, 2 cm/¾ inch, 1 cm/½ inch and 5 mm/¼ inch wide
crimping tool
greaseproof paper
greaseproof paper piping bag
No 1 writing nozzle
frill cutter
large and medium plunger blossom cutters
food colouring pen

1 Brush the cake with apricot jam, place on the cake board and cover the cake with marzipan. Tint the sugarpaste pale pink using a few drops of pink food colouring. Using two-thirds of the sugarpaste icing, cover the cake. Fit the widest ribbon around the cake board and the narrowest ribbon around the base of the cake. Secure with a bead of icing.

2 Using a crimping tool, crimp the top edge of the cake by pressing the crimper into the icing but not squeezing it together.

3 ▲ Cut a strip of greaseproof paper to fit around the cake and of the same height. Fold the paper into six equal divisions, position a plate half-way over the template and draw around the shape. Cut out the shape to form the template and reserve the cut-out piece. Fit the template around the cake and mark the shape with a scriber or pin. Remove the paper template.

4 Using a greaseproof paper piping bag fitted with a No 1 writing nozzle, fill with royal icing. Using some of the remaining sugarpaste icing, roll and cut out a frill, but cut out a larger centre circle to make a thinner frill. Frill the edges. Pipe a line of royal icing following one of the scalloped shapes marked on the cake and attach the frill. Repeat to make a total of six frills.

5 ▲ Using a cut-out piece of the template, mark ten 1 cm/½ inch lines in a semi-circle for the ribbon insertion cuts. Transfer these marks to the side of the cake under each frill and cut the slits. Cut the 1 cm/½ inch wide ribbon into pieces to fit the gaps and insert five pieces under each frill.

6 Mark a 10 cm/4 inch circle on top of the cake and mark 34 ribbon insertion lines. Cut the slits and insert 17 pieces of 1 cm/½ inch ribbon.

7 Knead all the sugarpaste icing trimmings together and tint half dark pink to match the ribbon, using pink and red food colouring. Cut out 22 large and 40 medium light plunger blossom flowers, and 24 medium and 6 large dark plunger blossom flowers. Pipe a bead of icing in the centre of each.

10 Secure the medium light pink flowers in between the ribbon inserts on top of the cake, and the small flowers on the side of the cake between the ribbon inserts. Secure the remaining light pink flowers between each frill. Leave the cake to dry.

8 ▲ Roll out a piece of dark pink sugarpaste icing thinly and cut out a round using the frill cutter. Frill the edges. Roll out the pale pink sugarpaste icing and cut out a 5 cm/2 inch fluted circle and place on top of the dark pink frill. Leave to dry. Arrange ten plunger blossom flowers at opposite sides of the plaque and secure with royal icing.

9 ▲ Using a food colouring pen, dot in the design and write the child's name across the centre. Place the plaque in position on top of the cake. Mark the dark centres on the blossom flowers with the food colouring pen. Attach the medium dark pink flowers to the top edge of the cake and the large ones in the centre of each frilled scallop.

Christening Sampler

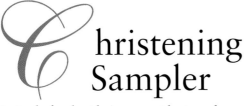

Instead of embroidering a sampler to welcome a new-born baby, why not make a sampler cake to celebrate?

INGREDIENTS
Serves 30
20 cm/8 in square Rich Fruit Cake
3 tbsp apricot jam, warmed and
sieved
450 g/1 lb marzipan
675 g/1½ lb/2 x quantity Sugarpaste
Icing
brown, blue, pink, yellow, orange,
green, cream and purple food
colourings

MATERIALS AND EQUIPMENT
25 cm/10 in square cake board
paintbrush
small heart-shaped biscuit cutter

Tip

Using the same techniques described here, you can change the overall design by modelling different figures and choosing different colours. You could also make a larger name plaque and pipe the baby's christian name on to it.

1 Brush the cake with the apricot jam. On a work surface lightly dusted with icing sugar, roll out the marzipan and use to cover the cake. Leave to dry for 12 hours.

2 Take two-thirds of the sugarpaste icing and cut off one-third of this. Roll out the smaller portion to the size of the top of the cake. Brush the top of the cake with a little water and cover with the icing.

3 ▲ Colour the larger portion of sugarpaste icing brown and divide into four equal amounts. Roll out each to the width of the cake side and about 1 cm/½ in longer than the height. Brush each cake side with a little water, then press the brown icing into place, folding over the extra at the top to represent a picture frame. Cut off each corner at an angle to make a mitred join. Reserve any trimmings. Place the cake on the cake board.

4 ▲ Paint the sides with brown food colouring thinned with a little water to represent wood grain.

5 ▲ Take the remaining sugarpaste icing and colour small amounts yellow, orange, brown, purple, cream, and two shades each of blue, green and pink. Leave a little white. Use these colours to shape the ducks, teddy bear, bulrushes, water, apple-blossom branch and leaves. Roll out a small piece of pink icing and cut out a heart with the small heart-shaped biscuit cutter. Roll out a small piece of white icing and cut out the baby's initial. For the border, roll out strips of light blue and yellow icing and cut into oblongs and squares. Make small balls and squares from the purple icing.

For the apple blossom, gently work together the two pinks and the white sugarpaste to give a marbled effect. Shape the flowers and add a small white ball in the centre of each. Leave all the shapes to dry on greaseproof paper. Then stick all the decorations on to the cake with a little water.

6 ▲ With any leftover coloured icing, roll out long strips of icing with your hands to make the embroidery threads. Form them into loops and use small strips of brown icing to hold the threads together. Arrange around the base of the cake.

Bunny and Bib Cake

This delicate cake may be made for a girl or a boy, using any pastel shade of icing. Make the decorations in advance and store in a warm, dry place. The bib may be kept as a keepsake.

INGREDIENTS
Serves 50
25 cm x 20 cm/10 x 8 inch oval Rich or Light Fruit Cake (make using quantities for a standard 25 cm/10 inch round cake)
60 ml/4 tbsp apricot jam, warmed and sieved
1.2 kg/2½ lb marzipan
1.3 kg/2¼ lb/2 x quantity Royal Icing
275 g/10 oz/½ quantity Petal Paste blue food colouring

MATERIALS AND EQUIPMENT
30 x 23 cm/12 x 9 inch oval silver cake board
card for template
small crimping tool
medium-sized heart-shaped plunger cutter
No 3 and No 1 writing nozzles
greaseproof paper piping bag
bunny-shaped cutter
blue food colouring pen
pale blue ribbon, 2 cm/¾ inch, 1 cm/½ inch, 5 mm/¼ inch and 3 mm/⅛ inch wide

1 Brush the cake with apricot jam, cover with marzipan and place on the cake board. Leave to dry for 12 hours. Flat ice the top and sides of the cake with three layers of smooth icing. Leave the cake until dry, then ice the cake board. Reserve the remaining royal icing for decorating the cake.

2 Tint the petal paste pale blue with a few drops of blue food colouring. Cut out a card template of the 'bib'. Roll out a small piece of petal paste very thinly. Place the template on top and cut around the shape using a pointed knife.

3 ▲ Using a small crimping tool, crimp the edge to give a fluted finish. Using the medium-sized heart-shaped plunger cutter, cut out five heart shapes around the edge of the bib. Use the end of a No 3 writing nozzle to cut out six small rounds between the heart shapes.

4 ▲ Half fill a greaseproof paper piping bag fitted with a No 1 writing nozzle with royal icing. Pipe fine threads of icing following the outlines of the cut-out shapes. Pipe alternate scrolls and three beads of icing as a border design, following the shape of the bib.

5 Pipe the child's name across the centre. Leave overnight to dry.

6 ▲ Roll out another piece of blue petal paste thinly and cut out 32 hearts using the plunger cutter. Then roll out some more icing thinly and use a tiny bunny cutter to cut out 16 bunny shapes. Mark their eyes using a blue food colouring pen. Leave all the cut-out shapes to dry overnight.

7 Measure and fit the wide blue ribbon around the cake board and secure with a pin. Measure and fit the 1 cm/½ inch wide ribbon around the base and the 5 mm/¼ inch wide ribbon around the top edge of the cake and secure each with a bead of royal icing. Secure alternate bunnies and hearts to the side of the cake between the ribbons with beads of royal icing. Secure 20 hearts around the top of the cake with royal icing.

8 Place the bib in the centre of the cake and support it with a piece of petal paste; arrange the remaining five bunnies around it. Tie a tiny bow in the fine ribbon, leave the ends long and pull over the scissors to curl the ends. Place in position at the neck of the bib and the side of the cake.

*B*irthday Bowl of Strawberries

*All kinds of fun designs can be painted on cakes with edible food colourings.
With this one the strawberry theme is carried on into the moulded
decorations too, providing a fresh, summery birthday cake.*

INGREDIENTS
Serves 20
*1 quantity Butter Icing
20 cm/8 inch petal-shaped Madeira
Cake (make using quantities for a
20 cm/8 inch round cake)
3 tbsp apricot jam, warmed and
sieved
675 g/1½ lb/2 x quantity Sugarpaste
Icing
pink, red, yellow, green and claret
food colourings
yellow powdered food colouring*

MATERIALS AND EQUIPMENT
*25 cm/10 inch petal-shaped cake
board
paint palette or small saucers
thin red and green ribbons*

1 Colour the butter icing pink. Cut the cake into three horizontal layers and sandwich together with the butter icing. Brush the cake with apricot jam. Roll out 500 g/1¼ lb of the sugarpaste icing on a work surface lightly dusted with icing sugar and use to cover the cake. Position on the cake board and leave to dry for 12 hours.

2 ▲ To make the strawberries, colour three-quarters of the remaining sugarpaste icing red, and equal portions of the rest yellow and green. Dust your fingers with cornflour to prevent sticking, and mould the red icing into strawberry shapes. Make tiny oval shapes from the yellow icing to represent seeds and lightly press on to the strawberries. Secure with water if necessary. Shape the green icing into small flat circles slightly bigger than the tops of the strawberries. Using scissors, make small cuts all the way round the circles and carefully curl the cut edges slightly. Attach to the tops of the strawberries, securing with a little water. Leave to dry on greaseproof paper.

3 ▲ Put the red, green, yellow and claret food colourings in a palette and water them down slightly. Draw or paint on an outline of the vase with the claret colour, then fill in the pattern.

4 ▲ Use a little powdered yellow food colouring to add highlights.

5 ▲ Finish painting the design, filling in the strawberries in the bowl and around the edge of the cake.

6 ▲ Decorate the cake with the ribbons. Secure two strawberries to the top of the cake, and arrange the others around the bottom edge.

Chocolate Fruit Birthday Cake

A moist chocolate Madeira cake is covered in marzipan and chocolate fudge icing. The fruits are moulded from coloured marzipan and make an eye-catching decoration.

INGREDIENTS
Serves 30
18 cm/7 inch square chocolate-flavour Madeira Cake (see Tip)
45 ml/3 tbsp apricot jam, warmed and sieved
450 g/1 lb marzipan
450 g/1 lb/1⅓ x quantity Fudge Frosting
red, yellow, orange, green and purple food colourings
whole cloves
angelica strips

MATERIALS AND EQUIPMENT
20 cm/8 inch square silver cake board
wire rack
nylon piping bag
medium-sized gâteau nozzle
yellow ribbon 1 cm/½ inch wide

1 Cut a slice off the top of the cake to level if necessary and invert on to the cake board. Brush evenly with apricot jam.

2 ▲ Roll out two-thirds of the marzipan thinly to a 25 cm/10 inch square. Place over the cake and smooth the top and sides. Trim off the excess marzipan around the base of the cake. Knead the trimmings together and reserve for making the marzipan fruits.

3 ▲ Place the cake on a wire rack over a tray and pour the freshly made fudge frosting over the cake, spreading quickly with a palette knife. Allow the excess icing to fall on the tray. Leave for 10 minutes, then place on the cake board.

4 ▲ Place the remaining frosting in a nylon piping bag fitted with a medium-sized gateau nozzle. Pipe a row of stars around the top edge and base of the cake. Leave to set.

5 ▲ Using the reserved marzipan, food colouring, cloves and angelica strips, model a selection of fruits.

6 Measure and fit the ribbon around the side of the cake and secure with a pin. Decorate the top with marzipan fruits.

Tip

To make an 18 cm/7 inch chocolate-flavour Madeira Cake, use 200 g/7 oz/1¾ cups plain flour plus 25 g/1 oz/2 tbsp cocoa powder in place of the full amount of plain flour.

Eighteenth Birthday Cake

A really striking cake for a lucky person celebrating their eighteenth birthday. Change the shape if you have difficulty hiring a diamond-shaped tin.

INGREDIENTS
Serves 80
34 x 20 cm/13½ x 8 inch diamond-shaped Rich or Light Fruit Cake (make using quantities for a standard 23 cm/ 9 inch round cake)
45 ml/3 tbsp apricot jam, warmed and sieved
1.2 kg/2½ lb marzipan
1.6 kg/3½ lb/4½ x quantity white Sugarpaste icing
black food colouring
30 ml/2 tbsp Royal Icing

MATERIALS AND EQUIPMENT
38 x 25 cm/15 x 10 inch diamond-shaped silver cake board
'1' and '8' numeral cutters or templates
small triangular cutter
very small round cutter
greaseproof paper piping bag
No 1 writing nozzle
white ribbon, 2.5 cm/1 inch wide
black ribbon, 3 mm/⅛ inch wide

1 Brush the cake with apricot jam and place on the cake board. Cover with marzipan.

2 Cover the cake using 1.2 kg/2½ lb/ 3⅓ x quantity sugarpaste icing. Knead the trimmings into the remaining sugarpaste and colour using black food colouring.

3 Roll out two-thirds of the black sugarpaste icing and cut into four strips the width and length of each section of the cake board. Brush the board with apricot jam and place each strip in position; trim to fit neatly.

4 ▲ Roll-out one-quarter of the remaining sugarpaste icing and cut out the number '18' using special biscuit cutters or by cutting round templates. Leave on a foam pad to dry.

5 ▲ Roll out some more icing thinly and cut out 40 triangles for the bow ties and 20 for the wine glasses.

6 ▲ Use a tiny round cutter or the end of a plain nozzle to cut out 20 music notes and 10 bases for the glasses, cut in half. Cut out thin strips of icing for the tails of the music notes and the stems of the glasses.

7 Using a greaseproof paper piping bag fitted with a No 1 writing nozzle, half-fill with black royal icing. Join the bow ties together with tiny beads of icing. Attach the music notes to their tails and the glasses to the stems and bases. Leave to dry.

8 ▲ Measure and fit the white ribbon around the cake board and secure with a pin. Arrange the motifs over the top and sides of the cake and attach each with a bead of icing. Make tiny bows using black ribbon; attach to the corners of the cake with beads of icing.

Twenty-first Birthday Cake

This cake looks good in white or any pale colour to suit the occasion. Add more colour with the ribbons and write your own personal message in the card.

INGREDIENTS
Serves 80
25 cm/10 inch round Rich
Fruit Cake
45 ml/3 tbsp apricot jam, warmed
and sieved
1.1 kg/2½ lb marzipan
1.4 kg/3 lb/2 x quantity Royal Icing
blue food colouring
575 g/1¼ lb/1 quantity petal paste

MATERIALS AND EQUIPMENT
30 cm/12 inch round silver
cake board
7.5 cm/3 inch square fluted cutter
5 cm/2 inch plain oval cutter
No 2 and 3 writing nozzles
club-shaped cocktail cutter
tiny petal cutter
royal blue ribbon, 3 mm/⅛ inch,
5 mm/¼ inch and 1 cm/½ inch wide
pale blue ribbon, 2 cm/¼ inch wide
looped royal blue ribbon, 1.5 cm/
⅝ inch wide
greaseproof paper piping bag
blue food colouring pen

3 ▲ Colour the petal paste pale blue with a few drops of blue food colouring. Roll out about one-third of the paste thinly on a surface sprinkled with cornflour. Cut out two squares using the square fluted cutter. Cut out an oval shape from one square using the plain oval cutter. Make two tiny holes using a No 2 writing nozzle on the left-hand edge, and match these on the plain square so that the ribbons will meet to tie the card together. Continue to make a cut-out pattern all around the card for the ribbon to thread through. Leave on a foam pad to dry.

5 ▲ To make the keys, roll out the paste thinly and cut two end shapes with the club cutter. Then, using a sharp knife, cut out two key shapes. Make a pattern on the keys using tiny cutters. Leave to dry.

6 Fit the pale blue ribbon and the 1 cm/ ½ inch royal blue ribbon around the board, securing with a pin. Fit a grease-proof paper piping bag with a No 3 writing nozzle and fill with blue icing. Fit the looped ribbon around the side of the cake and secure with a bead of icing.

1 Brush the cake with apricot jam, cover with marzipan and place on the cake board. Leave to dry for 12 hours.

2 Colour the royal icing pale blue with a few drops of blue food colouring. Flat-ice the top and sides of the cake with three layers of smooth royal icing. Leave the cake to dry, then ice the cake board. Reserve the remaining royal icing for decorating.

4 ▲ Roll out some more petal paste thinly and, using a club-shaped cocktail cutter, cut out 25 shapes, allowing extras for breakages. Use a tiny petal cutter to cut out three shapes on each piece. Leave to dry.

7 ▲ Arrange 18 cut-out sugar pieces around the top edge of the cake and secure each with a bead of icing. Leave to dry. Pipe a shell edging around the base of the cake, and beads of icing in between the cut-out pieces around the top edge.

10 Thread the remaining royal blue ribbon (5 mm/¼ inch) in and out of the cut-out sugar pieces on the top edge of the cake and join the ends together with a bead of icing underneath. Tie a bow and attach it to the side of the cake with a bead of icing. Arrange the card and one key on top of the cake and place the remaining key on the cake board. Secure each with a little icing. Leave the cake to dry.

8 ▲ Using the food colouring pen, write the message on the plain card and decorate the keys.

9 ▲ Thread the 3 mm/⅛ inch royal blue ribbon through the matching holes to join the card together – do not tie too tightly or the card will not open – and tie a small bow with long ends.

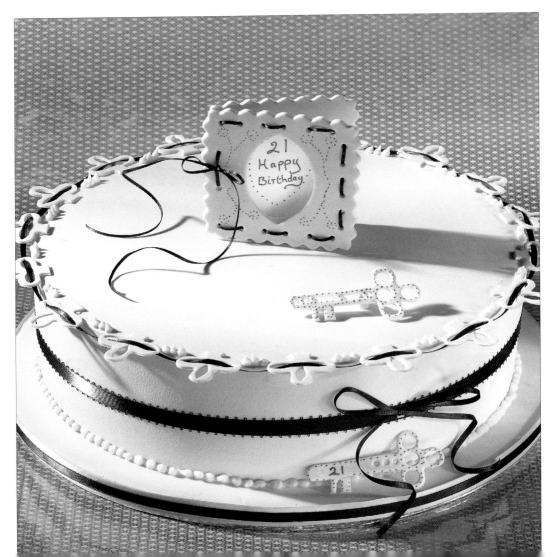

Flower Birthday Cake

A simple birthday cake decorated with piped sugar flowers and ribbons; use any mixture of flowers and ribbons, and pipe a birthday message on the top.

INGREDIENTS
Serves 40
*18 cm/7 inch round Light
Fruit Cake
30 ml/2 tbsp apricot jam, warmed
and sieved
675 g/1½ lb marzipan
1.1 kg/2½ lb/1⅔ x quantity Royal
Icing
yellow and orange food colourings*

MATERIALS AND EQUIPMENT
*23 cm/9 inch round silver
cake board
several greaseproof paper piping
bags
petal nozzle, No 1 and 2 writing
nozzles and medium star nozzle
flower nail
white ribbon, 2 cm/¾ inch wide
coral ribbon, 1 cm/½ inch and
5 mm/¼ inch wide*

1 Brush the cake with apricot jam and cover with marzipan. Place on the cake board. Leave to dry for 12 hours.

2 Flat-ice the top and side of the cake with three layers of smooth royal icing. Leave the cake to dry, then ice the cake board. Reserve the remaining royal icing for decorating the cake. Store the cake in a box until required.

3 ▲ Snip an inverted 'V' shape off the point of one greaseproof paper piping bag. Fit one with a petal nozzle, one with a No 1 writing nozzle, and another bag with a medium-sized star nozzle. Colour one-third of the icing yellow with yellow food colouring. Colour 15 ml/1 tbsp of icing orange with orange food colouring. Pipe the narcissi using the petal nozzle for the petals and the plain writing nozzle for the centres: make four white narcissi with yellow centres and nine yellow narcissi with orange centres.

4 ▲ Pipe nine simple white flowers using the snipped bag and add yellow centres with the plain nozzle. Peel the paper off the back of the flowers and arrange them on the top of the cake. Secure each flower with a little icing.

5 ▲ Fill the star nozzle with white icing and pipe a shell edging around the top edge and base of the cake. Using the No 2 writing nozzle and white icing, pipe the words 'Happy Birthday' on the right and left of the flower arrangement. Overpipe the writing using a No 1 nozzle and some orange icing.

6 ▲ Measure and fit the white ribbon around the cake board and secure with a pin. Fit the coral ribbon around the board and side of the cake, securing with a bead of royal icing. Tie a narrow ribbon bow and attach to the front of the cake with a bead of royal icing. Leave the cake to dry.

Fudge-frosted Starry Roll

Whether it's a birthday or another occasion you are wanting to celebrate, this sumptuous looking cake is sure to please.

INGREDIENTS
Serves 8
1 quantity Swiss Roll mix
½ quantity chocolate-flavour Butter Icing
50 g/2 oz white chocolate
50 g/2 oz plain chocolate
1½ x quantity Fudge Frosting

MATERIALS AND EQUIPMENT
23 x 33 cm/9 x 13 inch Swiss roll tin
small star cutter
several greaseproof paper piping bags
No 19 star nozzle

3 ▲ To make the chocolate decorations, cover a board with baking parchment and tape down at each corner. Melt the white chocolate, then pour on to the baking parchment. Spread the chocolate evenly with a palette knife and allow to stand until the surface is firm enough to cut, but not so hard that it will break. It should no longer feel sticky when touched with your finger. Press a small star cutter firmly through the chocolate and lift off the paper with a palette knife. Set aside.

4 ▲ Melt the plain chocolate and allow to cool slightly. Cover a rolling pin with baking parchment and attach it with tape. Fill a paper piping bag with the chocolate and cut a small piece off the pointed end in a straight line. Pipe lines of chocolate backwards and forwards over the baking parchment, to the size you choose. Make at least nine curls so you have extra in case of breakages. Leave the chocolate lace curls to set in a cool place, then carefully peel off the paper.

5 ▲ Make the fudge frosting. When cool enough to spread, cover the Swiss roll with about two-thirds of it, making swirls with a palette knife.

6 ▲ Fit a fresh paper piping bag with the No 19 star nozzle and spoon in the remaining frosting. Pipe diagonal lines, like a twisted rope, on either side of the roll and across both ends.

7 ▲ Position the lace curls in the icing, and arrange the stars. Transfer the cake to a serving plate and decorate with more stars.

1 Preheat the oven to 180°C/350°F/ Gas 4. Grease the tin, line the base with greaseproof paper and grease the paper. Spoon in the cake mixture and gently smooth the surface. Bake for 12–15 minutes, or until springy to the touch.

2 Turn out on to a sheet of greaseproof paper lightly sprinkled with caster sugar, peel off the lining paper and roll up the Swiss roll, leaving the lining paper inside. When cold, unroll carefully, remove the paper and spread the cake with the butter icing. Re-roll and set aside on a sheet of greaseproof paper on a wire rack.

The Beautiful Present Cake

For a best friend, mother, grandmother, aunt or sister, this beautiful cake can mark any special occasion.

INGREDIENTS
Serves 15–20
2 x quantity Quick-Mix Sponge
Cake mix
350 g/12 oz/1 quantity Butter
Icing
4 tbsp apricot jam, warmed and
sieved
575 g/1¼ lb marzipan
900 g/2 lb/2⅔ x quantity Sugarpaste
Icing
purple and pink food colourings

MATERIALS AND EQUIPMENT
23 cm/9 in square cake tin
25 cm/10 in square cake board
heart-shaped biscuit cutter
small round fluted cutter
pink food-colouring pen

1 Preheat the oven to 180°C/350°F/
Gas 4. Grease the tin, line the base
and sides with greaseproof paper and
grease the paper. Spoon the cake
mixture into the prepared tin and
smooth the surface. Bake in the centre
of the oven for 1¼–1½ hours, or until a
skewer inserted into the centre of the
cake comes out clean. Leave the cake in
the tin for 5 minutes, then turn out on
to a wire rack, peel off the lining paper
and leave to cool.

2 Cut the cake in half horizontally
and spread with the butter icing.
Sandwich the cake together and place in
the centre of the cake board. Brush the
cake with the apricot jam. On a work
surface lightly dusted with icing sugar,
roll out the marzipan to about a
5 mm/¼ in thickness and use to cover
the cake.

3 Colour about five-eighths of the
sugarpaste icing purple. On a work
surface lightly dusted with icing sugar,
roll out and use to cover the cake.

4 ▲ Using the heart-shaped cutter,
stamp out hearts from the
sugarpaste icing to make an even
pattern. Remove the hearts with a small,
sharp knife, taking care not to damage
the surrounding sugarpaste. Knead the
hearts together and reserve, wrapped in
clear film.

5 ▲ Colour the remaining sugarpaste
icing pink and roll out to a 5 mm/
¼ in thickness. Using the heart-shaped
cutter, cut out as many hearts as you
need to fill the spaces left by the purple
ones, re-rolling the pink sugarpaste as
necessary. Reserve the trimmings,
wrapped in clear film. Carefully insert
the pink hearts into the spaces.

6 Roll out the reserved pink
sugarpaste and cut into three strips
about 2 cm/¾ in wide and 30 cm/12 in
long. Lay one strip across the centre of
the cake and another at right angles
across the centre, brushing the strips
with a little water to secure. Reserve
the trimmings.

7 ▲ Divide the remaining strip of pink
sugarpaste into quarters and arrange
in the centre of the cake to make a bow.
Secure with a little water and reserve
the trimmings.

8 ▲ Roll out the remaining purple and
pink sugarpaste and cut out two
rounds from each colour using the small
round fluted cutter. With a cocktail stick,
carefully roll out the edges of the rounds
to make frilled petals. Use a little of the
purple sugarpaste to make two tiny balls
for the flower centres. Assemble the
flowers, securing with a little water and
position on the cake. Knead the pink and
purple trimmings together, roll out and
cut out a name tag. Write a message or a
name using the food-colouring pen and
position on the cake.

Cloth of Roses Cake

This cake says 'congratulations' for whatever reason - passing an exam, getting a new job, getting engaged, or for just achieving a life long ambition.

INGREDIENTS
Serves 20–25
20 cm/8 inch round Light Fruit Cake
3 tbsp apricot jam, warmed and sieved
675 g/1½ lb marzipan
900 g/2 lb/2⅔ x quantity Sugarpaste Icing
yellow, orange and green food colourings
115 g/4oz/⅙ quantity Royal Icing

MATERIALS AND EQUIPMENT
25 cm/10 inch cake board
7 cm/2¾ inch plain cutter
petal cutter
thin yellow ribbon

1 Brush the cake with apricot jam. Roll out the marzipan on a work surface lightly dusted with icing sugar and cover the cake. Leave for 12 hours.

2 Cut off 675 g/1½ lb of the sugarpaste icing and divide in half. Colour one-half very pale yellow and the other very pale orange. Wrap separately in clear film and set aside.

3 Cut out a template for the orange icing from greaseproof paper, as follows. Draw a 25 cm/10 inch circle using the plain cutter, draw half circles 2.5 cm/1 inch wide all around the outside of the large circle. Cut out the template.

4 Roll out the yellow sugarpaste icing on a work surface lightly dusted with icing sugar to the same length and height as the side of the cake. Brush the side of the cake with a little water and cover with the sugarpaste icing. Position the cake on the cake board.

5 ▲ Roll out the orange sugarpaste icing to about a 30 cm/12 inch circle. Place the template on the icing and cut out the scalloped shape.

6 ▲ Brush the top of the cake with water and cover with the orange icing so the scallops fall just over the edge. Bend them slightly to look like a cloth. Leave to dry overnight.

7 Meanwhile make the roses and leaves. Cut off about three-quarters of the remaining sugarpaste icing and divide into four portions. (Wrap the other piece in clear film and reserve for the leaves.) Colour the four portions pale yellow, deep yellow, orange, and marbled yellow and orange.

8 ▲ For each rose, dust your fingers with cornflour, take a small ball of coloured icing and form into a cone shape. For each petal, take a small piece of icing and work it with your fingers into a petal shape which is slightly thicker at the base. Wrap the petal around the cone so it sits above the top of it, pressing together to stick. Curl the ends of the petal back. Mould the next petal and attach so it just overlaps the first one. Curl the ends back. Repeat with several more petals, making them slightly larger each time. Cut off the base so the rose will stand on the cake. Make about 18 roses. Leave to dry on greaseproof paper.

9 ▲ Colour the reserved piece of sugarpaste icing green for the leaves. Roll out thinly and cut out leaves with a petal cutter. Make about 24 leaves. Leave to dry on greaseproof paper.

10 Arrange the leaves and roses, securing with a little royal icing. Decorate the cake with the ribbon.

Double Heart Engagement Cake

For a celebratory engagement party, these sumptuous cakes make the perfect centrepiece.

INGREDIENTS
Serves 20
2 x quantity chocolate-flavour Quick-Mix Sponge Cake mix
350 g/12 oz/12 squares plain chocolate
2 x quantity coffee-flavour Butter Icing
icing sugar, for sifting
fresh raspberries, to decorate

MATERIALS AND EQUIPMENT
2 x 20 cm/8 inch heart-shaped cake tins
2 x 23 cm/9 inch heart-shaped cake boards

1 Preheat the oven to 160°C/325°F/ Gas 3. Grease the tins, line the bases with greaseproof paper and grease the paper. Divide the cake mixture evenly between the tins and smooth the surfaces. Bake in the centre of the oven for 25–30 minutes or until firm to the touch. Turn out on to a wire rack, peel off the lining paper and leave to cool completely.

2 Meanwhile, melt the chocolate in a heatproof bowl over a saucepan of hot water (you may find it easier to work with half the chocolate at a time). Pour the melted chocolate on to a firm, smooth surface such as a marble or plastic laminate set on a slightly damp cloth to prevent slipping. Spread the chocolate out evenly with a large palette knife. Leave the chocolate to cool slightly. It should feel just set, but not hard.

3 ▲ To make the chocolate curls, hold a large sharp knife at a 45° angle to the chocolate and push it along the chocolate in short sawing movements from right to left and left to right. Remove the curls by sliding the point of the knife underneath each one and lifting off. Leave to firm on baking parchment. Repeat with remaining chocolate.

4 ▲ Cut each cake in half horizontally. Use about one-third of the butter icing to fill both cakes, then sandwich them together.

5 Use the remaining icing to coat the tops and sides of the cakes.

6 ▲ Place the cakes on the cake boards. Generously cover the tops and sides of the cakes with the chocolate curls, pressing them gently into the butter icing.

7 Sift a little icing sugar over the top of each cake and decorate with raspberries. Chill until ready to serve.

Chocolate-iced Anniversary Cake

This cake is special enough to celebrate any wedding anniversary. Tropical fruits and a glossy chocolate icing make it very appealing for all ages.

INGREDIENTS
Serves 12–15
20 cm/8 inch round Madeira Cake
1½ x quantity chocolate-flavour
Butter Icing
1 quantity Satin Chocolate Icing
chocolate buttons
selection of fresh fruits, such as
kiwi, nectarine or peach, apricot,
Cape gooseberries

MATERIALS AND EQUIPMENT
greaseproof paper piping bag
No 22 star nozzle
thin gold ribbon, about 5 mm/¼ in
wide
florist's wire

1 Cut the cake into three horizontal layers and sandwich together with about three-quarters of the chocolate butter icing. Place the cake on a wire rack with a baking sheet underneath.

2 ▲ Make the satin chocolate icing and immediately pour over the cake to coat completely. Working quickly, ease the icing gently over the surface of the cake, using a palette knife if necessary. Allow to set.

3 ▲ Transfer the cake to a serving plate. Fit a paper piping bag with the star nozzle and spoon in the remaining chocolate butter icing. Pipe scrolls around the top edge of the cake.

4 Cut several chocolate buttons into quarters and use to decorate the butter icing.

5 ▲ Prepare the fruit for the top of the cake. Peel and slice the kiwi and cut into quarters, and slice the nectarine or peach, apricot and gooseberries.

6 Arrange the fruit on top of the cake. For each ribbon decoration, make two small loops using the thin gold ribbon. Twist a piece of florist's wire around the ends of the ribbon to secure the loops. Trim the ends of the ribbon. Cut the wire to the length you want and use it to put the loops in position on the cake. Make about seven ribbon decorations. Remove the ribbons and wire before serving.

Rose Blossom Wedding Cake

The traditional white wedding cake, with its classic lines and elegant piping, is still a favourite choice for many brides and grooms.

INGREDIENTS
Serves 80
23 cm/9 inch square Rich Fruit Cake
15 cm/6 inch square Rich Fruit Cake
75 ml/7 tbsp apricot jam, warmed and sieved
1.5 kg/3½ lb marzipan
1.5 kg/3½ lb/2⅓ x quantity Royal Icing, to coat
675 g/1½ lb/1 quantity Royal Icing, to pipe
pink and green food colourings

MATERIALS AND EQUIPMENT
28 cm/11 inch square cake board
20 cm/8 inch square cake board
No 1 writing and No 42 nozzles
several greaseproof paper piping bags
thin pink ribbon
8 pink bows
3–4 cake pillars
about 12 miniature roses
few fern sprigs

1 Brush the cakes with the apricot jam and cover with marzipan, allowing 450 g/1 lb marzipan for the 15 cm/6 inch cake and the remainder for the 23 cm/ 9 inch cake. Place the cakes on the cake boards and leave to dry for 12 hours.

2 Make the royal icing for coating the cake. Secure the cakes to the cake boards with a little of the icing. Flat ice the cakes with three or four layers of smooth icing, allowing each layer to dry overnight before applying the next. The royal icing should be very dry before assembling the cake, so it can be made to this stage and stored in cardboard cake boxes for several days.

3 Make the royal icing for piping, and colour a small amount pale pink and another small portion pale green. To make the piped sugar pieces, draw the double-triangle design on a piece of greaseproof paper several times. You will need 40 pieces, but make extra in case of breakages. Tape the paper to a baking sheet or flat board and secure a piece of baking parchment over the top. Tape it down at the corners.

4 ▲ Fit a piping bag with a No 1 writing nozzle. Half-fill with white royal icing and fold over the top to seal. Pipe over each design, carefully following the outlines with a continuous thread of icing. Spoon a little of the pink icing and a little of the green icing into separate paper piping bags fitted with No 1 writing nozzles. Pipe pink dots on the corners of the top triangle in each design and green on the corners of the bottom triangle in each design. Leave to dry for at least two hours.

5 Mark four triangles on the top and side of each cake with a pin. Work from the centre of each side, so each triangle is 6 cm/2½ inches wide at the base and 4 cm/1½ inches high on the smaller cake, and 7.5 cm/3 inches wide at the base and 5 cm/2 inches high on the larger cake. Fit a paper piping bag with a clean No 1 writing nozzle and half-fill with some of the white icing. Using the pin marks as a guide, pipe double lines to outline the triangles.

6 ▲ Using the same nozzle, pipe cornelli inside all the triangles.

7 ▲ Fit a piping bag with a No 42 nozzle and half-fill with white icing. Pipe shells around the top and bottom edges of each cake, but not within the triangles.

8 Using the piping bags fitted with No 1 writing nozzles and filled with pink and green icing, pipe dots on the corners of each cake.

9 ▲ Remove the piped sugar pieces from the paper by carefully turning it back and lifting off each piece with a palette knife. Secure them to the cake and cake board with a little icing.

10 Decorate the cake with the ribbon and bows. Just before serving, assemble the cake with the cake pillars and decorate with the roses and fern sprigs.

*L*ucky Horseshoe

This horseshoe-shaped cake, made to wish 'good luck', is made from a round cake and the horseshoe shape is then cut out.

INGREDIENTS
Serves 30–35
25 cm/10 inch Rich Fruit Cake
4 tbsp apricot jam, warmed and sieved
800 g/1¾ lb marzipan
1 kg/2¼ lb/3 x quantity Sugarpaste Icing
peach and blue food colourings
silver balls
115 g/4 oz/⅛ quantity Royal Icing

MATERIALS AND EQUIPMENTS
28–30 cm/11–12 inch round cake board
crimping tool
large blossom cutter
small blossom cutter
pale blue ribbon, 3 mm/⅛ in wide

1 Draw a horseshoe shape on a sheet of greaseproof paper. Cut this shape out of the cake, using the template as a guide. Brush the cake with the apricot jam. Roll out 350 g/12 oz of the marzipan to a 25 cm/10 inch circle on a work surface lightly dusted with icing sugar. Using the template as a guide, cut out the shape and cover the top of the cake with the marzipan. Reserve the trimmings for the inside of the ring.

2 Measure the circumference of the cake as far as the openings of the horseshoe and the height of the side with string. Take the remaining marzipan and roll out for the side, using the string measurement as a guide. Use to cover the side. Using the same method and the reserved trimmings, cover the inside of the horseshoe. Position the cake on the board and leave to dry for 12 hours.

3 ▲ Colour 800 g/1¾ lb of the sugarpaste icing peach. Brush the marzipan lightly with water and cover the cake with the sugarpaste icing in the same way as described for the marzipan, covering first the top, then the side, then the inside of the horseshoe.

4 Using a crimping tool dipped in cornflour, carefully crimp the top edge of the cake.

5 Draw and measure the design for the ribbon insertion on the horseshoe template. Cut 13 pieces of pale blue ribbon fractionally longer than the size of each slit.

6 ▲ Place the template on the cake, securing with pins if necessary, and cut through the drawn lines into the icing with a scalpel to make slits for the ribbon. Remove the template.

7 ▲ With the aid of a pointed tool, insert one end of the ribbon into the first slit and the other end into the second slit. Leave a space and repeat, filling all the slits with the pieces of ribbon. Leave to dry for 12 hours.

8 ▲ Draw a small horseshoe shape on a piece of card and cut out. Take the remaining sugarpaste icing and colour one-half pale blue and leave the other half white. Roll out the blue icing on a work surface lightly dusted with icing sugar. Using the card template as a guide, cut out nine shapes with a sharp knife. Mark small lines around the centre of each horseshoe with the knife. Cut out 12 large and 15 small blossoms with the blossom cutters, then press a silver ball into the centres of the larger blossoms. Leave to dry on greaseproof paper. Repeat with the white icing.

9 Decorate the cake with the ribbon. Arrange the horseshoes and blossoms on the cake and board, securing with a little royal icing.

*T*ip

Save the discarded section of the round cake to use in the Truffle Mix, if wished. Horseshoe-shaped tins can be purchased or hired from cake decorating specialists.

*G*olden Wedding Heart Cake

Creamy gold colours, delicate frills and dainty iced blossoms give this cake a special celebratory appeal.

INGREDIENTS
Serves 30
23 cm/9 inch round Rich Fruit Cake
4 tbsp apricot jam, warmed and sieved
900 g/2 lb marzipan
900 g/2 lb/2⅔ x quantity Sugarpaste Icing
cream food colouring
115 g/4 oz/⅙ quantity Royal Icing

MATERIALS AND EQUIPMENT
28 cm/11 inch round cake board
crimping tool
small heart-shaped plunger tool
7.5 cm/3 inch plain cutter
dual large and small blossom cutter
stamens
frill cutter
foil-wrapped chocolate hearts

1 Brush the cake with apricot jam. Roll out the marzipan on a work surface lightly dusted with icing sugar and use it to cover the cake. Leave to dry for 12 hours.

2 Colour 675 g/1½ lb of the sugarpaste icing very pale cream. Roll out the icing on a work surface lightly dusted with icing sugar. Brush the marzipan with a little water and cover the cake with the sugarpaste icing. Position the cake on the cake board. Using a crimping tool dipped in cornflour, carefully crimp the top edge of the cake.

3 ▲ Divide the circumference of the top of the cake into eight equal sections, and stick pins in as markers. Use these as a guide to crimp evenly spaced slanting lines going from the top to the bottom edges of the cake. Using the plunger tool, emboss the bottom edge of the cake. Place the plain cutter lightly in the centre of the cake and use as a guide to emboss more hearts in a circle around the cutter. Leave the cake to dry for several hours.

4 ▲ Take the remaining sugarpaste icing and colour one-half cream and the other half pale cream. Retain half of each colour, and wrap the remainder in clear film. Roll out each colour evenly and thinly. Dip the end of the blossom cutter in cornflour and cut out the flower shapes. Make a pin hole in the centre of each larger flower as you make it. Leave to dry on a foam pad. When dry, pipe a little royal icing on to a stamen and thread it through the hole of each larger flower. This will hold it in position. Allow to dry.

5 ▲ To make the frills, roll out the two shades of reserved sugarpaste icing thinly. Using the frill cutter, cut out two rings from each colour.

6 ▲ Position the end of a wooden cocktail stick over 5 mm/¼ inch of the outer edge of the ring. Roll the stick firmly back and forth around the edge with your finger until the edge becomes thinner and begins to frill. Continue until the ring is completely frilled. Repeat with remaining rings. Using a sharp knife, cut each ring in half to make two frills. You should have four frills in each shade.

7 ▲ Using a little water, attach the frills in alternate shades next to the crimped lines running down the side of the cake. Crimp the edges of the deeper coloured frills.

8 Arrange the blossom flowers on the top and side of the cake, securing with a little royal icing. Before serving, place the chocolate hearts in the centre of the cake.

Trailing Orchid Wedding Cake

A special celebration such as a wedding deserves a very special cake.

INGREDIENTS
Serves 100
30 cm/12 inch round Madeira
Cake mix
25 cm/10 inch round Madeira
Cake mix
50 g/2 oz/2 squares plain
chocolate
50 g/2 oz/2 squares white
chocolate
7½ x quantity Butter Icing
1½ x quantity chocolate-flavour
Butter Icing

MATERIALS AND EQUIPMENT
30 cm/12 inch oval cake tin
25 cm/10 inch oval cake tin
about 22 rose leaves
plain scraper
several greaseproof paper piping
bags
No 4 writing and basket-weave
nozzles
35 cm/14 inch oval thick cake
board
25 cm/10 inch oval thin cake board
orchids

1 Grease the oval cake tins, line with a double thickness of greaseproof paper and grease the paper. Make the cakes one at a time and bake, following the baking times for the 30 cm/12 inch and 25 cm/10 inch round Madeira cakes. Leave to cool slightly in the tin, then turn out on to a wire rack, peel off the lining paper and leave to cool.

2 To make the chocolate leaves, wash and dry the rose leaves well on kitchen paper. Melt the chocolates in two separate heatproof bowls over pans of hot water.

3 ▲ Brush the underside of each leaf, some with plain, some with the white chocolate. Do not go over to the other side of the leaf. Place the leaves chocolate-side up on baking parchment, and leave to set in a cool place. Peel the leaf from the chocolate. Handle the chocolate as little as possible as the warmth of your hands will melt it. If the chocolate seems too thin, re-coat.

4 Make the butter icings in batches, whisking until smooth. Level off the tops of the cakes if they have domed. Cut each cake in half horizontally, then sandwich each one back together with some of the plain butter icing.

5 Invert each cake on to a board covered with greaseproof paper. Spread some of the plain butter icing over the sides and smooth with the scraper.

6 ▲ Spread the icing over the top of each cake. To make the surface really smooth, spread with a long metal palette knife which has been dipped into hot water.

7 ▲ To pipe the basket-weave design on each cake, spoon some of the chocolate-flavour butter icing into a greaseproof paper piping bag fitted with a No 4 writing nozzle. (You will need to work in batches with several piping bags.) Pipe a vertical line on the side of the cake from the base to the top of the cake. Pipe several more lines.

8 Spoon some of the plain butter icing into a fresh piping bag fitted with a basket-weave nozzle. (You will need to work in batches with several piping bags.) Across the second vertical line of chocolate icing, pipe 2 cm/¾ inch horizontal lines of basic butter icing, going across the vertical line at 1 cm/½ inch intervals. You will need about three horizontal lines across each vertical for the smaller cake and three to four for the larger one. Fill in the spaces between the horizontal lines with an alternating row of horizontal lines over the third chocolate vertical. Repeat until the sides of each cake have been covered with the design.

9 ▲ Transfer the larger cake to the thick cake board and the smaller cake to the thin one (you should not be able to see the thin board). Keeping the smaller cake on the thin board, position it on top of the larger cake, to one end. Using a piping bag fitted with a No 4 writing nozzle, pipe beads of chocolate butter icing round the top and bottom edges of each cake. Keep in a cool place overnight. On the day, arrange the chocolate leaves and orchids on the tops of each cake. Keep in a cool place until required.

Chocolate Leaf Wedding Cake

This cake has been designed for lovers of chocolate: a moist chocolate Madeira cake is covered with marzipan and chocolate-flavour sugarpaste. The decorations consist of pretty coral-coloured sugar flowers and assorted chocolate leaves.

INGREDIENTS
Serves 130

30 x 25 cm/12 x 10 inch oval, deep, chocolate-flavour Madeira Cake (see Tip)
25 x 20 cm/10 x 8 inch oval, deep, chocolate-flavour Madeira Cake
120 ml/4 fl oz/½ cup apricot jam, warmed and sieved
2.75 kg/6 lb marzipan
3.25 kg/7 lb/9 x quantity Sugarpaste Icing
450 g/1 lb/4 cups cocoa powder
350 g/12 oz/⅓ quantity Petal Paste
yellow and pink food colourings
175 g/6 oz/1 cup plain chocolate chips, melted
115 g/4 oz/¼ cup white chocolate chips, melted
115 g/4 oz/¼ cup milk chocolate chips, melted
115 g/4 oz/⅙ quantity Royal Icing

MATERIALS AND EQUIPMENT
35 x 30 cm/14 x 12 inch oval silver cake board
25 x 20 cm/10 x 8 inch thin oval silver cake board
flower cutter
30 peach pearl stamens
plunger blossom cutter
flower tape and wire
greaseproof paper piping bag
No 1 writing nozzle
peach ribbon, 2.5 cm/1 inch and 1 cm/½ inch wide
coral ribbon, 5 mm/¼ inch wide
light coral ribbon, 5 mm/¼ inch wide

To make the cakes
For a 30 x 25 cm/12 x 10 inch and a 25 x 20 cm/10 x 8 inch oval cake, use quantities of cake mix suitable for a 30 cm/12 inch and a 25 cm/10 inch round cake. Bake the cakes one at a time and store for up to a week before icing.

1 To level the cakes, cut a slice off the top of each. Invert the cakes on to their cake boards and brush with apricot jam. Cover each cake with marzipan and leave to dry for 12 hours.

2 Divide the sugarpaste icing into three pieces. Knead 115 g/4 oz/½ cup cocoa powder into each piece until the sugarpaste icing is evenly coloured, then knead all the pieces together. Cover the larger cake using half the sugarpaste icing, so there is plenty of icing to manipulate, dusting the surface with plenty of cocoa powder and using cocoa powder on your hands to smooth the surface. Repeat to cover the smaller cake and the large cake board. Store the cakes in boxes in a warm, dry place for up to a week.

3 ▲ To make the sugar flowers, divide the petal paste into three pieces. Using the yellow and pink food colourings, tint one piece pale, one piece medium and one piece dark coral. Make five roses, starting with dark centres and working out to pale petals.

4 Make 25 cut-out flowers of varying shades of coral paste and add stamens.

5 ▲ Make 40 plunger blossom flower sprays with the remaining stamens, wire and tape. Leave all the flowers to dry overnight and store in boxes in a warm, dry place. Using a piece of petal paste, press 30 blossom sprays in position to make an arrangement for the top of the cake.

Tip

To make a 30 x 25 cm/12 x 10 inch chocolate-flavour Madeira Cake, use 550 g/1¼ lb/5½ cups plain flour plus 75 g/3 oz/¼ cup cocoa powder in place of the full amount of plain flour. For a 25 x 20 cm/10 x 8 inch cake, use 450 g/1 lb/4 cups plain flour plus 65 g/2½ oz/½ cup cocoa powder.

6 ▲ To make the chocolate leaves, collect a variety of different-shaped leaves (rose, bay, camelia, fruit) and coat 30 with plain chocolate, 15 with white chocolate and 15 with milk chocolate. Store in a cool place until required, then peel off the leaves and keep the chocolate leaves separate on kitchen paper.

7 The day before the wedding, place the royal icing in a greaseproof paper piping bag fitted with a No 1 writing nozzle. Measure and fit the 2.5 cm/1 inch wide peach ribbon around the larger cake board, securing it at the back with a pin. Fit the 1 cm/½ inch wide peach ribbon around the base of the larger cake. Fix the coral ribbon over the top, and secure with a bead of royal icing. Arrange the cut-out flowers, roses and assorted chocolate leaves around the base of the cake, securing with royal icing.

8 Measure and fit another length of the 1 cm/½ inch wide peach ribbon around the base of the small cake with another coral ribbon over the top, securing with royal icing. Carefully place the cake in position on top of the larger cake so that the backs of the cakes are level.

9 Arrange the sprays of blossom, cut-out flowers and chocolate leaves at intervals around the base of the small cake on the edge of the larger cake. Secure all decorations with royal icing. Carefully remove the top cake. Place the sugar flower arrangement on the top of the cake and arrange the chocolate leaves so they come over the edge. Secure each leaf with royal icing. Using the remaining coral ribbon, the light coral ribbon and fine wire, make some ribbon loops with tails. Press these into the arrangement. Re-box the cakes until the next day, then re-assemble just before the reception.

Classic Wedding Cake

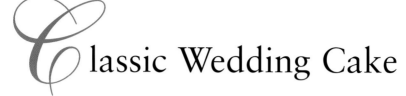

The sharp, classical lines of this royal-iced wedding cake give it a very regal appearance.
This traditional all-white cake has just a hint of peach in the ribbon decoration.

INGREDIENTS
Serves 100
30 cm/12 inch square Rich
Fruit Cake
75 ml/5 tbsp apricot jam, warmed
and sieved
1.8 kg/4 lb marzipan
2 kg/4½ lb/3 x quantity Royal Icing
(for covering)
900 g/2 lb/1⅓ x quantity Royal
Icing made with double-strength egg
albumen (for run-outs)

MATERIALS AND EQUIPMENT
35 cm/14 inch square silver cake
board
a sheet of perspex or glass
baking parchment
greaseproof paper piping bag
white ribbon, 2.5 cm/1 inch wide
peach ribbon, 2 cm/¼ inch and
5 mm/¼ inch wide
No 3 plain writing nozzle
medium star nozzle
fresh 'paper white' flowers
tiny vase

1 Brush the cake with apricot jam and cover with marzipan. Place the cake on the cake board and leave to dry for 12 hours.

2 Make the royal icing for covering the cake. Flat ice the top and sides of the cake with three or four smooth layers of royal icing. Leave the cake to dry overnight, then ice the cake board. Place in a cake box and store in a warm, dry place. Reserve the remaining royal icing for decoration.

3 ▲ Make the royal icing for the run-outs, unless you have plenty left over from the flat icing, in which case add double-strength egg albumen to dilute it. Draw templates for the side and corner pieces, cover with a piece of perspex or glass, and cover with baking parchment. Tape down to secure. As each run-out is piped and filled in, move the perspex or glass along to reveal the template, and repeat the procedure.

4 ▲ Make six corner pieces and six side pieces, allowing for breakages. Pipe in the details when dry.

5 Measure and fit the white and 2 cm/¾ inch peach ribbons around the cake board and sides of the cake, securing with beads of royal icing. Make some loops and bows from 5 mm/¼ inch peach ribbon for the top arrangement.

6 ▲ Carefully release the run-out pieces and half-fill a greaseproof paper piping bag fitted with a No 3 writing nozzle with the reserved royal icing. Pipe a line of icing at one corner. Carefully place a corner run-out in position; press very gently to make sure the run-out is secure. Repeat to attach all the corner pieces and the side pieces.

7 ▲ Pipe a bead edging in between the run-outs on the top edge of the cake. Using a medium-sized star nozzle, pipe a star edging around the base of the cake. Make a pretty arrangement of fresh flowers in a tiny vase to go on top of the cake, and decorate with thin peach ribbons and bows.

*M*idsummer Wedding Cake

This lovely meringue wedding cake is fresh and light, and is ideal for a summer wedding when all the soft fruits are in abundance. Picking your own fruits will add an extra personal touch.

INGREDIENTS
Serves 40
8 size 3 egg whites
5 ml/1 tsp cream of tartar
500 g/1 lb 2 oz/2¼ cups caster sugar
600 ml/1 pint/2½ cups
double cream
300 ml/½ pint/1¼ cups
whipping cream
350 g/12 oz/2 cups redcurrants
350 g/12 oz/2 cups white currants
350 g/12 oz/2 cups raspberries
350 g/12 oz/2 cups fraises des bois
or tiny strawberries
350 g/12 oz/2 cups blueberries
30 ml/2 tbsp Kirsch

MATERIALS AND EQUIPMENT
4 large baking sheets
baking parchment
nylon piping bags
1 cm/½ inch plain and small star
gâteau nozzles
looped white ribbon, 2 cm/
¾ inch wide
looped dark pink ribbon, 1 cm/
½ inch wide
30 cm/12 inch round silver
cake board
8 tiny pink rosebuds
plain dark pink ribbon, 5 mm/
¼ inch wide
plain light pink ribbon, 5 mm/
¼ inch wide
small fresh strawberry leaves

1 Preheat the oven to 110°C/225°F/ Gas ¼. Line two large baking sheets with baking parchment. Draw a 25 cm/ 10 inch circle on one sheet and 18 cm/ 7 inch and 15 cm/6 inch circles on the remaining sheet of paper. Invert the sheets of paper.

2 To make the meringue, whisk 4 egg whites and 2.5 ml/½ tsp cream of tartar until stiff. Gradually whisk in 250 g/9 oz/1 good cup of caster sugar, whisking really well between each addition, until the meringue stands up in stiff peaks. Place the meringue in a large nylon piping bag fitted with a 1 cm/½ inch plain gâteau nozzle.

3 ▲ Pipe a continuous circle of meringue following the marked lines on each circle. Then pipe a coil from the centre to the edge to fill in each round. Pipe leftover meringue into 5 small rounds in between the circles. Bake in the oven for 2–3 hours until the meringue is dry and the paper peels away easily from the base.

4 Meanwhile line two more baking sheets with baking parchment and draw a 23 cm/9 inch, a 10 cm/4 inch and a 5 cm/2 inch circle on one sheet of paper and a 20 cm/8 inch, a 13 cm/5 inch and a 7.5 cm/3 inch circle on the remaining sheet of paper. Invert the two papers.

5 Using the remaining egg whites, cream of tartar and sugar, make the meringue circles following the above instructions. When all the meringues are cold, cut around the paper to separate them. Store them in airtight containers on the paper in a warm, dry place until required.

6 ▲ Measure and fit the white and the wide pink ribbons around the edge of the cake board, securing them with a pin.

7 Place the creams in a bowl and whip until just thick; reserve one-third for piping. Whisk the remaining cream until slightly thicker.

8 ▲ Reserve several stems of red and white currants for decoration and remove the stems and hulls from the remaining fruits. Mix all the fruits together in a large bowl and sprinkle with Kirsch. Add the fruit to the cream and fold in until well blended. Place one-third of the reserved cream in a nylon piping bag fitted with a small star gâteau nozzle.

9 ▲ Place the largest circle of meringue on the cake board and spread evenly with the cream and fruit mixture to give about a 2 cm/¾ inch deep layer. Top with the next size of meringue round and spread with more of the filling. Cover with the next meringue layer and repeat to use all the layers.

10 ▲ Pipe small stars of cream in between the layers to seal in the filling and to decorate the joins. Pipe a swirl of cream on the top and arrange 4 tiny meringue rounds in a circle and one on the top.

11 ▲ Press redcurrants or other fruits into alternate cream stars and 4 tiny rosebuds around the top. Fit 3 dark and 3 light ribbon lengths from the top of the cake to the board. Decorate the board with reserved currants, leaves and rosebuds. Keep in a cold place for 4 hours.

*B*asket-weave Wedding Cake

This wonderful wedding cake can be made in any flavour. The butter icing design is really very easy and looks so special.

INGREDIENTS
Serves 150
1 x 25 cm/10 inch, 1 x 20 cm/8 inch and 1 x 15 cm/6 inch square Madeira Cake
2.75 kg/6 lb/8 x quantity Butter Icing

MATERIALS AND EQUIPMENT
30 cm/12 inch square cake board
20 cm/8 inch thin cake board
15 cm/6 inch thin cake board
12 greaseproof paper piping bags
basket and No 4 writing nozzles
lilac ribbon, 2.5 cm/1 inch wide
deep lilac ribbon, 5 mm/¼ inch wide
30 fresh freesias or other flowers

1 Make and bake the cakes one at a time, allow to cool, wrap in foil and store in a tin for up to a week before decorating. If the cake tops have domed, cut off a slice to level them, then invert the cakes on to their appropriate cake boards.

2 Make the butter icing in three batches. A food processor is worth using to obtain a very light texture and well-mixed icing. Spread each cake evenly with butter icing, dipping the palette knife in hot water for easy spreading. Use a side scraper to smooth the sides and the palette knife to smooth the top. Leave in a cool place to set for at least one hour.

*T*ip

It is quite a good idea to buy two larger thin cake boards to sit the smaller cakes on while they are being decorated, to keep the edges neat. Allow an extra 2.5–5 cm/1–2 inches.

3 Fit a basket-weave nozzle in one greaseproof paper piping bag and a No 4 writing nozzle in a second bag. Fill each with icing and fold down the tops.

4 ▲ Start piping the basket-weave design by piping a line of icing from the plain nozzle onto the corner of the large cake, from the base of the cake to the top. Using the basket-weave nozzle, pipe three horizontal lines across the vertical line, starting at the top of the cake and equally spacing the lines apart. Pipe another vertical line of icing on the edge of the horizontal lines, then pipe three horizontal lines across this between the spaces formed by the previous horizontal lines to form a basket-weave. Pipe all around the side of the cake and neaten the top edge with a shell border, using the basket-weave nozzle. Repeat for the second cake.

5 To decorate the small cake with piping, pipe the top first by starting on the edge with one straight plain line, then pipe across with the basket-weave nozzle, spacing the lines equally apart, about the width of the nozzle. When the top is complete, carry on working the design around the sides, making sure the top and side designs meet. Leave all the cakes overnight in a cold place to set before assembling the cake.

6 Measure and fit the wide and narrow lilac ribbons around the large board, securing with a pin. Use more narrow ribbon to tie eight small bows with long tails. Select the flowers and trim off the stems.

7 ▲ Carefully place the middle cake, still on its board, in position on the base cake. Use a palette knife at the back of the cake to position it. Place the top cake on its board in position, using the palette knife at the back.

8 ▲ Position the bows on the top and base corners of the cake. Place the flowers on each side of each cake, at the corners of the board and in a tiny arrangement on the top. Keep in a cool place; if the weather is warm, position the flowers at the last minute.

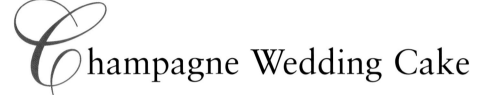

Champagne Wedding Cake

An unusual combination of colours – champagne sugarpaste icing and coffee-coloured ribbons and decorations – gives this cake an elegant, delicate appearance.

INGREDIENTS
Serves 120
1 x 25 cm/10 inch, 1 x 20 cm/8 inch and 1 x 15 cm/6 inch round Rich Fruit Cake
120 ml/4 fl oz/½ cup apricot jam, warmed and sieved
2.5 kg/5½ lb marzipan
3.25 kg/7 lb/9½ x quantity champagne-coloured Sugarpaste Icing
450 g/1 lb/⅓ quantity Royal Icing
575 g/1¼ lb/1 quantity Petal Paste
old gold and dark brown food colourings

MATERIALS AND EQUIPMENT
30 cm/12 inch, 25 cm/10 inch and 20 cm/8 inch round silver cake boards
greaseproof paper piping bags
No 0 and 1 writing nozzles
champagne ribbon, 2 cm/¾ inch wide
greaseproof paper
coffee ribbon, 1 cm/½ inch wide
frill cutter
crimping tool
coffee ribbon, 5 mm/¼ inch wide
champagne ribbon, 5 mm/¼ inch wide
6 champagne-coloured cake pillars
5 acrylic cake skewers
fresh cream or white flowers

1 Place each cake on its cake board and brush with apricot jam. Cover each cake with marzipan.

2 Reserving 900 g/2 lb/2½ x quantity sugarpaste icing for the cake boards, use the remainder to cover each cake smoothly, starting with the largest cake. Leave in boxes overnight to dry in a warm, dry place, without the cake boards. Knead enough sugarpaste icing and trimmings together to cover the cake boards. Replace the cakes on their boards and return to their boxes.

3 Make the royal icing and the petal paste. Tint both these icings with old gold food colouring to obtain the same champagne colour of the sugarpaste icing. Using a greaseproof paper piping bag fitted with a No 1 writing nozzle, half-fill with royal icing. Measure and fit the wide champagne-coloured ribbon around each cake board, securing it with a pin.

4 ▲ To make the templates, measure and fit a band of greaseproof paper the same height around each cake. Fold the largest strip of paper into six equal sections, the next size into five sections and the small band into four sections. Place a plate on the edge of each template so that it comes halfway down the width. Draw around the shape and cut out.

5 ▲ Fit the appropriate template around each cake and mark the scalloped shape with an icing marker or pin. Remove the template. Fit the wide coffee-coloured ribbon around the base of each cake and secure with a bead of royal icing.

6 ▲ Knead the remaining sugarpaste icing into the petal paste and, using a small piece at a time, make the frills one at a time. On the large cake pipe a line of icing following the design and apply the frill, pressing gently on to the cake. Once the first six frills have been fitted, apply the second layer of frills. Use a crimping tool to neaten the join. Repeat on each cake.

7 ▲ Pipe the bead and scroll design following the top edge of the frills and in between the frills at the base. Colour some of the royal icing dark brown and over-pipe the design using a No 0 writing nozzle. Tie 15 coffee-coloured bows and 15 champagne-coloured bows made from the fine ribbons and attach above and below the frills, where they join. Leave the cakes in their boxes to dry.

8 ▲ Just before the wedding, place the cake pillars in position on the large and middle tier cakes. Press the skewers through the pillars into the cake. Mark the skewers level with the top of the pillars and carefully remove. Cut off the excess skewer above the pillars. Reassemble the cakes with the skewers and pillars, carefully placing each cake on top of the other. Decorate with a fresh flower arrangement on top of the cake and insert flowers between the pillars.

Golden Wedding Cake

For 50 years of marriage, you must have a special cake. With a fine lace edging, embossed horseshoes, bells and flowers, this anniversary cake will be exactly right.

INGREDIENTS
Serves 80
23 cm/9 inch hexagonal Rich Fruit Cake (make using quantities for a standard 23 cm/9 inch round cake)
45 ml/3 tbsp apricot jam, warmed and sieved
1.1 kg/2½ lb marzipan
1.4 kg/3 lb/4 x quantity champagne-coloured Sugarpaste Icing
gold petal dust
375 g/13 oz/⅔ quantity Petal Paste
old gold food colouring
450 g/1 lb/⅓ quantity Royal Icing

MATERIALS AND EQUIPMENT
28 cm/11 inch hexagonal gold cake board
gold ribbon, 2.5 cm/1 inch wide
gold ribbon, 2 cm/¾ inch wide
horseshoe-shaped embossing tool
bell mould
foam pad
plunger blossom cutter
flower stamens
wire and tape
sheet of perspex or glass
baking parchment
greaseproof paper piping bag
No 0 writing nozzle
30 gold balls
'50' gold emblem
6 gold paper leaves

1 Brush the cake with apricot jam, place on the cake board and cover with marzipan. Using three-quarters of the sugarpaste icing, cover the cake smoothly.

2 Fit the wide ribbon around the base of the cake and secure with a pin. Measure and fit the narrower ribbon around the cake board, securing with a pin.

3 ▲ Using a horseshoe-shaped embossing tool and gold petal dust, emboss the sides of the cake with five horseshoes on each side and one on each corner. Place the cake in a box and leave in a warm place to dry.

4 Tint the petal paste to a champagne colour using old gold food colouring. Using a well cornfloured bell mould, fill with a small piece of petal paste, pressing into the mould and rubbing the paste against the mould to make the shape. Trim off the paste at the edge and tap to release.

5 Make three bells using two-thirds of the petal paste and leave to dry on a foam pad. Dust with gold petal dust when dry. Reserve just a little petal paste.

6 Using the remaining paste, blossom plunger and stamens, wire and tape, make up nine sprays of blossoms and leave to dry.

7 ▲ Tint the royal icing a champagne colour with old gold food colouring. Draw the lace design on a sheet of paper and cover with a sheet of perspex or glass. Cover this with a piece of baking parchment and secure with tape. Using a greaseproof paper piping bag fitted with a No 0 writing nozzle, half-fill with icing. Follow the lace shapes, piping with fine threads of icing. Move the lace designs and repeat to make 40 pieces, allowing for breakages.

8 Attach the lace pieces to the top edge of the cake with a few beads of icing. Secure gold balls in between, using icing to fix on. Press a small piece of petal paste into each bell shape and secure three sprays of blossoms just inside each bell opening. Arrange the bells in the centre of the cake, tilting them and supporting them on tiny pieces of petal paste.

9 Arrange lengths of 2.5 cm/1 inch gold ribbon in loops, and secure in the centre of the bells, with the '50' emblem on top. Place the leaves in pairs between the bells and secure with royal icing. Leave to set.

Silver Wedding Cake

This may look difficult, but it is really a simple cake to decorate once all the sugar pieces have been made.

INGREDIENTS
Serves 80
*25 cm/10 inch round Rich or Light
Fruit Cake
60 ml/4 tbsp apricot jam, warmed
and sieved
1.1 kg/2½ lb marzipan
1.4 kg/3 lb/2 x quantity Royal Icing
575 g/1¼ lb/1 quantity Petal Paste*

MATERIALS AND EQUIPMENT
*30 cm/12 inch round silver
cake board
white ribbon, 2.5 cm/1 inch wide
silver ribbon, 2.5 cm/1 inch wide
club cocktail cutter
tiny round cutter
greaseproof paper piping bag
No 1 writing nozzle
50 large silver balls
silver ribbon, 5 mm/¼ inch wide
7 silver leaves
'25' silver emblem*

1 Brush the cake with apricot jam and cover with marzipan. Place the cake on the cake board and leave for 12 hours to dry.

2 Flat-ice the top and sides of the cake with three or four smooth layers of royal icing. Leave to dry overnight, then ice the cake board. Place the cake in a box and dry in a warm, dry place. Reserve the remaining royal icing for decorations.

3 Measure and fit the white ribbon around the cake board and the wide silver ribbon around the sides of the cake; secure with a bead of icing.

4 ▲ Roll out small pieces of petal paste one at a time very thinly and, using a club cocktail cutter, cut out the sugar pieces. Using a tiny round cutter, cut four holes out of each sugar piece. Make about 65 cut-out sugar pieces, allowing for breakages, and leave flat to dry overnight.

5 ▲ Arrange 25 cut-out pieces around the top of the cake so that they fit evenly. Using a greaseproof paper piping bag fitted with a No 1 plain writing nozzle, half-fill with royal icing. Pipe small beads of icing on to the top edge of the cake and fit the sugar pieces in position. Repeat at the base of the cake, tilting the pieces upwards slightly. Pipe beads of icing between the sugar pieces and press a silver ball in position on each. Leave the cake in a box to dry overnight.

6 ▲ Measure the narrow silver ribbon to fit around the top edge of the sugar pieces, allowing enough to join. Very carefully thread the ribbon in and out of the sugar pieces, joining the ribbon at the back underneath the sugar pieces.

7 ▲ Arrange a circle of seven sugar pieces in the centre of the cake and secure each one with a bead of icing with seven silver balls in between. Thread a length of narrow ribbon through the sugar pieces as before. Place the silver leaves and '25' emblem in position and secure with icing.

ℬluebird Bon Voyage Cake

This cake is sure to see someone off on an exciting journey in a very special way.

INGREDIENTS
Serves 12–15
450 g/1 lb/⅔ quantity Royal Icing
blue food colouring
800 g/1¾ lb/2⅓ x quantity
Sugarpaste Icing
20 cm/8 inch round Madeira Cake
1 quantity Butter Icing
3 tbsp apricot jam, warmed and
sieved
silver balls

MATERIALS AND EQUIPMENT
25 cm/10 inch round cake board
greaseproof paper piping bags
No 1 writing nozzle
thin pale blue ribbon

1 Make up the royal icing, keeping about two-thirds softer for filling in, and the rest stiffer for the outlines and further piping. Colour the softer icing blue. Cover the icings and leave overnight. Stir before using.

2 ▲ On greaseproof paper, draw the birds several times in two sizes. Tape the paper to a baking sheet, then secure a piece of baking parchment over the top.

3 ▲ Fit a paper piping bag with a No 1 writing nozzle and spoon in some of the stiffer icing for piping the outlines. Pipe over the outlines of the birds with a continuous thread of icing.

4 ▲ Half-fill a fresh paper piping bag with the blue icing. Cut the pointed end off the bag in a straight line. Do not make the opening too large or the icing will flow too quickly. Pipe the icing into the outlines to fill, working from the outlines into the centre. Do not touch the outlines or they may break. To prevent air bubbles, keep the end of the bag in the icing. The icing should look overfilled and rounded, as it will shrink slightly as it dries.

5 Working quickly, brush through the icing to fill in any gaps and to ensure it goes right to the outlines. If any air bubbles appear, smooth them out or burst with a pin. Leave the run-outs on the paper for two days to dry.

6 ▲ Colour two-thirds of the sugar-paste icing blue and leave the rest white. Form the icing into small rolls and place them together on a work surface lightly dusted with icing sugar, alternating the colours. Form into a round and lightly knead together until the icing is marbled. Do not over-knead or you will lose the effect. Cut off about one-quarter of the sugarpaste icing, wrap in clear film and set aside.

7 Cut the cake horizontally into three even layers and sandwich together with the butter icing. Brush with the apricot jam. Roll out the marbled sugarpaste icing and use it to cover the cake. Roll out the reserved sugarpaste icing to a 25 cm/10 inch circle and use it to cover the cake board.

8 ▲ Position the cake to one edge of the board. Fit a piping bag with the writing nozzle and half-fill with the remaining stiffer royal icing. Pipe a wavy line all around the edge of the cake board. Working quickly before the icing dries, position the silver balls so they are evenly spaced in the icing.

9 Remove the birds from the greaseproof paper using a palette knife and secure them to the cake with a little royal icing. Pipe a bead of white icing on each for the eye and place a silver ball in the centre. Drape the ribbon between the birds' beaks, securing with icing.

$\mathcal{P}$ansy Retirement Cake

Sugar-frosted edible flowers make a very effective cake decoration. If pansies are not in season, use other edible flowers such as nasturtiums, roses or tiny daffodils to wish someone a happy retirement. Just co-ordinate the colour of the icing, piping and ribbon with the colour of the flowers.

INGREDIENTS
Serves 20–25
20 cm/8 inch round Light Fruit Cake
3 tbsp apricot jam, warmed and
sieved
675 g/1½ lb marzipan
1.1 kg/2½ lb/1⅔ x quantity
Royal Icing
orange food colouring
1 size 3 egg white, lightly beaten
caster sugar, for frosting
about 7 pansies (orange and purple)

MATERIALS AND EQUIPMENT
25 cm/10 inch round cake board
2 greaseproof paper piping bags
No 19 star and No 1
writing nozzles
2 cm/¾ inch wide purple ribbon
3 mm/⅛ inch wide dark
purple ribbon

3 ▲ To sugar-frost the pansies, have ready a small bowl with the egg white and a plate with caster sugar. Dry the pansies on kitchen paper. If possible, leave some stem attached. Evenly brush the pansies all over on both sides of the petals with the egg white. Holding the flowers by their stems, sprinkle them evenly with the sugar, then shake off any excess. Place the frosted flowers on a flat board or wire rack covered with greaseproof or kitchen paper and leave to dry in a warm place overnight.

5 ▲ Reverse the direction of the scrolls and pipe another row directly underneath the first row.

6 ▲ Pipe another row of scrolls around the bottom of the cake. Spoon the reserved orange icing into a fresh piping bag fitted with a No 1 writing nozzle. Pipe around the outline of the top of each scroll.

7 Using the same piping bag, pipe a row of single dots underneath the top row of reverse scrolls and a double row of dots above the bottom row of scrolls. Arrange the sugar-frosted pansies on top of the cake. Decorate with the ribbons, centring the narrow, darker ribbon on top of the wider one.

1 Brush the cake with the apricot jam. Roll out the marzipan on a work surface lightly dusted with icing sugar and cover the cake. Leave to dry for 12 hours.

2 Secure the cake to the cake board with a little of the royal icing. Colour one-quarter of the royal icing pale orange. Flat ice the cake with three or four layers of smooth icing, allowing each layer to dry overnight before applying the next, using the orange icing for the top and the white for the sides. Set aside a little of both icings in airtight containers, to decorate the cake.

4 ▲ Spoon the reserved white royal icing into a greaseproof paper piping bag fitted with a No 19 star nozzle. Pipe a row of scrolls around the top of the cake.

Retirement Cake

This easily decorated hexagonal cake bears good wishes for a happy retirement. With its plain lines and smart appearance, it would be equally suitable for a man or a woman.

INGREDIENTS
Serves 80
27 cm/10½ inch hexagonal Rich Fruit Cake (make using quantities for a standard 25 cm/10 inch round cake)
45 ml/3 tbsp apricot jam, warmed and sieved
1.1 kg/2½ lb marzipan
1.4 kg/3 lb/4 x quantity Sugarpaste Icing
ice-blue food colouring
115 g/4 oz/¼ quantity Royal Icing

MATERIALS AND EQUIPMENT
30 cm/12 inch hexagonal silver cake board
7.5 cm/3 inch square fluted cutter
No 3 writing nozzle
wooden dowel
light green looped ribbon, 2 cm/ ¼ inch wide
dark green looped ribbon, 5 mm/ ¼ inch wide
light green looped ribbon, 5 mm/ ¼ inch wide
light green ribbon, 3 mm/⅛ inch wide
dark green ribbon, 3 mm/⅛ inch wide
food colouring pen

1 Brush the cake with apricot jam. Cover with marzipan.

2 ▲ Add a few drops of blue food colouring to the sugarpaste icing.

3 ▲ Only partially knead in the colour to create a marbled effect. Cover the cake with the marbled sugarpaste icing and leave overnight to set.

4 ▲ Remove the cake from the board. Press the sugarpaste icing trimmings together and use to cover the cake board. Replace the cake carefully on the cake board and leave to dry. Roll out the remaining trimmings and cut out a square, using the fluted cutter. Make small holes around the border using a No 3 writing nozzle.

5 Leave to dry over a small piece of wooden dowel to shape.

6 ▲ Measure and fit the 2 cm/¾ inch wide light green looped ribbon around the cake board and secure with a pin. Measure and fit the 5 mm/¼ inch wide dark green looped ribbon around the board, base and the top of the cake. Secure with beads of royal icing. Cut six lengths of light and six lengths of dark green 5 mm/¼ inch looped ribbon the depth of the cake. Fit one strip of each coloured ribbon 5 cm/2 inches in from one corner on each side of the cake. Secure with beads of icing behind the bands of ribbon. Attach fine ribbon bows to the side ribbons.

7 Cut two strips of each ribbon to fit parallel across the top of the cake, leaving a space in the centre. Secure with beads of royal icing.

8 Using a food colouring pen, write the message or name on the plaque and place on the cake. Attach two bows to the sugar plaque. Thread the fine dark green ribbon in and out of the plaque and secure the ends underneath with icing. Attach fine ribbon bows to the top of the cake with beads of icing.

Cakes for Entertaining

*For the host eager to create the right impression, this
chapter contains cakes that cannot fail to win over even the
most demanding of social gatherings. Featuring sumptuous
desserts for dinner parties, from cappuccino cakes to
luxurious white chocolate cheesecakes, these recipes will
guarantee a spectacular finale to any meal.*

Chocolate Chestnut Roulade

A traditional version of the classic Bûche de Nöel, the famous and delicious French Christmas gâteau.

INGREDIENTS
Serves 6–8
225 g/8 oz plain chocolate
50 g/2 oz white chocolate
4 size 3 eggs, separated
114 g/4 oz/¹/₂ cup caster sugar, plus extra for dredging

For the Chestnut Filling
150 ml/¹/₄ pint/²/₃ cup double cream
1 x 225 g/8 oz can chestnut purée
4–5 tbsp icing sugar, plus extra for dredging
1–2 tbsp brandy

1 Preheat the oven to 180°C/350°F/ Gas 4. Grease a 23 × 33 cm/9 × 13 inch Swiss roll tin, line with greaseproof paper and grease the paper.

2 Place 50 g/2 oz of the plain chocolate and the white chocolate in two bowls and set over saucepans of hot water. Stir until melted.

3 ▲ Pour the plain chocolate on to a plastic chopping board and spread out evenly. When just set, do the same with the white chocolate. Leave to set.

4 To make the chocolate curls, hold a long, sharp knife at a 45° angle to the chocolate and push it along the chocolate, turning the knife in a circular motion. Carefully place the plain and white chocolate curls on a baking sheet lined with greaseproof paper and set aside until needed.

5 ▲ Place the remaining plain chocolate in another bowl set over a saucepan of hot water and stir until melted. Set aside. Place the egg yolks and caster sugar in a mixing bowl and beat with an electric mixer until thick and pale. Stir in the chocolate.

6 Whisk the egg whites in a clean dry bowl, until they hold stiff peaks. Fold into the chocolate mixture and then turn into the prepared tin. Bake in the centre of the oven for 15–20 minutes, or until risen and firm. Place on a wire rack, cover with a just-damp cloth and leave to cool completely.

7 Place a sheet of greaseproof paper on the work surface and sprinkle with a little caster sugar. Turn the roulade out on to the greaseproof paper. Peel away the lining paper and trim the edges of the roulade. Cover again with a just-damp cloth.

8 To make the filling, whip the double cream in a mixing bowl, until it holds soft peaks.

9 ▲ Place the chestnut purée and icing sugar in a clean bowl. Add the brandy and beat until smooth and evenly combined, then fold in the whipped cream.

10 ▲ Spread the mixture over the roulade, leaving a little border at the top edge. Roll up the roulade, using the greaseproof paper to help and transfer it to a serving plate. Top with the chocolate curls and sprinkle with sifted icing sugar, to serve.

Chocolate Gâteau Terrine

A spectacular finale to a special-occasion meal.
You'll find this is well worth the time and effort to make.

INGREDIENTS
Serves 10–12
115 g/4 oz/¹/₂ cup butter, softened
few drops of vanilla essence
115 g/4 oz/¹/₂ cup caster sugar
2 size 3 eggs
115 g/4 oz/1 cup self-raising flour,
sifted
50 ml/2 fl oz/¹/₄ cup milk
25 g/1 oz/¹/₂ cup desiccated
coconut, to decorate
fresh bud roses, or other flowers, to
decorate

For the Light Chocolate Filling
115 g/4 oz/¹/₂ cup butter, softened
2 tbsp icing sugar, sifted
75 g/3 oz/3 squares plain chocolate,
melted
225 ml/8 fl oz/1 cup double cream,
lightly whipped

For the Dark Chocolate Filling
115 g/4 oz/4 squares plain
chocolate, chopped
115 g/4 oz/¹/₂ cup butter
2 size 3 eggs
2 tbsp caster sugar
225 ml/8 fl oz/1 cup double cream,
lightly whipped
50 g/2 oz/¹/₂ cup cocoa powder
1 tbsp dark rum (optional)
2 tbsp gelatine powder dissolved in
2 tbsp hot water

For the White Chocolate Topping
225 g/8 oz/8 squares white
chocolate
115 g/4 oz/¹/₂ cup butter

1 Preheat the oven to 180°C/350°F/ Gas 4. Grease a 900 g/2 lb loaf tin, line the base and sides with greaseproof paper and grease the paper.

2 To make the cake, place the butter, vanilla essence and sugar in a mixing bowl and beat until light and fluffy. Add the eggs, one at a time, beating well after each addition. Sift the flour again and fold it and the milk into the cake mixture.

3 Transfer the cake mixture to the prepared tin and bake in the centre of the oven for 25–30 minutes or until a skewer inserted into the centre of the cake comes out clean. Leave the cake in the tin for about 5 minutes, then turn out on to a wire rack, peel off the lining paper and leave to cool completely.

4 ▲ To make the light chocolate filling, place the butter and icing sugar in a mixing bowl and beat until creamy. Add the chocolate and cream until evenly blended. Cover and set aside in the refrigerator, until required.

5 To make the dark chocolate filling, place the chocolate and butter in a small saucepan and heat very gently, stirring frequently, until melted. Set aside to cool. Place the eggs and sugar in a bowl and beat with an electric mixer until thick and frothy. Fold in the chocolate mixture, cream, cocoa, rum and dissolved gelatine until evenly blended.

6 ▲ To assemble the terrine, wash and dry the loaf tin, then line with clear film, allowing plenty of film to hang over the edges. Using a long serrated knife, cut the cake horizontally into three even layers.

7 ▲ Spread two of the layers with the light chocolate filling, then place one of these layers, filling side up, in the base of the tin.

8 Cover with half of the dark chocolate filling, then chill for about 10 minutes. Place the second light chocolate-topped layer in the terrine, filling side up. Spread over the remaining dark chocolate filling, then chill for another 10 minutes. Top with the remaining layer of cake and chill the terrine again for about 10 minutes.

9 To make the white chocolate topping, place the chocolate and butter in a small saucepan and heat very gently, stirring frequently, until melted and well blended. Allow to cool slightly.

10 To finish the terrine, turn it out on to a wire rack, removing the clear film. Trim the edges with a long, sharp knife, then pour over the white chocolate topping, spreading it evenly over the sides. Sprinkle the coconut over the top and sides. Allow to set before transferring the terrine to a serving plate and decorating with fresh bud roses.

Chocolate and Fresh Cherry Gâteau

The addition of spices to this attractive gâteau adds an exotic kick. A compôte of fresh cherries fills the hollowed-out centre, and the cake is coated with a rich chocolate icing. With the dipped cherries and chocolate-coated leaves, this is a cake for a special occasion.

INGREDIENTS
Serves 8
115 g/4 oz/½ cup butter
150 g/5 oz/⅔ cup caster sugar
3 size 3 eggs, lightly beaten
175 g/6 oz/1 cup plain chocolate chips, melted
60 ml/4 tbsp Kirsch
150 g/5 oz/1¼ cups self-raising flour
5 ml/1 tsp ground cinnamon
2.5 ml/½ tsp ground cloves
350 g/12 oz/2 cups fresh cherries, stoned and halved
45 ml/3 tbsp Morello cherry jam
5 ml/1 tsp lemon juice

For the Frosting
115 g/4 oz/⅔ cup plain chocolate chips
50 g/2 oz/4 tbsp butter
60 ml/4 tbsp double cream

To Decorate
75 g/3 oz/½ cup white chocolate chips
14–18 fresh cherries
a few rose leaves, washed and dried

1 Preheat the oven to 160°C/325°F/ Gas 3. Grease a 20 cm/8 inch springform cake tin, line the base with greaseproof paper and grease the paper. Dust the inside of the tin with flour.

2 Cream the butter and 115 g/4 oz/ ½ cup sugar together, until pale and light. Gradually beat in the eggs until incorporated. Stir in the melted chocolate and 30 ml/2 tbsp of the Kirsch.

3 Sift the flour and spices together and fold into the creamed mixture. Transfer to the prepared tin, smooth the surface and bake for 55–60 minutes or until a skewer inserted into the centre of the cake comes out clean. Remove from the oven and cool.

4 ▲ Meanwhile, prepare the filling. Place the halved cherries, remaining Kirsch and sugar in a small pan. Heat gently to dissolve the sugar, bring to the boil, cover and simmer for 10 minutes. Remove the lid and simmer for a further 10 minutes, until the mixture is thick and syrupy. Leave to cool.

5 ▲ Cut the cake in half. Using a saucer as a template, cut out a circle, about 1 cm/½ inch deep, from the centre of the bottom half. Crumble into the cherry syrup mixture, stirring well, to form a thick paste.

6 ▲ Use the mixture to fill the hollowed section of cake, smoothing over the surface. Cover with the top half of the cake.

7 Heat the jam and lemon juice and boil for 1 minute. Strain through a fine sieve and brush all over the cake.

8 To make the frosting, heat the chocolate, butter and cream in a small pan, until melted. Cool slightly, until the mixture starts to thicken. In one fluid motion, pour over the glazed cake, completely covering the top and sides. Smooth over the sides with a palette knife, if necessary. Leave to set in a cool place.

9 ▲ Melt the white chocolate chips in a small bowl over a pan of gently simmering water. Dip each cherry halfway into the white chocolate, so that it is half-white and half-red, and leave to set on baking parchment. Using a paintbrush, coat the underside of the rose leaves with a thick layer of the remaining chocolate. Leave to set on baking parchment.

10 ▲ When set, carefully peel away the leaves from the chocolate coating. Decorate the top of the cake with an arrangement of cherries and leaves.

White Chocolate Mousse Strawberry Cake

Layers of rich white chocolate mousse are enhanced by fresh strawberries and strawberry liqueur in this tempting gâteau.

INGREDIENTS

Serves 10

115 g/4 oz white chocolate, chopped
120 ml/4 fl oz/½ cup double cream
120 ml/4 fl oz/½ cup milk
15 ml/1 tbsp rum or vanilla essence
115 g/4 oz/½ cup butter, softened
175 g/6 oz/¾ cup granulated sugar
3 size 3 eggs
225 g/8 oz/2 cups plain flour
5 ml/1 tsp baking powder
pinch of salt
675 g/1½ lb fresh strawberries,
sliced, plus extra to decorate
750 ml/1¼ pints/3 cups whipping
cream
30 ml/2 tbsp rum or strawberry-
flavoured liqueur

For the Mousse Filling

250 g/9 oz white chocolate, chopped
350 ml/12 fl oz/1½ cups whipping or
double cream
30 ml/2 tbsp rum or strawberry-
flavoured liqueur

1 ▲ Preheat the oven to 180°C/350°F/ Gas 4. Grease two deep 23 cm/ 9 inch cake tins. Line the bases of the tins with baking parchment. Melt the chocolate and double cream in a double boiler over a low heat, stirring until smooth. Stir in the milk and rum or vanilla essence; set aside to cool.

2 ▲ In a large mixing bowl, beat the butter and sugar for 3–5 minutes until light and creamy, scraping the sides of the bowl occasionally. Add the eggs one at a time, beating well after each addition. In a small bowl, sift together the flour, baking powder and salt. Alternately add the flour and melted chocolate to the egg mixture, until just blended. Divide the mixture between the tins and spread evenly.

3 ▲ Bake for 20–25 minutes, or until a skewer inserted into the centre of one of the cakes comes out clean. Cool in the tins for 10 minutes. Turn the cakes out on to a wire rack, peel off the paper and leave to cool completely.

4 Prepare the filling. Melt the chocolate in the cream over a low heat until smooth, stirring frequently. Stir in the rum or liqueur and pour into a bowl. Chill until the mixture is just set. With a wire whisk, whip lightly until the mixture is mousse-like.

5 ▲ Slice both cake layers in half, making four layers. Place one layer on a plate and spread with one-third of the mousse. Arrange about one-third of the sliced strawberries over the mousse. Add two more layers in the same way, then cover with the last cake layer.

6 Whip the cream with the rum or liqueur. Spread about half the whipped cream over the top and sides of the cake. Use the remaining cream to pipe scrolls on top of the cake. Fill in the rest of the cake with the remaining strawberries.

Chocolate Cappuccino Cake

If you prefer, this cake can be left whole and rolled roulade-style, or the mixture can be baked in two 23 cm/9 inch tins and layered to make a round cake.

INGREDIENTS
Serves 8–10

175 g/6 oz plain chocolate, chopped
10 ml/2 tsp instant espresso powder
(or 15 ml/1 tbsp instant coffee
powder) dissolved in 45 ml/
3 tbsp boiling water
6 size 3 eggs, separated
150 g/5 oz/²/₃ cup granulated sugar
pinch of cream of tartar
cocoa for sifting

For the Coffee Cream Filling
175 ml/6 fl oz/³/₄ cup whipping or
double cream
25 g/1 oz/2 tbsp granulated sugar
225 g/8 oz/1 cup mascarpone or
cream cheese, softened
30 ml/2 tbsp coffee-flavour liqueur
25 g/1 oz plain chocolate, grated

For the Coffee Buttercream
4 size 3 egg yolks, at
room temperature
70 ml/5 tbsp light golden syrup
50 g/2 oz/¼ cup granulated sugar
225 g/8 oz/1 cup butter, cut into
small pieces and softened
15 ml/1 tbsp instant espresso
powder dissolved in 5–10 ml/
1–2 tsp boiling water
15–30 ml/1–2 tbsp coffee-
flavour liqueur

To Decorate
chocolate coffee beans

1 Preheat the oven to 180°C/350°F/
Gas 4. Grease a 40 x 27 cm/16 x
10½ inch baking tray. Line with baking
parchment, leaving a 5 cm/2 inch
overhang at each narrow end. Grease
the parchment. In the top of a double
boiler, over a low heat, heat the
chocolate and dissolved coffee powder
until melted and smooth, stirring
frequently. Set aside.

2 ▲ In a bowl with an electric mixer,
beat the egg yolks and sugar for
3–5 minutes, until thick and light-
coloured. Reduce speed to low and beat
in the chocolate mixture until blended.

3 ▲ In a large bowl with an electric
mixer with cleaned beaters, beat the
egg whites and cream of tartar until
stiff peaks begin to form. Do not
overbeat. Stir a spoonful of whites into
the chocolate mixture to lighten it, then
fold in the remaining whites.

4 Pour the batter into the prepared tin,
spreading into the corners and
smoothing the top evenly. Bake for
12–15 minutes until the cake springs
back when touched lightly with a
fingertip. Sprinkle a clean dish towel with
cocoa to cover and turn the cake out on
to the towel. Peel off the paper and cool.

5 ▲ Prepare the filling. In a medium
bowl with an electric mixer, whip
the cream and sugar until soft peaks
form. In another bowl, beat the
mascarpone or cream cheese and
liqueur until light and smooth. Stir in
the grated chocolate and fold in the
whipped cream. Cover and refrigerate
until ready for use.

6 ▲ Prepare the buttercream. In a
bowl with an electric mixer on high
speed, beat the yolks for 5–6 minutes
until thick and pale-coloured. In a
saucepan over medium heat, cook the
syrup and sugar until the mixture boils,
stirring constantly.

7 With the mixer on medium-low speed, slowly pour the hot syrup over the beaten yolks in a slow stream. Continue beating until the mixture feels cool, 5–6 minutes. Beat in the butter a few pieces at a time until the mixture is smooth. Beat in the dissolved coffee and liqueur. Refrigerate until ready to use, but bring to room temperature before spreading.

Tip

If you don't have any instant espresso powder, any instant coffee powder can be used for this cake.

8 ▲ Assemble the cake. With a serrated knife, trim off any crisp edges of cake. Cut the cake crosswise into three equal strips. Place one cake strip on a cake plate and spread with half the coffee cream filling. Cover with a second cake strip and the remaining filling. Top with the last cake strip.

9 ▲ Spoon about one third of the coffee buttercream into a small piping bag fitted with a small star nozzle. Spread the remaining buttercream on the top and sides of the cake. Pipe a lattice or scroll design on top and around the edges of the cake and decorate with chocolate coffee beans. Refrigerate the cake if you are not serving it immediately, but allow to stand at room temperature for 30 minutes before serving.

Gorgeous Chocolate Cake

*This recipe will definitely make you famous.
Make sure you serve it with paper and pens, as everyone will want
to take down the recipe.*

INGREDIENTS
Serves 8–10
175 g/6 oz/¾ cup butter, softened
115 g/4 oz/½ cup caster sugar
250 g/9 oz/9 squares plain
chocolate, melted
200 g/7 oz/2⅓ cups ground
almonds
4 size 3 eggs, separated
115 g/4 oz/4 squares white
chocolate, melted, to decorate

4 ▲ Place the remaining butter and remaining melted plain chocolate in a saucepan. Heat very gently, stirring constantly, until melted. Pour over the cake, allowing the topping to coat the sides too. Leave to set for at least an hour. To decorate, fill a piping bag with the melted white chocolate and snip the end. Drizzle all around the edges to make a double border. Use any remaining chocolate to make leaves (see Trailing Orchid Wedding cake, steps 2 and 3).

Tip

Place a large sheet of greaseproof paper or a baking sheet under the wire rack before pouring the chocolate topping over the cake. This will catch all the drips and keep the work surface clean.

3 ▲ Whisk the egg whites in another clean, dry bowl until stiff. Fold them into the chocolate mixture, then transfer to the prepared tin and smooth the surface. Bake for 50–55 minutes or until a skewer inserted into the centre of the cake comes out clean. Leave the cake in the tin for about 5 minutes, then turn out on to a wire rack, peel off the lining paper and leave to cool completely.

1 Preheat the oven to 180°C/350°F/ Gas 4. Grease a deep 21 cm/8½ inch springform cake tin, then line the base with greaseproof paper and grease the paper.

2 ▲ Place 115 g/4 oz/½ cup of the butter and all the sugar in a mixing bowl and beat until light and fluffy. Add two thirds of the plain chocolate, the ground almonds and the egg yolks and beat until evenly blended.

French Chocolate Cake

This very dense chocolate cake can be made up to three days before serving, but decorate it with icing sugar on the day it is to be served.

INGREDIENTS
Serves 10
250 g/9 oz dark chocolate, chopped
225 g/8 oz/1 cup butter, cut into pieces
90 g/3½ oz/½ cup granulated sugar
30 ml/2 tbsp brandy or orange-flavour liqueur
5 size 3 eggs
15 ml/1 tbsp plain flour
icing sugar for dusting
whipped or soured cream, for serving

1 Preheat the oven to 180°C/350°F/ Gas 4. Generously grease a 23 cm/ 9 inch springform tin. Line the bottom with baking parchment and grease the parchment. Wrap the outside of the tin in foil to prevent water seeping into the cake. In a saucepan over a low heat, melt the chocolate, butter and sugar, stirring frequently until smooth; cool slightly. Stir in the liqueur. In a large mixing bowl with an electric mixer, beat the eggs lightly. Beat in the flour then slowly beat in the chocolate mixture until well blended. Pour into the tin.

2 Place the tin in a large roasting tin and pour boiling water into the roasting tin, to come 2 cm/¾ inch up the side of the springform tin. Bake for 25–30 minutes until the edge of the cake is set, but the centre is still soft. Remove the tin from the water bath and remove the foil. Cool on a wire rack completely (the cake will sink in the centre and may crack).

3 ▲ Remove the side of the springform tin and turn the cake on to a wire rack. Remove the springform tin bottom and peel off the lining paper, so the bottom of the cake becomes the top.

4 ▲ Cut six to eight strips of baking parchment 2.5 cm/1 inch wide and place randomly over the cake, or make a lattice-style pattern if you wish. Dust the cake with icing sugar then carefully remove the paper. Serve with cream.

Death by Chocolate

There are many versions of this irresistible cake; here is a very rich one which is ideal for a large party, and guarantees there won't be a single slice left at the end of the evening.

INGREDIENTS
Serves 18–20
200 g/7 oz plain chocolate, chopped
115 g/4 oz/½ cup butter, diced
150 ml/¼ pint/⅔ cup water
275 g/10 oz/1⅓ cups granulated sugar
10 ml/2 tsp vanilla essence
2 size 3 eggs, separated
175 ml/6 fl oz/¾ cup soured cream
350 g/12 oz/3 cups plain flour
10 ml/2 tsp baking powder
5 ml/1 tsp bicarbonate of soda

For the Filling and Glaze
600 g/1 lb 5 oz plain chocolate, chopped
225 g/8 oz/1 cup butter
115 ml/8 tbsp brandy
215 g/7½ oz/¼ cup seedless raspberry jam
250 ml/8 fl oz/1 cup double cream

To Decorate
chocolate curls
raspberries
icing sugar, sifted, for dusting

1 Preheat the oven to 180°C/350°F/ Gas 4. Grease a 25 cm/10 inch springform tin and line the base with baking parchment. In a saucepan over a low heat, melt the chocolate, butter and water, stirring.

2 ▲ Remove from the heat, beat in the sugar and vanilla and cool. Beat the egg yolks lightly, then beat into the chocolate mixture; gently fold in the soured cream. Sift over the flour, baking powder and bicarbonate of soda, then fold in. Whisk the egg whites until stiff, then fold gently into the chocolate mixture.

3 ▲ Pour the mixture into the tin and bake for 50–60 minutes until the cake begins to shrink away from the side of the tin. Put the tin on a wire rack to cool for 10 minutes (the cake may sink in the centre; this is normal). Run a sharp knife around the edge of the cake, then remove the side of the tin. Invert the cake on the rack, remove the base of the tin and leave to cool completely. Wash and dry the tin.

4 ▲ Prepare the filling and glaze. Melt 400 g/14 oz of the chocolate with the butter and 60 ml/4 tbsp of the brandy. Cool, then chill until thickened. Cut the cake horizontally into three equal layers. Heat the raspberry jam and 15 ml/1 tbsp brandy, stirring until melted and smooth. Spread a thin layer over each cake layer and allow to set.

5 ▲ When the filling is spreadable, place the bottom cake layer back in the tin. Spread with half the filling and top with the second layer of cake, then spread with the remaining filling; top with the final cake layer, jam side down. Gently press the layers together, cover and chill for 4–6 hours or overnight.

6 ▲ Run a knife around the edge of the cake, then remove the side of the tin. Set the cake on a wire rack over a baking sheet. Bring the cream to the boil. Remove from the heat and add the remaining chocolate, stirring until melted. Stir in the remaining brandy and strain into a bowl. Leave to cool.

7 ▲ Whisk the chocolate mixture until it begins to hold its shape. Smooth it over the cake and leave to set. Slide the cake on to a serving plate and decorate with chocolate curls and raspberries. Dust with icing sugar. Serve at room temperature.

Tip

It's easy to make your own chocolate curls: bring a thick bar of chocolate to room temperature and pull a vegetable peeler firmly across the edge of the chocolate. Use a skewer or toothpick to transfer the curls to the cake, as fingers will melt them.

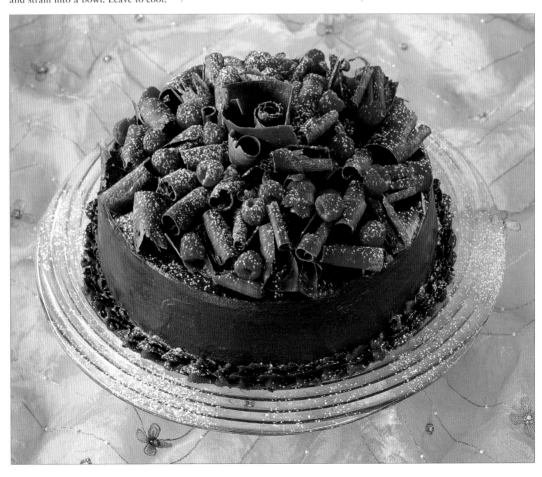

Luxury White Chocolate Cheesecake

Despite its pure, creamy-white looks, this is a wickedly indulgent cake. No white chocolate lover will be able to refuse a piece.

Ingredients
Serves 16–20
150 g/5 oz digestive biscuits
75 g/3 oz/½ cup blanched hazelnuts, toasted
50 g/2 oz/4 tbsp butter, melted
2.5 ml/½ tsp ground cinnamon

For the Filling
350 g/12 oz white chocolate, chopped
120 ml/4 fl oz/½ cup whipping or double cream
675 g/1½ lb/3 cups cream cheese, softened
50 g/2 oz/¼ cup granulated sugar
4 size 3 eggs
30 ml/2 tbsp hazelnut-flavour liqueur or 15 ml/1 tbsp vanilla essence

For the Topping
450 ml/15 fl oz/1¾ cup soured cream
50 g/2 oz/¼ cup granulated sugar
15 ml/1 tbsp hazelnut-flavour liqueur or 5 ml/1 tsp vanilla essence

To Decorate
white chocolate curls
cocoa for dusting (optional)

1 Preheat the oven to 180°C/350°F/ Gas 4. Lightly grease a 23 cm/9 inch springform tin. In a food processor, process the biscuits and hazelnuts until fine crumbs form. Pour in the butter and cinnamon. Process just until blended; do not over-mix.

2 Using the back of a spoon, press the mixture over the bottom and side of the tin to within 1 cm/½ inch of the top. Bake for 5–7 minutes, until just set. Place on a wire rack to cool. Lower the oven temperature to 150°C/300°F/ Gas 2.

3 ▲ Prepare the filling. In a small saucepan over a low heat, melt the white chocolate and cream until smooth, stirring frequently. Set aside to cool.

4 ▲ In a large bowl, beat the cream cheese and sugar with an electric mixer until smooth. Add the eggs one at a time, beating well after each addition and scraping the bowl occasionally. Slowly beat in the white chocolate mixture and liqueur or vanilla essence.

5 Pour into the baked crust. Place the tin on a baking sheet. Bake for 45–55 minutes, or until the edge of the cake is firm but the centre is still slightly soft; do not allow to brown. Leave on a wire rack while preparing the topping. Increase the oven temperature to 200°C/400°F/Gas 6.

6 ▲ Prepare the topping. In a small bowl whisk the soured cream, sugar and liqueur or vanilla. Pour over the cheesecake, spreading evenly, and return to the oven. Bake for a further 5–7 minutes. Turn off the oven, but do not open the door for 1 hour.

9 If you like, slide a sharp knife under the crust to separate the cake from the bottom. Alternatively, leave the bottom of the tin in place to avoid breaking the crust and serve the cake from it.

7 ▲ Place the cake, in the tin, on a wire rack to cool to room temperature. Run a sharp knife around the edge of the cake to separate it from the tin; this helps prevent cracking. Cool completely then refrigerate, loosely covered, overnight.

8 ▲ Decorate the top of the cake with chocolate curls and dust lightly with cocoa.

Tip

To ensure an even crust, use a metal spoon to press the crumbs to the bottom and side of the tin.

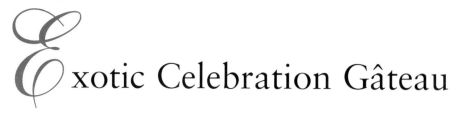

Exotic Celebration Gâteau

Use any tropical fruits you can find to make a spectacular display of colours and tastes.

INGREDIENTS
Serves 8–10
175 g/6 oz/¾ cup butter, softened
175 g/6 oz/¾ cup caster sugar
3 size 3 eggs, beaten
250 g/9 oz/2¼ cups self-raising flour
2–3 tbsp milk
6–8 tbsp light rum
425 ml/¾ pt/scant 2 cups double cream
25 g/1 oz/¼ cup icing sugar, sifted

To Decorate
450 g/1 lb mixed fresh exotic and soft fruits, such as figs, redcurrants, star fruit, kiwi fruit, etc.
6 tbsp apricot jam, warmed and sieved
2 tbsp warm water
sifted icing sugar

1 Preheat the oven to 190°C/375°F/ Gas 5. Grease and flour a deep 20 cm/8 inch ring mould.

2 ▲ Place the butter and sugar in a mixing bowl and beat until light and fluffy. Gradually beat in the eggs, then fold in the flour with the milk.

3 Spoon the cake mixture into the prepared tin and smooth the surface. Bake in the centre of the oven for about 45 minutes, or until a skewer inserted into the centre of the cake comes out clean. Turn out on to a wire rack and leave to cool completely.

4 ▲ Place the cake on a serving plate, then use a thin skewer to make holes randomly over the cake. Drizzle over the rum and allow to soak in.

5 ▲ Place the cream and icing sugar in a mixing bowl and beat with an electric mixer until the mixture holds soft peaks. Spread all over the top and sides of the cake.

6 Arrange the fruits attractively in the hollow centre of the cake, allowing the fruits to overhang the edges a little. Mix together the apricot jam and water, then use to brush evenly over the fruit. Sift over a little icing sugar, to decorate.

Chocolate Pecan Torte

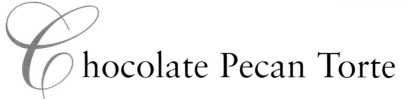

This torte uses finely ground nuts instead of flour. Toast, then cool the nuts before grinding finely in a food processor. Do not over-grind the nuts, as the oils will form a paste.

INGREDIENTS
Serves 16
200 g/7 oz dark or plain chocolate,
chopped
150 g/5 oz/⅔ cup butter, cut
into pieces
4 size 3 eggs
90 g/3½ oz/scant ½ cup caster sugar
10 ml/2 tsp vanilla essence
115 g/4 oz/1 cup ground pecans,
toasted
10 ml/2 tsp ground cinnamon

For the Chocolate Honey Glaze
115 g/4 oz dark or plain chocolate,
chopped
50 g/2 oz/4 tbsp butter, cut
into pieces
30 ml/2 tbsp honey
pinch of ground cinnamon

To Decorate
24 toasted pecan halves

3 ▲ Prepare the glaze. In a small saucepan over a low heat, melt the chocolate, butter, honey and cinnamon, stirring until smooth; remove from the heat. Carefully dip the toasted pecan halves halfway into the glaze and place on a baking parchment-lined baking sheet, until set. The glaze will have thickened slightly.

4 ▲ Remove the side from the springform tin and invert the cake on to a wire rack. Remove the tin bottom and lining paper. Pour the thickened glaze over the cake, tilting the rack slightly to spread the glaze. Use a palette knife to smooth the sides. Arrange the nuts around the outside edge of the torte and allow the glaze to set.

1 Preheat the oven to 180°C/350°F/ Gas 4. Grease a 20 cm/8 inch springform tin; line the bottom with baking parchment then grease the parchment. Wrap the outside of the tin with foil to prevent water seeping in. In a saucepan over a low heat, melt the chocolate and butter, stirring until smooth. Remove from the heat. In a mixing bowl, beat the eggs, sugar and vanilla with an electric mixer until frothy. Stir in the melted chocolate, toasted ground nuts and cinnamon. Pour into the prepared tin.

2 Place the foil-wrapped tin in a large roasting tin and pour boiling water into the roasting tin, to come 2 cm/ ¼ inch up the side of the springform tin. Bake for 25–30 minutes until the edge of the cake is set, but the centre is soft. Remove from the water bath and remove the foil. Cool on a wire rack.

Jewel Cake

*This pretty tea-time cake is excellent
served as an afternoon treat with tea or coffee.*

INGREDIENTS
Serves 10–15
115 g/4 oz/¹/₂ cup mixed coloured
glacé cherries, halved, washed and
dried
50 g/2 oz/¹/₄ cup stem ginger in
syrup, chopped, washed and dried
50 g/2 oz/¹/₃ cup chopped mixed
peel
115 g/4 oz/1 cup self-raising flour
75 g/3 oz/³/₄ cup plain flour
25 g/1 oz/3 tbsp cornflour
175 g/6 oz/³/₄ cup butter
175 g/6 oz/³/₄ cup caster sugar
3 size 3 eggs
finely grated zest of 1 orange

To Decorate
175 g/6 oz/1¹/₂ cups icing sugar,
sifted
2–3 tbsp freshly squeezed orange
juice
50 g/2 oz/¹/₄ cup mixed coloured
glacé cherries, chopped
25 g/1 oz/2¹/₂ tbsp mixed peel,
chopped

Tip

To ring the changes, bake the cake
in a 18 cm/7 inch round cake tin, if
wished. Use the same quantities of
ingredients and follow the method
as described here. Decorate with
crystallized citrus fruits instead of
the glacé cherries and mixed peel.

1 Preheat the oven to 180°C/350°F/
Gas 4. Grease a 900 g/2 lb loaf tin,
line the base and sides with greaseproof
paper and grease the paper.

2 ▲ Place the cherries, stem ginger
and mixed peel in a plastic bag with
25 g/1 oz/1 tbsp of the self-raising
flour and shake to coat evenly. Sift
the remaining flours and cornflour
into a small bowl.

3 ▲ Place the butter and sugar in a
mixing bowl and beat until light
and fluffy. Beat in the eggs, one at a
time, until evenly blended. Fold in the
sifted flours with the orange zest, then
stir in the dried fruit.

4 ▲ Transfer the cake mixture to the
prepared tin and bake in the centre
of the oven for about 1¹/₄ hours, or until
a skewer inserted into the centre of the
cake comes out clean. Leave the cake in
the tin for about 5 minutes, then turn
out on to a wire rack, peel off the lining
paper and leave to cool completely.

5 ▲ To decorate the cake, place the
icing sugar in a mixing bowl. Stir in
the orange juice and mix until smooth.
Drizzle the icing over the cake. Mix
together the chopped glacé cherries and
mixed peel in a small bowl, then use to
decorate the cake. Allow the icing to set
before serving.

Fresh Fruit Genoese

*This Italian classic, 'Genovese con Panne e Frutta',
can be made with any type of soft fresh fruit.*

INGREDIENTS
Serves 8–10
For the Sponge
175 g/6 oz/1½ cups plain flour,
sifted
pinch of salt
4 size 3 eggs
115 g/4 oz/½ cup caster sugar
6 tbsp orange-flavoured liqueur

For the Filling and Topping
600 ml/1 pint/2½ cups double
cream
4 tbsp vanilla sugar
450 g/1 lb fresh soft fruit, such as
raspberries, blueberries, cherries,
etc.
150 g/5 oz/1¼ cups shelled pistachio
nuts, finely chopped
4 tbsp apricot jam, warmed and
sieved, to glaze

Tip

To save time and money, use shop-bought chopped mixed nuts to coat the sides of the gâteau instead of pistachios.

1 Preheat the oven to 180°C/350°F/ Gas 4. Grease a 21 cm/8½ inch round springform cake tin, line the base with greaseproof paper and grease the paper.

2 ▲ Sift the flour and salt together three times, then set aside.

3 Place the eggs and sugar in a mixing bowl and beat with an electric mixer for about 10 minutes or until thick and pale.

4 ▲ Sift the reserved flour mixture into the mixing bowl, then fold in very gently. Transfer the cake mixture to the prepared tin. Bake in the centre of the oven for 30–35 minutes or until a skewer inserted into the centre of the cake comes out clean. Leave the cake in the tin for about 5 minutes, then turn out on to a wire rack, peel off the lining paper and leave to cool completely.

5 Cut the cake horizontally into two layers, and place the bottom layer on a serving plate. Sprinkle the orange-flavoured liqueur over both layers.

6 ▲ Place the double cream and vanilla sugar in a mixing bowl and beat with an electric mixer until it holds peaks.

7 ▲ Spread two-thirds of the cream mixture over the bottom layer of cake and top with half the fruit. Place the second layer of the cake on top and spread the remaining cream over the top and sides.

8 Using a knife, lightly press the chopped nuts evenly around the sides. Arrange the remaining fresh fruit on top and brush over a light glaze using the apricot jam.

Hazelnut Praline and Apricot Genoese

Genoese is the name associated with the most classic of all whisked sponge cakes. Here it is layered with an apricot- and maple-flavoured buttercream, and topped with apricots and whole praline-coated hazelnuts. Delicious and elegant, this is an ideal cake for any occasion.

INGREDIENTS
Serves 12
150 g/5 oz/1¼ cups plain flour
pinch of salt
4 size 3 eggs
115 g/4 oz/½ cup caster sugar
25 g/1 oz/2 tbsp toasted
ground hazelnuts

For the Praline
75 g/3 oz/6 tbsp granulated sugar
75 g/3 oz/¼ cup unblanched hazelnuts

For the Icing
6 size 3 egg yolks
175 g/6 oz/¾ cup caster sugar
150 ml/¼ pint/⅔ cup milk
350 g/12 oz/1½ cups butter, diced
30 ml/2 tbsp maple or golden syrup
15 ml/1 tbsp apricot brandy or
apricot juice from canned apricots

For the Topping
400 g/14 oz can apricot halves in
natural juice, drained
12 praline-coated hazelnuts

1 Preheat the oven to 180°C/350°F/
Gas 4. Grease a 23 cm/9 inch round
springform cake tin, line the base with
greaseproof paper and grease the paper.
Dust with flour. Oil a baking sheet.

2 Sift the flour and salt together three
times. Beat the eggs and sugar with
an electric mixer for about 10 minutes
or until thick and pale. Sift the flour
into the bowl, add the ground
hazelnuts and fold gently. Transfer the
mixture to the tin. Bake in the centre of
the oven for 30–35 minutes or until a
skewer inserted into the centre of the
cake comes out clean. Leave the cake in
the tin for 5 minutes, then turn out on
to a wire rack, peel off the lining paper
and leave to cool completely.

3 To make the praline, heat the
granulated sugar and nuts together
in a small heavy-based pan, until the
sugar melts. Increase the heat, and stir
with a wooden spoon until the sugar
turns golden. Be careful not to allow
the sugar to burn. Remove immediately
from the heat.

4 ▲ Carefully scoop out 12 coated
nuts with a metal spoon and place
separately on the oiled tray. Pour the
remaining mixture on to the tray and
set aside until completely cold and set
hard. Break this into pieces and grind in
a blender or food processor to form a
rough paste. Cover and set aside.

5 To make the icing, beat the egg
yolks and caster sugar together
until pale and thick. Heat the milk until
it just boils and pour over the creamed
mixture, still beating. Return to the pan
and stir over a low heat, until the
mixture coats the back of the spoon.
Do not let the mixture become too hot
or it will curdle. Remove from the heat
and strain through a fine sieve into a
large bowl.

6 Beat the mixture for 1–2 minutes,
until tepid. Gradually beat in the
butter, a little at a time, until the
mixture thickens and becomes glossy.
Beat in the maple syrup and apricot
brandy or fruit juice. (Just before the
mixture thickens it will appear to be
curdling. Continue beating and the
correct consistency will be achieved.)

7 ▲ Cut the cold cake into three equal
layers. Reserve four apricot halves
and chop the rest. Dry well and fold the
chopped fruit into one-third of the icing
along with 45 ml/3 tbsp of praline.

8 ▲ Place one layer of sponge cake
on a turntable, spread with half the
filling, top with the next layer of
sponge cake and repeat.

11 Fan the remaining apricot slices in the centre of the cake and top with a single praline-coated hazelnut.

9 ▲ Reserve a little of the remaining icing for decoration. Use the rest to cover the top and sides of the cake. Coat the sides with a further 45 ml/ 3 tbsp praline and swirl a pattern over the top with a palette knife.

10 ▲ Transfer the remaining icing to a piping bag fitted with a medium star nozzle and pipe 24 rosettes around the top of the cake. Decorate alternate rosettes with the reserved apricots, thinly sliced, and whole praline-coated nuts.

Iced Paradise Cake

A whisked sponge cake mixture is piped into fingers. These are then used to line a loaf tin to make a luxurious frozen gâteau, finished off with a coating of melted chocolate, butter and cream.

INGREDIENTS
Serves 12
For the Sponge Fingers
1 quantity Whisked Sponge Cake substituting 15 g/½ oz/2 tbsp plain flour with 15 g/½ oz/ 2 tbsp cornflour 90 ml/6 tbsp dark rum

For the Filling and Icing
250 g/9 oz/1½ cups plain chocolate chips 30 ml/2 tbsp golden syrup 30 ml/2 tbsp water 400 ml/14 fl oz/1⅔ cups double cream 115 g/4 oz/2 cups desiccated coconut, toasted 25 g/1 oz/2 tbsp butter 30 ml/2 tbsp single cream

To Decorate
25–50 g/1–2 oz/⅓ cup white chocolate chips desiccated coconut or coconut curls cocoa powder, for dusting

1 Preheat the oven to 200°C/400°F/ Gas 6. Grease and flour two baking trays. Line a 900 g/2 lb loaf tin with a layer of clear film.

2 ▲ Make the whisked sponge cake mixture and transfer to a piping bag fitted with a 1 cm/½ inch plain nozzle. Pipe 28–30, 7.5 cm/3 inch fingers on to the prepared trays and bake for 8–10 minutes until risen and springy to the touch. Remove from the oven, cool slightly and transfer to a wire rack to cool completely.

3 ▲ Line the base and sides of the prepared loaf tin with sponge fingers, trimming them as necessary to fit the tin. Brush with a little rum.

4 Melt 75 g/3 oz/½ cup of the chocolate chips, the syrup, water and 30 ml/2 tbsp rum in a bowl, over a pan of gently simmering water. Allow to cool slightly.

5 ▲ Whip the double cream until it holds its shape and stir in the chocolate mixture and toasted coconut. Pour into the tin, tap the bottom gently to clear any air bubbles, and place the remaining sponge fingers over the top. Brush over the remaining rum. Cover with clear film and freeze for several hours, until firm.

6 Melt the remaining chocolate, butter and cream in a bowl, over a pan of gently simmering water. Remove from the heat and cool slightly.

7 ▲ Remove the cake from the freezer and unmould on to a wire rack. Pour over the icing in one smooth motion, to coat the top and sides of the cake. Use a palette knife to smooth the sides, if necessary.

8 Refrigerate for 10–15 minutes, until the chocolate icing is set. (Alternatively, the cake can be returned to the freezer at this time and stored for up to 3 months.)

Tip

To make coconut curls, draw a swivel-bladed peeler along the curved edge of a fresh coconut piece. This will make thin wide curls with a brown edge. Use these to decorate the top of the cake.

9 ▲ To make the decorations, melt the white chocolate chips and transfer to a greaseproof paper piping bag. Snip the end off the bag and drizzle a pattern over the chocolate icing. Allow the cake to soften in the refrigerator for a further 20–30 minutes, or until a knife will cut through easily.

10 ▲ Just before serving, decorate the top with a little desiccated coconut or coconut curls, and dust lightly with cocoa powder.

Mocha Brazil Layer Torte

This wonderfully rich gâteau is a layered cake or torte, consisting of both sponge cake and meringue discs. The combination of mocha and brazil nuts is particularly successful and the simple decorations give an elegant finish to this classic European cake.

INGREDIENTS
Serves 12
3 size 3 egg whites
115 g/4 oz/½ cup caster sugar
45 ml/3 tbsp coffee essence
75 g/3 oz/¾ cup brazil nuts, toasted and finely ground
115 g/4 oz/⅔ cup plain chocolate chips
4 size 3 eggs
115 g/4 oz/½ cup caster sugar
115 g/4 oz/1 cup plain flour
5 ml/1 tsp baking powder

For the Icing
175 g/6 oz/1 cup plain chocolate chips
30 ml/2 tbsp coffee essence
30 ml/2 tbsp water
600 ml/1 pint/2½ cups double cream

To Decorate
50 g/2 oz/⅓ cup plain chocolate chips
12 chocolate-coated coffee beans

1 Preheat the oven to 150°C/300°F/ Gas 2. Draw 2 x 20 cm/8 inch circles on to a large sheet of baking parchment. Place on a baking tray. Grease a 20 cm/8 inch round springform tin and line the base with greaseproof paper. Grease the paper and flour the tin.

2 ▲ To make the meringue, whisk the egg whites until stiff and gradually whisk in the sugar, 15 g/½ oz/1 tbsp at a time, until thick and glossy. Fold in the coffee essence and nuts until evenly incorporated and transfer to a piping bag fitted with a 1 cm/½ inch plain nozzle. Starting in the centre, pipe circles of the meringue mixture on to the prepared paper.

3 ▲ Bake for 1¾–2 hours, until crisp and golden. Remove from the oven and transfer to a wire rack to cool completely. Peel away the baking parchment. Increase the oven temperature to 180°C/350°F/Gas 4.

4 ▲ To prepare the chocolate decorations, melt the chocolate chips and pour over a piece of baking parchment, spreading out to a very thin layer with a palette knife and leave to set.

5 To make the sponge, melt the chocolate chips and cool slightly. Whisk the eggs and sugar together in a bowl over a pan of gently simmering water, until very pale and thick and the whisk leaves a trail through the mixture. Remove from the heat, continue beating until cool and carefully stir in the melted chocolate. Sift the flour and baking powder together and fold into the whisked mixture, until incorporated. Transfer to the prepared tin and bake for 40–45 minutes, or until the mixture has risen and is springy to the touch.

6 Remove from the oven, cool in the tin for 10 minutes and transfer to a wire rack to cool completely.

7 To make the icing, melt the chocolate chips, coffee essence and water together in a bowl over a pan of gently simmering water, and remove from the heat. Whip the cream until it holds its shape and stir into the mocha mixture, until combined.

8 ▲ Place the cooled cake on a turntable and cut into three equal layers. Trim the meringue discs to the same size and assemble the gateau with a layer of sponge, a little of the icing and a meringue disc, finishing with a layer of sponge.

9 Reserve a little of the remaining icing for decoration; use the rest to completely coat the cake, forming a swirling pattern over the top.

10 ▲ Carefully peel away the paper from the set chocolate and cut out 12 triangles, 10 cm/4 inches long and 2.5 cm/1 inch wide at the top.

11 ▲ Transfer the reserved icing to a piping bag fitted with a large star nozzle, and pipe 24 small rosettes around the top edge of the cake. Top alternately with the coffee beans and chocolate triangles.

Coffee, Peach and Almond Daquoise

This is a traditional meringue gâteau. The meringue mixture is piped into rounds, baked, and layered with a classic buttercream and peach filling. The French name for this classic style of gâteau, 'succès', is then piped over the top of the finished cake.

INGREDIENTS
Serves 12
5 eggs, separated
425 g/15 oz/scant 2 cups caster sugar
15 g/½ oz/2 tbsp cornflour
175 g/6 oz/2 cups ground almonds, toasted
125 ml/4½ fl oz/good ½ cup milk
275 g/10 oz/1¼ cups butter, diced (at room temperature)
45–60 ml/3–4 tbsp coffee essence
2 x 400 g/14 oz cans peach halves in juice, drained

To Decorate
65 g/2½ oz/¼ cup flaked almonds, toasted
icing sugar
3 reserved peach halves
a few mint leaves (optional)

1 Preheat the oven to 150°C/300°F/ Gas 2. Draw 3 x 23 cm/9 inch circles on to three sheets of baking parchment. Place the sheets on separate baking trays.

2 Whisk the egg whites until stiff and gradually whisk in 275 g/10 oz/ 1¼ cups of the sugar, a little at a time, until thick and glossy. Fold in the cornflour and almonds until evenly incorporated. Transfer the mixture to a piping bag fitted with a 1 cm/½ inch plain nozzle.

3 Starting in the centre of the prepared circles, pipe the mixture in a continuous tight coil, finishing just within the lines. Bake for 1¾–2 hours until lightly golden and dried out. Remove from the oven and transfer to a wire rack to cool completely. Peel away the baking parchment.

4 Using the 5 egg yolks, the remaining 150 g/5 oz/¾ cup caster sugar, the milk and the diced butter, make the icing. See Hazelnut Praline and Apricot Genoese steps 5 and 6 for the method. Substitute the coffee essence for the syrup and brandy in that recipe.

5 ▲ Trim the meringue discs to 23 cm/9 inch circles, and crush the trimmings. Reserve three peach halves, chop the rest and fold into half the icing with the crushed meringue. Use this to sandwich together the three meringue discs.

6 ▲ Reserve a little icing for decoration. Coat the top and sides of the cake, and smooth over the sides with a palette knife.

7 ▲ Cover the top of the cake with toasted almond flakes and dust liberally with icing sugar.

8 ▲ Cut the reserved peaches into thin slices and use to decorate the outer edges of the cake. Garnish with mint leaves. Place the reserved icing in a piping bag fitted with a small star nozzle and use to pipe the word 'succès' in the centre of the cake.

Lemon Chiffon Cake

Lemon mousse provides a tangy filling for this light lemon sponge.
The curly lemon decorations add an extra 'bite' to every piece.

INGREDIENTS
Serves 8
2 size 3 eggs
75 g/3 oz/6 tbsp caster sugar
grated zest of 1 lemon
50 g/2 oz/½ cup plain flour, sifted

For the Filling
2 size 3 eggs, separated
75 g/3 oz/6 tbsp caster sugar
grated zest and juice of 1 lemon
30 ml/2 tbsp water
15 ml/1 tbsp powdered gelatine
120 ml/4 fl oz/½ cup fromage frais

For the Icing
115 g/4 oz/1 cup icing sugar, sifted
15 ml/1 tbsp lemon juice

To Decorate
blanched and shredded zest
of 1 lemon

1 ▲ Preheat the oven to 180°C/350°F/
Gas 4. Grease and line a 20 cm/8
inch round loose-bottom cake tin.
Whisk the eggs, sugar and lemon zest
together with an electric whisk until
thick and mousse-like. Gently fold in
the flour, then turn the mixture into the
prepared tin.

2 ▲ Bake for 20–25 minutes until the
cake springs back when lightly
pressed in the centre. Turn on to a wire
rack to cool. Once cold, split the cake
in half horizontally and return the
lower half to the clean cake tin. Set
the tin aside.

3 ▲ Make the filling. Place the egg
yolks, sugar, lemon zest and juice in
a bowl. Beat with an electric whisk
until thick, pale and creamy.

4 ▲ Pour the water into a small
heatproof bowl and sprinkle the
gelatine on top. Leave until spongy,
then place over simmering water and
stir until dissolved. Cool slightly, then
whisk into the yolk mixture. Fold in the
fromage frais. When the mixture begins
to set, quickly whisk the egg whites to
soft peaks. Fold a spoonful into the
mousse mixture to lighten it, then fold
in the rest.

5 ▲ Pour the lemon mousse over the
sponge in the cake tin, spreading it
to the edges. Set the second layer of
sponge on top and chill until set.

6 ◄Slide a palette knife dipped in hot water between the tin and the cake to loosen it, then carefully transfer the cake to a serving plate. Make the icing by adding enough lemon juice to the icing sugar to make a mixture thick enough to coat the back of a wooden spoon. Pour over the cake and spread evenly to the edges. Decorate with lemon shreds.

Tip

The mousse mixture should be just on the point of setting when the egg whites are added. This setting process can be speeded up by placing the bowl of mousse in a bowl of iced water.

Tia Maria Gâteau

This cake is a feather-light coffee sponge with a creamy liqueur-flavoured filling, perfect for a sophisticated dessert at the end of a dinner party.

INGREDIENTS
Serves 8
75 g/3 oz/¾ cup plain flour
30 ml/2 tbsp instant coffee powder
3 size 3 eggs
115 g/4 oz/½ cup caster sugar

For the Filling
175 g/6 oz/¾ cup low fat soft cheese
15 ml/1 tbsp clear honey
15 ml/1 tbsp Tia Maria
50 g/2 oz/¼ cup stem ginger,
roughly chopped

For the Icing
225 g/8 oz/2 cups icing sugar, sifted
10 ml/2 tsp coffee essence
15 ml/1 tbsp water
5 ml/1 tsp cocoa powder

To Decorate
coffee beans

1 ▲ Preheat the oven to 190°C/375°F/ Gas 5. Grease and line a deep 20 cm/8 inch round cake tin. Sift the flour and coffee powder together on to a sheet of greaseproof paper.

2 ▲ Whisk the eggs and sugar in a bowl with an electric whisk for about 2 minutes until the mixture is pale and leaves a thick trail when the beaters are lifted.

3 ▲ Gently fold in the flour mixture with a metal spoon, being careful not to knock out any air. Turn the mixture into the prepared tin. Bake the sponge for 30–35 minutes or until it springs back when lightly pressed. Turn on to a wire rack and leave to cool completely.

4 ▲ Make the filling. Mix the soft cheese with the honey in a bowl. Beat until smooth, then stir in the Tia Maria and chopped stem ginger.

5 ▲ Split the cake in half horizontally and sandwich the two halves together with the Tia Maria filling.

6 ◀ Make the icing. In a bowl, mix the icing sugar and coffee essence with enough of the water to make an icing which will coat the back of a wooden spoon. Pour three-quarters of the icing over the cake, spreading it evenly to the edges. Stir the cocoa into the remaining icing until smooth. Spoon into a piping bag fitted with a writing nozzle and pipe the mocha icing over the coffee icing. Decorate with coffee beans, if liked.

Tip

To make a Mocha Gâteau, replace the coffee powder with 30 ml/ 2 tbsp cocoa powder, sifting it with the flour. Omit the chopped ginger in the filling.

Apricot Brandy-snap Roulade

*A magnificent combination of soft
and crisp textures, this cake
looks impressive and is easy to prepare.*

INGREDIENTS
Serves 6–8
*4 size 3 eggs, separated
½ tbsp fresh orange juice
115 g/4 oz/½ cup caster sugar
175 g/6 oz/2 cups ground almonds
4 brandy-snap biscuits, crushed, to
decorate*

For the Filling
*150 g/5 oz canned apricots, drained
300 ml/½ pint/1¼ cups double
cream
25 g/1 oz/4 tbsp icing sugar*

3 ▲ Whisk the egg whites until they hold stiff peaks. Fold the egg whites into the almond mixture, then transfer to the Swiss roll tin and smooth the surface. Bake in the centre of the oven for about 20 minutes or until a skewer inserted into the centre comes out clean. Leave to cool in the tin, covered with a clean, just-damp cloth.

4 ▲ To make the filling, place the apricots in a blender or food processor and purée until smooth. Place the cream and icing sugar in a mixing bowl and whip until the cream holds soft peaks. Fold in the apricot purée.

5 Spread out the crushed brandy-snaps, on a sheet of greaseproof paper. Spread about one-third of the cream mixture over the cake, then invert it on to the crushed brandy-snaps. Peel away the lining paper.

6 Use the remaining cream mixture to cover the cake, then, using the greaseproof paper as a guide, tightly and neatly roll up the roulade from a short end. Transfer to a serving dish, sticking on any extra pieces of crushed brandy-snaps.

1 ▲ Preheat the oven to 190°C/375°F/ Gas 5. Grease a 33 × 23 cm/13 × 9 inch Swiss roll tin, line the base with greaseproof paper and grease the paper.

2 Place the egg yolks, orange juice and sugar in a mixing bowl and beat with an electric mixer for about 10 minutes until thick and pale. Fold in the ground almonds.

$\mathscr{S}$trawberry Cream Gâteau

Fresh raspberries also work well for this recipe.

INGREDIENTS
Serves 8–10
2 egg yolks
4 size 3 eggs
finely grated zest of 1 lemon
115 g/4 oz/½ cup caster sugar
115 g/4 oz/1 cup plain flour, sifted
115 g/4 oz/½ cup butter, melted

For the Strawberry Cream
225 g/8 oz/1½ cups fresh
strawberries, washed, dried and
hulled
275 ml/½ pint/1¼ cups double
cream
50 g/2 oz/½ cup icing sugar
1 tbsp strawberry liqueur or Kirsch

1 Preheat the oven to 150°C/300°F/ Gas 2. Grease a 20 cm/8 inch round cake tin, line the base with greaseproof paper and grease the paper.

2 Place the eggs yolks, egg, lemon zest and sugar in a mixing bowl and beat with an electric mixer for about 10 minutes or until thick and pale. Add the flour and melted butter. Whisk for a further minute, then transfer to the prepared cake tin.

3 ▲ Bake in the centre of the oven for 30–35 minutes or until a skewer inserted into the centre of the cake comes out clean. Turn out on to a wire rack, peel off the lining paper and leave to cool completely.

4 ▲ To make the strawberry cream, place all but one of the strawberries in a food processor or blender and purée until smooth. Place the double cream in a mixing bowl and whisk until it holds peaks. Fold the purée into the cream with the icing sugar and liqueur.

5 ▲ Place the cooled cake on a plate and spread the strawberry cream evenly over the top and sides, making swirls for an attractive finish. Decorate with the sliced reserved strawberry.

Seasonal Celebrations

What better way to welcome in the New Year or celebrate Christmas or Easter than with a really special cake? With the family gathered around, you really do have the perfect excuse to bake something special. Make a blackberry ring to usher in harvest time, celebrate Christmas French-style with a Bûche de Noël, or concoct a treat in the shape of a pumpkin to spook any Hallowe'en gathering.

Starry New Year Cake

Although it is not so traditional to welcome in the New Year with a cake as it is at Christmas, why not start a new tradition?

INGREDIENTS
Serves 15–20
23 cm/9 inch round Madeira Cake
2 x quantity Butter Icing
800 g/1¼ lb/2⅓ x quantity
Sugarpaste Icing
grape violet and mulberry food colourings
gold, lilac shimmer and primrose sparkle powdered food colourings

MATERIALS AND EQUIPMENT
star-shaped cutter
florist's wire
28 cm/11 inch round cake board
purple ribbon with gold stars

1 Cut the cake horizontally into three layers. Sandwich the layers together with three-quarters of the butter icing. Spread the remaining butter icing in a thin layer over the top and sides.

2 Colour 500 g/1¼ lb of the sugarpaste icing purple with the grape violet and a touch of the mulberry food colourings. Roll out on a work surface lightly dusted with icing sugar and cover the cake. Leave to dry overnight.

3 ▲ Place the cake on a sheet of greaseproof paper to protect the work surface. Water down a little of the gold and lilac shimmer powdered food colourings, then load up the end of a paintbrush with one of the colours. Position the brush over the area you want to colour, then flick your wrist in the direction of the cake, so the colour falls on to it in small beads. Repeat with the other colour until the whole cake is covered. Leave to dry.

4 To make the stars, divide the remaining sugarpaste icing into three portions. Colour one portion purple, the same as the coated cake, one portion with the lilac shimmer and one portion with the primrose sparkle. Roll out each colour separately to about 3 mm/⅛ inch thick. Cut out stars with the star-shaped cutter and place on a piece of greaseproof paper. You will need 30 stars total. Highlight the stars with the dry powdered colours, brushing gold on the purple stars, primrose on the yellow and lilac on the lilac stars. Using the watered-down gold and lilac colours, flick them on to each star as before.

5 ▲ While the icing is still soft, cut short lengths of florist's wire and carefully push them through the middle of 15 of the stars, but not all the way through. Leave to dry overnight.

6 ▲ Position the cake on the cake board or plate. Arrange three unwired stars in each colour in a diagonal line on the top edge of the cake, securing with a little water. Repeat to make four more groupings of the stars. Stick the wired stars at angles all over the top of the cake as you arrange the flat ones.

7 Decorate the base of the cake with the ribbon.

Greek New Year Cake

A gold coin wrapped in foil is baked into this cake and tradition holds that good luck will come to the person who finds it.

INGREDIENTS
Serves 8–10
275 g/10 oz/2½ cups plain flour
2 tsp baking powder
50 g/2 oz/⅔ cup ground almonds
225 g/8 oz/1 cup butter, softened
175 g/6 oz/¾ cup plus 2 tbsp caster sugar, plus a little extra
4 size 3 eggs
150 ml/¼ pint/⅔ cup fresh orange juice
50 g/2 oz/½ cup blanched almonds
1 tbsp sesame seeds

1 ▲ Preheat the oven to 180°C/350°F/ Gas 4. Grease a 23 cm/9 inch square cake tin, line the base and sides with greaseproof paper and grease the paper.

2 ▲ Sift the flour and baking powder into a mixing bowl and stir in the ground almonds.

3 ▲ In another mixing bowl, cream together the butter and sugar until light and fluffy. Beat in the eggs, one at a time, using an electric mixer. Fold in the flour mixture, alternating with the orange juice, until evenly combined.

4 ▲ Add a coin wrapped in foil if you wish to make the cake in the traditional manner, then spoon the cake mixture into the prepared tin and smooth the surface. Arrange the almonds on top, then sprinkle over the sesame seeds. Bake in the centre of the oven for 50–55 minutes or until a skewer inserted into the centre of the cake comes out clean. Leave to cool in the tin for about 5 minutes, then turn out on to a wire rack, peel off the lining paper and leave to cool completely. Serve cut into diamond shapes.

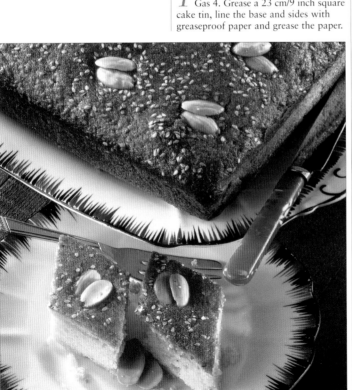

Valentine's Heart Cake

Cakes decorated with hearts can be very adaptable. Although this one was designed with Valentine's Day in mind, it could also be used to celebrate a birthday for someone special, an anniversary, or be made as two tiers for a wedding cake.

INGREDIENTS
Serves 30
20 cm/8 inch square Light Fruit Cake
3 tbsp apricot jam, warmed and
sieved
900 g/2 lb marzipan
1.5 kg/3 lb/2 x quantity Royal Icing
115 g/4 oz/¹/₃ quantity Sugarpaste
Icing
red food colouring

MATERIALS AND EQUIPMENT
1 x 25 cm/10 inch square
cake board
5 cm/2 inch heart-shaped cutter
2.5 cm/1 inch heart-shaped cutter
4 greaseproof paper piping bags
No 1 and No 2 writing and No 42
star nozzles
heart-patterned ribbon

1 Brush the cake with the apricot jam. Roll out the marzipan on a surface lightly dusted with icing sugar and cover the cake. Leave to dry for 12 hours.

2 Secure the cake to the cake board with a little of the royal icing. Flat ice the cake with three or four layers of smooth icing, allowing each layer to dry overnight before applying the next. Set aside a little of the royal icing in an airtight container for piping.

3 ▲ To make the heart decorations, colour the sugarpaste icing red. Roll out the red icing on a work surface lightly dusted with icing sugar and cut out 12 hearts with the 5 cm/2 inch heart-shaped cutter. Place the 2.5 cm/1 inch heart-shaped cutter in the centre of each larger heart and cut out a smaller heart, so you have 12 small hearts and 12 larger hollow hearts. Cut out four more smaller hearts from the red icing so you have 16 total. Place the hearts on a board covered with greaseproof paper.

4 ▲ Spoon a little of the reserved royal icing into a greaseproof paper piping bag fitted with a No 1 writing nozzle. Pipe wavy lines around the edges of four of the small hearts. Leave all the hearts to dry for several hours or overnight.

5 ▲ Spoon some more royal icing into a fresh piping bag fitted with a No 42 nozzle. Pipe swirls around the top and bottom edges of the cake with some of the royal icing.

6 ▲ Colour a heaped tablespoon of the remaining royal icing red and spoon into a fresh piping bag fitted with a clean No 1 writing nozzle. Pipe red dots on top of each white swirl of icing.

7 ▲ Arrange four of the large hearts on top of the cake, securing with a little royal icing.

8 Decorate with the ribbon. Spoon the remaining white royal icing into a fresh piping bag fitted with a No 2 writing nozzle. Pipe beads of icing down each side of the cake, above and below the ribbon. Allow all the piping to dry for several hours.

9 Arrange the remaining large hearts on top of the cake, securing with a little royal icing. Arrange the remaining small hearts on the sides.

Valentine's Box of Chocolates

This special cake would also make a wonderful gift for Mother's Day. Choose your favourite chocolates to go inside.

INGREDIENTS
Serves 10–12
1½ x quantity chocolate-flavour Quick-Mix Sponge Cake mix
275 g/10 oz yellow marzipan
8 tbsp apricot jam, warmed and sieved
900 g/2 lb/2⅔ x quantity Sugarpaste Icing
red food colouring
225 g/8 oz/about 16–20 hand-made chocolates

MATERIALS AND EQUIPMENT
heart-shaped cake tin
23 cm/9 inch square piece of stiff card
23 cm/9 inch square cake board
piece of string
small heart-shaped cutter
length of ribbon and a pin
petits fours cases

1 Preheat the oven to 180°C/350°F/ Gas 4. Grease the tin, line the base with greaseproof paper and grease the paper. Spoon the cake mixture into the tin and smooth the surface. Bake in the centre of the oven for 45–50 minutes, or until a skewer inserted into the centre of the cake comes out clean. Leave the cake in the tin for about 5 minutes, then turn out on to a wire rack, peel off the lining paper and leave to cool completely.

2 ▲ Place the cake on the piece of card and draw around it with a sharp pencil. Cut the heart shape out of the card and set aside. This will be used as the support for the box lid.

3 ▲ Using a large, sharp knife, cut through the cake horizontally just below where the cake starts to dome. Carefully lift the top section on to the heart-shaped card and place the bottom section on the cake board.

4 Use the piece of string to measure around the outside of the bottom section of cake.

5 ▲ On a work surface lightly dusted with icing sugar, roll out the marzipan into a long sausage shape to the same length as the string. Place the marzipan sausage on the cake around the outside edge. Brush both sections of the cake evenly with apricot jam.

6 Colour the sugarpaste icing red and cut off about one-third. Cut another portion from the larger piece, about 50 g/2 oz in weight. Wrap these two portions separately in clear film and set aside. On a work surface lightly dusted with icing sugar, roll out the icing to a 35 cm/14 inch square and use it to cover the bottom section of cake.

7 ▲ Stand the lid on a raised surface, such as a glass or bowl. Roll out the reserved one-third of sugarpaste icing to a 30 cm/12 inch square and cover the lid section of the cake. Roll out the remaining piece of icing and stamp out small hearts with the cutter. Stick them around the edge of the lid with a little water. Tie the ribbon in a bow and secure on top of the lid with the pin. Carefully lift the top section on to the heart-shaped card and place the bottom section on the cake board.

8 Place the chocolates in the *petits fours* cases and arrange in the bottom section of the cake. Position the lid, placing it slightly off centre, to reveal the chocolates inside. Remove the ribbon and pin before serving.

Sweetheart Cake

This romantic cake would be ideal for St Valentine's Day, or to celebrate an engagement or anniversary. Change the icing colours to suit the particular occasion.

INGREDIENTS
Serves 70
20 cm/8 inch heart-shaped, Light Fruit Cake (make using quantities for standard 23 cm/ 9 inch round cake)
30 ml/2 tbsp apricot jam, warmed and sieved
900 g/2 lb marzipan
900 g/2 lb/2⅔ x quantity Sugarpaste Icing
red food colouring
225 g/8 oz/⅓ quantity Royal Icing

MATERIALS AND EQUIPMENT
25 cm/10 inch silver heart-shaped cake board
large and medium-sized heart-shaped plunger cutters
red ribbon, 2.5 cm/1 inch and 5 mm/¼ inch wide
looped red ribbon, 1 cm/ ½ inch wide
greaseproof paper piping bag
medium star nozzle
fresh red rosebuds

1 ▲ Brush the cake with apricot jam, place on the cake board and cover with marzipan. Using about three-quarters of the sugarpaste icing, cover the cake smoothly.

2 ▲ Trim away the excess sugarpaste icing. Knead the trimmings together with the remaining sugarpaste icing and use to cover the cake board. Return the cake to the cake board and leave in a cake box to dry overnight.

3 ▲ Colour the remaining sugarpaste icing bright red with red food colouring. Roll out thinly and cut out 18 large and 21 medium-sized hearts. Leave flat to dry.

4 Measure and fit the wide ribbon around the cake board and secure with a pin. Fit a band of the looped ribbon around the side of the cake, securing with a bead of icing. Tie a bow with long tails in the narrow ribbon and attach to the side of the cake with a bead of icing.

5 ▲ Using a greaseproof paper piping bag fitted with a medium-sized star nozzle, fill using royal icing. Pipe a row of stars around the base of the cake and attach a medium-sized heart to alternate stars. Arrange the large red hearts around the top of the cake, and pipe a star to secure each one.

6 ▲ Choose several tiny rosebuds or one large rose and tie a bow with narrow ribbon. Place on top of the cake just before serving.

Heart Cake

This is a delightful variation of the Sweetheart Cake – a fun way to show someone special how you feel.

INGREDIENTS
Serves 8–10
225 g/8 oz/1 cup butter or margarine,
at room temperature
225 g/8 oz/1 cup sugar
4 eggs, at room temperature
175 g/6 oz/1½ cups flour
5 ml/1 tsp baking powder
2.5 ml/½ tsp baking soda
30 ml/2 tbsp milk
5 ml/1 tsp vanilla essence

To Decorate
3 egg whites
350 g/12 oz/1¼ cups granulated sugar
30 ml/2 tbsp cold water
30 ml/2 tbsp fresh lemon juice
1 ml/¼ tsp cream of tartar
pink food colouring
175–225 g/6–8 oz/1½–2 cups icing sugar

1 Preheat the oven to 180°C/350°F/ Gas 4. Line a 20 cm/8 inch heart-shaped tin with wax paper and grease.

2 ▲ With an electric mixer, cream the butter or margarine and sugar until light and fluffy. Add the eggs, one at a time, beating thoroughly after each addition.

3 Sift the flour, baking powder, and baking soda together. Fold the dry ingredients into the butter mixture in three batches, alternating with the milk. Stir in the vanilla.

4 ▲ Spoon the batter into the prepared pan and bake for 35–40 minutes. Let the cake stand for 5 minutes, then unmould and transfer to a rack to cool completely.

5 For the frosting, combine 2 of the egg whites, the granulated sugar, water, lemon juice, and cream of tartar in the top of a double boiler or in a bowl set over simmering water. With an electric mixer, beat until the mixture is thick and holds soft peaks, about 7 minutes. Remove from the heat and continue beating until the mixture is thick enough to spread. Tint the frosting with the pink food colouring.

6 ▲ Put the cake on a board, about 30 cm/12 inches square, covered in foil or in paper suitable for contact with food. Spread the frosting evenly on the cake. Smooth the top and sides. Leave to set 3–4 hours, or overnight.

7 ▲ For the paper piping bags, fold a 27 x 20 cm/11 x 8 inch sheet of parchment or wax paper in half diagonally, then cut into two pieces along the fold mark. Roll over the short side, so that it meets the right-angled corner and forms a cone. To form the piping bag, hold the cone in place with one hand, wrap the point of the long side of the triangle around the cone, and tuck inside, folding over twice to secure. Snip a hole in the pointed end and slip in a small metal piping tip to extend about ½ cm/¼ inch.

8 For the piped decorations, place 15 ml/1 tbsp of the remaining egg white in a bowl and whisk until frothy. Gradually beat in enough icing sugar to make a stiff mixture suitable for piping.

9 ▲ Spoon into a paper piping bag to half-fill. Fold over the top and squeeze to pipe decorations on the cake.

Simnel Cake

A traditional cake for Easter.

INGREDIENTS
Serves 10–12
225 g/8 oz/1 cup butter, softened
225 g/8 oz/1 cup caster sugar
4 size 3 eggs, beaten
550 g/1¼ lb/3 cups mixed dried
fruit
115 g/4 oz/½ cup glacé cherries
3 tbsp sherry (optional)
275 g/10 oz/2½ cups plain flour,
sifted
3 tsp ground mixed spice
1 tsp baking powder
675 g/1½ lb yellow marzipan
1 egg yolk, beaten
ribbons and sugared eggs, to
decorate

1 Preheat the oven to 160°C/325°F/
Gas 3. Grease a deep 20 cm/8 in
round cake tin, line with a double
thickness of greaseproof paper and
grease the paper.

2 Place the butter and sugar in a large
mixing bowl and beat until light
and fluffy. Gradually beat in the eggs.
Stir in the dried fruit, glacé cherries and
sherry, if using.

3 ▲ Sift together the flour, mixed
spice and baking powder, then fold
into the cake mixture. Set aside.

4 ▲ Cut off half of the marzipan and
roll out on a work surface lightly
dusted with icing sugar to a 20 cm/8
inch round. Spoon half of the cake
mixture into the prepared tin and
smooth the surface with the back of a
spoon. Place the marzipan round on
top, then add the other half of the cake
mixture and smooth the surface.

5 Bake in the centre of the oven for
about 2½ hours or until golden and
springy to the touch. Leave the cake in
the tin for about 15 minutes, then turn
out on to a wire rack, peel off the lining
paper and leave to cool completely.

6 ▲ Roll out the other half of the
marzipan to a round to fit on top of
the cooled cake. Brush the top of the
cake with a little of the egg yolk and
position the marzipan round on top.
Flute the edges of the marzipan and, if
liked, make a decorative pattern on top
with a fork. Brush with more egg yolk.

7 Put the cake on a baking sheet and
place under a grill for 5 minutes or
until the top is lightly browned. Leave
to cool completely before decorating
with ribbons and sugared eggs.

Easter Egg Nest Cakes

Celebrate Easter with a fresh-tasting lemon sponge, colourfully adorned with marzipan nests and chocolate eggs.

Ingredients
Serves 10
1 quantity lemon-flavour Quick-Mix Sponge Cake mix
350 g/12 oz/1 quantity lemon-flavour Butter Icing
225 g/8 oz marzipan
pink, green and purple food colourings
foil-wrapped chocolate eggs

MATERIALS AND EQUIPMENT
20 cm/8 inch ring mould
25 cm/10 inch cake board

1 Preheat the oven to 160°C/325°F/ Gas 3. Grease and flour the ring mould. Spoon the cake mixture into the mould and smooth the surface. Bake in the centre of the oven for about 25 minutes, or until firm to the touch. Turn out on to a wire rack and leave to cool completely.

2 ▲ Cut the cake in half horizontally and sandwich together with about one-third of the butter icing. Position the cake on the cake board. Spread the remaining icing over the outside of the cake to cover completely.

3 Smooth the top of the cake with a palette knife and swirl the icing around the side of the cake.

4 ▲ To make the marzipan plaits, divide the marzipan into three portions and colour it pink, green and purple. Cut each portion in half. Using one-half of each of the colours, roll each one out with your fingers on a work surface lightly dusted with icing sugar to make a thin sausage shape long enough to go around the bottom edge of the cake. Pinch the ends together at the top, then twist the individual strands into a rope. Pinch the other ends to seal neatly.

5 ▲ Place the rope on the cake board around the bottom edge of the cake.

6 To make the nests, take the remaining portions of coloured marzipan and divide each colour into five. Roll each piece into a rope about 16 cm/6½ inches long. Take a rope of each colour, pinch the ends together, twist to form a multi-coloured rope and pinch the other ends. Form the rope into a circle and repeat to make the remaining four nests.

7 ▲ Arrange the nests so they are evenly spaced on the top of the cake and place several chocolate eggs in the middle of each.

Easter Sponge Cake

For a special Easter celebration, serve your family this light lemon quick-mix sponge cake, decorated with lemon butter icing and cut-out marzipan flowers.

INGREDIENTS
Serves 10–12
1½ x quantity lemon-flavour Quick-mix Sponge Cake mix
675 g/1½ lb/2 x quantity lemon-flavour Butter Icing
50 g/2 oz/½ cup flaked almonds, toasted
50 g/2 oz marzipan
green, orange and yellow food colourings

MATERIALS AND EQUIPMENT
2 x 20 cm/8 inch sandwich tins
nylon piping bag
medium-sized gâteau nozzle
flower cutters

1 Preheat the oven to 160°C/325°F/ Gas 3. Grease the tins, line the bases with greaseproof paper and grease the paper. Divide the mixture between the tins and bake the cakes for 35–40 minutes until the cakes spring back when lightly pressed in the centre and are golden brown. Loosen the edges of the cakes with a palette knife, turn out, remove the lining paper and cool on a wire rack.

2 ▲ Sandwich the cakes together with one-quarter of the butter icing. Spread the side of the cake evenly with another one-quarter of icing.

3 ▲ Press the almonds on to the sides to cover evenly. Spread the top of the cake evenly with another one-quarter of icing and finish with a palette knife dipped in hot water, spreading backwards and forwards to give an even lined effect.

4 ▲ Place the remaining icing in a nylon piping bag fitted with a medium-sized gâteau nozzle and pipe a scroll edging.

5 ▲ Using the marzipan and food colourings, make ten green and eight orange marzipan flowers and six marzipan daffodils.

6 ▲ Arrange the marzipan flowers on the cake and leave the icing to set.

*E*aster Cake

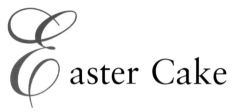

This delicious, spicy Easter fruit cake is covered with ribbons and miniature eggs made from chocolate modelling paste.

INGREDIENTS
Serves 16
125 g/4 oz/½ cup soft margarine
125 g/4 oz/½ cup light brown sugar
3 eggs
175 g/6 oz/1½ cups plain flour
2 tsp ground mixed spice
400 g/14 oz/3½ cups mixed dried fruit
50 g/2 oz/¼ cup glacé cherries, chopped
50 g/2 oz/¼ cup hazelnuts
3 tbsp apricot jam, warmed and sieved
450 g/1 lb marzipan
brown food colouring

For the Chocolate Moulding Icing
125 g/4 oz plain or milk chocolate
2 tbsp liquid glucose
1 egg white
450 g/1 lb/3½ cups icing sugar

For the Chocolate Modelling Paste
50 g/2 oz plain chocolate
50 g/2 oz white chocolate
2 tbsp liquid glucose
pink food colouring

MATERIALS AND EQUIPMENT
1.5 L/2½ pt pudding basin
25 cm/10 in round gold cake board
clean piece of sponge
several squares of gold foil

1 Preheat the oven to 150°C/300°F/ Gas 2. Grease the basin, line the base with greaseproof paper and grease the paper. Cream together the margarine and brown sugar and gradually add the eggs. Sift the remaining flour and the spice into the bowl and stir in the fruit and nuts.

2 Spoon the cake mixture into the prepared basin and smooth the surface. Bake in the centre of the oven for 1½ hours, or until a skewer inserted into the centre of the cake comes out clean. Turn the cake out on to a wire rack, peel off the lining paper and then leave to cool.

3 To make the chocolate moulding icing, break up the chocolate and place in a bowl with the glucose over a pan of hot water. Leave until melted, cool slightly then add the egg white. Gradually add the icing sugar, beating well after each addition, until too stiff to stir. Turn out on to a work surface lightly dusted with icing sugar and knead in the remaining sugar until stiff.

4 To make the modelling paste, melt the plain and white chocolate in separate bowls. Add half the glucose to the plain chocolate and mix to a stiff paste. Add some pink food colouring and the remaining glucose to the white chocolate and mix to a stiff paste. Wrap the pastes separately in clear film and chill until firm.

5 ▲ Cut a triangular wedge out of the cake. Place the cake on the board and brush with the apricot jam. On a work surface lightly dusted with icing sugar, roll out the marzipan and use to cover the cake, tucking the marzipan into the cut front section. Reserve the trimmings, wrapped in clear film.

6 On a work surface lightly dusted with cornflour, roll out the chocolate moulding icing and use to cover the cake. Cut two thin strips from the marzipan trimmings and stick on the inside edges of the cut-out wedge with a little water.

7 ▲ Thin the brown food colouring with water. Dip the sponge in the colour and pat over the surface of the icing. Leave to dry.

8 ▲ Lightly knead two-thirds of each of the modelling pastes and shape into 18 small eggs. Cover some of the eggs with gold foil and position them all inside the cut-out wedge. To make the bow, roll out the remaining modelling paste and cut two strips 2 cm/¾ in wide and 25 cm/10 in long from the dark paste and two strips 5 mm/¼ in wide and 20 cm/8 in long from the pink paste. Stick the pink strips to the dark ones with a little water. From these strips, cut two 13 cm/5 in lengths, press the ends together to form loops and secure to the cake. Secure two 8 cm/3 in length for ribbons ends and cover the centre of the bow with another small strip. Place a piece of crumpled kitchen foil under each strip until hardened.

*M*other's Day Basket

Every mother would love to receive a cake like this on Mother's Day. Choose fresh flowers to decorate the top and add ribbons to the basket handle for a pretty finish.

INGREDIENTS
Serves 12
1½ x quantity orange-flavour
Quick-mix Sponge Cake
900 g/2 lb/2⅔ x quantity orange-
flavour Butter Icing

MATERIALS AND EQUIPMENT
1 litre/2 pint fluted ovenproof glass
dish or brioche mould
15 cm/6 inch round thin silver
cake board
greaseproof paper piping bags
basket-weave nozzle
30 x 7.5 cm/12 x 3 inch strip
kitchen foil
mauve ribbon, 1 cm/½ inch wide
spotted mauve ribbon, 3 mm/
⅛ inch wide
fresh flowers

1 Lightly grease the dish. Line the base with greaseproof paper and grease the paper. Make the cake without any baking powder and bake in the oven for 75–85 minutes until well risen, golden brown and firm to the touch.

2 ▲ Spread the side of the cake with one-third of the orange-flavoured butter icing and place upside down on a board.

3 ▲ Make plenty of greaseproof paper piping bags and fit with a basket-weave nozzle. Half-fill with butter icing and pipe the sides with a basket-weave pattern (see Basket-weave Wedding Cake).

4 ▲ Invert the cake on to the cake board and spread the top with butter icing. Pipe a shell edging, using the basket-weave nozzle, to neaten the top edge. Continue to pipe the basket-weave icing across the top of the cake, starting at the edge. Leave the cake to set in a cool place.

5 ▲ Fold the strip of foil in half, then in half again; continue to fold until you have a strip several layers thick.

6 ▲ Using the plain ribbon, bind the strip to cover the foil; bend up the end to secure the ribbon. Bend the foil to make a handle; press into the icing.

7 ▲ Make a neat arrangement of fresh flowers tied with narrow ribbon and arrange on top of the cake just before serving. Tie a bow and pin it to the side of the cake.

Terracotta Flowerpot

Ideal for celebrating a gardener's birthday or Mother's Day, this cake is baked in a pudding basin for the flowerpot shape and filled with a colourful arrangement of icing flowers and foliage.

INGREDIENTS
Serves 15
3-egg quantity Madeira Cake mix
175 g/6 oz jam
175 g/6 oz/½ quantity Butter Icing
2 tbsp apricot jam, warmed and sieved
550 g/1¼ lb/1⅔ x quantity Sugarpaste Icing
125 g/4 oz/⅛ quantity Royal Icing
dark orange, black, red, silver, green, purple and yellow food colourings
2 chocolate-flake bars, coarsely crushed

MATERIALS AND EQUIPMENT
1.1 L/2 pt pudding basin
string
paintbrush
thin green wire
23 cm/9 in round cake board

1 Preheat the oven to 160°C/325°F/ Gas 3. Grease the basin, line the base with greaseproof paper and grease the paper. Spoon the cake mixture into the prepared basin and smooth the surface. Bake in the centre of the oven for 1¼ hours, or until a skewer inserted into the centre of the cake comes out clean. Cover with kitchen foil for the last 10 minutes if the top begins to brown. Turn the cake out on to a wire rack, peel off the lining paper and leave to cool.

2 Trim the top of the cake flat if it has domed. Cut the cake horizontally into three and fill with the jam and butter icing.

3 Cut out a shallow circle from the top of the cake, leaving a 1 cm/½ in rim around the edge.

4 ▲ Brush the outside of the cake and the rim with the apricot jam. Colour two-thirds of the sugarpaste icing dark orange. Measure the circumference of the cake at its widest part and the height, including a turnover for the rim, with string. On a work surface lightly dusted with icing sugar, roll out the icing to these measurements and use to cover the cake. Reserve any trimmings, wrapped in clear film. Leave the cake to dry for 12 hours.

5 ▲ Using the reserved trimmings, shape the decorations and handles for the flowerpot. Leave to dry on greaseproof paper. Sprinkle the crushed chocolate into the top of the flowerpot for soil.

6 Colour a small piece of the remaining sugarpaste icing a very pale orange, roll out into an oblong and fold over to make a seed bag. Colour a little of the icing black and make the seeds. Colour two more small pieces of icing red and silver and shape the trowel. Leave to dry on greaseproof paper.

7 ▲ Colour the remaining sugarpaste icing green, purple and a very small amount yellow. Mould individual flower petals with the purple icing and stick them together in flower shapes with royal icing. Roll out the yellow icing and cut out the flower centres with a small knife. Position in the centre of each flower with a small ball of yellow icing, securing with royal icing. Leave to dry on greaseproof paper.

8 ▲ Shape the leaves with the green icing using your fingers and mark the veins with a knife. Insert short pieces of wire up some of the stems so you can arrange them in the flowerpot. Leave to dry over the handle of a wooden spoon. Roll out any remaining green icing and snip to represent grass. Paint a design on the seed packet with food colourings.

9 Attach the dark-orange decorations to the flowerpot with royal icing. Arrange the leaves and flowers in the pot. Place the cake on the cake board and position the trowel, seed packet and grass around the outside. Remove the wire from the leaves before serving.

Mother's Day Bouquet

A piped bouquet of flowers can bring as much pleasure as a fresh one for a Mother's Day treat.

INGREDIENTS
Serves 8–10
1 quantity Quick-Mix Sponge Cake mix
2 x quantity Butter Icing
green, blue, yellow and pink food colourings

MATERIALS AND EQUIPMENT
2 × 18 cm/7 inch round cake tins
serrated scraper
5 greaseproof paper piping bags
No 3 writing and petal nozzles

1 Preheat the oven to 160°C/325°F/ Gas 3. Grease the cake tins, line the bases with greaseproof paper and grease the paper. Divide the cake mixture evenly between the tins and smooth the surfaces. Bake in the centre of the oven for about 20 minutes or until firm to the touch. Turn out on to a wire rack, peel off the lining paper and leave to cool.

2 ▲ Place one of the cakes on paper on a turntable. Use half to two-thirds of the butter icing to sandwich the cakes together and to coat the top and sides. Coat the top using a palette knife and the sides using the scraper.

3 Transfer the cake to a serving plate, then divide the remaining butter icing into four bowls and colour one portion green, one portion blue, one portion yellow and one portion pink. Spoon the blue icing into a greaseproof paper piping bag fitted with the No 3 writing nozzle. Pipe the vase on top of the cake in lines and beads.

4 ▲ Spoon the green icing into a fresh piping bag fitted with a clean No 3 writing nozzle. Pipe the flower stems coming out of the vase.

5 Spoon the pink icing into a fresh piping bag fitted with the petal nozzle. Pipe pink petals on the ends of some of the stems. Pipe beads of blue icing in the centres.

6 Spoon most of the yellow icing into a fresh piping bag fitted with a clean petal nozzle and pipe yellow flowers on the remaining stems. Pipe beads of blue icing in the centres.

7 ▲ Decorate the side of the cake. Pipe stems with leaves evenly spaced all around the side with the green icing, and pipe beads of the blue icing to make flowers at the end of each stem. Spoon the reserved yellow icing into a fresh piping bag fitted with a clean No 3 writing nozzle and pipe small beads in the centre of the blue flowers.

8 Pipe beads of green icing round the top and bottom edges of the cake.

Jazzy Chocolate Gâteau

This cake is made with Father's Day in mind, though really it can be made for anyone who loves chocolate.

INGREDIENTS
Serves 12–15
2 x quantity chocolate-flavour
Quick-Mix Sponge Cake mix
75 g/3 oz/3 squares plain chocolate
75 g/3 oz/3 squares white chocolate
½ quantity Fudge Frosting
½ quantity Glacé Icing
1 tsp weak coffee
8 tbsp chocolate hazelnut spread

MATERIALS AND EQUIPMENT
2 x 20 cm/8 inch round cake tins
greaseproof paper piping bag
No 1 writing nozzle

1 Preheat the oven to 160°C/325°F/ Gas 3. Grease the cake tins, line the bases with greaseproof paper and grease the paper. Divide the cake mixture evenly between the tins and smooth the surfaces. Bake in the centre of the oven for 20–30 minutes, or until firm to the touch. Turn out on to a wire rack, peel off the lining paper and leave to cool completely.

2 Meanwhile, cover a large baking sheet or board (or two smaller ones) with baking parchment and tape it down at each corner. Melt each chocolate in separate bowls over pans of hot water, stirring until smooth, then pour on to the baking parchment. Spread out the chocolates evenly with a palette knife. Allow to cool until the surfaces are firm enough to cut, but not so hard that they will break. The chocolate should no longer feel sticky when touched with your finger.

3 ▲ Cut out haphazard shapes of chocolate and set aside.

4 ▲ Make the fudge frosting and, when cool enough to spread, use to sandwich the two cakes together. Place the cake on a stand or plate.

5 Make the glacé icing, using 1 tsp weak coffee (to colour it very slightly) along with enough water to form a spreading consistency, and spread on top of the cake almost to the edges. Spread the side of the cake with enough chocolate hazelnut spread to cover.

6 ▲ Arrange the chocolate pieces around the side of the cake, pressing into the hazelnut spread to secure.

7 To decorate, spoon about 3 tbsp of the chocolate hazelnut spread into a piping bag fitted with a No 1 nozzle and pipe 'jazzy' lines over the glacé icing.

Father's Day Cake

Celebrate Father's Day with this coffee-flavour cake smothered in a rich coffee butterscotch frosting and decorated with piped chocolate and cut-out decorations.

INGREDIENTS
Serves 12
1½ x quantity coffee-flavour Quick
mix Sponge Cake (see Tip)
675 g/1½ lb/1½ x quantity coffee-
flavour Butterscotch Frosting
115 g/4 oz/⅔ cup plain
chocolate chips
30 ml/2 tbsp chocolate and
hazelnut spread

MATERIALS AND EQUIPMENT
deep 18 cm/7 inch square cake tin
20 cm/8 inch square silver cake
board
baking tray
greaseproof paper piping bags
star and No 2 writing nozzles

1 Grease the cake tin. Line with
greaseproof paper and grease the
paper. Make the cake and bake for
45–50 minutes until well risen, golden
brown and firm to the touch.

2 ▲ Place the cake on a rack over a
baking tray and pour the freshly
made frosting over to cover the cake
completely, allowing the excess frosting
to fall into the tray. Leave to set. Place
on the cake board.

3 ▲ Melt the chocolate, pour on to a
sheet of baking parchment and
spread evenly. As the chocolate begins
to set, place another sheet of baking
parchment on top and turn the
chocolate 'sandwich' over. Peel off the
baking parchment and turn the
chocolate sheet over.

4 ▲ Cut out seven 2.5 cm/1 inch
squares of chocolate with a sharp
knife and cut into 14 triangles.

5 ▲ Using a greaseproof paper piping
bag fitted with a star nozzle, half-
fill with chocolate and hazelnut spread.
Pipe a shell border around the base and
along the top edge of the cake.

6 ▲ Decorate the sides and top of the
cake with the chocolate cut-outs.
Using a No 2 writing nozzle, pipe
'Happy Father's Day' on the top.

Tip

To make a coffee-flavour Sponge
Cake, add 10 ml/2 tsp coffee
granules blended with 5 ml/1 tsp
boiling water to the cake mixture.

*H*arvest Blackberry Ring

Gracious blackberry branches twisting their way over the cake, and leaves tinged with reddish-brown, create an autumnal theme.

INGREDIENTS
Serves 20
1 quantity 18 cm/7 inch round
Light Fruit Cake mix
3 tbsp apricot jam, warmed and
sieved
450 g/1 lb marzipan
900 g/2 lb/2⅔ x quantity Sugarpaste
Icing
tangerine, purple, green and paprika
food colourings

MATERIALS AND EQUIPMENT
20 cm/8 inch ring mould
25 cm/10 inch round cake board

1 Preheat the oven to 150°C/300°f/ Gas 2. Grease the cake tin, line with greaseproof paper and grease the paper. Spoon in the cake mixture and smooth the surface with the back of a wet metal spoon. Bake in the centre of the oven for 1½–2 hours or until a skewer inserted in the centre of the cake comes out clean. Leave the cake to cool in the mould on a wire rack. When completely cool, turn out.

2 Brush the cake with the apricot jam. Measure half the circumference of the cake with a piece of string. Measure the height to include the top as well as the sides of the cake (see step 4 for guidance). Take three-quarters of the marzipan and cut in half. Cover the cake in two halves as follows. Roll out each piece of marzipan on a work surface lightly dusted with icing sugar and trim each using the string measurements as a guide. Trim and press the joins together to secure.

3 Measure the height and circumference of the inside of the ring with string. Cover the inside by rolling out the remaining one-quarter of marzipan. Trim to fit and press the joins together to secure. Position the cake on the board. Leave to dry for 12 hours.

4 ▲ Measure half the circumference of the cake with a piece of string. Measure the height to include the top as well as the sides of the cake.

5 ▲ Colour 675 g/1½ lb of the sugarpaste icing pale tangerine. Cut off three-quarters of this and cut in half. Keep the remaining icing well wrapped. Brush the marzipan lightly with water. Cover the top and sides of the cake in two pieces by rolling out each piece of icing. Trim and press the joins together.

6 Measure the height and circumference of the inside of the ring with string. Cover the inside of the ring by rolling out the remaining one-quarter of sugarpaste icing, using the string measurement as a guide. Trim to fit and press the joins together to secure.

7 ▲ Colour one-quarter of the white sugarpaste icing purple. To mould the blackberries, take a little of the purple icing and form into balls of different sizes for the bases. Make a number of smaller balls and stick them on the outside of the larger ones, securing with water. Place on a piece of greaseproof paper and leave to dry while making the leaves and branches.

8 ▲ Colour two-thirds of the remaining white sugarpaste icing green and the rest paprika. Reserve half of the green icing for the stems, and knead the remaining green and the paprika icing lightly together until marbled. Roll out and cut out leaf shapes. Make the branches by rolling the green icing into long thin strands.

9 To assemble, arrange the branches on the cake, securing them with a little water and twisting them as necessary, covering any joins in the icing where possible. Attach the leaves, bending them into shape, then arrange the blackberries on the cake attaching all with a little water.

Hallowe'en Pumpkin Patch

Pumpkins have sprung up all over this orange and chocolate cake, making it the ideal design to celebrate Hallowe'en.

Ingredients
Serves 12–15
2 x quantity chocolate-flavour
Quick-Mix Sponge Cake mix
175 g/6 oz/2 x quantity Sugarpaste
Icing
orange and brown food colourings
2 x quantity orange-flavour Butter
Icing
chocolate chips
angelica

MATERIALS AND EQUIPMENT
2 x 20 cm/8 inch round cake tins
23 cm/9 inch round cake board
serrated scraper
greaseproof paper piping bag
No 7 writing nozzle

1 Preheat the oven to 160°C/325°F/ Gas 3. Grease the cake tins, line the bases with greaseproof paper and grease the paper.

2 Divide the mixture between the tins and smooth the surfaces. Bake for 20–30 minutes or until firm to the touch. Turn out on to a wire rack, peel off the lining paper and leave to cool.

3 ▲ To make the pumpkins, colour a very small piece of the sugarpaste icing brown, and the rest orange. Dust your fingers with a little cornflour. Shape small balls of the orange icing the size of walnuts and some a bit smaller. Make the ridges with a wooden cocktail stick. Make the stems from the brown icing and press into the top of each pumpkin, securing with a little water. Paint highlights on each pumpkin with orange food colouring. Leave to dry on greaseproof paper.

4 Cut each cake in half horizontally. Use one-quarter of the butter icing to sandwich the cakes together. Place the cake on the cake board. Use about two-thirds of the remaining icing to coat the top and sides of the cake.

5 Texture the cake sides with a serrated scraper. Decorate the top with the same scraper, moving the scraper sideways to make undulations and a ridged spiral pattern in a slight fan shape. The texturing should resemble a ploughed field.

6 ▲ Fit a paper piping bag with the writing nozzle and spoon in the remaining butter icing. Pipe a twisted rope pattern around the top and bottom edges of the cake.

7 Decorate the piping with chocolate chips.

8 ▲ Cut the angelica into diamond shapes and arrange on the cake with the pumpkins.

Hallowe'en Coffin

A simple, spooky cake for the centrepiece of a Hallowe'en party.

INGREDIENTS
Serves 4–6
1 quantity Quick-Mix Sponge Cake
mix
5 tbsp apricot jam, warmed and
sieved
350 g/12 oz/1 quantity Sugarpaste
Icing
black food colouring
75 g/3 oz yellow marzipan
¼ quantity Butter Icing
golden caster sugar, for dusting

MATERIALS AND EQUIPMENT
900 g/2 lb loaf tin
23 cm/9 inch square piece of thick
card
small fluted oval cutter
small plastic skeleton and other
Hallowe'en toys
piping bag fitted with a small star
nozzle

5 Colour the sugarpaste icing black, then cut off about one-third and set aside, wrapped in clear film. Roll out the larger portion of sugarpaste icing on a work surface lightly dusted with icing sugar and use to cover the base of the coffin, easing it into the hollow and down the sides. Trim the edges. Roll out the remaining black icing and use to cover the lid. Trim the edges.

3 ▲ To make the lid of the coffin, slice about 1 cm/½ inch off the top of the cake. To make a base to reinforce the coffin and lid, place both pieces of cake on the card and draw around them with a pencil. Remove the cakes and cut out the shapes on the card. Brush the cakes with apricot jam.

4 Use a small, sharp knife to hollow out the base of the coffin, leaving about a 1 cm/½ inch border. Place the coffin and lid on the cards. Brush the cakes with apricot jam.

6 ▲ To make the coffin handles, pull off six small pieces of the marzipan and shape into sausages with rounded ends. To make the plaque on the lid, roll out the kneaded trimmings of marzipan thinly and stamp out a fluted oval with the cutter. Stick the handles and plaque in position with a little butter icing.

7 Lay the skeleton in the coffin. Colour the remaining butter icing black and use to pipe a small star border around the coffin and down the sides. Sprinkle with sifted caster sugar and decorate with the Hallowe'en toys.

1 Preheat the oven to 180°C/350°F/ Gas 4. Grease the tin, line the base and sides with greaseproof paper and grease the paper. Spoon the mixture into the tin and smooth the surface. Bake in the centre of the oven for 35– 40 minutes, or until a skewer inserted into the cake comes out clean. Leave the cake in the tin for 5 minutes, then turn out on to a rack, peel off the lining paper and leave to cool.

2 To shape the cake, use a large, sharp knife to slice off the risen surface to make it completely flat. Turn the cake upside-down and score the shape of the coffin in the cake. Cut off the two top corners at an angle, then cut diagonally down from the corners to the base of the coffin.

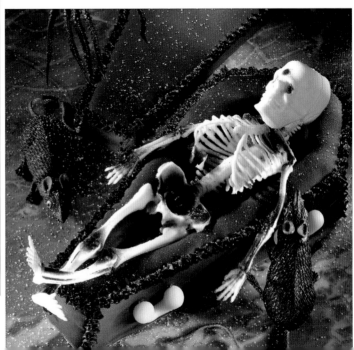

*H*allowe'en Pumpkin

Hallowe'en is a time for spooky cakes – witches may even burst out of them. This one is made in two pudding basins, making it easy to create a pumpkin effect. Make the cake and icing with your favourite flavour – and you are all set for a party full of eerie surprises.

INGREDIENTS
Serves 15
3-egg quantity Madeira Cake mix
250 g/9 oz/¾ quantity orange-
flavour Butter Icing
450 g/1 lb/1⅓ x quantity Sugarpaste
Icing
115 g/4 oz/¼ quantity Royal Icing
orange, black and yellow food
colourings

MATERIALS AND EQUIPMENT
2 x 1 litre/2 pint pudding basins
thin wooden skewer
thin paintbrush
23 cm/10 inch round cake board

1 Preheat the oven to 160°C/325°F/
Gas 3. Grease the pudding basins,
line the bottoms with greaseproof paper
and grease the paper. Divide the cake
mixture equally between them and bake
for 1¼ hours. Turn out and cool on a
wire rack.

2 Trim the widest ends of the cakes so
they will fit flat against one another
to make a round shape. Split each cake
in half horizontally and fill with some
of the butter icing, then stick the two
cakes together with butter icing to form
a pumpkin. Trim one of the narrow
ends slightly, to make the bottom of the
pumpkin. Cover the outside of the cake
with the remaining butter icing.

3 Take 350 g/12 oz of the sugarpaste
icing and colour it orange. Roll out
to cover the cake, trimming to fit where
necessary. Mould it gently with your
hands to give a smooth surface. Reserve
the trimmings.

4 ▲ With a thin wooden skewer,
mark the segments on to the
pumpkin. With a fine paintbrush and
watered-down orange food colouring,
paint on the markings for the pumpkin
skin. Use orange sugarpaste icing
trimmings to make the top of the cake
where the witch bursts out, by cutting
and tearing rolled-out pieces to create
jagged edges. Attach to the top of the
cake with a little water.

5 ▲ Take the remaining sugarpaste
icing and colour three-quarters black.
Of the remainder, colour a little yellow
and leave the rest white. Use some of the
black and white to make the witch,
moulding the head, arms and body
separately and securing with royal icing.
When set, roll out some black icing and
cut jagged edges to form a cape.

6 Drape the shapes over the arms and
body, securing with a little water.
Make the hat in two pieces – a circle
and a cone – and secure with royal
icing. Leave to dry on greaseproof
paper. Shape the cauldron, broomstick
and cat's head out of more of the black,
white and yellow icing, securing the
handle of the cauldron with royal icing
when dry. Leave all to dry completely
on greaseproof paper.

7 ▲ Use the remaining black icing for
the pumpkin features. Roll out and
cut out the eyes, nose and mouth with a
sharp knife. Attach to the pumpkin
with a little water. Place the cake on the
cake board, secure the witch on top of
the cake with royal icing and arrange
the cat, cauldron and broomstick
around the base.

Spiders' Web Cake

A spooky cake for any occasion, fancy dress or otherwise. Put as many spiders
as you like on the cake, but any leftover ones can be put on the children's plates
or arranged to look like they're crawling all over the table.

INGREDIENTS
Serves 6–8
1 quantity lemon-flavour Quick-
Mix Sponge Cake mix
1 quantity lemon-flavour Glacé
Icing
yellow and black food colourings

For the Spiders
115 g/4 oz/4 squares plain
chocolate, broken into pieces
150 ml/¼ pint/⅔ cup double cream
3 tbsp ground almonds
cocoa powder, for dusting
chocolate vermicelli
2–3 liquorice wheels, sweet centres
removed
15 g/½ oz Sugarpaste Icing

MATERIALS AND EQUIPMENT
900 g/2 lb fluted dome-shaped tin or
pudding basin
20 cm/8 inch cake board
small greaseproof paper piping bag
wooden skewer

1 Preheat the oven to 180°C/350°F/
Gas 4. Grease and flour the fluted
dome-shaped tin or pudding basin.
Spoon in the cake mixture and smooth
the surface. Bake in the centre of the
oven for 35–40 minutes or until a
skewer inserted into the centre of the
cake comes out clean.

2 ▲ Leave the cake in the tin for
about 5 minutes, then turn out on
to a wire rack and leave to cool
completely.

3 Place about 3 tbsp of the glacé icing
in a small bowl. Stir a few drops of
yellow food colouring into the larger
quantity of icing and colour the small
quantity black. Place the cake on the
cake board, dome side up, and pour
over the yellow icing, allowing it to run,
unevenly, down the sides. Fill the piping
bag with the black icing. Seal the bag
and snip the end, making a small hole
for the nozzle.

4 ▲ Starting on the top of the cake, in
the centre, drizzle the black icing
round the cake in a spiral, keeping the
line as continuous and as evenly spaced
as possible. Use the wooden skewer to
draw through the icing, downwards
from the centre at the top of the cake, to
make a web effect. Wipe away the
excess icing with a damp cloth, then
allow the icing to set at room
temperature.

5 To make the spiders, place the
chocolate and cream in a small,
heavy-based saucepan and heat gently,
stirring frequently, until the chocolate
melts. Transfer the mixture to a small
mixing bowl and allow to cool.

6 ▲ When cool, beat the mixture for
about 10 minutes or until thick and
pale. Stir in the ground almonds, then
chill until firm enough to handle. Dust
your hands with a little cocoa, then
make a ball the size of a large walnut
out of the chocolate mixture. Roll each
ball in chocolate vermicelli until evenly
coated. Repeat this process until all the
mixture is used.

7 ▲ To make the spiders' legs, cut the
liquorice into 4 cm/1½ inch lengths.
Make small cuts into the sides of each
spider, then insert the legs. To make the
spiders' eyes, pull off a piece of
sugarpaste icing about the size of a
hazelnut and colour it with black food
colouring. Use the white icing to make
tiny balls and the black icing to make
even smaller ones. Use a little water to
stick the eyes in place. Arrange the
spiders on and around the cake.

Ghostly Spectre

*This fun Hallowe'en cake is really simple to make, yet very effective.
Use an 18 cm/7 in square cake of your choice, such as a citrus or chocolate-
flavoured Madeira or a light fruit cake.*

INGREDIENTS
Serves 14
2 x quantity orange-flavoured
Quick-Mix Sponge Cake mix
900 g/2 lb/2⅔ x quantity Sugarpaste
Icing
black food colouring
350 g/12 oz/1 quantity Butter Icing

MATERIALS AND EQUIPMENT
18 cm/7 in square cake tin
300 ml/½ pt pudding basin
23 cm/9 in round cake board
paintbrush

3 ▲ Cut two small corners off the large cake and two larger wedges off the other two corners. Stand the large cake on the cake board and secure with a little butter icing. Halve the large cake trimmings and wedge around the base of the cake.

5 ▲ On a work surface lightly dusted with icing sugar, roll out the remaining sugarpaste icing to an oval shape about 51 cm/20 in long and 30 cm/12 in wide. Position over the cake, letting the icing fall into folds around the sides. Gently smooth the icing over the top half of the cake.

1 Preheat the oven to 150°C/300°F/ Gas 2. Grease the tin and the pudding basin, line the bases with greaseproof paper and grease the paper. Half-fill the basin with the cake mixture and turn the remainder into the tin. Smooth the surfaces and bake in the centre of the oven for 25 minutes for the basin and 1½ hours for the tin, or until a skewer inserted into the centre of the cakes comes out clean. Leave to cool for 5 minutes, then turn out on to a wire rack, peel off the lining paper and leave to cool.

2 Knead a little black food colouring into about one-eighth of the sugarpaste icing. On a work surface lightly dusted with icing sugar, roll out and use to cover the cake board.

4 ▲ Secure the small cake to the top of the large cake with a little of the butter icing for the head. Secure the small cake trimmings on either side of the head with butter icing for the shoulders. Use the remaining butter icing to cover the cake completely.

6 ▲ Using black food colouring, paint two oval eyes on to the head.

Glittering Star

With a quick flick of a paintbrush you can give a sparkling effect to this glittering cake. Add some shimmering stars and moons and you have a cake ready to celebrate a birthday, Christmas, Hallowe'en or silver wedding anniversary – for all the stars in your life.

INGREDIENTS
Serves 20–25
20 cm/8 inch round Rich Fruit Cake
2½ tbsp apricot jam, warmed
and sieved
675 g/1½ lb marzipan
450 g/1 lb/1⅓ x quantity
Sugarpaste Icing
silver, gold, lilac shimmer, red
sparkle, glitter green and primrose
sparkle powdered food colourings
115 g/4 oz/¼ quantity Royal Icing

MATERIALS AND EQUIPMENT
paintbrush
stiff paper for templates
25 cm/10 inch round cake board or
plate

1 Brush the cake with the apricot jam. Roll out two-thirds of the marzipan and cover the cake. Leave to dry for at least 12 hours.

2 Roll out the sugarpaste icing. Brush the marzipanned cake with a little water to dampen slightly and cover the cake with the sugarpaste icing. Leave to dry for several hours.

3 ▲ Place the cake on a large sheet of greaseproof paper. Water down a little powdered silver food colouring and, using a paintbrush loaded with the colour, flick this all over the cake to give a spattered effect. Allow to dry.

4 ▲ Make templates out of stiff paper in two or three different-sized moon shapes and three or four irregular star shapes. Take the remaining marzipan, divide into six pieces and colour silver, gold, lilac, pink, green and yellow. Roll out each colour and cut into stars and moons using the templates as a guide, cutting some of the stars in half.

5 ▲ Place the cut-out shapes on the greaseproof paper and brush each with its own colour in powdered form to add more glitter. Allow to dry for several hours.

6 ▲ Position the cake on the cake board, securing underneath with a dab of royal icing, or place on a plate. Arrange the stars and moons at different angles all over the cake, attaching with royal icing, and position the halved stars upright as though coming out of the cake. Allow to set.

Glazed Christmas Ring

A good, rich fruit cake is a must at Christmas. This one is particularly festive with its vibrant, glazed fruit and nut topping. Made here in a ring mould, it gives the cake an unusual shape, but it is equally successfully made in a 25 cm/10 inch round cake tin. If using the latter, cook for an extra 15–30 minutes, checking the centre with a skewer.

INGREDIENTS
Serves 16–20

225 g/8 oz/1⅓ cups sultanas
175 g/6 oz/1 cup raisins
175 g/6 oz/1 cup currants
175 g/6 oz/1 cup dried figs, chopped
90 ml/6 tbsp whisky
45 ml/3 tbsp orange juice
225 g/8 oz/1 cup butter
225 g/8 oz/1 cup dark brown sugar
5 size 3 eggs
250 g/9 oz/2 cups plain flour
15 ml/1 tbsp baking powder
15 ml/1 tbsp ground mixed spice
115 g/4 oz/½ cup glacé
cherries, chopped
115 g/4 oz/1 cup brazil nuts, chopped
50 g/2 oz/scant ½ cup cut peel
50 g/2 oz/⅓ cup ground almonds
grated zest and juice of 1 orange
30 ml/2 tbsp orange marmalade

To Decorate

150 g/5 oz/½ cup orange marmalade
15 ml/1 tbsp orange juice
175 g/6 oz/¼ cup glacé cherries
75 g/3 oz/¼ cup whole brazil nuts
115 g/4 oz/⅔ cup dried figs, halved

1 Place the sultanas, raisins, currants and figs in a large bowl. Pour over 60 ml/4 tbsp of the whisky and the orange juice and leave to marinate overnight.

2 Preheat the oven to 160°C/325°F/Gas 3. Grease a 25 cm/10 inch ring mould and line with a double layer of greaseproof paper; grease the paper.

3 Cream the butter and sugar together until pale and light. Beat in the eggs one at a time, beating well after each addition, until incorporated. Add some flour if the mixture starts to curdle.

4 ▲ Sift the remaining flour, baking powder and mixed spice together. Fold into the creamed mixture, alternating with the remaining ingredients, except for the whisky. Transfer the mixture to the prepared tin, smooth the surface, making a small dip in the centre. Bake for 1 hour, reduce the oven temperature to 150°C/300°F/Gas 2 and bake for a further 1¾–2 hours. Test with a skewer, to ensure the cake is cooked.

5 ▲ Remove from the oven, prick the cake all over with a skewer and pour over the reserved whisky. Leave to cool in the tin for 30 minutes and then transfer to a wire rack to cool completely.

6 ▲ To decorate, heat the marmalade and orange juice together and boil gently for 3 minutes. Stir in the cherries, nuts and figs. Remove from the heat and cool slightly.

7 ▲ Spoon the glazed fruits and nuts over the cake in an attractive pattern and leave to set.

Bûche de Noël

This is the traditional French Christmas cake, filled with a purée of chestnuts, flavoured with honey and brandy, and coated with a classic chocolate ganache. The meringue mushrooms add a whimsical touch to the decoration of this festive cake.

INGREDIENTS
Serves 8
1 size 3 egg white
50 g/2 oz/¼ cup caster sugar, plus extra for sprinkling
¼ quantity Whisked Sponge Cake mixture substituting 25 g/1 oz/ 2 tbsp plain flour with 25 g/1 oz/ 2 tbsp cocoa powder

For the Filling and Icing
225 g/8 oz unsweetened chestnut purée
30 ml/2 tbsp clear honey
30 ml/2 tbsp brandy
300 ml/½ pint/1¼ cups double cream
150 g/5 oz/scant 1 cup plain chocolate chips

To Decorate
4 chocolate flakes, crumbled icing sugar holly leaves

1 Preheat the oven to 110°C/225°F/ Gas ¼. Grease a baking tray, line with greaseproof paper and grease the paper. Grease a 33 x 23 cm/13 x 9 inch Swiss roll tin, line with greaseproof paper and grease the paper.

2 To make the meringue mushrooms, whisk the egg white until stiff and gradually beat in the sugar a little at a time, until thick and glossy. Transfer to the piping bag. Pipe eight tall 'stalks' and eight shorter 'caps' on to the prepared baking tray. Bake for 2½–3 hours, until crisp and dried out. Remove from the oven and leave to cool completely. Increase the temperature to 200°C/400°F/Gas 6.

3 Make the whisked sponge cake mixture and transfer to the prepared Swiss roll tin. Bake for 10–12 minutes until risen and springy to the touch.

4 Lay a sheet of baking parchment on a lightly dampened dish towel and sprinkle liberally with caster sugar. Turn the cake over on to the paper and leave to cool completely with the tin in place.

5 To make the filling, blend the chestnut purée with the honey and brandy in a food processor until smooth, and gradually blend in half the cream until thick. Chill until required.

6 To make the icing, heat the chocolate and remaining cream in a small pan over a low heat, until melted. Transfer to a bowl, cool and chill for 1 hour. Remove from the refrigerator and beat until thick.

7 ▲ Remove the Swiss roll tin and peel away the lining paper from the sponge. Spread with all but 30 ml/ 2 tbsp chestnut filling, leaving a border around the edges. Roll up from one narrow end, to form a roll. Transfer to a cake board.

8 Coat the top and sides of the roll with the icing, leaving the ends plain. Swirl a pattern over the icing with a palette knife, to resemble tree bark. Sprinkle the crumbled flakes over the rest of the board.

9 ▲ Remove the meringue 'stalks' and 'caps' from the baking tray. Transfer the reserved chestnut filling to the piping bag, fitted with the star nozzle. Pipe a swirl on to the underside of each mushroom 'cap'. Press gently on to the 'stalks' to form the mushroom decorations.

10 Place a small cluster of mushrooms on top of the chocolate log, arranging the rest around the board. Sprinkle over a little icing sugar and add a few festive holly leaves if wished.

Marbled Cracker Cake

Here is a Christmas cake decorated in an untraditional way.
The cake can be made well ahead of Christmas and then decorated nearer the time.

INGREDIENTS
Serves 20–25
20 cm/8 inch round Rich Fruit Cake
3 tbsp apricot jam, warmed and sieved
675 g/1½ lb marzipan
800 g/1¼ lb/2⅓ x quantity Sugarpaste Icing
red and green food colourings
edible gold balls

MATERIALS AND EQUIPMENT
wooden cocktail sticks
25 cm/10 inch round cake board
red, green and gold thin gift wrapping ribbon
3 red and 3 green ribbon bows

1 Brush the cake with the jam. Roll out the marzipan on a work surface lightly dusted with icing sugar and cover the cake. Leave to dry for 12 hours.

2 ▲ Take 500 g/1¼ lb of the sugarpaste icing and form a smooth roll. Put some red food colouring on the end of a cocktail stick and dab a few drops on to the icing. Repeat with the green. Knead just a few times. Roll out the sugarpaste, on a work surface lightly dusted with icing sugar, until marbled.

3 Brush the marzipan with a little water and cover with the icing. Position the cake on the cake board.

4 ▲ Colour half of the remaining sugarpaste icing red and the rest green. Roll about half of the red icing into five 5 x 1 cm/2 x ½ inch rectangles for the crackers. Roll half of the green icing into a 13 x 1 cm/5 x ½ inch roll and cut off ten 1 cm/½ inch lengths. These are the ends of the crackers. Attach two green ends to each red cracker with a little water. Gather together any icing trimmings. Roll out a small piece of green icing thinly and cut into two 13 x 1 cm/5 x ½ inch strips. Cut each strip into five diamonds. Attach two green diamonds to each cracker, then press a gold ball in the centre. Leave to dry on greaseproof paper for several hours or overnight.

5 ▲ Meanwhile, roll out the remaining red and green icings, including any trimmings, into 1 cm/½ inch wide strips. Cut each strip into diamonds – you will need about 24 diamonds in each colour.

6 ▲ Attach alternate red and green diamonds around the top and base of the cake, securing with water.

7 ▲ Cut the ribbons into about 10 cm/4 inch lengths. Run the blade of a pair of scissors or a sharp knife down the length of them to curl.

8 Arrange the crackers in a pile on top of the cake and decorate with the curled ribbons. Attach the bows in alternate colours with a little softened sugarpaste icing, evenly spaced between the diamonds around the top edge of the cake.

Tip

Add the colour to the icing sparingly at first because the colour becomes more intense as the icing stands. It is advisable to leave the icing for about 10 minutes to see if it is the shade you need.

Christmas Tree Cake

No piping is involved in this bright and colourful Christmas tree cake, making it a good choice for all the family to help decorate.

INGREDIENTS
Serves 20 – 25
20 cm/8 inch round Rich Fruit Cake
3 tbsp apricot jam, warmed and
sieved
900 g/2 lb marzipan
green, red, yellow and purple food
colourings
225 g/8 oz/¹⁄₃ quantity Royal Icing
silver balls

MATERIALS AND EQUIPMENT
25 cm/10 inch round cake board

1 Brush the cake with the apricot jam. Colour 675 g/1½ lb of the marzipan green. Roll out the green marzipan on a work surface lightly dusted with icing sugar and use it to cover the cake. Leave to dry for 12 hours.

2 ▲ Make the royal icing. Secure the cake to the cake board with a little of the icing. Spread the icing evenly on the side of the cake to cover just half way up. Starting at the bottom of the cake, press the flat side of a palette knife into the icing, then pull away sharply to form a peak. Repeat until the iced area is covered with peaks.

3 ▲ Draw three Christmas tree shapes in different sizes on to a piece of card and cut out. Take half of the remaining marzipan and colour it a slightly deeper shade of green than the top. Using the card templates as a guide, cut out three Christmas tree shapes. Arrange the trees on top of the cake.

4 ▲ Divide the remaining marzipan into three portions and colour it red, yellow and purple. Use a little of the marzipan to make five 9 cm/3 inch rolls from each colour. Loop the coloured lengths alternately around the top edge of the cake, pressing on to the top to secure firmly.

5 ▲ Make small balls from red marzipan and press on to the end of each loop.

6 ▲ Use the remaining marzipan to make the tree decorations. Roll the red marzipan into a thin rope and cut into eight 2.5 cm/1 inch lengths for the candles. Shape eight flames from the yellow icing and stick on the end of each candle. Mould 11 small balls from the purple icing and press a silver ball into the centre of each.

7 Arrange the candles and balls on the trees, securing them with a little water if necessary.

Noël Christmas Cake

For those who prefer a traditional royal-iced cake, this is a simple design using only one icing and easy-to-pipe decorations.

INGREDIENTS
Serves 50
20 cm/8 inch round Rich Fruit Cake
30 ml/2 tbsp apricot jam, warmed
and sieved
800 g/1¾ lb marzipan
900 g/2 lb/1⅓ x quantity
Royal Icing
red and green food colourings

MATERIALS AND EQUIPMENT
23 cm/9 inch round silver
cake board
greaseproof paper piping bag
No 0 and No 1 writing nozzles
44 large gold balls
gold ribbon, 2 cm/¾ inch wide
red ribbon, 5 mm/¼ inch wide

1 Brush the cake with apricot jam, cover with marzipan and place on the cake board. Leave to dry for at least 12 hours.

2 ▲ Flat ice the top of the cake with two layers of royal icing and leave until dry. Ice the sides of the cake and, using a palette knife, peak the royal icing, leaving a space around the centre of the side to fit the ribbon. Reserve the remaining royal icing for decorating.

3 ▲ Using a greaseproof paper piping bag fitted with a No 1 writing nozzle, half-fill with royal icing. Pipe beads of icing around the top edge of the cake and attach a gold ball on every other bead of icing.

4 Write 'NOEL' across the cake and then pipe holly leaves, stems and berries around the cake.

5 ▲ Measure and fit the gold ribbon around the side of the cake, taking care not to break the peaks. Press into the icing. Measure and fit the red ribbon over the top of the gold, and secure with a bead of icing. Tie a neat red bow and attach it to the front of the cake. Use more ribbon to fit around the cake board, securing with a pin. Leave overnight to dry.

6 ▲ Colour 30 ml/2 tbsp of the royal icing bright green and 15 ml/1 tbsp bright red with food colouring. Use a greaseproof paper piping bag and a No 0 writing nozzle. Overpipe 'NOEL' in red.

7 ▲ Pipe the holly berries and alternate dots around the edge of the cake in red and overpipe the holly in green. Leave to dry.

Christmas Stocking Cake

A bright and happy cake to make for Christmas. You can make the stocking and parcel decorations in advance, and assemble the cake nearer the time.

INGREDIENTS
Serves 50
20 cm/8 inch square Rich Fruit Cake
45 ml/3 tbsp apricot jam, warmed
and sieved
900 g/2 lb marzipan
1.1 kg/2½ lb/3 x quantity
Sugarpaste Icing
115 g/4 oz/⅙ quantity Royal Icing
red and green food colourings

MATERIALS AND EQUIPMENT
25 cm/10 inch square silver cake board
red ribbon, 2 cm/¼ inch wide
green ribbon, 2 cm/¼ inch wide
card for template

1 Brush the cake with apricot jam and place on the cake board. Cover the cake with marzipan. Reserve 225 g/8 oz sugarpaste icing for decorations, and use the remainder to cover the cake smoothly. Place the cake in a box and leave to dry in a warm place. Measure and fit the red ribbon around the board, securing with a pin, and the green ribbon around the cake, securing with royal icing.

2 ▲ Knead the sugarpaste icing trimmings together. Reserve 115 g/4 oz and cut the remainder in half; colour one half red and the other green with food colouring. Draw a template for the stocking on card and cut out. Roll out a piece of white sugarpaste icing and cut out round the template.

3 ▲ Roll out the red and green sugarpaste icing to 5mm/¼ inch thick and cut each into seven 1 cm/½ inch strips. Remove alternate green strips and replace with red strips. Gently roll the stripy sugarpaste icing together.

4 ▲ Use the template to cut out a striped stocking shape, allowing an extra 5 mm/¼ inch all around.

5 Brush the white stocking with apricot jam and, using a palette knife, lift the striped stocking and place over the white one. Press lightly together and leave to dry.

6 Shape the remaining white sugarpaste icing into four parcel shapes and trim each with thin strips of red and green sugarpaste icing ribbons.

7 ▲ Knead the remaining green and red sugarpaste icing, keeping the colours separate. Roll out each into a 20 cm/8 inch strip, 1 cm/½ inch wide. Cut each into two 5 mm/¼ inch strips. Pipe a bead of royal icing on to each corner of the cake, press alternate green and red strips in position and trim to size. Shape four red and four green balls and press in position where the sugarpaste icing strips join, securing with a little royal icing.

8 ▲ Arrange the stocking and parcels in position on the top of the cake. Leave to dry.

Mini Christmas Cakes

These little cakes make a welcome gift, especially for friends or relatives on their own. Gift-wrap them in pretty boxes tied with ribbon.

INGREDIENTS
Makes 9
20 cm/8 inch square Rich
Fruit Cake
45 ml/3 tbsp apricot jam, warmed
and sieved
675 g/1½ lb marzipan
450 g/1 lb/1⅓ x quantity
Sugarpaste Icing
675 g/1½ lb/1 quantity Royal Icing
red, green and yellow
food colourings

MATERIALS AND EQUIPMENT
3 silver, 3 red and 3 gold 10 cm/
4 inch thin cake boards
small crimping tool
holly leaf cutter
red ribbon, 2 cm/¼ inch and 5 mm/
¼ inch wide
green ribbon, 2 cm/¼ inch and
5 mm/¼ inch wide
18 gold leaves
3 gold candles
gold ribbon, 2 cm/¼ inch wide

1 Cut the cake into three strips each way to make nine square cakes. Brush each with apricot jam and place on a cake board.

2 Cut the marzipan into nine pieces. Cut two-thirds off one piece and roll out a strip long enough and wide enough to cover the sides of one cake. Trim to size and wrap around the cake, keeping a good square shape. Roll out the remaining one-third of the marzipan large enough to fit the top. Invert the cake on to the square, trim to shape and replace on to the cake board. Repeat to cover all the cakes with marzipan. Knead all the trimmings together and reserve for decorations.

3 ▲ Cut the sugarpaste icing into three pieces. On a lightly sugared surface, roll out one piece at a time large enough to cover the top and sides of a cake. Cover the three cakes on the red cake boards. Carefully crimp the top edges of each cake using a small crimping tool.

4 ▲ Cover the three cakes on the gold boards with royal icing and peak the surfaces to finish, working on one cake at a time. Leave a plain strip around the sides to fit the ribbons.

5 Cut the marzipan trimmings into three portions. Colour one piece red, one green and the other yellow. Roll out the green marzipan thinly and cut out 36 leaves, using a holly leaf cutter. Mark the veins with a knife and bend the leaves into shape. Make lots of tiny red berries, and form the remaining red marzipan into nine candle shapes – three small, three medium and three large. Shape nine flames from the yellow marzipan.

6 ▲ Arrange the candles, flames, holly leaves and berries on the sugarpaste cakes and tie each with a wide red ribbon and a bow. Secure all the decorations with a little royal icing.

7 Arrange a holly garland with a few berries on each of the plain marzipan cakes. Tie each marzipan cake with wide green and fine red and green ribbon and a double bow.

8 Arrange six gold leaves on each peaked royal icing cake. Position a gold candle in the centre and the gold ribbon around each cake with a bow. Leave all the cakes to set overnight before gift-wrapping them.

$\mathcal{H}$and-painted Christmas Cake

An unusual Christmas cake which is thoroughly enjoyable to make, provided that you like painting and have a reasonably steady hand.

INGREDIENTS
Serves 35
25 cm/10 inch round Rich Fruit Cake, covered with 1.1 kg/ 2½ lb marzipan
1.4 kg/3 lb/4 x quantity Sugarpaste Icing
red, yellow, green and mauve food colourings

MATERIALS AND EQUIPMENT
33 cm/13 inch round gold cake board
baking parchment
dressmakers' pins
fine paintbrush
red ribbon, 2.5 cm/1 inch wide
red candle

1 ▲ Place the cake on the cake board. Reserve 115 g/4 oz of the sugarpaste icing and use the remainder to cover the cake. Colour the reserved sugarpaste icing red and roll out thinly on a surface dusted with icing sugar. Dampen the surface of the cake board and cover with strips of icing. Smooth down gently and trim off the excess around the edge of the board. Leave for at least 24 hours to harden.

2 ▲ Draw a template for one-quarter of the design on baking parchment, using the photograph as a guide. Make a pin mark in the exact centre of the cake. Lay the template on top of the cake so that the apex of the template meets the pin mark. Using a pin, press the template lines on to the surface of the cake so that a faint marking can be seen on the cake. Move the template round and repeat on the remaining three-quarters of the cake.

3 Cut another piece of baking parchment to fit around the circumference of the cake and 6 cm/ 2½ inch wide. Lay around the side of the cake so that the base of the template rests on the cake board, securing the ends with pins. Using a pin, mark a line on the icing around the top edge of the template. Cut the template in half lengthways and reposition around the cake as before. Mark another line around the top edge of the template, halfway down the sides of the cake. Remove the template.

4 ▲ Place a little of each food colouring on a large flat plate and thin each with a little water. Paint a red triangle on the cake next to the central circle to within 1 mm/¹⁄₁₆ inch of the template markings. Paint another triangle opposite the first. Fill in the centres with yellow. Use the green and mauve colours to fill the remaining triangles around the central circle.

5 Using a clean paintbrush dampened with water, lightly 'smudge' the red and yellow colours together. Repeat on the green and mauve triangles.

6 ▲ Using this technique, build up a design over the top and sides of the cake. Leave the area between the two marked lines around the cake blank and attach the ribbon. Place a candle in the centre, using a little icing sugar mixed to a paste with water as glue.

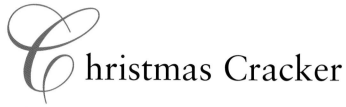hristmas Cracker

A festive cake that is fun to make and fun to eat. To make sure it is really fresh for your Christmas party, the cake can be made and decorated a day or two ahead of time, then cut in half on the day and arranged on the cake board with the colourful decorations to serve.

INGREDIENTS
Serves 8
1 quantity Whisked Sponge Cake
225 g/8 oz/1 cup jam, for filling
30 ml/2 tbsp apricot jam, warmed
and sieved
700 g/1½ lb/2 x quantity Sugarpaste
Icing
Christmas red, mint green, yellow,
black and blue food colourings

To Decorate
red, gold, green and pink foil-wrapped
chocolate eggs, coins and bars

MATERIALS AND EQUIPMENT
33 x 23 cm/13 x 9 inch Swiss
roll tin
small round cutter
2 small red candles
33–35 cm/13–14 inch cake board

1 Preheat the oven to 180°C/350°F/ Gas 4. Grease the Swiss roll tin, line with greaseproof paper and grease the paper. Spoon the cake mixture into the prepared tin and bake in the preheated oven for 20–25 minutes. Allow to cool, spread with the jam and make into a roll. Cut 2.5 cm/1 inch off each end of the Swiss roll. Cut each piece in half. Set aside. Brush the outside of the roll with the apricot jam.

2 ▲ Take 450 g/1 lb sugarpaste icing and colour it red. Roll it out so it is 15 cm/6 inches longer than the length of the trimmed cake, and wide enough to wrap around it. Position the cake in the centre of the red sugarpaste icing and wrap around to cover, keeping the join underneath. Secure with water and trim where necessary.

3 ▲ Pinch the icing slightly where it meets the ends of the cake to resemble a cracker, and place the reserved pieces of cake inside each end of the icing to support them. Using any red icing trimmings, cut out two circles the same diameter as the ends of the cracker. Dampen the edges and position one at each end of the cracker, pressing together to seal.

4 Use the remaining icing as follows: colour most of it green and yellow for the decorations, leave a little white for the snowman, and colour a very small amount black and blue. Roll out the green and yellow icing. Cut strips with a knife and small circles with a small cutter or the end of a large piping nozzle to decorate the cracker. Arrange the decorations on the cracker, securing with a little water.

5 ▲ Make the snowman with the white icing. Shape the body, head, arms and legs separately, then assemble securing the pieces with a little water. Shape the hat, eyes and mouth from the black icing, the bow tie from the green, buttons from the red, and a nose from the blue. Position these on the snowman, securing with a little water. Press two small red candles into his arms to hold. Leave to set.

6 When ready to serve, cut the cake in half, making jagged edges, and position on the cake board. Sit the snowman on top of one half and arrange the wrapped sweets around the board.

Marzipan Bell Cake

An unusual Christmas cake, this is decorated purely with marzipan which gives a Christmas feel without the sweetness of icing.

INGREDIENTS
Serves 40
18 cm/7 inch round Rich or Light
Fruit Cake
30 ml/2 tbsp apricot jam, warmed
and sieved
900 g/2 lb marzipan
green, yellow and red
food colourings

MATERIALS AND EQUIPMENT
20 cm/8 inch round silver cake board
crimping tool
bell cutter
holly leaf cutter
red ribbon, 2 cm/¼ inch and 5 mm/
¼ inch wide
green ribbon, 5 mm/¼ inch wide

1 Brush the cake with apricot glaze and place on the cake board.

2 Colour two-thirds of the marzipan pale green with a few drops of green food colouring. Knead until evenly coloured.

3 Roll out the marzipan to a 23 cm/ 9 inch circle and place over the cake, smoothing across the top and down the side. Trim the excess away from the base of the cake.

4 ▲ Use a crimping tool to make a scalloped pattern on the top edge.

5 Colour a small piece of marzipan bright yellow, a small piece bright red and the remaining marzipan bright green. Roll out the yellow marzipan and using a bell cutter, cut out two bells and mould two clappers.

6 ▲ Using some green marzipan, cut two pencil-thin lengths and form into bell ropes, bending them into shape. Roll out the remaining green marzipan and using a holly cutter, cut out 11 holly leaves. Mark the veins with a knife and bend them to shape. Using the red marzipan, shape some tiny red berries and also two thin strips to wind around the ends of the bell ropes. Leave the decorations to dry.

7 Measure and fit the wide red and fine green ribbon around the side of the cake, securing each with a pin. Tie a neat double bow from red and green fine ribbon and attach to the side with a bead of icing.

8 ▲ Arrange the bells, clappers, bell ropes, holly leaves and berries on top of the cake and secure each with a little icing.

Animal Cakes

*This chapter contains a wide range of ideas to amuse
children of all ages. From tropical parrots to dinosaurs,
from appealing puppies to crazy caterpillars, this section
will encourage you to bring a little bit of fun into baking
that will brighten up any occasion.*

*L*adybird Cake

*Create a little animal magic and make this cake
for a nature lover or gardener.*

INGREDIENTS
Serves 10–12
*1½ x quantity lemon-flavoured
Quick-Mix Sponge Cake mix
175 g/6 oz/½ quantity lemon-
flavoured Butter Icing
2 tbsp apricot jam, warmed and
sieved
4 tbsp lemon curd, warmed
1 kg/2¼ lb/3 x quantity Sugarpaste
Icing
red, black and green food
colourings
5 marshmallows
50 g/2 oz yellow marzipan
edible ladybird icing decorations
(optional)*

MATERIALS AND EQUIPMENT
*1.1 L/2 pt ovenproof mixing bowl
28 cm/11 in round cake board
4 cm/1½ in and 5 cm/2 in plain
round biscuit cutters
garlic press
2 pipe cleaners*

1 Preheat the oven to 180°C/350°F/
Gas 4. Grease the bowl, line the
base with greaseproof paper and grease
the paper. Spoon the cake mixture into
the prepared bowl and smooth the
surface. Bake in the centre of the oven
for 55–60 minutes, or until a skewer
inserted into the centre of the cake
comes out clean. Leave the cake in the
basin for 5 minutes, then turn out on to
a wire rack, peel off the lining paper
and leave to cool.

2 ▲ Cut the cake in half horizontally
and sandwich together with the
butter icing. Cut off about one-third of
the cake and brush both pieces of cake
with the lemon curd.

3 ▲ Colour a little less than half of
the sugarpaste icing red. On a work
surface lightly dusted with icing sugar,
roll out to about a 5 mm/¼ in thickness
and use to cover the large piece of cake.
Using a wooden skewer or the back of a
knife, make an indentation down the
centre of the cake for the wing casings.

4 Colour just over half of the
remaining sugarpaste icing black.
Roll out three-quarters of the icing and
use to cover the small piece of cake.
Place the cakes on the cake board and
assemble the ladybird's head and body,
gently pressing them together to secure.

5 Roll out a little of the white
sugarpaste icing and cut out two
circles for the eyes, using the 5 cm/2 in
round biscuit cutter. Stick in position
with a little water.

6 ▲ Roll out the reserved black
sugarpaste icing and cut out eight
circles, using the 4 cm/1½ in round
biscuit cutter. Stick one on each eye
and stick the rest on to the body with
a little water. Reserve the trimmings.

7 Colour the remaining sugarpaste
icing green. To make the grass,
break off small pieces and squeeze
through the garlic press. Trim off with a
knife. Brush the cake board with a little
water and position the grass.

8 ▲ To make the marshmallow
flowers, roll the marzipan into a
2 cm/¾ in long sausage shape and cut
into slices. Set aside. On a work surface
lightly dusted with icing sugar, flatten
each marshmallow with a rolling pin.
Snip around the marshmallows to make
petals. Press a marzipan circle into the
centre of each flower.

9 To make the antennae, paint the pipe
cleaners with black food colouring
and press a small ball of the reserved
black sugarpaste icing on to the end of
each one. Bend each pipe cleaner slightly
and insert into the cake between the head
and the body. Arrange the ladybird
decorations around the cake, if using.

*R*ainbow Snake Cake

This wild cake doesn't need any cooking and its heavy texture and sweet flavour make it an excellent party cake. For a large party, double the ingredients to make an extra big snake.

INGREDIENTS
Serves 10–15
675 g/1½ lb white marzipan
red, yellow, orange, purple and
green food colouring
1 quantity Truffle Cake mix
2 round red sweets
125 g/4 oz/2 cups desiccated
coconut
jelly snake sweets (optional)

MATERIALS AND EQUIPMENT
5 cocktail sticks
25 cm/10 in round cake board
small piece of thin red card, cut into
a tongue shape
small star-shaped biscuit cutter

2 ▲ On a work surface lightly dusted with icing sugar, roll out each piece of marzipan into a sausage shape with your hands. They should be about 1 cm/½ in in diameter. Line up the sausage shapes next to one another and twist together the two outside sausages on either side. Firmly push the twists up against the middle sausage.

4 ▲ Spoon the truffle mix evenly down the centre of the marzipan and mould into a sausage shape. Starting at one end, gather up the sides of the marzipan around the cake mixture and pinch the sides together firmly to seal. Shape the head and the tail.

1 ▲ Divide the marzipan into five equal portions and colour one portion red, one portion yellow, one orange, one purple and one green. Remove a tiny ball of icing from the green portion and reserve, wrapped in clear film.

3 ▲ Roll out the marzipan, making short, sharp downward movements with the rolling pin. Starting at one end, roll out the marzipan a little at a time until about 15 cm/6 in wide. Keep the width even all along the snake. Carefully slide a heavy, sharp knife underneath the marzipan and flip the marzipan over.

5 ▲ Carefully coil the snake on to the cake board. Make a small incision for the mouth and insert the red card tongue. Roll out the reserved green marzipan and cut out two eyes using the small star biscuit cutter. Stick the eyes to the head with a little water and press the red sweets on top.

6 Place the desiccated coconut in a bowl and add a few drops of green food colouring and a little water. Stir until the coconut is flecked with green. Scatter around the snake on the cake board for grass.

*E*lephant Cake

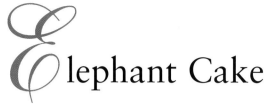

Any medium-sized roasting tin will work for this cake, but one with rounded edges is preferable as this improves the finished result.

INGREDIENTS
Serves 10–12
1½ x quantity lemon-flavour Quick-Mix Sponge Cake mix
1 quantity lemon-flavour Butter Icing (optional)
8 tbsp apricot jam, warmed and sieved
900 g/2 lb/2⅔ x quantity Sugarpaste Icing
pink, blue and grey food colourings

MATERIALS AND EQUIPMENT
30 x 23 cm/12 x 9 inch roasting tin
18 cm/7 inch round cake tin, or card, to use as a template
40 cm/16 inch round cake board, with a support for the trunk, or 40 x 25 cm/16 x 10 inch square cake board (optional)
wooden cocktail stick
medium-size round cutter (optional)
bow made from pretty ribbon
pin

1 Preheat the oven to 180°C/350°F/ Gas 4. Grease the roasting tin, line the base and sides with greaseproof paper and grease the paper. Spoon in the cake mixture and smooth the surface. Bake in the centre of the oven for 45–50 minutes or until a skewer inserted into the centre of the cake comes out clean. Leave in the tin for about 5 minutes, then turn out on to a wire rack, peel off the lining paper and leave to cool completely.

2 ▲ Place the cake, dome side down, on the work surface and position the template in the centre on the flat surface. Use a sharp knife to cut around the template, holding it steady and firm as you cut. Lift out the cut-out circle, keeping the outside piece intact.

3 ▲ Use the template to cut out the elephant's trunk. Place the template close to one edge of the short side of the remaining cake and cut out a crescent shape. Cut off one end of the crescent to make the elephant's mouth. Cut off the other end of the cake, just past the rounded corners, to make the ear. Discard the two small, middle sections of cake. Cut horizontally through the face, ear, trunk and mouth sections of the cake, then sandwich them back together with lemon butter icing, if you are using it.

4 ▲ Assemble the cake on a board or directly on the table. Place the ear piece on one side of the round face, then place the flat edge of the trunk section up against the face, opposite the ear. Place the mouth section in the space between the trunk and the face. Brush the whole surface with jam.

5 Cut off about 50 g/2 oz of sugarpaste icing and set aside, wrapped in clear film. Cut off another 175 g/6 oz of sugarpaste icing and colour it pink, and 15 g/½ oz and colour it blue. Set aside, wrapped in clear film. Colour the remaining icing grey, cut off about 75 g/3 oz and set aside. Dust the work surface with icing sugar then roll out the larger portion of grey icing into a 50 × 25 cm/20 × 10 inch rectangle. Use this to cover the entire cake. Smooth down the sides and edges, snipping with scissors or cutting the icing in the places where it overlaps. Trim the edges.

6 To make the ear piece, roll out the reserved portion of grey icing into a 20 × 10 cm/8 × 4 inch rectangle, then roll it in small sections with the cocktail stick, to give a ruffled effect (see Teddy Bear Christening cake, step 7). Lay this section on top of the ear, slightly off centre. Cut off about 150 g/5 oz of the pink icing and roll it out to a slightly smaller rectangle, then repeat the ruffling process with the cocktail stick. Lay this piece on top of the grey ruffle.

7 Roll out the reserved blue and white icings and cut out the eye parts, using the round cutter, if preferred. Stick in place with a little water, placing a small round ball of the remaining pink icing in the centre. Roll out the remaining pink icing and cut out a triangular piece for the mouth. Shape the remaining white icing into a tusk and then stick them both in place with a little water. Finally, position the bow, securing in place with the pin, which must be removed before serving the cake.

$\mathcal{I}$ndian Elephant

Make this cake to celebrate a birthday, to wish someone 'Bon Voyage' or for a festive occasion. Be as colourful as you like with the decorations.

INGREDIENTS
Serves 30
30 cm/12 in square Madeira Cake
675 g/1½ lb/2 x quantity Butter Icing
225 g/8 oz marzipan
black, green, yellow and pink food colourings
chocolate coins, silver balls, coloured and white chocolate buttons and two sweets
125 g/4 oz/2 cups desiccated coconut
2 tbsp apricot jam, warmed and sieved

MATERIALS AND EQUIPMENT
stiff paper for template
36 cm/14 in square cake board

1 ▲ Make a template from stiff paper in the shape of an elephant. Trace off the design from the photograph of the finished cake and enlarge by 150%, if wished. Place the template on top of the cake and cut out the shape with a sharp knife. Position the cake on the cake board.

2 ▲ Colour the butter icing pale grey using the black food colouring. Cover the top and sides of the cake with the icing and swirl with a palette knife.

3 ▲ Using a cocktail stick and black food colouring, swirl black highlights into the icing.

4 ▲ On a work surface lightly dusted with icing sugar, roll out half of the marzipan and cut out shapes for the elephant's tusk, headpiece and blanket. Place them in position on the cake. Colour the remaining marzipan green, yellow and pink. Roll out thinly and cut out patterns for the blanket, headpiece, trunk and tail. Roll small balls of yellow and pink marzipan to make the ankle bracelets.

5 ▲ Place all the decorations, including the silver balls, chocolate coins and coloured chocolate buttons, in position. Cut the white chocolate buttons in half and use for the toenails and the sweets for the eye.

6 Mix a little green food colouring into the coconut. Brush the cake board with a little apricot jam and sprinkle with the coconut for grass.

Fish Cake

A very easy, but colourful cake, perfect for a small child's birthday party. Candles can be pressed into the icing covering the board.

INGREDIENTS
Serves 8
1 quantity Quick-mix Sponge
Cake mix
450 g/1 lb/1⅓ x quantity
Sugarpaste Icing
blue, orange, red, mauve and green
food colourings
350 g/12 oz/1 quantity Butter Icing
1 blue sweet

MATERIALS AND EQUIPMENT
large ovenproof mixing bowl
large oval cake board
palette knife
2.5 cm/1 inch plain biscuit cutter
greaseproof paper piping bag

1 Preheat the oven to 160°C/325°F/Gas 3. Grease the mixing bowl and line the base with greaseproof paper. Spoon the cake mixture into the prepared bowl, level the surface and bake for 40–50 minutes until just firm. Turn out and let cool.

2 Colour two-thirds of the sugarpaste icing blue and roll out very thinly on a surface dusted with sugar. Lightly dampen the cake board and cover with the sugarpaste icing. Trim off the excess.

3 ▲ Invert the cake and trim to create a fish shape. Trim the edges to give sloping sides. Place on the board.

4 ▲ Colour all but 15 ml/1 tbsp of the butter icing orange. Cover the cake completely with the orange butter icing and smooth down with a palette knife. Score curved lines for scales with the palette knife, starting from the tail end and working up towards the head.

5 ▲ Colour half the remaining sugarpaste icing red. Shape and position two lips. Thinly roll the remainder and cut out the tail and fins. Mark with lines using a knife and position on the fish.

6 Roll a small ball of white sugarpaste icing, flatten slightly and position for the eye. Press the blue sweet into the centre.

7 Colour a small ball of sugarpaste icing mauve, cut out crescent-shaped scales using a biscuit cutter and place on the fish. Colour the remaining sugarpaste icing green, roll out and cut long strips. Twist each strip and arrange them around the board.

8 ▲ Place the reserved butter icing in a piping bag and snip off the end. Pipe small circles on the cake board around the fish to look like bubbles.

Tip

For a sea-themed birthday party you could decorate small cupcakes with fish designs and other watery motifs, to be given as a gift to take home at the end of the afternoon.

Porcupine Cake

Melt-in-the-mouth strips of flaky chocolate bars give this porcupine its spiky coat, and a quick-mix moist chocolate cake makes the base. It's a fun cake for a children's or adults' party.

INGREDIENTS
Serves 15
1½ x quantity chocolate-flavour
Quick-mix Sponge Cake
575 g/1¼ lb/1⅔ x quantity
chocolate-flavour Butter Icing
5–6 chocolate flake bars
50 g/2 oz marzipan
black, green, cream, brown and
red food colourings

MATERIALS AND EQUIPMENT
greaseproof paper
1 litre/2 pint pudding basin
600 ml/1 pint/2½ cup pudding basin
35 cm/14 inch long rectangular
cake board
cocktail stick
fine paintbrush

1 Preheat the oven to 160°C/325°F/ Gas 3. Grease the pudding basins and line the bottoms with greaseproof paper. Grease the paper. Spoon the cake mixture into both basins to two-thirds full. Bake, allowing 55 minutes–1 hour for the larger basin and 35–40 minutes for the smaller basin. Turn out and allow to cool on a wire rack.

2 ▲ Place both cakes on a surface so the widest ends are underneath. Slice pieces from the smaller cake to create a pointed nose at one end.

3 ▲ Place the larger cake on the cake board behind the smaller one. Cut one of the cut-off slices in half and position either side, between the larger and small cake, to fill in the side gaps. Place the other cut-off piece on top to fill in the top gap, securing all with a little butter icing.

4 ▲ Spread the remaining butter icing all over the cake. On the pointed face part, make markings with a cocktail stick.

5 ▲ Break or cut the flake bars into thin strips and stick into the butter icing over the body of the porcupine to represent spikes.

6 Reserve a small portion of marzipan. Divide the remainder into three and colour one portion black, one green and one cream. Colour a tiny portion of the reserved, white marzipan brown for the apple stems. With the cream marzipan shape the ears and feet, using black and white make the eyes, and with the rest of the black shape the nose and the claws for the feet. With the green marzipan make the apples, painting on red markings with a fine paintbrush. Position the stems. Place everything except the apples in place on the porcupine cake. Finally, place the apples on the board by the front of the porcupine.

Tropical Parrot

Create a tropical feel to your celebration with this colourful, exotic cake, whether for a Bon Voyage to faraway places or a simple birthday celebration. The cake is made from one round Madeira cake, cutting out three easy shapes to give the parrot's body, tail and the branch it sits on. You can then be as decorative as you like with the markings and foliage.

Ingredients
Serves 15
20 cm/8 inch round Madeira Cake
450 g/1 lb/1⅓ quantity
Sugarpaste Icing
red, brown, yellow, pink, orange,
blue, purple, black and
green food colourings
500 g/1 lb 4 oz/1½ x quantity
Butter Icing

Materials and Equipment
stiff paper for templates
35 cm/14 inch square cake board

1 ▲ Make templates out of a circle of stiff paper, using the photograph as a guide, for the parrot's body, tail and branch. Place the templates on top of the cake and cut out the shapes with a sharp knife.

2 Take the sugarpaste icing and colour about one-third red. Colour a quarter of the remaining piece brown and the rest yellow, pink, orange, blue, purple, black, green and light green. Leave a small amount white.

3 ▲ Slice each piece of cake (body, tail and branch) in half horizontally and fill with some of the butter icing. Use the remaining butter icing to coat the outsides of the cake. Measure the length and depth of the cake which forms the branch. Roll out the brown icing in one piece large enough to cover it. Position over the cake branch and trim to fit.

4 Measure the length and depth of the sides of the parrot's body. Roll out some of the red icing and cut strips to match the measurements. Press on to the butter icing to fix in position. Roll out a piece of red icing for the top of the parrot's body, using the template as a guide. Leave out the face, beak and blue body parts.

5 Position the red sugarpaste icing on the butter icing, reserving the trimmings. Roll out a piece of white and some black icing for the face and beak, cut to fit and ease into position with your fingers. Do the same with a piece of blue icing to finish off the body and cover the tailpiece using the rest of the reserved red icing.

6 ▲ Roll out the other coloured pieces of icing. Cut out pieces in the shape of feathers, some with jagged edges. Press these into position on the body and tail, easing to fit with your fingers. Secure with a little water, bending and twisting some of the 'feathers' to create different angles and heights. Cut out leaf and flower shapes for the branch out of the green and pink icings.

7 ▲ Place the iced parrot pieces in position on the cake board. Make the eye for the parrot. Secure the eye on to the head with water, and use water to fix the leaves and flowers on the branch. If wished, colour an additional 115 g/4 oz/⅓ quantity sugarpaste icing green. Roll and cut out more leaves to decorate the cake board.

$\mathcal{D}$aisy Cow

A really fun cake to make for a child who loves animals or the countryside.

INGREDIENTS
Serves 10–12
1½ x quantity Quick-Mix Sponge
Cake mix
9 tbsp apricot jam, warmed and
sieved
1.67 kg/3 lb 12 oz/5 x quantity
Sugarpaste Icing
black, brown, blue, yellow and red
food colourings

MATERIALA AND EQUIPMENT
2 x deep 18 cm/7 inch round cake
tins
25 x 33 cm/10 x 13 inch cake board
4 cm/1½ inch and 2.5 cm/1 inch
plain round pastry cutters
6 cm/2½ inch fluted round pastry
cutter
wooden cocktail stick
25 cm/10 inch florist's wire covered
in florist's tape

1 Preheat the oven to 180°C/350°F/
Gas 4. Grease the tins, line the bases
with greaseproof paper and grease the
paper. Divide the cake mixture equally
between the two tins and smooth the
surfaces. Bake in the centre of the oven
for 30–35 minutes or until a skewer
inserted into the centre of each cake
comes out clean. Turn out on to wire
racks, peel off the lining paper and leave
to cool completely.

2 ▲ Using a sharp, pointed knife, cut
a crescent-shaped piece from the
side of one cake, then cut it in half to
make the cow's ears.

3 ▲ This is how the cake should be
assembled. On the work surface,
brush the cake with apricot jam and
push the two rounds together to make
the face.

4 Colour 950 g/2 lb 2 oz of the
sugarpaste icing with black food
colouring. Cut off 500 g/1 lb 2 oz and
set aside, wrapped in clear film. Roll
out the remainder on a work surface
dusted with icing sugar into a rectangle
about 5 mm/¼ inch thick. Roll out two-
thirds of the white icing, then cut into
rounds using plain round cutters. Place
some of the rounds of white icing in a
random pattern on the rolled-out black
icing and roll again lightly with the
rolling pin to flatten them into the
surface. Cover the cow's face with the
black and white icing, trimming it
neatly around the bottom edge. Brush
the cake board evenly with apricot jam.
Roll out 275 g/10 oz of the reserved
black icing into an oblong large enough
to cover the cake board.

5 Arrange the circles of white icing on
top of the black icing and roll lightly
into the surface. Lay over the cake board
and trim the edges. Set aside 50 g/2 oz of
the black icing, break off two marble-
size pieces and set aside from the rest for
the cow's eyes. Roll out the icing that is
left and use to cover the ear shapes.

6 Carefully lift the cow's head on to
the cake board, set aside 90 g/3½
oz of the white icing then roll out the
rest thinly. Cut out a pear shape for the
cow's nose. Brush the back with a little
water and stick on to the cake. Roll two
small pieces of white icing into walnut-
size balls, then flatten with a rolling pin
and reserve for the eyes.

7 To make the cow's eyes, colour
40 g/1½ oz sugarpaste icing brown,
then cut out two rounds with the
4 cm/1½ inch round pastry cutter.
Colour 25 g/1 oz icing blue, then cut
out two rounds with the 2.5 cm/1 inch
round cutter. Assemble the cow's eyes
from the brown and blue rounds and
the reserved white and black icings.
Stick them in place with a little water.

8 Divide the reserved 50 g/2 oz of the
black sugarpaste icing in half, and
roll out one half thinly into a rectangle
of about 15 × 10 cm/6 × 4 inches. Cut
along the icing at intervals, leaving a
1 cm /½ inch border along the top, to
create the fringe. Position between the
ears. Divide the remaining sugarpaste
icing in half and use for the nose.

9 ▲ Colour 25 g/1 oz of the remaining
icing bright yellow and the rest red.
Roll two-thirds of the red icing into a
sausage shape, to make a mouth. To
make the flower, roll out the remaining
red icing and cut out a 6 cm/2½ inch
round, using the fluted cutter.

10 Roll the edge of the red icing using
a cocktail stick to make it frilly (see
Teddy Bear Christening Cake, step 7).
Roll the yellow icing into a ball to finish
off the flower. Push the florist's wire
through the cake. Remove before serving.

inosaur Cake

For a dino-crazy kid, this cake is just the ticket.
Put it on a cake board or build a little scene using bits
and pieces from around the house and garden.

INGREDIENTS
Serves 8–10
1 quantity Quick-Mix Sponge
Cake mix
½ quantity Butter Icing
1 quantity Truffle Cake mix
900 g/2 lb/2⅔ x quantity
Sugarpaste Icing
pink, yellow, green and black food
colourings
4 tbsp apricot jam, warmed and
sieved

MATERIALS AND EQUIPMENT
900 g/2 lb heart-shaped tin
5 x 25 cm/2 x 10 inch piece of card
small block of wood, for raising
the cake

1 Preheat the oven to 180°C/350°F/
Gas 4. Grease the heart-shaped tin,
line the base with greaseproof paper
and grease the paper. Spoon in the cake
mixture and smooth the surface. Bake
in the centre of the oven for 35–40
minutes or until a skewer inserted into
the centre of the cake comes out clean.
Turn out on to a wire rack, peel off the
lining paper and leave to cool
completely.

2 ▲ Cut the heart-shaped cake in half
vertically, then sandwich the halves
together with the butter icing so they
form a half heart shape. Place the cake
in the centre of the strip of card,
positioned on the long, straight side.
Stand the cake on the small block of
wood to raise it up slightly.

3 ▲ Divide the truffle mixture in half.
Shape one portion into the tail,
making it thicker and flattened at one
end and more pointed at the other.
This will fit on the pointed end of the
cake. Mould the other half of the truffle
cake mix into the head shape, starting
with a ball and then flattening one side,
so the diameter matches the width of
the head end of the cake. Mould the
other end of the head into a pointed
shape for the nose.

4 Place the head and tail in
position at either end of the cake,
moulding the truffle cake mix on to
the cake a little. Cut off about 500 g/
1¼ lb of the sugarpaste icing and
colour it pink. Lightly dust the work
surface with icing sugar and roll out
the icing to a long, thin, rectangular
shape. Brush the cake evenly with jam
and cover the dinosaur with the icing in
one piece from head to toe. Smooth
down the sides and edges with your
hands, then trim.

5 ▲ To make the dinosaur's legs,
cut off about 115 g/4 oz of the
remaining sugarpaste icing and colour it
yellow. Remove about 25 g/1 oz and set
aside, wrapped in clear film. Use the
remainder to roll out 10 evenly sized
balls, each about the size of a small
walnut. Squeeze together two balls for
each of the back legs and three for each
of the front ones. Indent the toes with a
fork, then using a little water stick the
legs on the dinosaur.

6 ▲ Use the reserved yellow
sugarpaste icing to make one small
and three large horns, then stick these in
place with a little water. Cut off about
75 g/3 oz of the remaining icing and
colour it green. Divide it into about 11
evenly sized pieces and shape each into a
cone. Stick these on to the dinosaur with
a little water. Divide the remaining icing
in half and colour one portion black.
Use the white and black icings to make
the mouth, eyes and eyebrows for the
dinosaur. Stick on with a little water.

$\mathcal{D}$ucks on a Pond

A real treat at a children's party. A scrumptious combination of coconut cake, jelly and cream.

INGREDIENTS
Serves 8–10
1 quantity Quick-Mix Sponge Cake mix
575 ml/1 pint/2½ cups double cream
green, yellow and red food colourings
225 g/8 oz/4 cups desiccated coconut
1 x 135 g/4½ oz packet of green jelly, made up to the manufacturer's instructions
200 g/7 oz/½ quantity Sugarpaste Icing
a few tiny sweets
75 g/3 oz marzipan
5 pink marshmallows

MATERIALS AND EQUIPMENT
18 cm/7 inch flan tin
23 cm/9 inch round cake board
duck-shaped cutter
cocktail sticks
garlic press

1 Preheat the oven to 180°C/350°F/ Gas 4. Grease the flan tin, line the base with greaseproof paper and grease the paper. Spoon the cake mixture into the prepared tin and smooth the surface. Bake in the centre of the oven for 35–40 minutes or until firm to the touch. Leave the cake in the tin for about 3 minutes, then turn out on to a wire rack, peel off the lining paper and leave to cool completely.

2 ▲ Add a few drops of green food colouring to the double cream, and beat until it holds soft peaks. Place the cake on the cake board and spread the cream evenly over the cake.

3 ▲ To make the grassy bank, place the coconut in a bowl and add a few drops of green food colouring diluted with a dash of water. Stir until the coconut is speckled green and white.

4 ▲ Cut up the set jelly into 1 cm/ ½ inch pieces. Carefully place the jelly pieces in the centre of the cake.

5 To make the ducks, take 75 g/3 oz of the sugarpaste icing and colour it yellow. Roll out on a work surface lightly dusted with icing sugar until about 5 mm/¼ inch thick.

6 ▲ Using a duck-shaped cutter, stamp out the ducks, then skewer the bottom of each one with a cocktail stick. Lay the ducks on a baking sheet and leave them in a warm, dry place to harden.

7 Use the tiny sweets, or sugarpaste icing, for the ducks' eyes, securing with a drop of water. Take off a small piece of marzipan, about the size of a hazelnut, then colour the remainder green and shape into a frog, using a small, sharp knife to open the mouth and make the feet. Colour the reserved piece of marzipan red, shape into the frog's tongue and secure in position with a little water. Use sweets or blue and white sugarpaste icing for the eyes. Place the frog on the cake board.

8 To make the grass, colour the remaining sugarpaste icing green and push through a garlic press, cutting it off with a small, sharp knife. Place the grass around the pond. To make the flowers, flatten the marshmallows with a rolling pin, then snip the edges with scissors to make the petals. Place the flowers around the pond and put a coloured sweet in the centre of each. The wooden cocktail sticks must be removed from the ducks before serving.

Puppies in Love

*Out of one Swiss roll come two gorgeous puppy dogs.
This cake looks extremely impressive, without
being too difficult to prepare.*

INGREDIENTS
Serves 8–10
*1 quantity chocolate-flavour Swiss
Roll mix
¼ quantity chocolate-flavour
Butter Icing
115 g/4 oz yellow marzipan
green, brown, pink and red food
colourings
75 g/3 oz/1½ cups desiccated
coconut
450 g/1 lb/1⅓ x quantity
Sugarpaste Icing
4 tbsp apricot jam, warmed and
sieved*

MATERIALS AND EQUIPMENT
*33 x 23 cm/13 x 9 inch Swiss
roll tin
25 cm/10 inch square cake board
small round cutter
10 cm/4 inch piece of thin ribbon*

1 Preheat the oven to 180°C/350°F/
Gas 4. Grease the Swiss roll tin, line
with greaseproof paper and grease the
paper. Spoon in the cake mixture and
smooth the surface. Bake in the centre
of the oven for about 12 minutes or
until springy when touched in the
centre. Leave to cool in the tin, on a
wire rack, covered with a clean, just-
damp cloth. Then invert the cake on to
a sheet of greaseproof paper, dredged
with icing sugar.

2 Trim the edges of the cake, then
spread with the chocolate butter
icing, reserving a tiny amount. Roll up
the Swiss roll, using the greaseproof
paper as a guide, then cut in half
widthways.

3 ▲ To make the faces, cut the
marzipan in half and roll each portion
into a ball, then into a squat cone shape.
Use a little of the reserved butter icing to
stick the faces on to the bodies.

4 Place a few drops of green food
colouring in a bowl with the
desiccated coconut. Add a few drops of
water and stir until the coconut is
flecked with green and white. Scatter it
over the cake board then position the
two puppies a little apart on the board.

5 Cut off about 25 g/1 oz of the
sugarpaste icing and set aside,
wrapped in clear film. Colour half the
remaining icing brown and half pink.
Cut off about 50 g/2 oz from each
colour and wrap in clear film.

6 ▲ Lightly dust the work surface
with icing sugar and roll out the
larger portions of brown and pink
icings into 11 × 35 cm/4½ × 14 inch
rectangles. Cut in half widthways and
trim the edges. Cover all four sections
with clear film and set aside.

7 ▲ Roll out the reserved pieces of
brown and white icings, then use
the small round cutter to stamp out
several shapes. Gather up the icing
trimmings and set aside, wrapped in
clear film. Stick the white rounds on to
one of the brown rectangles, then the
brown rounds on to one of the pink
rectangles, using a little water. Use a
rolling pin to press them in slightly.

8 Use a sharp knife to slash all four
icing rectangles along the two short
edges. Brush the body of each puppy
with jam, then lay the brown icing
without spots over one body, and the
pink icing without spots over the other.
Place a little water on the back of each,
then put the brown spotty icing over
the brown dog and the pink spotty
icing over the pink dog.

9 ▲ Roll half of the reserved icings in
your hands to make little tails. Stick
them in place with a little reserved
butter icing. Make a little fringe from
the brown icing for the brown puppy,
and tie a few strands of pink icing
together with the ribbon to make a
fringe for the pink puppy. Stick them in
place with a little water.

10 Use the remaining pieces of
sugarpaste icing to make the
facial features for each puppy, choosing
your own expressions, then stick them in
place with some water. The little
heart-shaped food bowl is an optional
extra, or you can make a small bone, if
you prefer.

$\mathcal{L}$ion Cake

For an animal lover or a celebration cake for a Leo, this cake is quick and surprisingly easy to make.

INGREDIENTS
Serves 10–15
1½ x quantity Quick-Mix Sponge
Cake mix
1 quantity orange-flavour Butter
Icing
orange and red food colourings
675 g/1½ lb yellow marzipan
50 g/2 oz/⅛ quantity Sugarpaste
Icing
red or orange liquorice bootlaces
long and round marshmallows

MATERIALS AND EQUIPMENT
25 x 30 cm/10 x 12 inch roasting tin
30 cm/12 inch square cake board
cheese grater
small heart-shaped cutter

1 Preheat the oven to 180°C/350°F/ Gas 4. Grease the roasting tin, line the base and sides with greaseproof paper and grease the paper. Spoon the cake mixture into the prepared tin and smooth the surface. Bake in the centre of the oven for 45–50 minutes, or until a skewer inserted into the centre of the cake comes out clean. Leave the cake in the tin for about 5 minutes, then turn out on to a wire rack, peel off the lining paper and leave to cool completely.

2 ▲ Place the cake, base side up, on the work surface. Use a small, sharp knife to cut around the edge of the cake in an uneven scallop design. You may need to do this several times in order to cut through to the bottom. Discard the excess cake from the edges. Turn the cake over and trim the top so that it sits squarely.

3 ▲ Place the cake on the cake board. Mix the orange-flavour butter icing in a bowl together with the orange colouring. Spoon the butter icing on top of the cake and spread evenly over the surface and down the sides, using a small palette knife.

4 On a work surface lightly dusted with icing sugar, roll out about 115 g/4 oz of marzipan to a 15 cm/ 6 inch square. Place the marzipan square in the centre of the cake, gently pressing down to secure.

5 ▲ Grate the remaining marzipan on to a sheet of greaseproof paper. Use a palette knife to lift the grated marzipan carefully on to the cake, evenly covering the sides and top up to the edges of the face panel.

6 ▲ Colour the sugarpaste icing red, then roll out on a work surface lightly dusted with icing sugar. Use the heart-shaped cutter to stamp out the lion's nose and position on the cake, securing it with a little water. Take a little of the excess sugarpaste icing and use your fingers to roll out two thin, short strands for the mouth. Position on the cake, securing with water.

7 Cut the liquorice sticks into graduated lengths, and place on the cake for the whiskers. For the eyes, flatten two round marshmallows and place on the cake, securing with water.

8 ▲ To make the eyebrows, cut the long marshmallows into 5 cm/2 in lengths, and snip along one side. Place them on the cake, securing with water.

eepo Rabbits

*An easy cake to make for a chocoholic who loves rabbits.
All the fun is in the decorating.*

INGREDIENTS
Serves 6–8
For the Toadstools
*2 size 3 egg whites
25 g/1 oz/2 tbsp caster sugar*

For the Cake
*1 quantity Swiss Roll cake mix
1 quantity chocolate-flavour Butter
Icing
150 g/5 oz/2½ cups desiccated
coconut
25 g/1 oz/3 tbsp cocoa powder, plus
a little extra for dusting
225 g/8 oz/⅔ quantity Sugarpaste
Icing
pink, yellow, green and brown food
colourings*

*MATERIALS AND EQUIPMENT
piping bag fitted with a small round
nozzle
23 x 33 cm/9 x 13 inch Swiss roll
tin
23 cm/9 inch square cake board
small rabbit cutter
small butterfly cutter
1 cocktail stick
small leaf cutter*

1 Preheat the oven to 135°C/275°F/
Gas 1. To make the meringue
toadstools, place a sheet of baking
parchment on a baking sheet. Place the
egg whites in a clean, dry mixing bowl
and whisk until they hold soft peaks.
Whisk in half of the sugar, then add the
rest. Whisk until the mixture holds stiff
peaks. Fill the piping bag with the
meringue mixture and pipe several
small rounds and several 2.5 cm/1 inch
stalks. Bake for about 1 hour, or until
dry. Leave to cool completely.

2 ▲ To assemble the toadstools,
gently press a stalk into a small
meringue round. Set aside. Increase the
oven temperature to 180°C/350°F/Gas 4.

3 Grease the tin, line the base and
sides with greaseproof paper and
grease the paper. Spoon the cake
mixture into the tin and smooth the
surface. Bake in the centre of the oven
for about 12 minutes, or until firm to
the touch. Leave the cake in the tin,
covered, to cool completely.

4 Lay a sheet of greaseproof paper on
the work surface and sprinkle with
icing sugar. Tip the cake on to the
greaseproof paper and remove the lining
paper. Spread with about one-third of
the butter icing and roll up. Cut off one-
third of the roll and stand the larger
section on the cake board, sticking it in
place with a little butter icing.

5 ▲ Position the smaller log next to
the larger one, then cover both in
the remaining butter icing. Peak and
swirl the icing quite unevenly to make it
look like bark.

6 Place the coconut in a bowl and sift
in the cocoa powder. Stir well until
evenly blended. Spoon the coconut all
around the cake.

7 ▲ Take half of the sugarpaste icing
and divide into two portions.
Colour one portion pink. Roll out each
piece on a work surface lightly dusted
with icing sugar until about 5 mm/
¼ inch thick. Stamp out two rabbits in
each colour. Use the pink and white
trimmings to make tiny balls for the
eyes, securing them in place with a little
water. Place the rabbits on a baking
sheet and leave until dried out.

8 Cut off about one-quarter of the
remaining sugarpaste icing and
colour it yellow. Roll out until about
5 mm/¼ inch thick and stamp out a
butterfly. Use the cocktail stick to
indent the centre of the butterfly gently
and fold it a little. Press half of the
cocktail stick through the base of the
butterfly. Place the butterfly on the
baking sheet with the rabbits, resting
one wing on the edge of the baking
sheet so that it dries in that position.

9 Cut off one-third of the remaining
sugarpaste icing and colour it green.
Roll it out thinly, then cut it into strips
using scissors and snip the strips into
pointed sections to make the grass.
Position the pieces of grass randomly
in the coconut around the cake.

10 Colour the remaining icing
brown and roll out thinly. Cut
out several leaf shapes, and then use
a small, sharp knife to make the leaf
indentations. Gently twist and bend the
leaves a little, then place them in the
coconut. Reserve the trimmings.

11 To assemble the rabbits, use a
little of the reserved brown icing
to stick them securely in place around
the cake. Press the butterfly's cocktail
stick into the back of the cake. Finally,
position the meringue toadstools and
dust them with a little cocoa powder.

Cat in a Basket

The pretty woven pattern of the basket is quite simple to do but is surprisingly realistic. The marzipan cat can be painted in appropriate colours to make it a portrait of your own family pet.

INGREDIENTS
Serves 8
18 cm/7 inch round Madeira Cake
115 g/4 oz/⅓ quantity Butter Icing
30 ml/2 tbsp apricot jam, warmed and sieved
350 g/12 oz pink marzipan
225 g/8 oz green marzipan
225 g/8 oz yellow marzipan
115 g/4 oz/⅓ quantity Sugarpaste Icing
brown food colouring

MATERIALS AND EQUIPMENT
23 cm/9 inch round cake board
fine paintbrush

1 ▲ Split the cake and fill with butter icing. Place on the cake board. Measure the circumference of the cake with string, fold in half and measure (this will give the length of the marzipan strips to be cut). Brush the cake with apricot jam.

2 Roll out the pink marzipan to a large rectangle. Cut into five 1 cm/ ½ inch strips, long enough to fit half way round the cake. Roll out the green marzipan and cut into 7.5 cm/3 inch lengths of the same width.

3 ▲ Fold back alternate pink strips and lay a green strip across widthways. Fold back the pink strips over the green strip to form the weave, fold back the second lot of pink strips and repeat the process. Press lightly to join.

4 ▲ Trim the basket weave and press on to the sides of the cake, joining the edges neatly.

5 ▲ Using the yellow marzipan, model a cat about 10 cm/4 inches across. Leave to dry overnight.

6 Roll out the sugarpaste icing, cut out a 23 cm/9 inch diameter circle and place on the cake, arranging it in folds to look like a blanket. Sit the cat in the centre of the cake.

7 ▲ Roll any leftover pink and green marzipan into long ropes. Twist together and lay around the edge of the basket then press on neatly. With a fine paintbrush and brown colouring, paint the face and markings on the cat.

*M*ouse in Bed

This cake is suitable for almost any age. The quilt and sheets may reflect a child's favourite colour.
Make the mouse well ahead to allow it time to dry.

INGREDIENTS
Serves 10
1½ x quantity Quick-mix Sponge
Cake baked in a 20 cm/8 inch
square tin
115 g/4 oz/½ quantity Butter Icing
2 tbsp apricot jam, warmed
and sieved
450 g/1 lb marzipan
675 g/1½ lb/2 x quantity
Sugarpaste Icing
blue and pink food colourings

MATERIALS AND EQUIPMENT
25 cm/10 inch square cake board
flower cutter
pink and blue food colouring pens

1 ▲ Split the cake and fill with butter icing. Cut 5 cm/2 inches off one side and reserve; the cake should measure 20 x 15 cm/8 x 6 inches. Place on the cake board and brush with apricot jam. Cover with marzipan. With the reserved cake, cut a pillow to fit the bed and cover with marzipan, pressing a hollow in the middle for the head. Cut a mound for the body and legs of the mouse and cover with marzipan. Leave to dry overnight.

2 ▲ Cover the cake and pillow with sugarpaste icing. Lightly press a fork around the edge to make a frill around the pillow. Roll out 350 g/12 oz sugarpaste icing and cut into 7.5 cm/ 3 inch wide strips to make a valance. Attach to the side of the bed with a little water and arrange in drapes.

3 ▲ To make the top sheet and quilt; colour 75 g/3 oz sugarpaste icing pale blue and roll out to an 18 cm/ 7 inch square to cover the bed. Lightly mark a diamond pattern with the back of a knife and press a flower cutter into the diamonds to mark. Put the pillow and body on top of the cake and cover with the quilt.

4 ▲ Roll out a little white sugarpaste and cut a 2.5 x 19 cm/1 x 7½ inch strip for the sheet. Mark along one length to resemble a seam and place over the quilt, tucking it in at the top.

5 ▲ Colour a little marzipan pink and make the head and paws.

6 ▲ Put the mouse's paws over the edge of the sheet. Draw facial markings with food colouring pens.

The Beehive

The perfect cake for an outdoors spring or summer party.
Take the bees along separately on their wires and
insert them into the cake at the picnic.

INGREDIENTS
Serves 8–10
1 quantity Quick-Mix Sponge
Cake mix
900 g/2 lb yellow marzipan
5 tbsp apricot jam, warmed and
sieved
black food colouring
25 g/1 oz sugarpaste icing

MATERIALS AND EQUIPMENT
900 g/2 lb pudding basin
23 cm/9 inch fluted or round cake
board
20 cm/8 inch square of rice paper
florist's wire covered in florist's tape

1 Preheat the oven to 180°C/350°F/ Gas 4. Grease and flour the pudding basin. Spoon in the cake mixture and smooth the surface. Bake in the centre of the oven for 40–45 minutes or until a skewer inserted into the centre of the cake comes out clean. Leave the cake in the basin for about 5 minutes, then turn out on to a wire rack and leave to cool completely.

2 Cut off about 175 g/6 oz of marzipan and set aside, wrapped in clear film. Knead the remainder on a work surface lightly dusted with icing sugar, then roll it out into a long, thin sausage shape. If it breaks when it gets too long, make more than one sausage. Place the cake, dome side up, on the cake board and brush evenly with apricot jam.

3 ▲ Starting at the back of the base, coil the marzipan sausage around the cake, keeping it neat and tight all the way to the top. Any joins that have to be made should be placed at the back of the cake.

4 ▲ Using a small, sharp knife, cut an arched doorway at the front of the cake. Remove the cut-out section and cut away some of the inside cake to make a hollow. Brush the crumbs away from the doorway.

5 ▲ To make six bees, divide the reserved marzipan in half and colour one portion black. Set aside a cherry-sized ball of black marzipan, and wrap in clear film. Divide both the black and the yellow marzipan into 12 small balls. To make a bee, pinch together two balls of each colour, alternately placed. Stick them together with a little water, if necessary. Cut the rice paper into six pairs of rounded wings, then stick them to the bees with a tiny drop of water.

6 ▲ Use the reserved black marzipan and sugarpaste icing to make the facial features. Then cut the florist's wire into various lengths and then use it to pierce the bees from underneath. Once secure, press the other end of the wire into the cake in various places. The wires must be removed before serving.

ℬumble Bee

This friendly bee looks effective, but is very quick and simple to construct. If time is very short you can decorate the board with ready-made sugar flowers instead of making them.

INGREDIENTS
Serves 10
1 quantity Quick-mix Sponge Cake baked in a 20 cm/8 inch round tin
115 g/4 oz/⅓ quantity Butter Icing
2 tbsp apricot jam, warmed and sieved
350 g/12 oz marzipan
500 g/1 lb 4 oz/1½ x quantity Sugarpaste Icing
yellow, black, blue, pink and green food colourings
50 g/2 oz/1 cup desiccated coconut
115 g/4 oz/⅛ quantity Royal Icing

MATERIALS AND EQUIPMENT
25 cm/10 inch square cake board
paper doiley
sticky tape
pipe cleaner

1 ▲ Split the cake and fill with butter icing. Cut in half, sandwich both halves together and stand upright on the cake board. Trim the ends to shape the head and tail. Brush with apricot jam and cover with marzipan. Colour two-thirds of the sugarpaste icing yellow, roll out and use to cover the cake. Reserve the trimmings.

2 ▲ Colour two-thirds of the remaining sugarpaste icing black. Roll out and cut out three stripes 2.5 x 25 cm/1 x 10 inches. Leave about 10 cm/4 inches for the head from the end of the cake and position the stripes evenly spaced behind the head sticking them with a little water. Roll out and cut eyes, mouth and daisies from the sugarpaste icing. Colour and stick on with a little water.

3 ▲ Put the coconut into a bowl and mix in a drop of green colouring. Cover the cake board with royal icing, then sprinkle over the coconut to look like grass. Place the daisies on the board. To make the wings, cut the doiley in half, wrap each half into a cone shape and stick together with sticky tape. Cut the pipe cleaner in half and stick the pieces into the cake just behind the head. Place the wings over the pipe cleaners.

Teddy's Birthday

This is a perfect cake for anyone who loves teddies. To get a really smooth, flat finish to the cake, use an icing smoother on the top.

INGREDIENTS
Serves 10
1 quantity Quick-mix Sponge Cake
baked in a 20 cm/8 inch round tin
115 g/4 oz/⅓ quantity Butter Icing
30 ml/2 tbsp apricot jam, warmed
and sieved
350 g/12 oz marzipan
450 g/1 lb/1⅓ x quantity
Sugarpaste Icing
brown, red, blue and black
food colourings
115 g/4 oz/⅛ quantity Royal Icing
silver balls

MATERIALS AND EQUIPMENT
25 cm/10 inch round cake board
greaseproof paper
ribbon, 2.5 cm/1 inch wide
greaseproof paper piping bag
No 7 shell nozzle
No 7 star nozzle
birthday cake candles

2 ▲ Colour one-third of the remaining sugarpaste icing pale brown. Colour a piece pink, a piece red, some blue and a tiny piece black. Using the template, cut out the pieces and place in position on the cake. Stick down by lifting the edges carefully and brushing the undersides with a little water. Roll small ovals for the eyes and stick in place with the other face shapes.

3 ▲ Tie the ribbon round the cake. Colour the royal icing blue and pipe the border around the base of the cake with the shell nozzle and tiny stars around the small cake with the star nozzle. Decorate the icing with silver balls. Put the candles on the cake.

1 ▲ Split the cake and fill with butter icing. Place on the cake board and brush with apricot jam. Cover with marzipan. Roll out two-thirds of the sugarpaste icing and use to cover the cake. Make a template on greaseproof paper using the photograph as a guide, and mark the design on top of the cake.

Hickory Dickory Dock

This appealing cake is based on the nursery rhyme. Small children love the jolly clockface, and the sugar mouse can be given as a prize.

INGREDIENTS
Serves 12–15
2 x quantity Quick-mix Sponge Cake baked in a 20 cm/8 inch round tin and a 15 cm/6 inch square tin
225 g/8 oz/⅔ quantity Butter Icing
3 tbsp apricot jam, warmed and sieved
675 g/1½ lb marzipan
550 g/1¼ lb/1⅔ x quantity Sugarpaste Icing
brown, gold, red, blue and black food colourings
2 silver balls
115 g/4 oz/⅙ quantity Royal Icing

MATERIALS AND EQUIPMENT
25 x 35 cm/10 x 14 inch cake board
paintbrush
plastic mouse mould
10 cm/4 inch piece of string
greaseproof paper
greaseproof paper piping bag
No 1 writing nozzle

1 ▲ Split the cakes and fill with butter icing. Cut two wedges off one end of the square cake, 6 cm/2½ inches from the corner.

2 ▲ Use a cake tin as a guide to cut a semi-circle from the opposite end of the square cake to fit around the round cake. Place on the cake board and brush with apricot jam. Cover with marzipan. Colour four-fifths of the sugarpaste icing brown. Roll out and use to cover the cake. Reserve the trimmings.

3 ▲ Roll out half the remaining sugarpaste icing and cut a 15 cm/6 inch circle for the face and a window for the pendulum. Cut out a 5 cm/2 inch long pendulum and 5 cm/2 inch and 6 cm/2½ inch long hands.

4 ▲ Paint the pendulum and hands gold and leave to dry overnight.

5 ▲ Colour most of the remaining sugarpaste icing pink and mould a mouse with a string tail and silver balls for eyes. Leave to dry overnight on greaseproof paper.

6 ▲ Stick on the clock face with a little water. Using a template, mark the numbers and face on the clock. Colour the royal icing black and pipe the numbers with a No 1 nozzle. Stick on the window with a little water. Roll out the excess brown sugarpaste icing into long sausages and edge the face and the window. Colour the remaining sugarpaste icing blue, red and black. Roll out and cut the eyes, pupils, eyebrows, mouth and centre. Stick on the hands, features and pendulum with a little water. Stick on the mouse.

ip

If you are making this cake for a children's party, you may want to model extra mice from pink sugarpaste icing for the children to take home.

Noah's Ark

This charming cake is decorated with small purchased animals, about 4 cm/1½ inches high, available from party and cake decorating shops. Children will love to take home one of the novelties, as a reminder of the party.

INGREDIENTS
Serves 10
1½ x quantity Quick-mix Sponge Cake baked in a 20 cm/8 inch square cake tin
115 g/4 oz/⅓ quantity Butter Icing
30 ml/2 tbsp apricot jam, warmed and sieved
450 g/1 lb marzipan
450 g/1 lb/1⅓ x quantity Sugarpaste Icing, coloured light brown
115 g/4 oz/⅙ quantity Royal Icing
yellow and blue food colourings
chocolate mint stick

MATERIALS AND EQUIPMENT
25 cm/10 inch square cake board
rice paper
small animal cake ornaments

1 ▲ Split the cake and fill with butter icing. Cut a rectangle 20 x 13 cm/ 8 x 5 inches and cut to shape the hull of the boat. Place diagonally on the cake board.

2 ▲ Cut a smaller rectangle 10 x 6 cm/ 4 x 2½ inch for the cabin and a triangular roof from the remaining piece of cake. Sandwich together with butter icing or apricot jam.

3 ▲ Brush the three pieces of cake with apricot jam and cover with marzipan then cover the hull and cabin with brown sugarpaste icing. Sandwich together with butter icing and place in position on the hull. Roll a long sausage from the remaining brown sugarpaste icing and stick round the edge of the hull with a little water. Mark planks of wood with the back of a knife. Leave to dry overnight.

4 ▲ Colour one-third of the royal icing yellow and spread over the roof with a palette knife. Roughen it with a skewer to look like thatch.

5 ▲ Colour the remaining royal icing pale blue and spread over the cake board, making rough waves. Stick a rice paper flag on to the chocolate mint stick and press on the back of the boat. Stick the small animals on to the deck with dabs of icing.

$\mathcal{M}$agic Rabbit

This cheery rabbit bursting from a top hat is the perfect centrepiece for a party with a magic theme. For an extra surprise, cover the cake with a silk handkerchief, to be pulled away by the guest of honour.

INGREDIENTS
Serves 10
1½ x quantity Quick-mix Sponge
Cake baked in 2 x 15 cm/6 inch
round cake tins
225 g/8 oz/⅔ quantity Butter Icing
115 g/4 oz/⅙ quantity Royal Icing
45 ml/3 tbsp apricot jam, warmed
and sieved
675 g/1½ lb marzipan
675 g/1½ lb/2 x quantity Sugarpaste
Icing, coloured grey
black and pink food colourings
silver balls

MATERIALS AND EQUIPMENT
25 cm/10 inch square cake board
wooden spoons
pink ribbon
greaseproof paper piping bag
small star nozzle
No 1 writing nozzle

2 ▲ With the remaining grey sugarpaste icing, roll out to a 15 cm/ 6 inch circle, cut a cross in the centre, place on the hat and curl triangles over a spoon handle to shape. Smooth the join around the edge of the hat.

4 ▲ Stick the rabbit in the centre of the hat with a little royal icing. Tie the ribbon round the hat. Pipe a border of royal icing around the top and base of the hat and decorate with silver balls while the icing is still wet.

1 ▲ Split the cakes and fill with butter icing. Stick on the centre of the cake board with a little royal icing. Brush with apricot jam. Cover with two-thirds of the marzipan. Roll out the grey icing and use about three-quarters to cover the cake. Roll out the remaining sugarpaste icing to a 20 cm/8 inch round. Cut a 15 cm/6 inch circle from the centre, and lower the ring carefully over the cake. Shape the sides of the brim and hold in place to dry.

3 ▲ Colour the remaining marzipan pink. Shape the rabbit's head, about 5 cm/2 inches in diameter, shaping a slightly pointed face. Mark the position of the eyes, nose and mouth. Shape the ears around the handle of a wooden spoon and leave to dry separately overnight.

5 ▲ Colour the remaining royal icing black and use to pipe two eyes and a smiling mouth.

Frog Prince

This smartly dressed frog, with his golden crown and happy smile,
makes a perfect cake for a birthday princess.

INGREDIENTS
Serves 8
1 quantity Quick-mix Sponge Cake
baked in a 20 cm/8 inch round
cake tin
115 g/4 oz/⅓ quantity Butter Icing
30 ml/ 2 tbsp apricot jam, warmed
and sieved
450 g/1 lb marzipan
550 g/1¼ lb/1⅔ x quantity
Sugarpaste Icing
115 g/4 oz/⅙ quantity Royal Icing
green, red, black and gold
food colourings

MATERIALS AND EQUIPMENT
25 cm/10 inch square cake board

1 ▲ Split the cake and fill with butter
icing. Cut it in half and sandwich
both halves together with apricot jam.
Stand upright diagonally across the
cake board.

2 ▲ Brush the cake with apricot jam
and cover with marzipan. Reserve
115 g/4 oz/⅓ quantity of sugarpaste
icing and colour the rest green. Cover
the cake with the green sugarpaste. To
make the legs and feet, roll green
sugarpaste icing into 20 cm/8 inch
lengths about 1 cm/½ inch in diameter.
Fold in half for the back legs and stick
on with a little water.

3 The front legs are rolled into
10 cm/4 inch lengths, folded in half
and pinched to taper to the foot end.
The feet are made in the same way, cut
to 4 cm/1½ inch lengths and pinched
together to tapered ends. Stick in place
with a little royal icing. Roll balls for
the eyes and stick in place on top of
the cake.

4 ▲ Roll out the reserved sugarpaste
icing. Cut a strip 5 x 19 cm/2 x
7½ inches and mark one edge at 2.5 cm/
1 inch intervals, then cut out triangles to
make the crown shape. Wrap around a
glass dusted with cornflour and moisten
the edges to join. Leave to dry (this
may take up to 2 days).

5 Cut a 10 cm/4 inch circle for the
white shirt. Stick in place and trim
the edge level with the cake board. Cut
white circles and stick to the eyes.
Colour a little sugarpaste pink, roll into
a sausage and stick on for the mouth.
Colour a little sugarpaste black, roll out
and cut pupils for the eyes and bow tie
and stick in place.

6 ▲ Paint the crown gold and stick
into position with royal icing.

Crazy Caterpillar

A no-bake cake made from sponge cake crumbs, home-made or bought. You can double the quantity for an extra-large party, but remember the cake is rich and heavy in texture so you only serve a small amount. One ball per person is more than enough!

INGREDIENTS
Serves 11
1 quantity Truffle Cake mix
675 g/1½ lb yellow marzipan
green, brown and orange food colourings
selection of coloured liquorice sticks, or sweets, for the feet
green-coloured desiccated coconut (see Puppies in Love, step 4), for the grass
small flowers, to decorate (optional)

MATERIALS AND EQUIPMENT
40 x 20 cm/16 x 8 inch cake board (optional)
small round fluted cutter
round fluted aspic cutter

1 ▲ Using slightly damp hands, roll the truffle cake mixture into balls about the size of a large walnut. Place them on a baking sheet as you make them, then cover with clear film and set to one side.

2 ▲ Divide the marzipan into three equal portions, then colour one portion green, one portion brown and the other portion orange. Remove a small amount of orange and green marzipan, to make the face features, and set aside, covered with clear film.

3 ▲ Roll each colour of marzipan into a sausage shape about 45 cm/18 inches long on a work surface lightly dusted with icing sugar. Make sure the sausage shape is even all the way along; if it breaks, compress the marzipan into a ball and start again.

4 ▲ Place the three long sausages side-by-side on the work surface. Starting at one end, hold them together firmly and start to turn them in a twisting motion — do not squeeze. Place the twist back on the work surface, then use a rolling pin to push and roll the twist gently until it is flat and the colours merge. It should be about 50 cm/20 inches long.

5 Lay the truffle balls all along the length of the marzipan strip, then wrap the marzipan evenly around the balls, sealing the join by pinching the marzipan together. (An extra pair of hands is useful for this stage.) Turn the caterpillar over so the join is underneath, tucking in and cutting off any excess marzipan from the ends. Lift the caterpillar on to the cake board, if using, otherwise position it on the table, curving it slightly.

6 Roll out the reserved orange and green marzipan thinly and use the fluted cutters to stamp out rounds for the eyes. Use a little water to stick the smaller green rounds on the orange rounds, then stick them on to one end of the caterpillar to make the face. Roll a tiny piece of orange marzipan into a little sausage, shape and stick it on to make the mouth. Cut the liquorice sticks into small pieces and position them along either side, to make the feet. Scatter the green-coloured coconut all around. Add a few flowers, if you like.

*F*un and Games

Baking does not always have to be a serious business all the time. Celebrate any event with a novel cake design that will provide an amusing twist to traditional occasions. Using a range of colours and icing techniques, cakes can be fashioned into almost any design you could dream of. From a pinball machine to an army tank, from space ships to circus clowns, your imagination really is the only limit.

Artist's Box and Palette

*Making cakes is an art in itself, and this cake proves it. It is
the perfect celebration cake for artists of all ages.*

INGREDIENTS
Serves 30
20 cm/8 in square Rich Fruit Cake
*3 tbsp apricot jam, warmed and
sieved*
450 g/1 lb marzipan
*800 g/1¼ lb/2⅓ x quantity
Sugarpaste Icing*
*125 g/4 oz/⅛ quantity Royal Icing
brown, yellow, blue, black, silver,
orange, green and purple food
colourings*

MATERIALS AND EQUIPMENT
stiff paper for template
25 cm/10 in square cake board
paintbrush

1 Brush the cake with the apricot jam.
On a work surface lightly dusted
with icing sugar, roll out the marzipan
and use to cover the cake. Leave to dry
for 12 hours.

2 Make a template out of stiff paper
in the shape of an artist's palette
that will fit the top of the cake. Colour
just less than one-quarter of the
sugarpaste icing a pale brown. On a
work surface lightly dusted with icing
sugar, roll out to the size of the template
and cut out the palette shape.

3 Colour about two-thirds of the
remaining sugarpaste icing brown.
Roll out, brush the marzipanned cake
with a little water and cover the cake
with the icing. Place the cake on the
cake board and leave to dry for
several hours.

4 ▲ With the remaining sugarpaste
icing, leave half white and divide
the remainder into seven equal
portions. Colour these yellow, blue,
black, silver, orange, green and purple.
Shape the box handle with black icing
and the box clips and paintbrush
ferrules with silver icing. Shape the
paintbrush bristles with orange icing
and mark the hairs of the bristles with
a knife. Shape the paintbrush handles in
various colours and attach the handles,
ferrules and bristles with a little royal
icing. Leave all the pieces to dry on
greaseproof paper for several hours.

5 ▲ Make two paint tubes from some
of the white icing. Roll out an
oblong shape for each one and then
wrap these around 'sausages' of icing,
sealing the edges with a little water.
Paint lettering and coloured bands on
the tubes with food colouring.

6 ▲ Shape the squeezed-out paint in
various colours and attach one to
each of the paint tubes with a little royal
icing. Leave all the pieces to dry on
greaseproof paper for several hours.

7 Using the remaining white icing, roll
out two small rectangles for sheets
of paper and brush on patterns with
watered-down food colouring. Leave
the sheets to dry on greaseproof paper
for several hours.

8 ▲ Paint wood markings on to the
cake box with watered-down brown
food colouring and leave to dry. To
assemble the cake, attach the handles
and clips to the front side of the box
and the palette to the top of the cake
with a little royal icing. Position the
paintbrushes, tubes, squeezed-out paint
and the sheets of paper on the cake and
around the cake board.

Strawberry Cake

A summer-time cake or for someone who's simply mad about strawberries!

INGREDIENTS
Serves 10–12
*1 quantity Quick-Mix Sponge
Cake mix
650 g/1 lb 7oz marzipan
green, red and yellow food
colourings
caster sugar, to dredge*

MATERIALS AND EQUIPMENT
*900 g/2 lb heart-shaped tin
30 cm/12 inch round cake board
icing smoother*

Tip

You can also sandwich the cake with a half quantity of strawberry-flavour Butter Icing before brushing it with apricot jam for extra flavour! Use a long, serrated knife and cut the cake horizontally into two layers.

1 Preheat the oven to 180°C/350°F/ Gas 4. Grease the heart-shaped tin, line the base with greaseproof paper and grease the paper. Spoon in the cake mixture and smooth the surface. Bake in the centre of the oven for 35–40 minutes or until a skewer inserted into the centre of the cake comes out clean.

2 Leave in the tin for about 5 minutes, then turn out on to a wire rack, peel off the lining paper and leave to cool completely.

3 ▲ Cut off about 175 g/6 oz of the marzipan and colour it green. Brush the cake board with a little apricot jam, then roll out the green marzipan on the work surface lightly dusted with icing sugar and use to cover the cake board. Trim the edges. Use an icing smoother to make the marzipan as flat and as smooth as possible.

4 ▲ Evenly brush the remaining apricot jam over the top and sides of the cake. Position the cake on the cake board. Cut off about 275 g/10 oz of the remaining marzipan and colour it red. Roll it out to about 5 mm/¼ inch thick and use to cover the cake, smoothing down the sides and edges. Trim the edges. Use the handle of a teaspoon to indent the strawberry evenly and lightly all over.

5 To make the stalk, cut off another 175 g/6 oz of marzipan and colour it bright green. Cut it in half and roll out one portion into a 10 × 15 cm/4 × 6 inch rectangle. Use a sharp knife to cut 'V' shapes out of the rectangle, leaving a 2.5 cm/1 inch border across the top, to form the calyx. Position this on the cake, curling and moving the sections to make them look more realistic.

6 ▲ Roll the other half of the green marzipan in your hands into a sausage shape about 13 cm/5 inches long. Bend it slightly, then position it on the cake to form the stalk.

7 ▲ To make the strawberry seeds, colour the remaining marzipan yellow. Pull off tiny pieces about the size of an apple pip and roll them into little tear-shaped seeds. Place them in the indentations all over the strawberry. Dust the cake and board with sifted caster sugar.

Sailing Boat

Make this cake for someone who loves sailing or is going on a journey – you can even personalize the cake with a rice paper name tag flag, written with a food colouring pen.

INGREDIENTS
Serves 10–12
1½ x quantity Quick-mix Sponge
Cake mix
60 ml/4 tbsp apricot jam, warmed
and sieved
450 g/1 lb/1⅓ x quantity
Sugarpaste Icing
350 g/12 oz/1 quantity Butter Icing
coloured blue
1 sheet of rice paper
1 grissini
1 black liquorice wheel, with an
orange sweet in the centre
1 blue sherbet 'flying saucer'
9 short candy sticks
4 Polo mints
1 red liquorice 'bootlace'
1 black liquorice 'bootlace'

MATERIALS AND EQUIPMENT
900 g/2 lb loaf tin
33 x 18 cm/13 x 7 inch cake board
cocktail stick
black food colouring pen

1 Preheat the oven to 180°C/350°F/ Gas 4. Grease the loaf tin. Line the base and sides with greaseproof paper and grease the paper. Spoon the cake mixture into the prepared tin and smooth the top with a plastic spatula. Bake in the preheated oven for 55–60 minutes, or until a skewer inserted into the centre of the cake comes out clean. Leave for 5 minutes before turning out on to a wire rack to cool.

2 ▲ Slice a thin layer off the top of the cake to make it perfectly flat. Trim one end to make a pointed bow. Using a small sharp knife, cut a shallow hollow from the centre of the cake, leaving a 1 cm/½ inch border.

3 ▲ Brush the cake all over with the apricot jam. Roll out the sugarpaste icing to a 35 x 23 cm/14 x 9 inch rectangle and lay over the cake. Gently ease the sugarpaste icing into the hollow middle and down the sides of the cake, until completely and evenly covered. Trim the edges at the base.

4 Cover the cake board with the blue butter icing, peaking it to resemble a rough sea. Position the cake on the iced board. Cut the rice paper into two tall triangular sails. Using a small brush, apply a little water along the length of the grissini and secure the rice paper sails to it. Insert the mast into the front of the hollowed compartment at the bow of the boat.

5 Cut a small flag shape from the remaining rice paper and personalize it with the recipient's name using the food colouring pen. Stick the flag on to the cocktail stick using a little water and position it at the stern of the boat.

6 Uncoil the liquorice wheel and remove the sweet from the centre. Use the liquorice to make a fender all around the outside of the boat, securing it with a little water. Trim the excess liquorice and use the remainder to line the seating area in the same way. Position the sweet from the centre of the wheel to one side of the boat for the searchlight. Place the sherbet flying saucer at the back of the seating area for the cushion.

7 ▲ Insert seven of the short candy sticks around the bow of the boat, leaving a little space between each one and allowing them to stand about 2.5 cm/1 inch above the surface of the cake. Insert the remaining two short candy sticks at either side of the stern of the boat and hang two Polo mints on each, for the life belts. Use the bootlace liquorice strips to tie loosely in and out of the candy sticks at the bow of the boat for the guard rail. Trim away any excess, if necessary.

Shirt and Tie Cake

Instead of buying the man in your life a shirt and tie for his birthday, make him a cake for a deliciously novel surprise.

INGREDIENTS
Serves 20–30
2 x quantity Quick-mix Sponge
Cake mix
350 g/12 oz/1 quantity coffee-flavour
Butter Icing
90 ml/6 tbsp apricot jam, warmed
and sieved
icing sugar, for dusting
1 kg/2 lb 4 oz/3 x quantity
Sugarpaste Icing
blue food colouring
115 g/4 oz/1 cup icing sugar, sifted
45–60 ml/3–4 tbsp water

MATERIALS AND EQUIPMENT
19 x 27 cm/7½ x 10½ inch
roasting tin
30 x 33 cm/12 x 13 inch cake board
steel ruler
wooden skewer
greaseproof paper piping bag fitted
with a small round nozzle
40 x 5 cm/16 x 2 inch piece of flexible
card, the short ends cut at an angle,
for the collar
paintbrush
'Happy Birthday' cake decoration
blue tissue paper

1 Preheat the oven to 180°C/350°F/
Gas 4. Grease the roasting tin. Line
the base and sides with greaseproof
paper and grease the paper. Spoon the
mixture into the tin and smooth the
surface. Bake in the preheated oven for
1¼–1½ hours, or until a skewer inserted
into the centre of the cake comes out
clean. Leave for 5 minutes before
turning out on to a wire rack to cool.

2 Cut the cake in half horizontally and
spread with the coffee-flavour butter
icing. Sandwich together with the top
half of the sponge cake. Brush the cake
evenly with apricot jam and lightly dust
the work surface with icing sugar.

3 Colour 675 g/1½ lb/2 x quantity
sugarpaste icing light blue. Roll out
the light blue sugarpaste icing to about
5 mm/¼ inch thick and use to cover the
cake, gently easing the sugarpaste icing
down the sides and corners. Trim away
any excess icing. Place the cake on the
cake board.

4 ▲ Using a steel ruler, make grooves
down the length and sides of the
cake, in straight lines, about 2.5 cm/
1 inch apart. Use a wooden skewer to
re-indent the grooves, rolling the skewer
slightly from side to side to make the
channels deeper and slightly wider.

5 ▲ Mix the icing sugar and water
together in a small bowl to make a
just thick glacé icing and use to fill the
piping bag fitted with the small, round
nozzle. Pipe lines of glacé icing into the
grooves on the top and sides of the
cake, moving slowly and evenly.

6 ▲ To make the collar, roll out
225 g/8 oz/⅔ quantity sugarpaste
icing, on a work surface lightly dusted
with icing sugar, to a 40.5 x 10 cm/
16½ x 4 inch rectangle. Lay the piece of
card for the collar on top, placing it
along one edge of the sugarpaste icing.
Brush a little water around the edges of
the sugarpaste icing, then carefully lift
the other edge of the sugarpaste icing
and fold over the card to encase it
completely. Trim the two short ends to
match the angles of the card. Carefully
lift the collar and gently bend it round
and position on the cake, applying a
little water to help secure it in place.

7 Colour the remaining sugarpaste
icing dark blue. To make the tie, cut
off one-third of the dark blue
sugarpaste icing and shape into a
pyramid for the tie knot. Position the
knot. Lightly dust the work surface
with icing sugar and roll out the
remaining dark blue sugarpaste icing to
about 5 mm/¼ inch thick.

8 Cut out a tie piece to fit under the
knot and long enough to hang over
the edge of the cake, making it slightly
wider at the end where you cut a point.
Position the tie piece, tucking it under
the knot and applying a little water to
secure it in place. Finish the cake with
the 'Happy Birthday' decoration and
tissue paper.

Liquorice Sweet Cake

If liquorice sweets are a favourite, this is a cake to fantasize over. Larger than life, its base is a Madeira cake filled with butter icing, and it is topped with look-alike liquorice sweets.

INGREDIENTS
Serves 15–20
20 cm/8 inch square Madeira cake
15 cm/6 inch square Madeira cake
675 g/1½ lb/2 x quantity
Butter Icing
45 ml/3 tbsp apricot jam, warmed
and sieved
350 g/12 oz marzipan
800 g/1¾ lb/2⅓ x quantity
Sugarpaste Icing
egg-yellow, black, blue and
mulberry food colourings

MATERIALS AND EQUIPMENT
25 cm/10 inch square cake board
4.5 cm/1¼ inch round cutter

1 Cut both the cakes horizontally into three. Fill with the butter icing, reserving a little to coat the outsides of the smaller cake. Wrap and set aside the smaller cake.

2 Brush the 20 cm/8 inch cake with the apricot jam. Roll out the marzipan and cover the cake. Position the cake on the cake board, securing underneath with a little butter icing. Leave to dry for 12 hours.

3 Take 350 g/12 oz/1 quantity sugarpaste icing and colour it yellow. Take 115 g/4 oz/⅓ quantity sugarpaste icing and colour half black and leave the other half white. Brush the marzipanned cake lightly with water. Roll out the yellow icing; cover the top and down one third of the sides of the cake.

4 ▲ Roll out the white icing and cut a strip wide and long enough to cover the sides of the bottom one-third of the cake. Position on the cake, securing the join with a little water. Roll out the black icing to a strip wide enough and long enough to fill the central third strip, between the yellow and white strips. Position on the cake.

5 Cut the 15 cm/6 inch cake into three equal strips. Divide two of the strips each into three squares. From the remaining strip cut out two circles (about 4.5 cm/1¼ inches), using a cutter as a guide.

6 Take another 115 g/4 oz/⅓ quantity sugarpaste icing and colour it black. Take the remaining sugarpaste icing and divide into four equal amounts: colour blue, pink, yellow and leave one portion white.

7 Coat the outsides of the cut-out cake pieces with the reserved butter icing. Make the square liquorice sweets for the top of the cake using the coloured icings, rolling out strips for the sides and squares to coat the tops. Secure any of the strip joins with a little water.

8 ▲ Make small balls of pink and blue icing for the round sweets, attaching them by lightly pressing into the butter icing.

9 ▲ To make the small rolls for the edges of the cake, roll out any black sugarpaste icing trimmings into a strip about 18 x 13 cm/7 x 5 inches. With your fingers, roll out 18 cm/7 inch long sausage shapes of yellow, pink, white and blue icing. Position one of the colours down the length of the black strip, roll over to form a filled roll, securing the join underneath with water. Slice into three across. Repeat with the remaining colours.

10 Arrange the smaller liquorice sweets in a pile on top and around the edges of the large cake.

Camping Tent

The perfect cake for a child who enjoys camping. You may find it easier to cover the sides of the cake first, and then the top, rather than all in one.

INGREDIENTS
Serves 8–10
1½ x quantity Quick-mix Sponge
Cake baked in a 20 cm/8 inch
square cake tin
115 g/4 oz/⅓ quantity Butter Icing
60 ml/4 tbsp apricot jam, warmed
and sieved
450 g/1 lb marzipan
500 g/1¼ lb/1½ x quantity
Sugarpaste Icing
brown, orange, green, red, yellow
and blue food colourings
115 g/4 oz/⅛ quantity Royal Icing
50 g/2 oz/1 cup desiccated coconut
chocolate matchsticks

MATERIALS AND EQUIPMENT
25 cm/10 inch square cake board
wooden cocktail sticks
fine paintbrush
greaseproof paper piping bag
No 1 writing nozzle
basket weave nozzle
toy football and mug

1 ▲ Split the cake and fill with a little butter icing. Cut the cake in half. Cut one half in two diagonally from the top right edge to the bottom left edge to form the roof of the tent.

2 ▲ Stick the two wedges, back to back, on top of the oblong with apricot jam to form the tent. Measure the height from the 'ground' and trim off at 10 cm/4 inches high. Use these trimmings on either side of the base. Place the cake diagonally and brush with apricot jam. Cover with marzipan, reserving 50 g/2 oz.

3 ▲ Colour 50 g/2 oz/⅛ quantity sugarpaste icing brown and the remainder orange. Cover one end of the tent with brown sugarpaste and the rest with orange. It is easier to cut the opening for the tent separately and then stick it on with a little water. Cut a 7.5 cm/ 3 inch slit down the front of the tent, lay over the brown sugarpaste, then trim off the excess and smooth the joins at the top. Fold back the sides and secure with royal icing. Leave to dry.

4 Stick halved cocktail sticks in the corners as pegs and in the ridge as poles.

5 ▲ Put the coconut in a bowl and mix in a little green colouring. Spread the cake board with a thin layer of royal icing and sprinkle with the coconut to look like grass.

6 ▲ Colour 50 g/2 oz marzipan flesh coloured, roll a ball for the head, a tiny wedge for the nose and shape the body and arms. Paint a blue T-shirt on to the body and leave to dry. Colour some of the royal icing brown and pipe on the hair with a basket weave nozzle. Pipe on the mouth and eyes. Make a bonfire beside the tent with broken chocolate matchsticks, and add the toy football and mug to complete the scene.

Dart Board

Start the decoration several days before this cake is needed, as lots of patience and time is required. If the cake is well sealed to begin with, the decoration can be worked on in stages.

INGREDIENTS
Serves 10–12
*1½ x quantity Quick-mix Sponge
Cake baked in a 25 cm/10 inch
round cake tin
175 g/6 oz/½ quantity Butter Icing
45 ml/3 tbsp apricot jam, warmed
and sieved
450 g/1 lb marzipan
550 g/1¼ lb/1⅔ x quantity
Sugarpaste Icing
black, yellow, red and silver food
colourings
115 g/4 oz/⅛ quantity Royal Icing*

MATERIALS AND EQUIPMENT
*30 cm/12 inch round cake board
greaseproof paper
icing smoother
1 cm/½ inch round cutter
greaseproof paper piping bag
No 1 writing nozzle
fine paintbrush
candles*

2 Draw a 20 cm/8 inch circle on a piece of greaseproof paper, cut out and fold in quarters. Divide each quarter into five equal portions and draw in lines to meet in the centre. Place the template on the cake and mark the centre and the edge of each wedge on the cake.

3 ▲ Mark the wedges on the top of the cake with a sharp knife. Colour most of the remaining sugarpaste icing yellow, roll out and cut out wedges, using the template as a guide. Place on alternate sections but do not stick in place yet. Repeat with the rest of the black sugarpaste icing.

4 ▲ Carefully cut 3 mm/⅛ inch off the wide end of each wedge and swap the colours. Mark a 13 cm/5 inch circle in the centre of the board and cut out 3 mm/⅛ inch pieces to swap with adjoining colours. Stick in place and use an icing smoother to flatten.

5 ▲ Colour the last piece of sugarpaste icing red. Use the cutter to remove the centre for the bull's eye. Cut out and stick on a red sugarpaste bull's eye and surround with a thin strip of black sugarpaste icing. Roll the remaining black icing into a long sausage to fit around the base of the cake and stick all the way round with a little water.

6 ▲ Mark numbers on the board and pipe on with royal icing using a No 1 nozzle. Leave to dry, then paint the numbers with silver food colouring. Stick candles into the cake at an angle to resemble darts.

1 Split the cake and fill with butter icing. Put on to the cake board and brush with apricot jam. Cover with marzipan. Colour 450 g/1 lb/1⅓ x quantity sugarpaste icing black. On a work surface lightly dusted with icing sugar, roll out and use about three-quarters of the icing to cover the cake.

Space Ship

For this cake the triangles for the jets should be covered separately, then stuck into position after the cake is decorated.

INGREDIENTS
Serves 10–12
2 x quantity Quick-mix Sponge
Cake baked in a 25 cm/10 inch
square cake tin
225 g/8 oz/⅔ quantity Butter Icing
75 ml/5 tbsp apricot jam, warmed
and sieved
350 g/12 oz marzipan
450 g/1 lb/1⅓ x quantity
Sugarpaste Icing
blue, pink and black food
colourings

MATERIALS AND EQUIPMENT
30 cm/12 inch square cake board
2.5 cm/1 inch plain round cutter
candles
gold paper stars

1 ▲ Split the cake and fill with a little butter icing. With a sharp serrated knife, cut a 10 cm/4 inch piece diagonally across the middle of the cake and about 25 cm/10 inches long.

2 ▲ Shape the nose and cut the remaining cake in to three 7.5 cm/3 inch triangles for the sides and top of the ship. Cut two smaller triangles for the boosters and any remaining cake to fit down the middle of the space ship. Assemble diagonally across the cake board and brush with apricot jam. Cover with a layer of marzipan.

3 ▲ On a work surface, dusted with icing sugar, roll out about three-quarters of the sugarpaste icing and use to cover the cake and the small triangles for the boosters. Colour one-third of the remaining sugarpaste icing blue, one-third pink and one-third black. Wrap each separately in clear film. Roll out the blue and cut in 1 cm/½ inch strips. Stick in a continuous line around the base of the cake with a little water and outline the triangles. Cut a 2.5 cm/1 inch strip and stick down the centre of the space ship.

4 ▲ Roll out the pink sugarpaste icing and cut out shapes to decorate the ship. Roll out the black sugarpaste icing and cut out windows, circles, name and numbers. Stick in place with a little water.

5 ▲ With any leftover sugarpaste icing, make candle holders by shaping into small cubes. Stick the candles into them then stick on to the board. Decorate the board with gold stars.

Chess Board

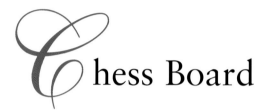

For this cake to look most effective, the squares have to have very sharp edges, so take care to neaten them as you stick them into position.

INGREDIENTS
Serves 12

1½ x quantity Quick-mix Sponge
Cake baked in a 25 cm/10 inch
square cake tin
225 g/8 oz/⅓ quantity Butter Icing
45 ml/3 tbsp apricot jam, warmed
and sieved
800 g/1¾ lb marzipan
550 g/1¼ lb/1⅔ x quantity
Sugarpaste Icing
black and red food colourings
silver balls
115 g/4 oz/⅙ quantity Royal Icing

MATERIALS AND EQUIPMENT

30 cm/12 inch square cake board
greaseproof paper piping bag
No 8 star nozzle

1 ▲ Split the cake and fill with butter icing. Place on the cake board and brush with apricot jam. Roll out 450 g/1 lb marzipan and cover the cake. On a work surface dusted with icing sugar, roll out 450 g/1 lb/1⅓ x quantity sugarpaste icing and use to cover the cake. Leave to dry overnight.

2 ▲ Divide the remaining marzipan in half and colour one half black and the other half red. To shape the chess pieces, work with one colour at a time. Roll 50 g/2 oz marzipan into a sausage and cut into eight equal pieces then shape into pawns. Divide 75 g/3 oz marzipan into six equal pieces then shape into two castles, two knights and two bishops. Divide 25 g/1 oz marzipan in half and shape a queen and a king. Decorate with silver balls. Leave to dry overnight.

3 ▲ Mark the cake into eight 3 cm/1¼ inch squares along each side, leaving a border around the edge. Divide the board into 64 equal squares using a sharp knife.

4 ▲ Colour the remaining sugarpaste icing black, roll out and cut into 3 cm/1¼ inch squares. Stick on to alternate squares on the board with a little water, starting with a black square in the bottom left hand corner and finishing with another black square in the top right hand corner.

5 ▲ Cut 1 cm/½ inch black strips to edge the board and stick in place with a little water. Pipe a border round the base of the cake with royal icing. Place the chess pieces in position.

Mobile Phone Cake

Mobile phones keep getting smaller, but this delicious cake will always stay the same size.

INGREDIENTS
Serves 8–10
1 quantity Quick-Mix Sponge Cake mix
2 tbsp apricot jam, warmed and sieved
350 g/12 oz/1 quantity Sugarpaste Icing
black food colouring
10 small square sweets
1–2 striped liquorice sweets
2–3 tbsp icing sugar
$^{1}/_{2}$–1 tsp water

MATERIALS AND EQUIPMENT
900 g/2 lb loaf tin
23 x 18 cm/9 x 7 in cake board
diamond-shaped biscuit cutter
piping bag fitted with a small plain nozzle

Tip

The dial pad is made from small sweets. However, you could increase the quantity of sugarpaste icing slightly, colour it as wished, then cut it to shape.

1 Preheat the oven to 180°C/350°F/ Gas 4. Grease the tin, line with greaseproof paper and grease the paper. Spoon the cake mixture into the prepared tin and smooth the surface. Bake in the centre of the oven for 40–50 minutes, or until a skewer inserted into the centre of the cake comes out clean. Leave the cake in the tin for 5 minutes, then turn out on to a wire rack, peel off the lining paper and leave to cool.

2 ▲ Turn the cake upside-down and starting about 2.5 cm/1 in along the cake, slice into it, across and at an angle, about 1 cm/½ in deep. Cut out this wedge, then slice horizontally along the length of the cake, stopping about 2.5 cm/1 in away from the end. Withdraw the knife and re-insert it at the end of the cake and slice vertically into the cake to meet up with the horizontal cut. Remove the inner piece of cake and discard.

3 ▲ Place the cake on the cake board and brush the cake evenly with the apricot jam. Colour three-quarters of the sugarpaste icing black. On a work surface lightly dusted with icing sugar, roll out to a 5 mm/¼ in thickness and use to cover the cake. Trim away any excess sugarpaste and reserve, wrapped in clear film.

4 ▲ Colour the remaining sugarpaste icing grey with a little black food colouring. On a work surface lightly dusted with icing sugar, roll out to a 5 mm/¼ in thickness. Cut out an oblong to fit the centre of the cake, leaving a 1 cm/½ in border. Cut out another piece about 2.5 cm/1 in square and stamp out the centre of the square using the diamond-shaped biscuit cutter. Stick all the pieces on the phone with a little water, placing the diamond at the bottom of the phone and the square at the top.

5 ▲ Position the sweets and a strip of kitchen foil for the dial pad. To make the glacé icing, mix the icing sugar with the water and black food colouring to a piping consistency. Fill the piping bag and pipe border lines around the edges of the phone and the grey pieces. Pipe the numbers on the keys.

6 Knead the reserved black sugarpaste icing and, with your hands, roll into a sausage shape for the aerial. Indent the top with a knife and position at the top of the phone to one side. Secure with a little water.

Personal Stereo

This loud cake in noisy colours will be a smash hit!
The cake board is optional.

INGREDIENTS
Serves 4–6
1 quantity chocolate-flavour Quick-Mix Sponge Cake mix
¼ quantity chocolate-flavour Butter Icing
4 tbsp apricot jam, warmed and sieved
350 g/12 oz/1 quantity Sugarpaste Icing
orange, green, purple and black food colourings
3 sweets, for the buttons
2 liquorice sweets, for the cassette holes
2 long liquorice bootlaces
2 liquorice wheels

EQUIPMENT AND MATERIALS
20 x 13 cm/8 x 5 inch shallow cake tin
edible black ink pen

1 Preheat the oven to 180°C/350°F/ Gas 4. Grease the cake tin, line the base and sides with greaseproof paper and grease the paper. Spoon in the cake mixture and smooth the surface. Bake in the centre of the oven for 35–40 minutes or until a skewer inserted into the centre of the cake comes out clean. Turn out on to a wire rack, peel off the lining paper and leave to cool completely. Trim the top of the cake to make it perfectly flat, then cut horizontally in half.

2 ▲ Spread the chocolate butter icing over one half, then top with the other half. Brush the cake evenly with the apricot jam. Colour about 250 g/ 9 oz of the sugarpaste icing orange. Lightly dust the work surface with icing sugar and roll out the icing until it is large enough to cover the cake. Smooth and ease it over the sides and edges. Trim the edges.

3 ▲ Colour about 50 g/2 oz of the remaining sugarpaste icing green. Colour all but a small ball of the remaining icing purple, then colour the small ball black. Roll out the green and purple icings thinly. Cut the green icing into a rectangle about 1 cm/½ inch smaller than the top surface of the cake. Stick it in place with a little water. Cut the purple icing into a 2.5 x 10 cm/1 x 4 inch strip and stick in place on top of the green rectangle with a little water.

4 Press the sweets for the buttons into one side of the cake through the orange icing, then position the liquorice sweets for the cassette holes, sticking them in place with a little water. Use the edible ink pen to draw tiny lines around the sweets.

5 Cut a few short pieces off the bootlace liquorice and stick on the personal stereo with a little water. Stick the reserved piece of black icing in place at the side of the cake with a little water.

6 ▲ To make the headphones, unravel a little of each of the liquorice wheels and place in position on the table or board, if you are using. Overlap the unravelled ends of the liquorice wheels, sticking them together with a little water. Use a pin or thin metal skewer to make a small hole in the bottoms of the liquorice wheels, then press a liquorice bootlaces into each one. Brush three-quarters of the liquorice bootlace with a little water and stick them together with your fingers, removing the excess water. Press the joined end into the black icing on the cake.

*H*ot Dog Cake

Make a meal of a cake! This hot dog tastes nothing like the real thing – it is much more delicious and looks very attractive when cut into slices.

INGREDIENTS
Serves 6–8
1 quantity Swiss Roll mix
icing sugar, to dredge
½ quantity coffee-flavour Butter Icing
⅓ quantity Truffle Cake Mix
6 tbsp apricot jam, warmed and sieved
450 g/1 lb/1⅓ x quantity **Sugarpaste** Icing
brown **and** red food colouring
1–2 tbsp toasted sesame seeds
¼ **quantity** Glacé Icing

MATERIALS AND EQUIPMENT
23 x 33 cm/9 x 13 inch Swiss roll tin
2 small greaseproof paper piping bags

1 Preheat the oven to 180°C/350°F/ Gas 4. Grease the tin, line the base and sides with greaseproof paper and grease the paper. Spoon the cake mixture into the tin and smooth the surface. Bake in the centre of the oven for about 12 minutes or until springy to the touch. Cover and leave to cool.

2 Turn the cake out on to greaseproof paper dusted with icing sugar and remove the lining paper. Spread over the butter icing, then roll the cake up using the greaseproof paper.

3 ▲ Shape the truffle cake mix into a sausage about 23 cm/9 inches long.

4 Place the Swiss roll on the work surface and slice along the middle lengthways, almost through to the bottom. Ease the two halves apart to resemble a partially opened bun.

5 Colour the sugarpaste icing brown, then cut off about 50 g/2 oz and set aside, wrapped in clear film. Roll out the rest on a work surface lightly dusted with icing sugar until about 5mm/¼ inch thick and use to cover the bun. Ease the icing into the centre and down the sides of the cake.

6 ▲ Dilute a few drops of brown food colouring in a little water and paint the top of the bun very lightly to give a toasted effect. Dab on a little colour, then rub it around gently with a finger until blended in. Carefully place the truffle cake sausage in position.

7 ▲ Divide the glacé icing between two small bowls. Colour one half brown and the other red. Fill the piping bags with the icings and snip off the ends with scissors. Pipe red icing along the sausage for the ketchup, then overlay with brown icing for the mustard. Sprinkle the sesame seeds over the bun.

8 Roll out the reserved brown sugarpaste icing and cut thin strips to resemble onion rings. Place on the cake so that the joins lie under the sausage. Carefully place the cake on a napkin and serving plate, with a knife and fork.

Circus Cake

This design is very easy to achieve. The miniature circus ornaments measure 5 cm/2 inches high and can be bought from party shops, although anything similar can be used.

INGREDIENTS
Serves 10–12
1 quantity Quick-mix Sponge Cake
baked in a 20 cm/8 inch round
cake tin
115 g/4 oz/¹⁄₃ x quantity Butter Icing
45 ml/3 tbsp apricot jam, warmed
and sieved
450 g/1 lb marzipan
450 g/1 lb/1¹⁄₃ x quantity
Sugarpaste Icing
red and blue food colourings
115 g/4 oz/¹⁄₁₆ quantity Royal Icing
silver balls
3 digestive biscuits

MATERIALS AND EQUIPMENT
25 cm/10 inch round cake board
greaseproof paper piping bag
No 5 star nozzle
small plastic circus ornaments

1 ▲ Split the cake and fill with a little butter icing. Place on the cake board and brush with apricot jam. Cover with a layer of marzipan. Roll out half the sugarpaste icing on a surface dusted with icing sugar and use to cover the cake. Colour 115 g/4 oz/¹⁄₃ quantity sugarpaste icing pink, roll into a rope and stick around the top edge of the cake to make a wall.

2 ▲ Colour half the remaining sugarpaste red and the other half blue. Roll out each colour and cut into twelve 2.5 cm/1 inch squares. Stick alternately at an angle around the side of the cake with a little water. Pipe stars around the base of the cake with royal icing and stick in silver balls.

3 ▲ Crush the digestive biscuits by pressing through a sieve to make the sawdust. Scatter over the top of the cake and place small circus ornaments on top.

Clown Cake

Made from a clown-shaped tin, this is a quick and easy
cake to make and decorate. Choose your own nozzle shapes for the designs,
following the contours of the cake.

INGREDIENTS
Serves 10–15
1½ x quantity Quick-Mix Sponge
Cake mix
115 g/4 oz/⅓ quantity Sugarpaste
Icing
2 x quantity Butter Icing
yellow, red, pink and blue food
colourings
small coloured sweets, for the
features

MATERIALS AND EQUIPMENT
900 g/2 lb clown-shaped cake tin
25 x 30 cm/10 x 12 inch cake board
greaseproof paper piping bags
small star, small plain
and large star nozzles
small party hat

1 ▲ Preheat the oven to 180°C/350°F/
Gas 4. Grease the cake tin
generously. Spoon in the cake mixture
and smooth the surface. Bake in the
centre of the oven for 45–50 minutes or
until a skewer inserted into the centre of
the cake comes out clean. Leave for 5
minutes before turning out on to a wire
rack to cool.

2 ▲ To make a template for the
clown's face, hold a piece of
greaseproof paper firmly over the face
on the cooled tin. Draw around the
outline using a pencil and cut around
the shape.

3 ▲ On a work surface lightly
dusted with icing sugar, roll out the
sugarpaste icing to about 5 mm/¼ inch
thick, then place the greaseproof paper
template on top. Use a small sharp knife
to cut around the outline of the
template. Place the cut-out sugarpaste
on a baking sheet and cover with
clear film.

4 To colour the butter icing, place
about one-third of the icing in a
small mixing bowl and colour it yellow.
Place another third in another mixing
bowl and colour it red. Divide the
remaining butter icing between two
small bowls and colour one pink and
the other blue.

5 ▲ Place the cake on the cake board.
Fit a small star nozzle in a paper
piping bag and fill it with the yellow
butter icing. Use to pipe along the
contours of the hair on the clown's
head. Place the cut-out sugarpaste
template in position on the cake, then
place a small plain nozzle in another
piping bag and fill with the red butter
icing. Use it to pipe decoratively around
the neck and torso area of the clown.
Pipe around the mouth, then change the
nozzle to a large star shape and pipe in
the nose.

6 Place a small star nozzle in another
small piping bag and fill with the
pink icing. Use to pipe a star border
around the edges of the sugarpaste
template. Place a large star nozzle in
another piping bag and fill with the blue
icing. Use to pipe in the buttons and the
clown's eyes. Place the sweets in the
centres of the eyes, nose and buttons.
Position the hat.

Magic Carpet Cake

The Master of the Lamp can also be made out of coloured sugarpaste icing, instead of marzipan, if you prefer.

Ingredients
Serves 8–10
1 quantity Quick-Mix Sponge
Cake mix
675 g/1½ lb/2 x quantity
Sugarpaste Icing
*blue, brown, red, orange, yellow,
purple and black food colourings*
115 g/4 oz/4 squares milk or plain
chocolate, melted
350 g/12 oz white marzipan
*small sweet or diamond-shaped
cake decoration
small brightly coloured feather*

MATERIALS AND EQUIPMENT
23 x 15 cm/6 x 9 inch cake tin
33 cm/13 inch round cake board
2.5 cm/1 inch and 6 cm/2½ inch
round fluted pastry cutters
small piece of yellow crepe paper

1 Preheat the oven to 180°C/350°F/ Gas 4. Grease the cake tin, line the base and sides with greaseproof paper and grease the paper. Spoon in the cake mixture and smooth the surface. Bake in the centre of the oven for 30–35 minutes or until a skewer inserted into the centre of the cake comes out clean. Turn out on to a wire rack, peel off the lining paper and leave to cool completely.

2 Colour 275 g/10 oz sugarpaste icing with blue food colouring. Remove a piece about the size of a walnut and set aside, wrapped in clear film. Roll out the rest of the blue icing thinly on a surface dusted with icing sugar into a round about the same size as the cake board.

3 ▲ Roll out about 150 g/5 oz of white icing and cut out rounds using the pastry cutters. Arrange these on the blue icing to resemble clouds, then roll lightly into the icing. Brush the cake board lightly with water and cover with the blue and white icing, smoothing it with your hands to exclude air bubbles. Leave the icing draped over the edge of the board, if liked, or trim level with the edge of the board.

4 ▲ Colour 175 g/6 oz sugarpaste icing dark brown, then roll it out thinly into an oblong large enough to cover the top and sides of the cake generously. Trim the edges. Knead the trimmings into a ball and set aside, wrapped in clear film. Brush the cake with melted chocolate, then place on the cake board. Drape the brown icing over the top of the cake, being careful not to flatten it at the sides too much.

5 Divide 75 g/3 oz sugarpaste icing into two equal pieces. Colour one piece red and the other orange. Then unwrap the reserved pieces of blue and brown icing.

6 Divide each of the four colours into three or four smaller pieces, then knead them together to make a marbled ball of icing. Roll it out into a rectangle slightly larger than the top of the cake. Trim the edges, then lay over the brown icing and stick into place with water.

7 ▲ Colour 75 g/3 oz marzipan yellow, then roll most of it into a long, thin sausage shape. Press it around the edge of the carpet to make a trim. Decorate with small balls of yellow marzipan. Snip pieces of yellow crepe paper with scissors to make tassels. Push into the small balls of icing.

8 ▲ To make the figure, roll about 75 g/3 oz of white marzipan into a pear shape, then cut in half to make two legs. Bend the legs into a sitting position. Colour 65 g/2½ oz marzipan dark brown and shape into a head, body and arms. Make the eyes and mouth from tiny pieces of coloured icing or marzipan and press on to the face. Press the head and body on to the legs. Colour 25 g/1 oz of marzipan purple and use it to make the jacket. Press the arms on to the figure.

9 Colour small pieces of marzipan black and deep red or purple and use to make hair and a hat respectively. Colour the remaining marzipan bright orange. Roll a tiny piece into a ball and press on to the hat. Decorate with a tiny diamond-shaped sweet or cake decoration and coloured feather. Use the rest of the orange marzipan to make slippers and a lamp. Position the figure and the lamp on the carpet.

Jack-in-the-Box Cake

*An impressive, colourful cake which will
delight a small party of young children. This cake does
require a little extra time and patience, so be sure to start the cake
well in advance and not on the morning of the party!*

INGREDIENTS
Serves 6–8
1 quantity chocolate-flavour Quick-
Mix Sponge Cake Mix
6 tbsp apricot jam, warmed and
sieved
1 kg/2¼ lb/3 x quantity Sugarpaste
Icing
purple, yellow, orange and green
food colourings
1 large round doughnut
1 small round doughnut
2 marshmallow sweets, for the eyes
2 coloured sweets, for the buttons

MATERIALS AND EQUIPMENT
deep 10 cm/4 inch square cake tin
18 cm/7 inch cake board
9 cm/3½ inch square piece of stiff
card
3 cocktail sticks
garlic press
ice-cream cornet
balloon
small star cutter
butterfly cutter
wooden skewer

1 Preheat the oven to 180°C/350°F/
Gas 4. Grease the cake tin, line the
base and sides with greaseproof paper
and grease the paper. Spoon the cake
mixture into the prepared tin and
smooth the surface. Bake in the centre
of the oven for 35–40 minutes, or until
a skewer inserted into the centre of the
cake comes out clean. Leave the cake in
the tin for about 5 minutes, then turn
out on to a wire rack, peel off the lining
paper and leave to cool completely.

2 ▲ Place the cake on the work
surface and cut a 2.5 cm/1 inch slice
off the top for the lid. Use a small, sharp
knife to hollow out the centre of the box
section of cake, leaving a 1 cm/½ inch
border. Spread a little apricot jam in the
centre of the cake board and some on
the square piece of card. Place the
bottom section of cake on the cake
board and position the lid on the card.
Brush the box and lid with apricot jam.

3 ▲ Pull off a walnut-sized piece of
sugarpaste icing, wrap in clear film
and set aside. Then take about half of
the remaining sugarpaste icing and
marble in the purple food colouring.
Cut off about one-quarter of the
marbled icing and roll out on a surface
lightly dusted with icing sugar to about
a 15 cm/6 inch square. Use to cover the
lid section of the cake, wrapping the
icing around the card. Set aside, card
side down. Reserve the trimmings.

4 Roll out the remaining marbled
icing and use to cover the box
section of cake, lightly pressing the icing
into the hollow. Reserve the trimmings.

5 Colour about half of the remaining
sugarpaste icing yellow and pull off
two pieces, each the size of a cherry.
Wrap these in clear film and set aside.
Cut a thin slice off the side of the large
doughnut for the body to give it a flat
base. Lay it down on the work surface
and place the small doughnut above it
for the head. Brush the head and body
with jam. Roll out the large portion of
yellow sugarpaste icing until about
5mm/¼ inch thick and use to cover the
head and body of the clown. Wrap the
icing around the back and pinch it
together to seal.

6 ▲ Pierce a cocktail stick into the
base of the body, leaving about half
of it exposed. Place the body in position
on the box section of the cake, pressing
the exposed cocktail stick into the cake
for extra stability.

7 ▲ Cut off about half of the
remaining sugarpaste icing and
colour it orange. Push about one-
quarter of this through a garlic press on
to a sheet of greaseproof paper for the
hair. Stick it on to the clown's head
with a little water. Use the remaining
orange icing to make one hand, the
nose, mouth and a few spots for the
bow tie. Allow the hand to dry out on
a baking sheet, but cover the other
features with clear film and set aside.

8 ▲ Colour the remaining sugarpaste icing green. To make the hat, cut off about 15 g/½ oz of the green icing and roll out into a thin strip. Brush the pointed end of the ice-cream cornet with a little apricot jam, then roll the strip of green sugarpaste icing around it, starting at the pointed end and working downwards. Use scissors to cut off the excess cornet. Stick the hat in position on the clown's head with a little water. Reserve any trimmings.

9 Use the reserved piece of yellow sugarpaste icing to make two small ovals for the arms. Thread each one on to a cocktail stick and carefully press the hand on to one of them. Press the cocktail sticks into the body of the clown. Tie a slightly blown up balloon on to the arm without the hand.

10 Roll out the remaining piece of white sugarpaste icing and stamp out two small stars with the star cutter. Use a little water to stick them in place for the eyes. Stick the marshmallow sweets on top.

11 Position the orange nose and mouth, sticking them in place with a little water. Roll out the remaining green icing to about 5mm/ ¼ inch thick and stamp out a butterfly and six small stars with the cutters. Stick the reserved red spots on to the butterfly bow tie, using a little water, then place the bow tie on the clown in the same way. Place the green stars around the edges of the cake board. Stick the two coloured sweets in place for the clown's buttons, using a little more water.

12 To position the lid, carefully sit it, card side out, on the back edge of the box section of the cake. Use the wooden skewer and the reserved icing trimmings to support the lid and hold it in place. This stage is best completed when the cake is in position on the table and unlikely to be moved again.

Happy Clown

This fun clown can be made with tiny edible flowers or letters stuck on to the sides of the box.

INGREDIENTS
Serves 6–8
*1 quantity Quick-mix Sponge Cake
baked in a 15 cm/6 inch square
cake tin
50 g/2 oz/¼ quantity Butter Icing
45 ml/3 tbsp apricot jam, warmed
and sieved
350 g/12 oz marzipan
450 g/1 lb/1⅓ x quantity
Sugarpaste Icing
ice cream cone
115 g/4 oz/⅓ quantity Royal Icing
blue, black, green, red and yellow
food colourings
silver balls*

MATERIALS AND EQUIPMENT
*20 cm/8 inch round cake board
frill cutter
plain round cutter
wooden cocktail stick
cotton wool
No 8 star nozzle*

1 ▲ Split the cake and fill with butter icing. Cut a 5 cm/2 inch rectangle from two sides of the cake to create a 10 cm/4 inch square, a 5 cm/2 inch square and two rectangles. Sandwich the rectangles together on top of the large square to make a cube. Place on the cake board and brush with apricot jam. Cover with a layer of marzipan.

2 On a work surface dusted with icing sugar, roll out three-quarters of the sugarpaste icing and use to cover the cake. Shape the remaining cube of cake into a ball for the head. Brush with apricot jam, cover with marzipan then with sugarpaste icing. Leave to dry overnight.

3 ▲ Cut the top off the ice cream cone. Stick the wide part of the cone in the centre of the cake with a little royal icing, then stick on the head.

4 ▲ Colour a small piece of sugarpaste icing blue, roll out and cut a fluted circle with a small inner circle. (The depth of the frill will depend on the size of the central hole; the smaller the centre, the wider the frill.) Cut one side and open out then roll the fluted edge with a wooden cocktail stick to stretch it. Attach it to the neck with royal icing, carefully arranging the folds with a cocktail stick and supporting with cotton wool while they dry. Make a second frill in the same way.

5 ▲ Stick the ice cream cone hat on the head with a little royal icing. Cut eyes from blue sugarpaste icing and stick on with a little water. Colour pieces of sugarpaste icing black, green and red and roll out. Cut and stick on black eyes. Cut a semi-circle of green, stick around the back of the head and snip with sharp scissors to give spikey hair (or cut two short lengths). Cut out a red nose, a mouth and numbers for the sides of the box. Stick these on with a little water.

6 ▲ Colour the remaining royal icing yellow and pipe stars round the edges of the cube and pompons on the hat, sticking in silver balls as you go.

Treasure Chest

Allow yourself a few days before the party to make this cake. The lock and handles are made separately, then left to dry for 48 hours before sticking on to the cake.

INGREDIENTS
Serves 8–10
1½ x quantity Quick-mix Sponge
Cake baked in a 20 cm/8 inch
square cake tin
115 g/4 oz/⅓ quantity Butter Icing
60 ml/4 tbsp apricot jam, warmed
and sieved
350 g/12 oz marzipan
350 g/12 oz/1 quantity
Sugarpaste Icing
brown, green and black
food colourings
50 g/2 oz/1 cup desiccated coconut
115 g/4 oz/⅙ quantity Royal Icing
edible gold dusting powder
silver balls
chocolate coins

MATERIALS AND EQUIPMENT
30 cm/12 inch round cake board
fine paintbrush

1 ▲ Split the cake and fill with butter icing. Cut the cake in half and sandwich the halves on top of each other. Place on the cake board.

2 ▲ Cut the top to shape the rounded lid and brush with apricot jam. Cover with a layer of marzipan. Colour all but a small piece of the sugarpaste icing brown. On a work surface dusted with icing sugar, roll out the icing and use to cover the cake.

3 ▲ Mark the lid of the treasure chest with a sharp knife.

4 ▲ Roll out the trimmings of the brown sugarpaste icing and stick on four 5 mm/¼ inch wide strips with water.

5 ▲ Put the coconut in a bowl and mix in a few drops of green colouring. Spread a little royal icing over the cake board and press the coconut into it to look like grass.

6 ▲ From the remaining sugarpaste icing, cut out the padlock and handles. Cut a keyhole shape from the padlock and shape the handles over a small box. Leave to dry. Stick the padlock and handles into place with royal icing. Paint them gold and stick silver balls on the handles and padlock with a little royal icing to look like nails. Arrange the chocolate money around the chest on the grass.

*S*and Castle

Crushed digestive biscuits are used to cover this fun cake. It is ideal for children who do not like the richness of butter icing as only a very small amount is used to sandwich the cake.

INGREDIENTS
Serves 8–10
1½ x quantity Quick-mix Sponge
Cake baked in 2 x 15 cm/6 inch
round cake tins
115 g/4 oz/⅓ quantity Butter Icing
60 ml/4 tbsp apricot jam, warmed
and sieved
115 g/4 oz digestive biscuits
115 g/4 oz/¹⁄₁₆ quantity Royal Icing
blue food colouring
sweets

MATERIALS AND EQUIPMENT
25 cm/10 inch square cake board
rice paper
plastic drinking straw
candles

2 ▲ Cut 4 x 3 cm/1¼ inch cubes from the reserved piece and stick on for the turrets. Brush with apricot jam.

3 Crush the digestive biscuits and press through a sieve to make the 'sand'.

4 ▲ Press on the crushed biscuits, using a palette knife to get a smooth finish. Colour some royal icing blue and spread around the sand castle on the board to make a moat. Spread a little royal icing around the board and sprinkle on sand. Make a flag with rice paper and half a straw and stick into the cake. Stick candles into each turret and arrange the sweets on the board.

1 ▲ Split the cakes and sandwich all the layers together with butter icing. Place in the centre of the cake board. Cut 3 cm/1¼ inches off the top just above the filling and shape the rest of the cake with slightly sloping sides.

Ice-Cream Cornets

Individual cakes make a change for a party, the idea being that each guest has one to themselves. You could even put a candle in the special person's one.

INGREDIENTS
Makes 9
1 quantity Quick-Mix Sponge Cake mix
9 ice-cream cornets
1 quantity Butter Icing
red, green and brown food colourings
selection of coloured vermicelli, wafers, chocolate sticks, etc.

MATERIALS AND EQUIPMENT
9 fairy cake paper cases
bun tin

Tip

To have 3 sets of 3 ice cream cakes placed on the table, you will need 3 egg boxes, which hold 12 eggs each. Place a ball of marzipan in 3 evenly spaced holes in the up-turned egg box. Cover the box in foil, then pierce the foil and make a small hole with your finger where the marzipan balls are. Insert the iced ice cream cornets, pressing them in gently, so they stand securely.

1 Preheat the oven to 180°C/350°F/ Gas 4. Place the paper cases in the bun tin, then spoon in the cake mixture until they are all at least half full. Bake in the centre of the oven for about 20 minutes or until the cakes have risen and are golden. Transfer the cakes to a wire rack to cool completely. Remove the cases.

2 ▲ Gently press a fairy cake into a cornet, taking care not to damage the cornet. If the bases of the cakes are a little large to insert into the cornets, trim them down with a small, sharp knife. The cakes should feel quite secure once inserted into the cornets.

3 Divide the butter icing into three small bowls and colour one portion pale red, one portion green and one portion brown.

4 ▲ Using a small palette knife, spread each cake with some of one of the icings. Place in the ice-cream stand (see Tip). Continue coating the cornets, making sure the icing isn't too smooth so it looks like ice cream.

5 ▲ To insert a wafer or chocolate stick into an ice cream, use a small, sharp knife to make a hole or incision through the icing and into the cake, then insert the wafer or stick. Add the finishing touches by sprinkling over some coloured vermicelli.

*P*izza Cake

*Quick, easy and impressive – this deliciously sweet cake is a definite winner
for pizza fanatics everywhere. Serve in small wedges.*

INGREDIENTS
Serves 8–10
*1 quantity Quick-Mix Sponge Cake
mix
350 g/12 oz/1 quantity Butter Icing
175 g/6 oz yellow marzipan
1 tbsp desiccated coconut
red and green food colouring
icing sugar
25 g/1 oz sugarpaste icing*

MATERIALS AND EQUIPMENT
*23 cm/9 in shallow round cake tin
25 cm/10 in pizza plate
cheese grater*

*T*ip

This recipe can be adapted easily for peperoni pizza fanatics. You will need an extra 175 g/6 oz/½ quantity of sugarpaste icing. Colour with brown food colouring, then roll out to a thick sausage shape with your hands. Slice thinly and add to the pizza cake as an extra topping ingredient.

1 Preheat the oven to 180°C/350°F/ Gas 4. Grease the tin, line the base with greaseproof paper and grease the paper. Spoon the cake mixture into the prepared tin and smooth the surface. Bake in the centre of the oven for 40–50 minutes, or until a skewer inserted into the centre of the cake comes out clean. Leave the cake in the tin for 5 minutes, then turn out on to a wire rack, peel off the lining paper and leave to cool.

2 ▲ Colour the butter icing red. Place the cake on the pizza plate and spread evenly with the butter icing to represent the tomato topping. Leave a 1 cm/½ in border around the edge of the cake.

3 ▲ Knead the marzipan for a few minutes to soften it slightly, then grate it. Sprinkle over the red butter icing to represent cheese.

4 ▲ Colour the sugarpaste icing green. On a work surface lightly dusted with icing sugar, roll out to about a 5 mm/¼ in thickness. Cut out two leaf shapes freehand or cut around a real leaf. Mark the veins with a knife and add to the pizza cake for the garnish.

5 ▲ Place the desiccated coconut in a small bowl and colour with green food colouring. Scatter over the pizza cake to represent chopped herbs.

*M*arket Stall

An open-air market stall is the theme for this cake, bursting with colourful produce. Vary this design if you like, adding as wide a variety of fruit and vegetables as you can think of.

INGREDIENTS
Serves 30
30 cm/8 in square Rich Fruit Cake
3 tbsp apricot jam, warmed and sieved
900 g/2 lb marzipan
450 g/1 lb/1⅓ x quantity Sugarpaste Icing
125 g/4 oz/⅙ quantity Royal Icing
brown, green, red, orange, yellow, peach, purple, pink and black food colourings

MATERIALS AND EQUIPMENT
25 cm/10 in square cake board
piping bag fitted with a small plain nozzle
paintbrush

1 Slice 4 cm/1½ in off one side of the cake. Brush the cake pieces with the apricot jam. Take half of the marzipan and cut off one-quarter. On a work surface lightly dusted with icing sugar, roll out the small piece of marzipan and use to cover one long side, the top and the two short sides of the cake slice. Roll out the larger piece of marzipan and use to cover the large piece of cake. Leave to dry for 12 hours.

2 ▲ Colour half of the sugarpaste icing brown and other half green. Using three-quarters of the brown icing, cover three sides of the large cake (not the cut side), brushing the marzipan first with a little water. With the remaining brown icing, cover the marzipanned sides of the cake slice in the same way. With the brown trimmings, roll out and cut narrow dividers to fit the top of the cake. Leave to dry on greaseproof paper for several hours.

3 ▲ Place the large piece of cake on the cake board, with the cake slice in front to form a step. Stick the cakes together and to the cake board with a little royal icing.

4 ▲ Measure the length and width of the cake, including the step. Roll out the green sugarpaste icing to about 4 cm/1½ in wider and longer than the measured length. Brush the marzipan tops with a little water and cover the cakes loosely with the green icing. Allow the icing to fall naturally into folds over the edges of the cake. Leave to dry for several hours.

5 ▲ Take the remaining marzipan, reserve a little for the stall-holder, and colour the rest red, orange, yellow, green, brown, peach and purple. Use these colours to shape the fruits and vegetables. Add markings with a paintbrush and food colouring to the melons, peaches and potatoes. For the front of the stall, shape baskets and a potato sack out of different shades of brown. For the stall-holder, colour the reserved marzipan pink, purple, black and flesh-coloured and shape the head, body and arms separately. Stick the figure together with a little royal icing. Make the hands, the facial features and hair, and press on with a little water. Place a melon in the stall-holder's arms. Leave all the marzipan shapes to dry on greaseproof paper for several hours. Assemble on the cake just before serving, attaching the dividers, baskets and the stall-holder to the cake with royal icing.

Pinball Machine

The design of this stylish machine is well suited to the clean, sharp lines of sugarpaste icing.

INGREDIENTS
Serves 12
2 x quantity Quick-mix Sponge
Cake baked in a 25 cm/10 inch
square cake tin
225 g/8 oz/⅔ quantity Butter Icing
60 ml/4 tbsp apricot jam, warmed
and sieved
450 g/1 lb marzipan
115 g/4 oz/⅙ quantity
Royal Icing
450 g/1 lb/1⅓ x quantity
Sugarpaste Icing
yellow, blue, green and pink food
colourings
sweets
2 ice cream fan wafers

MATERIALS AND EQUIPMENT
30 cm/12 inch square cake board
20 cm/8 inch cake tin
greaseproof paper
greaseproof paper piping bag
No 1 writing nozzle

1 ▲ Split the cake and fill with butter icing. Cut off a 5 cm/2 inch strip from one side and reserve.

2 ▲ Using a sharp serrated knife, cut a thin wedge off the top of the cake, diagonally along its length, to end just above the halfway mark. This will give a sloping top.

3 ▲ Using a 20 cm/8 inch cake tin as a guide, cut an arched back from the reserved cake. Brush cakes with apricot jam. Cover separately with marzipan and place on the cake board, sticking together with royal icing. Leave to dry overnight.

4 ▲ Roll out two-thirds of the sugarpaste icing and use to cover the cake. Leave to dry. Using a template, mark out a design on top of the cake. Colour the remaining sugarpaste icing in different colours, roll out and cut to fit each section. Stick with water and smooth the joins carefully.

5 ▲ Use royal icing to stick different coloured sweets on the cake as buffers, flippers, lights and knobs. Roll some blue sugarpaste icing into a long sausage and use to edge the pinball table and divider. Cut a zig-zag design for the sides and a small screen for the back. Stick these on with a little water. Stick the ice cream fans at the back of the screen. Load the pinball sweets. The name on the screen can be added with run-out letters or piping.

Computer Game

This is a small cake to give to a computer game fanatic. The fine rope is made by rolling the
sugarpaste on a smooth surface with a perspex smoother to give a neat continuous finish.

INGREDIENTS
Serves 6
1 quantity Quick-mix Sponge Cake
baked in a 15 cm/6 inch square
cake tin
115 g/4 oz/¹⁄₃ quantity Butter Icing
30 ml/2 tbsp apricot jam, warmed
and sieved
225 g/8 oz marzipan
350 g/12 oz/1 quantity
Sugarpaste Icing
black, blue, red and yellow
food colourings
a little royal icing

MATERIALS AND EQUIPMENT
20 cm/8 inch square cake board
cocktail stick
perspex icing smoother
fine paintbrush

1 ▲ Split the cake and fill with butter icing. With a sharp serrated knife, cut 2.5 cm/1 inch off one side of the cake and 1 cm/½ inch off the other. Round the corners slightly. Place on the cake board and brush with apricot jam. Cover with marzipan.

2 ▲ Colour two-thirds of the sugarpaste icing black. Roll out on a work surface dusted with icing sugar and use to cover the cake. With a cocktail stick, mark the speaker holes and position of the screen and knobs. Colour half the remaining sugarpaste icing pale blue, roll out and cut out a 6 cm/2½ inch square for the screen. Stick it in the centre of the game with a little water. Colour a small piece of sugarpaste icing red and the rest yellow. Cut out the start switch 2.5 cm/1 inch long from the red and the controls from the yellow. Stick into position with a little water. Edge the screen and the base with the remaining black sugarpaste.

3 ▲ With a fine paintbrush, draw the game on the screen with a little blue colour. Pipe letters on to the buttons with a little royal icing.

Sheet of Music

This cake is ideal for musicians young and old. As it requires very delicate piping, it is advisable to practise first before attempting the decoration.

INGREDIENTS
Serves 12
2 x quantity Quick-mix Sponge
Cake baked in a 25 cm/10 inch
square cake tin
225 g/8 oz/⅔ quantity Butter Icing
45 ml/3 tbsp apricot jam, warmed
and sieved
450 g/1 lb marzipan
450 g/1 lb/1⅓ x quantity
Sugarpaste Icing
115 g/4 oz/⅞ quantity Royal Icing
black food colouring

MATERIALS AND EQUIPMENT
25 x 30 cm/10 x 12 inch
cake board
greaseproof paper
greaseproof paper piping bags
No 0 writing nozzle
No 7 shell nozzle
ribbon

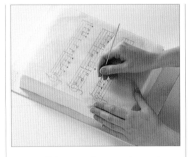

2 ▲ With a template, mark out the sheet of music and the person's name on the top of the cake.

3 ▲ Pipe the staves and bars with white royal icing and a No 0 nozzle, then colour a little of the remaining royal icing black and pipe the clefs, name and notes. Pipe a royal icing border around the base with the shell nozzle and tie a ribbon around the sides.

1 ▲ Split the cake and fill with a little butter icing. Cut 5 cm/2 inches off one side of the cake so that it measures 20 x 25 cm/8 x 10 inches. Place on the cake board and brush with apricot jam. Cover with a layer of marzipan. On a work surface dusted with icing sugar, roll out the sugarpaste icing and use to cover the cake. Leave to dry overnight.

ℬanjo Cake

The perfect cake for the musician in the family. It can be set on a large tray or you could cut out card for a template to support it.

INGREDIENTS
Serves 15–20
2 x quantity Quick-Mix Sponge
Cake mix
115 g/4 oz/6 tbsp seedless raspberry
jam, warmed
900 g/2 lb/2⅔ x quantity Sugarpaste
Icing
lime green food colouring
2 coloured sticks of liquorice
4 round lollipops
4 tbsp coloured vermicelli
piece of flat green liquorice
2 long red liquorice bootlaces
4 long green liquorice bootlaces
sugarpaste stars, or other decoration

MATERIALS AND EQUIPMENT
20 cm/8 inch round cake tin
18 cm/7 inch square cake tin
54 cm/21 inch stiff card
5 cm/2 inch round cutter
ribbon and 2 pins, for the strap

1 Preheat the oven to 180°C/350°F/ Gas 4. Grease the tins, line the bases with greaseproof paper and grease the paper. Divide the cake mixture between the two tins and smooth the surfaces. Bake for 35–40 minutes, or until firm to the touch. Turn out on to a wire rack, peel off the lining paper and leave to cool completely.

2 ▲ Cut off the dome from the round cake and place bottom side up on the work surface. Cut the dome off the square cake, then cut in half down the middle. Place the cakes together to form the banjo shape, then draw around them on to stiff card. Cut out the shape to make the reinforcing template.

3 ▲ Use the cutter to stamp out a shallow hollow from the centre of the round cake. Place both cakes on the card base and brush with the raspberry jam. Colour the sugarpaste icing with the lime green food colouring and roll out on a work surface lightly dusted with icing sugar to about a 62 x 25 cm/ 25 x 10 inch rectangle. Use to cover the banjo in one piece, easing the icing into the hollow and down the sides. Make finger indentations along the length of the neck of the banjo.

4 ▲ Cut off four 1 cm/½ inch pieces from one of the sticks of liquorice and press into the cake at the top end of the neck to resemble stays for the strings. Place the remains of the liquorice stick with the other one at the base of the banjo, next to the hollow. Dip the lollipops in water, then in the coloured vermicelli to coat. Press the lollipops into the sides of the neck end so that they line up with the pieces of liquorice stick forming the stays.

5 Place the two flat pieces of liquorice side by side at the base, securing with a little water. Cut the red liquorice bootlace into about 5 cm/2 inch lengths and position them along the length of the banjo neck, in the indentations. Use a little water to stick them in place, if necessary.

6 ▲ Dip the green liquorice bootlaces in hot water, then stretch and smooth each one until perfectly straight. Wrap one end of the banjo strings around the liquorice sticks at the top of the neck end and bring the other ends down so they meet together on the flat liquorice at the rounded end. Secure the ribbon strap with pins pushed through each end and into the cake. Decorate the banjo with sugarpaste stars and more coloured vermicelli, if wished. The pins *must* be removed from the cake before serving.

*D*rum Cake

The ropes can be made by rolling by hand on a smooth work surface, but a perspex smoother gives a much better result.

INGREDIENTS
Serves 8
1 quantity Quick-mix Sponge Cake baked in a deep 15 cm/6 inch round cake tin
50 g/2 oz/¼ quantity Butter Icing
30 ml/2 tbsp apricot jam, warmed and sieved
350 g/12 oz marzipan
450 g/1 lb/1⅓ x quantity Sugarpaste Icing
red, blue and yellow food colourings

MATERIALS AND EQUIPMENT
20 cm/8 inch round cake board

1 ▲ Split the cake and fill with a little butter icing. Place on the cake board and brush with apricot jam. Cover with a layer of marzipan and leave to dry overnight. Colour half the sugarpaste icing red. Roll out to 25 x 30 cm/ 10 x 12 inches and cut in half. Stick to the sides of the cake with water.

2 Roll out a circle of white sugarpaste icing to fit the top of the cake and divide the rest in half. Colour one half blue and the other yellow. Divide the blue into four equal pieces and roll each piece into a sausage long enough to go halfway round the cake. Stick around the base and the top of the cake with a little water.

3 ▲ Mark the cake into six around the top and bottom using a disc of greaseproof paper folded in six wedges.

4 ▲ Roll the yellow sugarpaste icing into strands long enough to cross diagonally from top to bottom to form the drum strings. Roll the rest of the yellow sugarpaste icing into 12 small balls and stick where the strings join the drum. Using red and white sugarpaste icing, knead together until streaky and roll two balls and sticks 15 cm/6 inches long. Dry overnight. Stick together with royal icing to make the drumsticks and place on top of the drum.

Army Tank

Create an authentic camouflaged tank by combining green and brown sugarpaste icing. The chocolate flake makes a not-too-threatening gun.

INGREDIENTS
Serves 12
*2 x quantity Quick-mix Sponge
Cake baked in a 25 cm/10 inch
square cake tin
225 g/8 oz/⅔ quantity Butter Icing
60 ml/4 tbsp apricot jam, warmed
and sieved
450 g/1 lb marzipan
450 g/1 lb/1⅓ x quantity
Sugarpaste Icing
green and brown food colourings
chocolate flake
liquorice wheels
115 g/4 oz/⅛ quantity Royal Icing
round biscuits
sweets*

MATERIALS AND EQUIPMENT
25 x 35 cm/10 x 14 inch cake board

1 Split the cake and fill with butter icing. Cut off a 15 cm/6 inch rectangle from one side of the cake. Cut a smaller rectangle 15 x 7.5 cm/ 6 x 3 inches and stick on the top.

2 ▲ Using a sharp serrated knife, shape the sloping top and cut a 2.5 cm/ 1 inch piece from both ends between the tracks. Shape the rounded ends for the wheels and tracks. Assemble the cake on the cake board and brush with apricot jam. Cover with a layer of marzipan.

3 Colour 350 g/12 oz/1 quantity sugarpaste icing green and the remainder brown. On a work surface dusted with icing sugar roll out the green sugarpaste icing to about a 25 cm/10 inch square. Break small pieces of brown icing and place all over the green. Flatten and roll out together to give the camouflage effect.

4 Turn the icing over, brush off the excess icing sugar and repeat on the underside. Continue to roll out until the sugarpaste icing is about 3 mm/ ⅛ inch thick. Lay it over the cake, gently pressing over the turret and down the sides of the tracks on both sides.

5 ▲ Carefully mould over the tracks, cutting away the excess. Cut a piece into a 6 cm/2½ inch disc and stick on with a little water for the hatch on top. Cut a small hole for the gun and stick the chocolate flake in for the gun. Unroll some liquorice wheels and stick on the strips for the tracks, using a little royal icing. Stick on biscuits for the wheels and sweets for the lights and portholes.

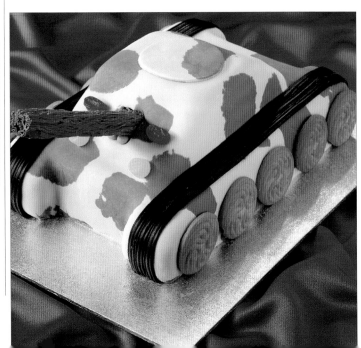

Box of Chocolates

This sophisticated looking cake is perfect for an older child's birthday and will delight all chocolate lovers. For a younger child you could adapt the idea and fill the box with the birthday person's favourite sweets.

INGREDIENTS
Serves 6–8
1 quantity chocolate-flavour Quick-mix Sponge Cake baked in a 15 cm/6 inch square cake tin
50 g/2 oz/¹⁄₆ quantity Butter Icing
45 ml/3 tbsp apricot jam, warmed and sieved
350 g/12 oz marzipan
350 g/12 oz/1 quantity Sugarpaste Icing
red food colouring
chocolates

MATERIALS AND EQUIPMENT
20 cm/8 inch square cake board
small paper sweet cases
gold and red ribbon, 4 cm/
1½ inches wide

2 ▲ Colour two-thirds of the sugarpaste icing red and set aside. Roll out the remainder on a work surface dusted with icing sugar and cut into an 18 cm/7 inch square. Lay it in the hollow dip and trim off the excess. Roll out the red sugarpaste icing and cover the sides.

3 ▲ Put the chocolates into paper cases and arrange in the box. Tie the ribbon around the sides and tie a big bow.

1 ▲ Split the cake and fill with a little butter icing. With a sharp knife, cut a shallow square from the top of the cake, leaving a 1 cm/½ inch border around the edge. Place on the cake board and brush with apricot jam. Cover with a layer of marzipan.

*G*ift-wrapped Parcel

If you do not have a tiny flower cutter for the design on the wrapping paper you could press a small decorative button into the sugarpaste icing while still soft to create a pattern.

INGREDIENTS
Serves 6–8
1 quantity Quick-mix Sponge Cake baked in a 15 cm/6 inch square cake tin
50 g/2 oz/¼ quantity Butter Icing
45 ml/3 tbsp apricot jam, warmed and sieved
450 g/1 lb marzipan
350 g/12 oz/1 quantity Sugarpaste Icing
yellow, red and green food colourings
115 g/4 oz/¼ quantity Royal Icing

MATERIALS AND EQUIPMENT
20 cm/8 inch square cake board
small flower cutter
wooden spoon
greaseproof paper piping bag
No 1 writing nozzle

1 Split the cake and fill with butter icing. Place on the cake board and brush with apricot jam. Cover with half the marzipan. Colour the sugarpaste icing pale yellow and roll out on a work surface dusted with icing sugar. Use to cover the cake, turning in the corners neatly to look like wrapping paper. Mark the paper with a small flower cutter.

2 Divide the remaining marzipan in half, colour one half pink and the other pale green. Roll out the pink marzipan and cut into four 2.5 x 18 cm/1 x 7 inch strips. Roll out the green marzipan and cut into four 1 cm/½ inch strips the same length. Centre the green strips on top of the pink strips and stick on to the cake with a little water. Cut two 5 cm/2 inch strips from each colour and cut a V from the ends to form the ends of the ribbon. Stick in place and leave to dry overnight.

3 ▲ Cut the rest of the green into 2.5 x 7.5 cm/1 x 3 inch lengths and the pink into 1 x 7.5 cm/½ x 3 inch lengths. Centre the pink on top of the green, fold in half, stick the ends together and slip over the handle of a wooden spoon, dusted with cornflour. Leave to dry overnight. Cut the ends in V shapes to fit neatly together. Cut a piece for the join in the centre, and fold in half with the join at the bottom.

4 ▲ Carefully remove the bows from the wooden spoon and stick in position with royal icing.

Children's Party Cakes

There can be no better way to celebrate a child's birthday than with a special cake. An imaginative design can provide a focal point for a party theme, and this chapter should give inspiration to any parent. The cake decorating ideas here range from pirate hats and monsters from outer space to fairy castles and ballerinas. Easy-to-follow instructions ensure you achieve the cake of your choice with the minimum of fuss, and guarantee your child's party will be a hit!

Flickering Birthday Candle Cake

*Stripy icing candles are flickering and ready to blow out on
this birthday celebration cake for all ages.*

INGREDIENTS
Serves 15–20
*20 cm/8 inch square Madeira Cake
1 quantity Butter Icing
3 tbsp apricot jam, warmed and
sieved
800 g/1¼ lb/2⅓ x quantity
Sugarpaste Icing
pink, yellow, purple and jade food
colourings
edible silver balls, to decorate*

MATERIALS AND EQUIPMENT
*23 cm/9 inch square cake board
leaf cutter
small round cutter
pink and purple food colouring pens
5 mm/¼ inch wide jade-coloured
ribbon*

1 Cut the cake horizontally into three
layers, using a long serrated knife.
Sandwich the layers together with the
butter icing and brush the cake with the
apricot jam. Roll out 500 g/1¼ lb of the
sugarpaste icing on a work surface
lightly dusted with icing sugar and use
to cover the cake. Position on the cake
board.

2 Divide the remaining sugarpaste
into four portions and colour one
portion pink, one portion yellow, one
portion pale purple and one portion
jade. Roll out the jade icing and cut into
six 1 cm/½ inch wide strips of slightly
different lengths, but each long enough
to go over the side and on to the top of
the cake. Make a diagonal cut at one
end of each strip.

3 ▲ Roll out the yellow icing and cut
out six candle flames with the leaf
cutter. Place a silver ball in each flame.
Set aside the remaining yellow icing,
wrapped in clear film. Arrange the
candles on top of the cake, securing with
a little water. Mould small strips,
fractionally longer than the width of
each candle, from the yellow and purple
icings. Arrange alternate colours on the
candles at a slight angle, securing with
water. Position the flames at the end of
each jade strip, also securing with water.

4 ▲ Roll out the pink and remaining
purple icings, then cut out wavy
pieces with a sharp knife. Attach to the
cake, above the candles, with a little
water. Gather together the pink icing
trimmings and roll into a ball.

5 ▲ Using the leftover yellow and
pink icings, make the decorations
for the sides of the cake. Roll out the
yellow icing and cut out circles with the
small round cutter or the end of a
piping nozzle. Make small balls from
the pink icing and attach to the yellow
circles with a little water. Press a silver
ball in the centre of each pink ball.

6 Arrange the decorations around the
bottom edge of the cake, securing
with water.

7 ▲ Using food colouring pens,
draw wavy lines and dots coming
from the purple and pink wavy icings.
Decorate the sides of the cake board
with the ribbon, securing at the back
with a little softened sugarpaste.

ℬirthday Balloons

A colourful cake for a child's birthday party, made using either a sponge cake or fruit cake base.

INGREDIENTS
Serves 10–12
20 cm/8 inch round Quick-mix
Sponge Cake or Light Fruit Cake,
covered with 800 g/1¾ lb marzipan,
if liked
900 g/2 lb/2⅔ x quantity
Sugarpaste Icing
red, green and yellow
food colourings
3 size 3 eggs
2 size 3 egg whites
450 g/1 lb/4 cups icing sugar

MATERIALS AND EQUIPMENT
25 cm/10 inch round cake board
3 bamboo skewers, 25 cm/10
inches, 24 cm/9½ inches and
23 cm/9 inches long
small star cutter
baking parchment
greaseproof paper piping bags
fine writing nozzle
narrow ribbon
candles

1 Place the cake on the cake board.
Colour 50 g/2 oz/¼ quantity
sugarpaste icing red, 50 g/2 oz/
¼ quantity green and 115 g/4 oz/
⅓ quantity yellow. Roll out the
remaining icing on a surface dusted
with icing sugar and use to cover the
cake. Use half the yellow icing to cover
the cake board.

2 Using the tip of a skewer or the end
of a paintbrush, make a small hole
in the pointed end of one egg. Stir the
egg lightly inside then tip out into a
bowl. Repeat with the remaining eggs.
Carefully wash and dry the shells. (The
eggs should be strained before using.)

3 ▲ Roll out the red sugarpaste icing
to about 12 cm/4½ inches diameter
and use to cover one of the egg shells,
trimming off any excess around the
pointed ends. Keep smoothing the icing
in the palms of the hands. Push a
bamboo skewer up through the hole
and rest in a tall glass to harden.
Repeat on the other egg shells with the
green and yellow sugarpaste icing.

4 ▲ Roll out the red, green and
yellow trimmings and cut out a
small star shape from each. Dampen
lightly, then thread on to the skewers
and secure to the bases of the balloons,
matching the colours, for the knots on
each balloon.

5 Draw 16 balloon shapes on a large
sheet of baking parchment. Beat the
egg whites with the icing sugar until
smooth and divide among four bowls.
Add red colouring to one bowl, green
to the second and yellow to the third,
leaving the last white. Cover each with
clear film to prevent a crust forming.

6 ▲ Place the white icing in a piping
bag fitted with a plain writing
nozzle and use to pipe over the traced
outlines. Leave to harden slightly. Thin
the green icing with a little water to the
consistency of pouring cream. Place in a
greaseproof paper piping bag and snip
off the end. Use to fill a third of the
balloon shapes. Repeat with the red
and yellow icings. Leave the run-outs
for at least 24 hours to harden.

7 Carefully peel the balloons off the
baking parchment and secure
around the sides of the cake. Pipe
narrow strings for the balloons with
white icing.

8 ▲ Press the large balloons into the
top of the cake and decorate with
the ribbon. Press the candles into the
icing around the top edge.

Candle Cake

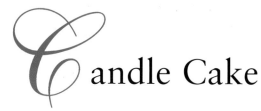

Marbled icing is so effective that little other decoration is required. This design combines blue and orange but any other strong colour combination is equally effective. It makes a lovely cake for a child's first birthday.

INGREDIENTS
Serves 20
20 cm/8 inch round Rich Fruit Cake, covered with 800 g/ 1¼ lb marzipan
900 g/2 lb/2⅔ x quantity Sugarpaste Icing
orange, blue and green food colourings

MATERIALS AND EQUIPMENT
25 cm/10 inch round silver cake board
1 bamboo skewer
2 household candles
clear film

1 Place the cake on the cake board. Colour 115 g/4 oz/⅓ quantity of the sugarpaste icing orange and reserve. Reserve another 115 g/4 oz/⅓ quantity of white sugarpaste icing. Divide the remaining icing into three parts. Knead the orange colouring into one piece until deep orange but still streaked with colour. Knead a mixture of blue and green coloured icing into another piece until streaky. Leave the remaining piece white.

2 ▲ Lightly dust the work surface with icing sugar. Roll long sausages of icing in the three colours and lay on the work surface.

3 ▲ Twist the colours together and knead for several seconds until the strips of colour are secured together but retain their individual colours.

4 Roll out the marbled icing and use to cover the cake, trimming off the excess around the base.

5 ▲ Take a small piece of the reserved orange sugarpaste icing, about the size of a large grape, and shape into a candle flame. Thread on to the end of a bamboo skewer. Thinly roll the remaining orange sugarpaste icing and use to cover the board around cake. Re-roll the trimmings and cut another strip, 1 cm/½ inch wide. Secure over the orange icing around the cake. Cut another strip, 5 mm/¼ inch wide, and use to complete the border.

6 ▲ Wrap the candles in clear film, twisting the ends together. (One candle is prepared as a spare.) Roll the reserved white sugarpaste icing to a long thin strip cut vertically into two sections, each about 5 mm/¼ inch wide. Starting from one end of a covered candle, coil the icing around the candle, trimming off any excess icing at the end. Leave for at least 48 hours to harden completely.

7 To release the icing, untwist the clear film and gently push out the candle inside. Carefully peel away the clear film.

8 ▲ Place a dot of white icing in the centre of the cake and use to secure the icing candle. Push the bamboo skewer down through the centre of the cake to finish.

n Apple Tree

*For this unusual centrepiece, choose whichever fruit you prefer. You could make
the apples green instead of red, or have a mixture of red and green apples or golden pears.*

INGREDIENTS
Serves 10–12
*1 quantity chocolate-flavour Quick-
Mix Sponge Cake mix
1 quantity chocolate-flavour Swiss
Roll, baked and rolled with ¼
quantity chocolate-flavour
Butter Icing
¼ quantity chocolate-flavour
Butter Icing
½ quantity Butter Icing, coloured
green with food colouring
225 g/8 oz marzipan
red and green food colouring
green-coloured desiccated coconut
(see Puppies in Love, step 4)
tiny fresh flowers, to decorate
(optional)*

MATERIALS AND EQUIPMENT
*450 g/1 lb fluted round cake tin or
pudding basin
15 cm/6 inch round cake board
wooden cocktail stick
2 x 30 cm/12 inch lengths of florist's
wire
florist's tape
greaseproof paper piping bag
leaf nozzle*

1 Preheat the oven to 180°F/350°C/
Gas 4. Grease and flour the tin or
pudding basin. Spoon in the cake
mixture and smooth the surface. Bake in
the centre of the oven for 35–40 minutes
or until a skewer inserted into the centre
of the cake comes out clean. Leave in the
tin for about 5 minutes, then turn out on
to a wire rack and leave to cool.

2 ▲ Arrange the Swiss roll on the
card template or cake board (see
Tip), trimming it, if necessary. Spread
the chocolate butter icing over the tree
trunk, making swirls. Use about three-
quarters of the green butter icing for the
top of the tree, making it peak and
swirl. Position on top of the tree trunk.

3 ▲ Colour about 25 g/1 oz of the
marzipan green. Colour the
remainder red, then roll it into cherry-
size balls. Roll the green marzipan into
tiny sausage shapes to make the stalks
and leaves. Use the cocktail stick to
make tiny holes in the tops of the
apples, then insert the stalks and leaves.

4 ▲ Twist the florist's tape around
the florist's wire, then cut it into
7.5 cm/3 inch lengths. Press the lengths
of wire through the apples, bending the
ends so the apples cannot fall off when
hanging. Press the hanging apples into
the tree, reserving the extra apples to
scatter around the bottom.

5 ▲ Use the remaining green butter
icing to fill the piping bag. Practise
piping the leaves on a piece of
greaseproof paper before piping leaves
all over the tree top. Scatter the green
desiccated coconut around the base of
the tree and pipe a few extra leaves.
Add a few tiny fresh flowers for effect,
if liked. The wires must be removed
from the cake before serving.

ip

To stand the tree up at a slight
angle, you can cut out a template of
thick card from around the un-iced
cake. Then decorate the cake on
the card and prop it up on a small
block of wood. Alternatively, decorate the cake flat on a cake board.

A Basket of Flowers

This attractive arrangement of flowers looks very impressive, yet none of the stages are very difficult to do.

INGREDIENTS
Serves 10–12
1½ x quantity orange-flavour
Quick-Mix Sponge Cake mix
2 x quantity orange-flavour Butter
Icing
orange, yellow, pink, red, black and
green food colourings
900 g/2 lb/2⅔ x quantity Sugarpaste
Icing

MATERIALS AND EQUIPMENT
deep 20 cm/8 inch round cake tin
20 cm/8 inch oval cake board
3 greaseproof paper piping bags
small round nozzle
small straight serrated nozzle
selection of small flower and leaf
cutters
30 cm/12 inch piece of strong wire,
bent to a curve with the two ends
about 20 cm/8 inch apart
plasticine

1 Preheat the oven to 180°C/350°F/
Gas 4. Grease the cake tin, line the
base with greaseproof paper and grease
the paper. Spoon the cake mixture into
the prepared tin and smooth the surface.
Bake in the centre of the oven for 45–
50 minutes or until a skewer inserted
into the centre of the cake comes out
clean. Turn out on to a wire rack, peel
off the lining paper and leave the cake
to cool completely.

2 Place the butter icing in a bowl and
beat in a few drops of orange food
colouring. Cut the cake in half down
the middle and spread the bottom of
one half with a little of the butter icing.
Sandwich with the other half of the
cake, base to base.

3 Cut a thin slice from the bottom of
the sandwiched cake. Place a little
butter icing on the cake board and
position the cake on top, with the large
flat surface facing upwards.

4 ▲ Spread more of the butter icing
over the cut surface of the cake,
covering right up to the edges.

5 Place about 4 tbsp of the butter
icing in a small bowl and colour it
with a little more orange food colouring
to make it a slightly deeper colour. Fit a
paper piping bag with the small round
nozzle and fill with the deeper orange
butter icing. Pipe a decorative border
around the top edge of the basket.

6 Fit the clean round nozzle into a
fresh paper piping bag and fill with
the lighter orange butter icing. Pipe
vertical lines about 2.5 cm/1 inch apart
all around the sides of the cake. Fit a
fresh paper piping bag with the serrated
nozzle and fill with more orange butter
icing. Starting at the top of the cake
pipe short lines alternately crossing
over, then stopping at the vertical lines
to give a basket-weave effect.

7 Divide the sugarpaste icing into
two. Cut one of the portions in
half and colour one half pale orange
and the other half darker orange. Wrap
these separately in clear film and set
aside. Divide the other portion of
sugarpaste icing into five equal
amounts. Colour these yellow, pink,
red, black and green.

8 ▲ Roll out the yellow, pink and red
portions on a work surface lightly
dusted with icing sugar and use the
flower cutters to stamp out the flower
shapes. Place some of the flowers in an
egg carton so they dry curved and place
others on a baking sheet so they dry
flat. Leave the flowers for at least 2
hours to dry out.

9 Use a little of the orange, yellow
and black sugarpaste icings to roll
into tiny balls to make the centres of the
flowers, sticking them in place with a
little water.

10 Roll out the green icing and use a
leaf-shaped cutter to stamp out
leaves, indenting them with a small
sharp knife and curling them slightly to
give them more interest. Place them on
the baking sheet to dry out.

11 When dry, arrange the flowers
and leaves attractively on top of
the basket and the cake board.

12 ▲ To make the handle for the
basket, roll the two shades of
orange sugarpaste icing into balls about
the size of small marbles. Thread these
alternately on to the curved piece of
wire, leaving about 2.5 cm/1 inch of
wire exposed at each end. Stand the
handle in two pieces of plasticine stuck
to the work surface or a baking sheet,
supported by a tea towel pushed under
the handle to stop it falling over. Leave
to dry for at least 2 hours. To finish,
gently press the handle into the cake,
pushing it in until secure.

Telephone Cake

A great idea for a first or second birthday, as the telephone is an endless source of amusement for many toddlers.

Ingredients
Serves 8–10
1 quantity chocolate-flavour Quick-Mix Sponge Cake mix
6 tbsp apricot jam, warmed and sieved
550 g/1¼ lb/1⅔ x quantity Sugarpaste Icing
1 quantity Butter Icing
red, blue, yellow and green food colourings
black liquorice ribbon

Materials and Equipment
18 cm/7 inch square cake tin
20 cm/8 inch square cake board
3 greaseproof paper piping bags
small round cutter

3 ▲ Brush the centre of the main cake with apricot jam and reposition the top of the cake, leaving space to replace the receiver rest.

4 ▲ To shape the receiver rest, cut a 1 cm/½ inch cross out of the centre of this portion, then cut away the four end corners. Brush the base with apricot jam and position on the cake.

5 ▲ Brush the top surface of the cake evenly with apricot jam. On a work surface lightly dusted with icing sugar, roll out 350 g/12 oz of the sugarpaste icing to a 30 cm/12 inch square and use to cover the telephone cake. Place the cake on the cake board.

6 ▲ Divide the butter icing into three separate bowls, colouring one red, one blue and one yellow. Fill the piping bags with the coloured butter icings and snip the end off each one to make a small hole. Pipe spots in all three colours evenly over the cake.

7 Colour 175 g/6 oz of the remaining sugarpaste icing green. Cut off about 25 g/1 oz and set aside, wrapped in clear film. Brush the receiver piece of cake with a little apricot jam, then roll out the larger piece of green sugarpaste icing and use to cover the receiver. Position the receiver on the cake.

8 Take a small piece of the remaining green sugarpaste icing and roll it into a ball. Stick it on to the side of the receiver with a little water.

9 Roll out the remaining green sugarpaste icing and cut out a flower pot shape, measuring approximately 7.5 cm/3 inches across the top. Place on the front of the telephone, sticking it down with a little water. For the dial, colour the remaining sugarpaste icing red and roll out to a 7.5 cm/3 inch round, or stamp it out using a cutter. Use a tiny round cutter to stamp out the finger holes, then position the dial on the cake. Use any remaining butter cream to pipe in the numbers.

10 To make the telephone cord, twist the piece of liquorice around a pencil until tightly coiled and leave it for about 10 minutes. Carefully remove the pencil, and press one end of the liquorice into the ball of green sugarpaste icing on the receiver and the other end into the back of the cake.

1 Preheat the oven to 180°C/350°F/Gas 4. Grease the tin, line with greaseproof paper and grease the paper. Spoon the mixture into the tin and smooth the surface. Bake in the centre of the oven for 35–40 minutes or until firm. Turn out and leave to cool.

2 ▲ Cut off a 4 cm/1½ inch strip for the receiver. Cut the main body of the telephone in half. Cut about one-quarter off the top half of the main body of the telephone for the receiver rest.

*D*umper Truck

Any large, round biscuits will work well for the wheels, and all sorts of coloured sweets can go in the truck.

INGREDIENTS
Serves 8–10
1½ x quantity Quick-Mix Sponge
Cake mix
6 tbsp apricot jam, warmed and
sieved
900 g/2 lb/2⅔ x quantity Sugarpaste
Icing
yellow, red and blue food colouring
icing sugar, to dredge
sandwich wafer biscuits
4 coconut swirl biscuits
115 g/4 oz coloured sweets
5 cm/2 inch piece blue liquorice
stick
demerara sugar, for the sand

MATERIALS AND EQUIPMENT
900 g/2 lb loaf tin
30 x 18 cm/12 x 7 inch cake board
18 x 7.5 cm/7 x 3 inch piece of cake
card, brushed with apricot jam
small crescent-shaped cutter

1 Preheat the oven to 180°C/350°F/ Gas 4. Grease the tin, line the base and sides with greaseproof paper and grease the paper. Spoon the cake mixture into the tin and smooth the surface. Bake in the centre of the oven for 40–45 minutes or until a skewer inserted into the centre of the cake comes out clean. Turn out on to a wire rack, peel off the lining paper and leave to cool completely.

2 Using a large, sharp knife, cut off the top of the cake to make a flat surface. Then cut off one-third of the cake to make the cabin of the truck.

3 ▲ Take the larger piece of cake, and, with the cut side up, cut a hollow in the centre, leaving a 1 cm/½ inch border. Brush the hollowed cake evenly with apricot jam.

4 ▲ Colour 350 g/12 oz of the sugarpaste icing yellow and remove a piece about the size of a walnut. Set aside, wrapped in clear film. Roll out the remainder on a work surface lightly dusted with icing sugar until about 5mm/¼ inch thick. Use to cover the hollowed out piece of cake, carefully pressing it into the hollow. Trim the bottom edges and set aside.

5 Colour 350 g/12 oz of the sugarpaste icing red. Cut off one-third of this and set aside, wrapped in clear film. Roll out the rest on a work surface until about 5mm/¼ inch thick. Use to cover the remaining piece of cake and trim the edges.

6 Take the reserved red icing, break off a piece the size of a walnut and wrap in clear film. Roll out the rest and use to cover the cake card.

7 ▲ Brush the wafers with a little apricot jam and stick them together in two equal piles. Place the piles on the cake board, about 7.5 cm/3 inches apart. Place the red-covered cake card on top of the wafers. Place a little of the remaining white sugarpaste icing about halfway along the covered card in order to tip the dumper part of the truck slightly. Place the dumper on top, with the cabin in front. Stand the coconut biscuits in position for the wheels.

8 ▲ Roll out the reserved piece of yellow sugarpaste icing to make a 5 x 2.5 cm/2 x 1 inch rectangle. Colour the remaining white sugarpaste icing with blue food colouring and roll out thinly. Use the crescent-shaped cutter to stamp out the eyes. Make simple ones, or overlay with white crescent shapes for detail.

9 Roll out the reserved red sugarpaste icing thinly and stamp out a mouth shape with an appropriate cutter. Use a little water to stick the yellow panel on to the front of the truck, then stick on the features in the same way.

10 To finish, fill the dumper part of the truck with brightly coloured sweets and push a piece of coloured liquorice into the top of the cabin. Scatter the sugar around the base of the dumper truck to resemble sand.

Train Cake

This quick-and-easy train cake is made from a shaped tin, so all you need to do is decorate it!

INGREDIENTS
Serves 8–10
1½ x quantity Quick-Mix Sponge
Cake mix
yellow food colouring
2 x quantity Butter Icing
red liquorice bootlaces
6–8 tbsp coloured vermicelli
4 liquorice wheels

MATERIALS AND EQUIPMENT
train-shaped cake tin
25 x 38 cm/10 x 15 inch cake board
2 fabric piping bags
small round and small star nozzles
pink and white cotton wool balls

Tip

When applying butter icing to a cake, it is a good idea to have a small bowl of very hot water at the ready to dip your palette knife into. This will ensure you get a really smooth finish on the cake.

1 Preheat the oven to 180°C/350°F/ Gas 4. Grease and flour the cake tin and stand firmly on a greased baking sheet. Grease some strips of foil and press along the edges of the cake tin to prevent the cake mixture escaping. Spoon the cake mixture into the prepared tin and smooth the surface. Bake in the centre of the oven for 40–45 minutes or until a skewer inserted into the centre of the cake comes out clean. Leave the cake to cool in the tin.

2 ▲ Slice off the top surface of the cake to make it perfectly flat. Run a knife around the edges of the cake to release it from the tin, then turn out the cake and place on the cake board.

3 ▲ Add a few drops of yellow food colouring to the butter icing and beat well until evenly blended.

4 ▲ Using a palette knife, cover the cake smoothly with about half the butter icing.

5 ▲ Fit a piping bag with a round nozzle and fill with about one-quarter of the remaining butter icing. Pipe a straight border around the edges of the cake. Repeat the process to make a double-edged border.

6 ▲ Position the red liquorice bootlaces around the edge of the cake, on top of the piped border. Snip the bootlaces with scissors as you bend them around the curves on the train.

7 Fit a piping bag with a small star nozzle and fill with the remaining butter icing. Pipe small stars evenly over the top of the cake. Add extra details to the train with the liquorice, or by piping, if you like. Use a palette knife to press on the coloured vermicelli all around the sides of the cake.

8 Pull a few balls of cotton wool apart for the steam and stick in position with a little butter icing. Press the liquorice wheels in place.

Merry-go-round Cake

Choose your own figures to sit on the merry-go-round, from chocolate animals to jelly bears.
Remember to position the top of the cake at the last minute for the best results.

INGREDIENTS
Serves 16–20
1½ x quantity lemon-flavour Quick-
mix Sponge Cake mix
60 ml/4 tbsp apricot jam, warmed
and sieved
575 g/1¼ lb/1⅔ x quantity
Sugarpaste Icing
orange and yellow food colourings
8 x 18 cm/7 inch long candy sticks
sweet figures

MATERIALS AND EQUIPMENT
2 x 20 cm/8 inch round sandwich
cake tins
23 cm/9 inch round scalloped
cake board
18 cm/7 inch round piece of
stiff card
cocktail stick
star-shaped biscuit cutters in 2 sizes

1 Preheat the oven to 180°C/350°F/
Gas 4. Grease the sandwich tins.
Line the bases with greaseproof paper
and grease the paper. Spoon two-thirds
of the mixture into one tin and the
other third into the other tin. Smooth
the surfaces with a plastic spatula. Bake
for 55–60 minutes, or until a skewer
inserted into the centre of each cake
comes out clean. Leave for 5 minutes
before turning out on to a wire rack
to cool.

2 ▲ Place the larger cake, upside-
down, on the scalloped cake board
to make the base of the merry-go-
round, and place the smaller cake,
right-side up, on the piece of card.
Brush both cakes evenly with apricot
jam and set aside. Lightly dust the
work surface with icing sugar and place
450 g/1 lb/1⅓ x quantity sugarpaste
icing on it. Using the cocktail stick,
apply a few spots of orange food
colouring to the sugarpaste icing.

3 ▲ To achieve the marbled effect in
the sugarpaste icing, roll into a
sausage shape on the work surface.
Fold the sausage shape in half and
continue to roll out until it reaches its
original length. Fold over again and roll
out again into a sausage shape. Continue
this process until the sugarpaste is
streaked with the orange colour.

4 Divide the marbled sugarpaste icing
into two-thirds and one third. Roll
out the larger portion on the work
surface lightly dusted with icing sugar
and use to cover the larger cake. Repeat
with the smaller portion of marbled
sugarpaste icing and use to cover the
smaller cake. Trim away any excess
sugarpaste icing and reserve, wrapped
in clear film.

5 ▲ Using one of the candy sticks,
make eight holes, evenly spaced,
around the edge of the larger cake,
leaving about a 2 cm/¼ inch border.
Press the upright stick right through the
cake to the board.

6 Knead the reserved marbled
sugarpaste icing until the orange
colour is evenly blended, then roll out
on the work surface lightly dusted with
icing sugar. Using the smaller star
cutter, cut out nine stars. Cover with
clear film and set aside. Colour 115 g/
4 oz/⅓ quantity sugarpaste icing yellow.
Roll out on a surface lightly dusted
with icing sugar and cut out nine stars
with the larger star cutter. Sit the
smaller cake on an upturned bowl and
stick eight large and eight small stars
around the edge of the cake, using a
little water to secure. Stick the
remaining stars on top of the cake.

7 ▲ To secure the sweet figures to the candy sticks, stick tiny balls of the excess sugarpaste icing behind the figures and then lightly press on to the sticks. Leave to set for about 30 minutes. Place the candy sticks in the holes on the larger cake.

8 ▲ To assemble the cake, carefully lift the smaller cake, with its card base, on to the candy sticks, making sure it balances before letting go.

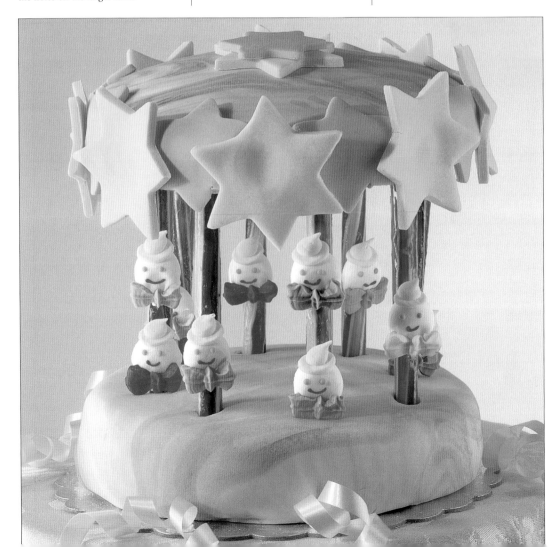

Racing Circuit

A simple ring cake makes the perfect base for this teddy-bear racing track. Choose the flattest and widest side of the cake for the top (this will depend on the shape of your ring mould), so there's plenty of room for the icing cars to race around on.

INGREDIENTS
Serves 12
1 quantity Quick-mix Sponge Cake mix
350 g/12 oz/1 quantity Butter Icing
500 g/1 lb 4 oz/1½ x quantity Sugarpaste Icing
black, blue, yellow, green, orange, red and purple food colourings
115 g/4 oz/⅛ quantity Royal Icing, for fixing
selection of miniature liquorice sweets, dolly mixtures and teddy bears
115 g/4 oz liquorice wheels

MATERIALS AND EQUIPMENT
20 cm/8 inch ring mould
25 cm/10 inch round cake board
wooden skewer
fine paintbrush
greaseproof paper

1 Preheat the oven to 160°C/325°F/ Gas 3. Spoon the cake mixture into a greased ring mould. Bake for 35–40 minutes. Turn out and cool on a wire rack.

2 ▲ Cut the cake in half horizontally and fill with some of the butter icing. Cover the outside of the cake with the remaining butter icing, having the widest part of the cake on top.

3 Cut 350 g/12 oz/1 quantity of the sugarpaste icing in half. To coat the inside of the ring, cut one half of the icing in half again and roll out to the measured circumference and height (reserve the other piece for the top). Press in position over the butter icing. Roll out the reserved piece for the top to the measured diameter and width (you may find this easier to do in two halves), pressing in position and easing into shape over the butter icing.

4 ▲ Take the half piece of icing reserved for coating the outside and roll out to the measured circumference and height. Press in position round the outside of the cake, reserving the trimmings. Place the cake on the cake board.

5 ▲ Take the reserved white icing trimmings and roll out to an oblong for the flag. Cut the wooden skewer to a height of about 13 cm/5 inches and fold one end of the flag round it, securing with a little water. With black food colouring and a fine paintbrush paint on a chequered pattern. Colour a small piece of icing black, make into a ball and stick on top of the skewer. Create a few folds in the flag and leave to dry on greaseproof paper.

6 ▲ Colour the remaining sugarpaste icing blue, yellow, green, orange, red and a very small amount purple. Shape each car in two pieces, attaching in the centre with royal icing where the seat joins the body of the car. Add decorations and headlights and attach dolly mixture wheels with royal icing. Place a candy teddy bear in each car and leave to set.

7 ◄ Unwind the liquorice wheels, removing the centre sweets. Lay the liquorice around the top of the cake to represent the track, leaving a gap in the middle and securing the strips with royal icing. Secure one strip round the bottom of the cake also.

8 Cut some of the liquorice into small strips and attach round the middle of the outside of the cake with some royal icing.

9 Arrange small liquorice sweets around the bottom of the cake. Position the cars on top of the cake on the tracks and attach the flag to the outside with royal icing.

$\mathcal{B}$alloons

This is a simple yet effective design that can be adapted to any age.

INGREDIENTS
Serves 8
1 quantity Quick-mix Sponge Cake
baked in a 20 cm/8 inch round
cake tin
115 g/4 oz/⅓ quantity Butter Icing
45 ml/3 tbsp apricot jam, warmed
and sieved
450 g/1 lb marzipan
450 g/1 lb/1⅓ x quantity
Sugarpaste Icing
pink, blue, green and yellow
food colourings
115 g/4 oz/⅛ quantity Royal Icing

MATERIALS AND EQUIPMENT
25 cm/10 inch cake board
ribbon
greaseproof paper piping bag
No 2 writing nozzle
No 7 star nozzle
candles

3 ▲ Tie the ribbon round the cake. With yellow icing and a No 2 writing nozzle, pipe on the strings, attaching them to the balloons. Using the star nozzle, pipe a border around the base of the cake.

4 ▲ Pipe a number on to each balloon. Place the candles on the cake.

1 Split the cake and fill with butter icing. Place on the cake board and brush with apricot jam. Cover with a layer of marzipan. On a work surface dusted with icing sugar, roll out 350 g/12 oz/1 quantity sugarpaste icing and use to cover the cake.

2 ▲ Divide the remaining sugarpaste icing into three pieces; colour one pink, one blue and the other green. Roll out and, using a template, cut out a balloon from each colour. Stick on to the cake with a little water, rubbing the edges gently with a finger to round off straight edges.

Treasure Map

Allow several days to paint the map because each colour must dry completely before adding another. Use a fairly dry paintbrush to apply the colour.

INGREDIENTS
Serves 12
2 x quantity Quick-mix Sponge Cake baked in a 25 cm/10 inch square cake tin
225 g/8 oz/⅓ quantity Butter Icing
60 ml/4 tbsp apricot jam, warmed and sieved
450 g/1 lb marzipan
675 g/1½ lb/2 x quantity Sugarpaste Icing
yellow, brown, paprika, green, blue, red and black food colourings
115 g/4 oz/⅙ quantity Royal Icing

MATERIALS AND EQUIPMENT
25 x 35 cm/10 x 14 inch cake board
fine paintbrush
greaseproof paper
greaseproof paper piping bag
No 7 shell nozzle
No 1 writing nozzle

1 ▲ Split the cake and fill with butter icing. Cut into a 20 x 25 cm/8 x 10 inch rectangle and place on the cake board. Brush with apricot jam. Cover with a layer of marzipan. On a work surface dusted with icing sugar, roll out 450 g/1 lb/1⅓ quantity sugarpaste icing and use to cover the cake. Colour the remaining sugarpaste icing yellow and roll out. Mark out the island, river, lake, mountains and trees on top of the cake.

2 ▲ With brown and paprika colours and a fine paintbrush, paint the edges of the map to look old and smudge the colours together with kitchen paper. Paint the island pale green and the water around the island, river and lake pale blue. Dry overnight before painting on other details, otherwise the colours will run.

3 ▲ Pipe a border of royal icing around the base of the cake with a shell nozzle. Colour a little royal icing red and, using a No 1 nozzle, pipe the path to the treasure, finishing with the letter 'X'. Colour some icing green and pipe on grass and trees. Colour some icing black and pipe on a North sign.

*P*irate's Hat

Pirates are an enduringly popular theme for children's parties and this cake will be much admired. Surround it with lots of stolen treasures.

INGREDIENTS
Serves 12
2 x quantity Quick-mix Sponge
Cake baked in a 25 cm/10 inch
round cake tin
225 g/8 oz/⅔ quantity Butter Icing
60 ml/4 tbsp apricot jam, warmed
and sieved
450 g/1 lb marzipan
575 g/1¼ lb/1⅔ x quantity
Sugarpaste Icing
black and gold food colourings
chocolate money
jewel sweets

MATERIALS AND EQUIPMENT
30 cm/12 inch square cake board
greaseproof paper
fine paintbrush

1 ▲ Split the cake and fill with butter icing. Cut in half and sandwich the halves together. Stand upright diagonally across the cake board and use a template to cut shallow dips to create the crown of the hat. Brush with apricot jam.

2 Cut a strip of marzipan to lay over the top of the cake to neaten the joints. Cover the whole cake with a layer of marzipan. Colour 450 g/1 lb/1⅓ quantity sugarpaste icing black. On a work surface dusted with icing sugar, roll out the sugarpaste icing and use to cover the cake.

3 ▲ Roll out the remaining sugarpaste icing, cut 1 cm/½ inch strips and stick in place around the brim of the hat with a little water.

4 ▲ Mark the strip with a fork to look like braid. Using the template, mark the skull and crossbones on to the hat. Cut the shapes out of the white sugarpaste and stick in place with a little water. Paint the braid strip around the hat gold and arrange the chocolate money and sweets around the board.

*N*umber 6 Cake

Use the round tin as a guide to cut the square cake to fit neatly around the round cake.

INGREDIENTS
Serves 12
*2 x quantity Quick-mix Sponge
Cake baked in a 15 cm/6 inch
round and a 15 cm/6 in square
cake tin
115 g/4 oz/⅓ quantity Butter Icing
75 ml/5 tbsp apricot jam, warmed
and sieved
450 g/1 lb marzipan
500 g/1¼ lb/1½ x quantity
Sugarpaste Icing
yellow and green food colourings
115 g/4 oz/⅒ quantity Royal Icing*

MATERIALS AND EQUIPMENT
*25 x 35 cm/10 x 14 inch cake
board
7.5 cm/3 inch fluted cutter
greaseproof paper piping bags
No 1 writing nozzle
No 8 star nozzle
plastic train set with 6 candles*

3 ▲ Colour most of the sugarpaste icing pale yellow. On a work surface dusted with icing sugar, roll out and use to cover the cake. Mark a 7.5 cm/ 3 inch circle in the centre of the round cake. Colour the reserved sugarpaste icing pale green, roll out and cut out a fluted circle. Stick in place with water and leave to dry overnight.

4 Mark the track 2 cm/¼ inch wide (or the width of the train). Colour the royal icing yellow and pipe the track with a No 1 writing nozzle.

5 Using a star nozzle, pipe a border around the base and top of the cake. Pipe the name on the green circle and attach the train with royal icing.

1 ▲ Split the cake and fill with a little butter icing. Cut the square cake in half and cut a rounded end from one oblong to fit neatly around the round cake. Trim the cakes to the same depth and assemble on the cake board as shown, and brush with apricot jam.

2 Cover with a thin layer of marzipan. Smooth any joins and make sure surface is flat.

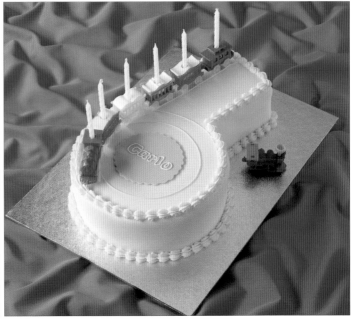

Clown Face

Children love this happy clown. His frilly collar is quite easy to make, but you do have to work quickly before the sugarpaste icing dries.

INGREDIENTS
Serves 10
*1 quantity Quick-mix Sponge Cake
baked in a 20 cm/8 inch round cake tin
115 g/4 oz/⅓ quantity Butter Icing
45 ml/3 tbsp apricot jam, warmed
and sieved
450 g/1 lb marzipan
450 g/1 lb/1⅓ x quantity
Sugarpaste Icing
115 g/4 oz/⅙ quantity Royal Icing
silver balls
pink, red, green, blue and black
food colourings*

MATERIALS AND EQUIPMENT
*25 cm/10 inch round cake board
greaseproof paper piping bag
No 8 star nozzle
frill cutter
cocktail stick
small round cutter
cotton wool
candles*

1 ▲ Split the cake and fill with butter icing. Place in the centre of the cake board and brush with apricot jam. Cover with a thin layer of marzipan. On a work surface lightly dusted with icing sugar, roll out about half the sugarpaste icing and use to cover the cake. Mark the position of the features on the top of the cake. Pipe stars around the base of the cake with royal icing, placing silver balls as you work, and leave to dry overnight.

2 ▲ Colour half the remaining sugarpaste icing pale pink, roll out and with the use of a template, cut out the shape of the face. Lay on the cake with the top of the head touching one edge of the cake.

3 ▲ Colour the remaining pink sugarpaste icing red, roll out and cut out the nose. Roll out some of the white sugarpaste icing, cut out the eyes and mouth and stick on the face with the nose, using a little water. Roll a little of the red sugarpaste icing into a thin sausage and cut to fit the mouth. Stick in place with a little water.

4 ▲ Roll out the rest of the red sugarpaste icing, cut in thin strands for hair and stick in place with water.

5 ▲ Colour most of the remaining sugarpaste icing pale green and roll out thinly. Cut out a frill using a frill cutter. Cut through one side and roll along the fluted edge with a cocktail stick to stretch it. Stick on the cake with a little water and arrange the frills. Repeat to make three layers of frills, holding them in place with cotton wool until dry.

6 Colour a little sugarpaste icing blue, roll and cut out eyes and stick in place with a little water. Colour the rest of the sugarpaste icing black, roll and cut out the eyes and eyebrows, then stick in position. Place the candles at the top of the head.

ite Cake

This cheerful kite has a bright and happy clown's face, and is a great favourite with children of all ages.

INGREDIENTS
Serves 10
1½ x quantity Quick-mix Sponge Cake baked in a 25 cm/10 inch square cake tin
225 g/8 oz/⅓ quantity Butter Icing
45 ml/3 tbsp apricot jam, warmed and sieved
450 g/1 lb marzipan
675 g/1½ lb/2 x quantity Sugarpaste Icing
yellow, red, green, blue and black food colourings
115 g/4 oz/⅙ quantity Royal Icing

MATERIALS AND EQUIPMENT
30 cm/12 inch square cake board
greaseproof paper
piping bag
No 8 star nozzle

1 ▲ Split the cake and fill with butter icing. Mark 15 cm/6 inches from one corner down two sides and using a ruler from this point cut down to the opposite corner on both sides to make the kite shape. Place diagonally on the cake board and brush with apricot jam. Cover with marzipan.

2 ▲ Colour 450 g/1 lb/1⅓ quantity sugarpaste icing pale yellow. Roll out and use to cover the cake. Using a template, mark the face on the kite. Divide the remaining sugarpaste icing into four and colour them red, green, blue and black. Wrap each separately in clear film. Using royal icing pipe a border of shells around the base of the cake.

3 ▲ Using a template, cut out the face, bow tie and buttons and stick in place with a little water.

4 ▲ To make the kite's tail, roll out each colour separately and cut two 4 x 1 cm/1½ x ½ inch lengths from the blue, red and green sugarpaste icing. Pinch them to shape into bows.

5 ▲ Roll the yellow sugarpaste icing into a long rope and lay it on the board in a wavy line from the narrow end of the kite and stick the bows in place with water. Roll balls of yellow sugarpaste icing, stick to the board with a little royal icing and press in the candles.

Fairy Castle

Allow plenty of time to cover the cake with royal icing as it is quite a delicate job. If the icing dries too quickly, dip the palette knife into hot water to help smooth the surface.

INGREDIENTS
Serves 10–12
1 quantity Quick-mix Sponge Cake baked in a 20 cm/8 inch round cake tin
115 g/4 oz/⅓ quantity Butter Icing
90 ml/6 tbsp apricot jam, warmed and sieved
675 g/1½ lb marzipan
8 mini Swiss rolls
675 g/1½ lb/1 quantity Royal Icing
pink, blue and green food colourings
jelly diamonds
4 ice cream cones
2 ice cream wafers
50 g/2 oz/1 cup desiccated coconut
marshmallows

MATERIALS AND EQUIPMENT
30 cm/12 inch square cake board
cocktail stick

2 ▲ Colour two-thirds of the royal icing pale pink and spread evenly over the cake. Cover the extra pieces of Swiss roll in icing and stick round the top of the cake. Using a cocktail stick, score the walls with brick patterns and stick jelly diamonds on the corner towers as windows. Cut the ice cream cones to fit the turrets and stick them in place. Leave to dry overnight.

4 ▲ Cut the wafers to shape for the gates, stick to the cake and cover with blue icing, marking planks with the back of a knife.

5 ▲ Put the coconut in a bowl and mix in a few drops of green colouring. Spread the board with the remaining royal icing and sprinkle over the coconut. Stick the marshmallows on the small turrets with royal icing.

1 ▲ Split the cake and fill with butter icing. Place in the centre of the board and brush with apricot jam. Cover with a layer of marzipan. Cover the Swiss rolls separately with marzipan. Stick four at regular intervals around the cake. Cut the remaining Swiss rolls in half.

3 ▲ Colour half the remaining royal icing pale blue and spread thinly over the cones, using a fork to pattern the icing.

Fire Engine

This jolly fire engine is simplicity itself as the decorations are mainly bought sweets and novelties.

INGREDIENTS
Serves 8–10
1½ x quantity Quick-mix Sponge
Cake baked in a 20 cm/8 inch
square cake tin
115 g/4 oz/⅓ quantity Butter Icing
45 ml/3 tbsp apricot jam, warmed
and sieved
350 g/12 oz marzipan
450 g/1 lb/1⅓ x quantity
Sugarpaste Icing
red, black and green
food colourings
liquorice wheels
115 g/4 oz/⅙ quantity Royal Icing
sweets
50 g/2 oz/1 cup desiccated coconut

MATERIALS AND EQUIPMENT
25 cm/10 inch round cake board
greaseproof paper piping bag
No 2 writing nozzle
2 silver bells
candles

1 ▲ Split the cake and fill with a little
butter icing. Cut in half and
sandwich one half on top of the other.
Place on the cake board.

2 ▲ Trim a thin wedge off the front
edge to make a sloping windscreen.
Brush the cake with apricot jam and
cover with marzipan. Colour 350 g/
12 oz/1 quantity sugarpaste icing bright
red. Roll out on a work surface dusted
with icing sugar and use to cover
the cake.

3 ▲ Mark the positions of the
windows, ladder and wheels.

4 ▲ To make the ladder, unwind
some liquorice wheels and cut the
liquorice into two strips and short
pieces for the rungs. Colour half the
royal icing black and stick the ladder
to the top of the cake with royal icing.
Roll out the remaining sugarpaste icing,
cut out and stick on the windows with
a little water.

5 ▲ Pipe round the windows in black
royal icing. Stick sweets in place for
headlights, lamps and wheels and stick
the silver bells on the roof. Put the
coconut in a bowl and mix in a few
drops of green food colouring. Spread a
little white royal icing over the cake
board and sprinkle with coconut. Stick
sweets to the board with royal icing
and press in the candles.

$\mathcal{B}$arley Twist

This delicately decorated cake would be a lovely centrepiece for a party to welcome a new baby. Sugarpaste twists will dry quickly so have the cake marked out in sections before you attempt to make the swags around the sides.

INGREDIENTS
Serves 8–10
1 quantity Quick-mix Sponge Cake baked in a 20 cm/8 inch round cake tin
115 g/4 oz/⅓ quantity Butter Icing
45 ml/3 tbsp apricot jam, warmed and sieved
450 g/1 lb marzipan
575 g/1¼ lb/1⅔ x quantity Sugarpaste Icing
yellow and blue food colourings
115 g/4 oz/¼ quantity Royal Icing
pink dusting powder

MATERIALS AND EQUIPMENT
25 cm/10 inch round cake board
greaseproof paper piping bag
No 1 writing nozzle
6 small blue bows

1 ▲ Split the cake and fill with butter icing. Place on the board and brush with apricot jam. Cover with a thin layer of marzipan. Colour 450 g/1 lb/1⅓ x quantity sugarpaste icing pale yellow. On a work surface dusted with icing sugar, roll it out and use to cover the cake, extending it over the board. Measure the circumference of the cake with a piece of string and cut a strip of paper of the same length and depth as the cake. Fold the paper into six sections, mark with a deep scallop and cut in the top edge. Use to mark the swags on the side of the cake with a sharp needle.

2 ▲ Colour 40 g/1½ oz/3 tbsp of the remaining sugarpaste pale blue and roll out thinly. Wet a paintbrush with water, remove excess on kitchen paper and brush lightly over the sugarpaste icing. Roll out thinly the same quantity of white sugarpaste icing, lay this on top and press together. Roll out together to a 20 cm/8 inch square.

3 ▲ Cut 5 mm/¼ inch strips, carefully twist each one, moisten the swag marks with water and stick in place.

$\mathscr{T}$ip

The powder tints should be mixed with a drop of vodka or gin as they evaporate more quickly than water and do not have a chance to dissolve the delicate icing.

4 ▲ Using a template, mark the knitting in the centre of the cake. Cut out the jersey from white sugarpaste icing and stick into place with a little water.

5 Roll a little white sugarpaste into a ball and colour another amount blue. Roll into two tapering 7.5 cm/3 inch long needles with a small ball for the end of each. Dry overnight.

6 ▲ Stick the needles and ball in position and, with royal icing and a No 1 writing nozzle, pipe knitting and stitches over the needles and a trail of wool over the ball. Pipe wool over the ball. Pipe a border around the base of the cake. Stick small bows around the edge of the cake with a little royal icing and carefully brush the knitting with powder tints.

Cloth Cake

This beautiful cake for an older child uses the elegant draping qualities of sugarpaste icing to make a covering that looks like an embroidered tablecloth.

INGREDIENTS
Serves 8–10
1 quantity Quick-mix Sponge Cake baked in a 20 cm/8 inch round cake tin
115 g/4 oz/¹⁄₃ quantity Butter Icing
60 ml/3 tbsp apricot jam, warmed and sieved
450 g/1 lb marzipan
675 g/1¹⁄₂ lb/2 x quantity Sugarpaste Icing
red food colouring
115 g/4 oz/¹⁄₄ quantity Royal Icing

MATERIALS AND EQUIPMENT
25 cm/10 inch round cake board
decorative teaspoon
8 wooden cocktail sticks
knitting needle or skewer
greaseproof paper piping bags
No 0 writing nozzle
No 2 writing nozzle
No 1 writing nozzle
8 small red bows

1 Split the cake and fill with butter icing. Place on the board and brush with apricot jam. Cover with a layer of marzipan. Colour two-thirds of the sugarpaste icing red. On a work surface dusted with icing sugar, roll the red sugarpaste out and use to cover the cake, extending it over the board. Reserve a little for the base of the cake. Brush the lower edge of the cake with a thin band of water.

2 ▲ Roll the reserved red sugarpaste into a thin rope long enough to go round the cake. Lay it neatly around the base of the cake and cut off the excess. Mark with the decorative handle of a spoon. Leave to dry overnight.

3 ▲ Roll out the white sugarpaste icing to a 25 cm/10 inch circle, place over the cake and quickly form drapes over wooden cocktail sticks at eight equal positions around the cake.

4 Mark a 10 cm/4 inch circle in the centre of the cake. Make a template of the small flower design and transfer to the cake with a needle. Press a fine knitting needle or skewer into the sugarpaste icing to make the flowers. The red colour should show through – do not press quite so deeply for the stems and leaves.

5 ▲ Mark the child's name in the centre. Colour a little royal icing with red food colouring and pipe with a No 0 writing nozzle.

6 ▲ Stick on the bows with a dab of royal icing. With a No 2 writing nozzle and white royal icing, pipe around the circle in the centre. With a No 1 writing nozzle, pipe small dots around the edge of the cloth to finish.

$\mathcal{N}$umber 7 Cake

Any combination of colours works well for this marbled cake.

INGREDIENTS
Serves 8–10
1½ x quantity Quick-Mix Sponge
Cake mix
1 quantity orange-flavour Butter
Icing
4 tbsp apricot jam, warmed and
sieved
675 g/1½ lb/2 x quantity
Sugarpaste Icing
green and blue food colourings

MATERIALS AND EQUIPMENT
23 x 30 cm/9 x 12 inch roasting tin
25 x 33 cm/10 x 13 inch cake board
small No 7 cutter

2 ▲ Working with the cake flat side up, lightly mark out the shape of the number seven on the cake. Cut through the cake, starting at the bottom end and working up.

3 ▲ Slice through the cake horizontally, then carefully lift off the top layer and place on the work surface. Place the bottom layer of cake on the cake board and spread with the butter icing. Reassemble the cake.

$\mathcal{T}$ip

If you feel unsure about shaping the number seven cake freehand, you can purchase or hire shaped cake tins from specialist cake decorating shops.

1 Preheat the oven to 180°C/350°F/ Gas 4. Grease the roasting tin, line the base and sides with greaseproof paper and grease the paper. Spoon the cake mixture into the prepared tin and smooth the surface. Bake in the centre of the oven for 45–50 minutes, or until a skewer inserted into the centre of the cake comes out clean. Leave the cake in the tin for about 5 minutes, then turn out on to a wire rack, peel off the lining paper and leave to cool completely.

4 Brush the cake evenly with apricot jam. Divide the sugarpaste icing into three equal portions. Leave one portion white, colour one blue and the last green. Cut off about 50 g/2 oz from each of the blue and green icings, wrap each separately in clear film and set aside. Marble the remaining blue and green with the white portion of sugarpaste icing.

5 ▲ Roll out the marbled icing on a work surface lightly dusted with icing sugar to a rectangle 35 × 28 cm/ 14 × 11 inches and use to cover the number seven. Smooth the icing with a cake smoother or with your hands.

6 ▲ Use the cutter to cut random shapes out of the covered cake. Press the cutter into the icing carefully, but firmly. Remove the cutter and the shape should be wedged in the cutter. Poke out the shape with a cocktail stick and discard. This stage needs to be done immediately after the cake has been covered, or the sugarpaste icing will start drying out.

7 ▲ Roll out the reserved blue and green coloured sugarpaste icing and use the cutter to stamp out a combination of blue and green shapes. Use these to replace the stamped out shapes from the cake, pressing them in gently to fill the holes.

Paddling Pool

*This fun cake will need at least a day's preparation before the party; the bather,
boat and duck are modelled from marzipan and sugarpaste and left to dry overnight before
arranging them in partly dried royal icing.*

INGREDIENTS
Serves 8–10
*1 quantity Quick-mix Sponge Cake
baked in a deep 15 cm/6 inch round
cake tin
50 g/2 oz/¼ quantity Butter Icing
45 ml/3 tbsp apricot jam, warmed
and sieved
350 g/12 oz marzipan
450 g/1 lb/1⅓ x quantity
Sugarpaste Icing
blue, red, yellow, green and brown
food colourings
115 g/4 oz/¼ quantity Royal Icing*

MATERIALS AND EQUIPMENT
*20 cm/8 inch round cake board
drinking straw
sheet of rice paper
greaseproof paper piping bag
basket weave nozzle
No 1 writing nozzle*

1 Split the cake and fill with a little butter icing. Place in the centre of the cake board and brush with apricot glaze. Cover with a layer of marzipan. Roll out about three-quarters of the sugarpaste icing on a work surface dusted with icing sugar and use to cover the cake. Divide the remaining sugarpaste icing into four pieces and colour them blue, red, yellow and green. Shape a small duck from the yellow, a 4 cm/1½ inch rubber ring from the red and a boat from the green. Roll the remains of each colour into two sausages long enough to go half way round the cake. Stick to the sides of the cake with a little water, flattening slightly and smoothing the joins so the stripes come to the top of the cake.

2 ▲ Colour 50 g/2 oz marzipan flesh colour and shape into a small child with a head, half a body, arms and feet. Place in the rubber ring and leave to dry overnight. Cut a mast for the boat from a drinking straw and thread on a square rice-paper sail.

3 ▲ Colour two-thirds of the royal icing blue and spread on top of the cake to resemble water, placing the child, duck and boat in the water. Colour a little royal icing brown and pipe on the child's hair using a basket weave pipe. Pipe the eyes and mouth.

Toy Car

This little car can be made for any age. You could add a personalized number plate with the child's name and age to the back of the car.

INGREDIENTS
Serves 8–10
1 quantity Quick-mix Sponge Cake baked in a 20 cm/8 inch round cake tin
115 g/4 oz/⅓ quantity Butter Icing
45 ml/3 tbsp apricot jam, warmed and sieved
450 g/1 lb marzipan
575 g/1¼ lb/1⅔ x quantity Sugarpaste Icing
red, yellow and black food colourings
115 g/4 oz/⅙ quantity Royal Icing
sweets

MATERIALS AND EQUIPMENT
25 cm/10 inch round cake board
4 cm/1½ inch plain round cutter
2 cm/¾ inch plain round cutter
greaseproof paper piping bag
No 1 writing nozzle
candles

2 ▲ Colour a small piece of sugarpaste icing red and the rest yellow. Roll out the yellow icing on a work surface dusted with icing sugar and use to cover the cake. Mark the doors and windows on to the car with a sharp skewer.

3 ▲ Roll out the red sugarpaste icing and cut out four 4 cm/1½ inch wheels with a cutter. Stick in place with water. Mark the centre of each wheel with a smaller cutter. Colour the royal icing black and pipe around the doors and windows. Stick on sweets for headlights with a little royal icing. Stick the candles into sweets with royal icing.

1 ▲ Split the cake and fill with a little butter icing. Cut in half and sandwich the halves upright together. With a sharp serrated knife, cut a shallow dip to create the windscreen and to shape the bonnet. Place on the cake board and brush with apricot jam. Cut a strip of marzipan to cover the top of the cake to level the joins. Then cover the whole cake with an even layer of marzipan.

Nurse's Set

This is a simple cake to make. Any toy medical equipment is suitable to use, but make sure it doesn't get confused with the edible bits!

INGREDIENTS
Serves 12–15
1½ x quantity chocolate-flavour Quick-Mix Sponge Cake mix
8 tbsp apricot jam, warmed and sieved
675 g/1½ lb/2 x quantity Sugarpaste Icing
pink and red food colourings

MATERIALS AND EQUIPMENT
35 x 20 cm/14 x 8 inch roasting tin
25 cm/10 inch square cake board
selection of toy medical equipment

1 Preheat the oven to 180°C/350°F/ Gas 4. Grease the roasting tin, line the base and sides with greaseproof paper and grease the paper. Spoon in the cake mixture and smooth the surface. Bake in the centre of the oven for 45–50 minutes or until a skewer inserted into the centre of the cake comes out clean. Leave the cake in the tin for about 5 minutes, then turn out on to a wire rack, peel off the lining paper and leave to cool completely.

2 ▲ Place the cake, dome side down, and cut in half widthways.

3 ▲ Turn one half of the cake dome side up, then use a small, sharp knife to indent a border about 1 cm/½ inch in from the edge and about the same measurement deep, around the three uncut edges. Cut out the centre in strips, keeping the edges neat. Brush the tops and sides of both halves of the cake with the apricot jam.

4 Cut off about 150 g/5 oz of the sugarpaste icing and colour it deep pink. Cut off about 15 g/½ oz from this and shape into a small handle for the box. Carefully wrap in clear film and set aside. Lightly dust the work surface with icing sugar and roll out the remaining pink icing and use to cover the cake board. Trim the edges. Cut off about 15 g/½ oz from the remaining white icing and colour it red. Cover with clear film and set aside. Colour the remaining icing light pink and divide into two portions, one slightly bigger than the other.

5 Roll out the slightly bigger portion of light pink icing and use to cover the base of the nurse's box, gently easing it into the hollow and along the edges. Trim the edges, then position the covered cake on the cake board.

6 ▲ Roll out the other portion of light pink icing and use to cover the lid of the box, using your hands to ease it over the edges. Trim the edges. Place on top of the other cake, back a little and slightly turned to an angle.

7 ▲ Stick the handle on to the bottom section of the box, using a little water. Roll out the red icing and cut out a small cross. Use a little water to stick the cross on the lid of the box. Carefully insert a few toy items into the box, allowing them to hang over the edges a little. Arrange any other items of toy medical equipment around the board and cake when it is positioned on the table.

$\mathcal{M}$ermaid Cake

Pretty, elegant and chocolatey! Every little girl's dream.

INGREDIENTS
Serves 6–8
1 quantity chocolate-flavour Quick-
Mix Sponge Cake mix
450 g/1 lb plain chocolate
25 g/1 oz/3 cups unflavoured
popcorn
450 g/1 lb/1⅓ x quantity Sugarpaste
Icing
lilac and pink food colouring
3 tbsp apricot jam, warmed and
sieved
1 egg white, lightly beaten
demerara sugar

MATERIALS AND EQUIPMENT
900 g/2 lb loaf tin
30 x 15 cm/12 x 6 inch cake board
doll, similar in dimensions to a
'Barbie' or 'Sindy' doll
small crescent-shaped cutter
small fluted round cutter
15 cm/6 inch piece of thin lilac
ribbon

1 ▲ Preheat the oven to 180°C/350°F/
Gas 4. Grease the tin, line the base
and sides with greaseproof paper and
grease the paper. Spoon the cake
mixture into the prepared tin and
smooth the surface. Bake in the centre
of the oven for 35–40 minutes, or until
a skewer inserted into the centre of the
cake comes out clean. Leave the cake in
the tin for about 5 minutes, then turn
out on to a wire rack, peel off the lining
paper and leave to cool.

2 ▲ Turn the cake dome side up and
place on the cake board. Melt the
chocolate in a bowl placed over hot
water. Add the popcorn and stir until
evenly coated. Spoon the popcorn
around the sides of the cake and on the
cake board. Spread any remaining
melted chocolate over the top of the
cake until evenly covered. Set aside at
room temperature.

3 Cut off about one-quarter of the
sugarpaste icing. Colour the larger
piece lilac and the smaller piece pink.
Cut off about one-third of the lilac
icing, wrap this and the pink icing
separately in clear film and set aside.

4 ▲ On a work surface lightly dusted
with icing sugar, roll out the larger
portion of lilac sugarpaste icing to an
oblong shape wide enough to wrap
around the doll's legs and about 5 cm/
2 inches longer. Brush the doll from the
waist down with the apricot jam, then
wrap her in the rolled out sugarpaste
icing, lightly pinching and squeezing
it around her legs to make it stick.
Working downwards towards her feet,
pinch the end of the tail to form a fin
shape, curling the ends slightly.

5 ▲ Position the mermaid on the
cake, moving her slightly until she
feels secure and then pressing down
firmly. Roll out the reserved lilac and
pink sugarpaste icing and use the
crescent-shaped cutter to stamp out the
scales. Cover the scales and the reserved
trimmings with clear film to prevent
them drying out. Starting at the fin end
of the tail, brush the scales with a tiny
amount of egg white and stick on to the
tail, overlapping all the time, until the
tail is completely covered.

6 Re-roll the reserved icing trimmings
and use the small fluted cutter to
stamp out a shell-shaped bra top for the
mermaid. Make indentations on the top
with the back of a knife, then stick in
place with a little extra apricot jam. Use
the ribbon to tie up the mermaid's hair.

7 Position the cake on the serving
table or large board, then scatter the
demerara sugar around the base of the
cake for the sand and add a few real
shells, if you like. Remove the doll
before serving the cake.

$\mathcal{T}$ip

For an even more chocolatey version of this cake, cut the sponge
into three horizontally and use 1
quantity chocolate-flavour Butter
Icing to spread between the layers.
Reassemble the cake and then cover
with chocolate popcorn.

Helicopter Cake

Perfect for a party of boys or girls who are partial to helicopters. The cake involves a little creative use of non-edible items which must be removed before eating.

INGREDIENTS
Serves 6–8
1 quantity Quick-Mix Sponge Cake mix
2 fan wafers
6–8 tbsp apricot jam, warmed and sieved
450 g/12 oz/1 quantity Sugarpaste Icing
red, blue and black food colourings small round sweet
¼ quantity Butter Icing
2 sweets, for the headlights
2 x 15 cm/6 inch pieces of flat liquorice
4 x 2.5 cm/1 inch pieces of liquorice sticks
50 g/2 oz/1 cup toasted desiccated coconut

MATERIALS AND EQUIPMENT
900 g/2 lb loaf tin
small round cutter
2 wooden skewers
wood glue
small wooden block, to raise helicopter
18 cm/7 inch square cake board
13 cm/5 inch piece of white ribbon
piping bag fitted with a small plain nozzle

1 Preheat the oven to 180°C/350°F/ Gas 4. Grease the tin, line with greaseproof paper and grease the paper. Spoon the cake mixture into the prepared tin and smooth the surface. Bake in the centre of the oven for 35– 40 minutes, or until a skewer inserted into the centre of the cake comes out clean. Turn out on to a wire rack, peel off the lining paper and leave to cool.

2 ▲ To shape the cake, stand it flat side down and use a large, sharp knife to cut it into the shape of a teardrop. Trim the sides from top to bottom so that the top is wider than the bottom. Turn the cake on its side, and cut a wedge shape out of the back part.

3 ▲ Invert the cake so the flat side is uppermost. Use the cutter to stamp out a hole for the cockpit, indenting about 2.5 cm/1 inch. Remove the round piece and reserve.

4 Cut a thin slice from each of the wafers, reserve one for the tail fin and discard the other slice. Cut each wafer in half lengthways. Measure the long side of one of the wafers and then cut the wooden skewers double that length. Glue the skewers together in the centre to form a cross and set aside.

5 Remove a small piece of sugarpaste icing. Take another piece of icing about the size of an egg and colour it deep blue. Wrap these pieces in clear film and set aside.

6 Colour the remaining sugarpaste icing pale blue. Remove an egg-sized piece, wrap in clear film and set aside. Brush the cake with apricot jam. Roll out the pale blue sugarpaste on a work surface lightly dusted with icing sugar and use to cover the helicopter. Position the covered cake on the small block of wood on the cake board.

7 To make the propeller support, brush the reserved piece of round cake cut out for the pilot's cockpit with apricot jam. Roll out the reserved pale blue sugarpaste icing and cover the round cake. Reserve the trimmings. Position the propeller support on the helicopter, halfway between the cockpit and the tail, sticking it in place with a spot of jam. Place the crossed skewers on top of the propeller support and secure them in place with a little of the pale blue icing. Place the wafers over the skewers, securing them underneath with more icing. Place the small round sweet on top.

8 ▲ To make the pilot, shape the dark blue sugarpaste icing into a small head and body to fit into the cockpit. Colour a little of the reserved white icing red for the nose and mouth and use white icing for the buttons. Stick the details in place with a little water. Shape some of the reserved pale blue icing into the pilot's hat and place on his head, securing with a little water if necessary. Sit the pilot in his seat and tie the ribbon scarf around his neck.

9 Colour the butter icing black and fill the piping bag. First pipe in the pilot's eyes, then pipe the zigzag and straight borders around the helicopter. Stick the headlight sweets in position with a little of the remaining butter icing and stick the tail fin on in the same way. To make the landing feet, smooth out the flat pieces of liquorice and fold in half lengthways. Position on the cake board, wedged in with the liquorice sticks. Scatter the desiccated coconut around the cake board.

oll's House

Little children love this cake. You can pipe their age on the door and the same number of candles can be added to the cake if you wish.

INGREDIENTS
Serves 10–12
2 x quantity Quick-mix Sponge
Cake baked in a 25 cm/10 inch
square cake tin
225 g/8 oz/²/₃ quantity Butter Icing
60 ml/4 tbsp apricot jam, warmed
and sieved
450 g/1 lb marzipan
450 g/1 lb/1¹/₃ x quantity
Sugarpaste Icing
red, yellow, blue, black, green and
gold food colourings
115 g/4 oz/¹/₄ quantity Royal Icing

MATERIALS AND EQUIPMENT
30 cm/12 inch square cake board
paintbrush
greaseproof paper piping bag
No 2 writing nozzle
flower decorations

1 ▲ Split the cake and fill with butter icing. Cut 6 cm/2½ inch triangles off two corners then use these pieces to make a chimney. Shape the top of the roof. Place on the cake board and brush with apricot jam. Cover with a layer of marzipan.

2 ▲ On a work surface dusted with icing sugar, roll out three-quarters of the sugarpaste icing and use to cover the house. Using a pastry wheel, mark the roof to look like thatch. Mark the chimney with the back of a knife to look like bricks.

3 ▲ Paint the chimney red and the roof yellow.

4 ▲ Mark the door 7.5 x 12 cm/3 x 4½ inches and the windows 6 cm/ 2½ inches square. Colour 25 g/1 oz/ 2 tbsp of sugarpaste icing with red food colouring, cut out and stick on the door with a little water. Colour a small piece blue, cut out and stick on for the top fanlight. Paint on the curtains with blue food colouring. Colour half the royal icing black and pipe the window frames and panes, around the door and the fanlight.

5 ▲ Colour the remaining royal icing green. Pipe the flower stems under the windows and the climber up the wall and on to the roof. Stick the flowers in place with a little icing and pipe green flower centres. Pipe the knocker, the handle and the age of the child on the door. Leave to dry for 1 hour. Paint the knocker, handle and number with gold food colouring.

Fairy Cake

This is one of the more advanced cakes and requires a lot of skill and patience. Allow yourself plenty of time if you are attempting the techniques for the first time.

INGREDIENTS
Serves 8–10
1 quantity Quick-mix Sponge Cake baked in a 20 cm/8 inch round cake tin
115 g/4 oz/⅓ quantity Butter Icing
45 ml/3 tbsp apricot jam, warmed and sieved
450 g/1 lb marzipan
450 g/1 lb/1⅓ x quantity Sugarpaste Icing
blue, pink, yellow and gold food colourings
115 g/4 oz/⅛ quantity Royal Icing
silver balls

MATERIALS AND EQUIPMENT
25 cm/10 inch round cake board
greaseproof paper piping bags
No 1 writing nozzle
fine paintbrush
twinkle pink sparkle lustre powder
frill cutter
small round cutter
wooden cocktail stick
cotton wool
No 7 star nozzle
silver ribbon

1 Split the cake and fill with butter icing. Place on the board and brush with apricot jam. Cover with a thin layer of marzipan. Colour most of the sugarpaste icing pale blue and roll out on a surface dusted with icing sugar to cover the cake. Leave to dry overnight. Using a template, carefully mark the position of the fairy on to the cake. As royal icing dries quickly, work only on about 2.5 cm/1 inch sections of the fairy's wings at a time. Fill a piping bag with a No 1 writing nozzle with white royal icing and carefully pipe over the outline of each wing section.

2 ▲ Pipe a second line just inside that and with a damp paintbrush, brush long strokes from the edges towards the centre, leaving more icing at the edges and fading away to a thin film near the base of the wings. Leave to dry for 1 hour. Brush with dry lustre powder (not dissolved in spirit).

3 ▲ Colour a little sugarpaste icing flesh colour, roll and cut out the body. Lay carefully in position. Dampen a paintbrush, remove the excess water on kitchen paper and carefully brush under the arms, legs and head to stick. Round off any sharp edges by rubbing gently with a finger. Cut out the bodice and shoes from white sugarpaste and stick in place. Cut out a wand and star and leave to dry.

4 Work quickly to make the tutu, as thin sugarpaste dries quickly and will crack easily. Each frill must be made separately. Roll out a small piece of sugarpaste to 3 mm/⅛ inch thick and cut out a fluted circle with a small plain inner circle. (The depth of the frill will be governed by the size of the central hole; the smaller the central hole, the wider the frill.)

5 ▲ Cut into quarters and with a wooden cocktail stick, roll along the fluted edge to stretch it and give fullness.

6 Attach the frills to the waist with a little water. Repeat with the other layers, tucking the sides under neatly. Use a wooden cocktail stick to arrange the frills and small pieces of cotton wool to hold the folds of the skirt in place until dry. Leave to dry overnight. Brush a little lustre powder over the edge of the tutu. Paint on the hair and face, stick on the wand and star and paint the star gold. Pipe a border of royal icing round the edge of the board with a star nozzle and place a silver ball on each point. Leave to dry. Colour a little royal icing yellow and pipe over the hair. Paint with a touch of gold colouring.

Ballerina Cake

This cake shows how you can adapt the design of the Fairy Cake to make a ballerina. The delicate pink flowers look especially pretty against the white icing background.

INGREDIENTS
Serves 8–10
*1 quantity Quick-mix Sponge Cake
baked in a 20 cm/8 inch round
cake tin
115 g/4 oz/⅓ quantity Butter Icing
45 ml/3 tbsp apricot jam, warmed
and sieved
450 g/1 lb marzipan
450 g/1 lb/1⅓ x quantity
Sugarpaste Icing
pink, yellow, green and
blue food colourings
115 g/4 oz/⅙ quantity Royal Icing*

MATERIALS AND EQUIPMENT
*25 cm/10 inch round cake board
plunger blossom cutters
frill cutter
small round cutter
wooden cocktail stick
cotton wool
greaseproof paper piping bag
No 1 writing nozzle
fine paintbrush
No 7 shell nozzle
ribbon*

1 Split the cake and fill with butter icing. Place on the board and brush with apricot jam. Cover with a layer of marzipan. On a work surface dusted with icing sugar, roll out three-quarters of the sugarpaste icing and use to cover the cake. Leave to dry overnight. Divide the remaining sugarpaste icing into three: colour one flesh tones and the other two contrasting pinks for the tutu and flowers. Roll out each colour separately and cut out 12 flowers and 3 tiny flowers from the paler pink sugarpaste icing for the headdress. Leave aside to dry.

2 ▲ Make a template for the ballerina and carefully mark her position on the cake. Cut out the body from flesh coloured sugarpaste icing and stick into position with a little water. Round off the edges by rubbing gently with a finger. Cut out a bodice from the darker pink sugarpaste icing and stick in place.

3 To make the tutu, work quickly as the thin sugarpaste dries quickly and will crack. Roll out the darker pink sugarpaste icing to 3 mm/⅛ inch thick and cut out a fluted circle with a small plain inner circle.

4 ▲ Cut the circle into quarters and, with a wooden cocktail stick, roll along the fluted edge to stretch it and give fullness.

5 ▲ Attach the frills to the waist with a little water. Repeat with two more layers, using a cocktail stick to shape the frills and cotton wool to hold them in place until dry. For the final layer, use the paler pink and cover with a short dark frill, as the bodice extension. Leave to dry overnight.

6 ▲ Attach flowers to make a hoop. Colour a little royal icing green and pipe tiny leaves in between. Paint on the face and hair. Colour a little royal icing yellow and pipe over the hair. Stick three tiny flowers in place around the head. Cut pale pink sugarpaste shoes and stick in place with water, and paint ribbons. Colour a little royal icing dark pink and pipe the flower centres on the hoop and headdress. Pipe white royal icing around the base of the cake with the shell nozzle and tie round the ribbon.

Royal Crown

The most difficult part of this cake is supporting the covered ice cream wafers with cocktail sticks while they dry in place. Plenty of royal icing can be used to smooth the joins and help to support the pieces.

INGREDIENTS
Serves 12–14
2 x quantity Quick-mix Sponge
Cake baked in a 20 cm/8 inch
round cake tin and a 15 cm/6 inch
round cake tin
175 g/6 oz/½ quantity Butter Icing
75 ml/5 tbsp apricot jam, warmed
and sieved
450 g/1 lb marzipan
575 g/1¼ lb/1⅔ x quantity
Sugarpaste Icing
red food colouring
450 g/1 lb/⅓ quantity Royal Icing
small black jelly sweets
4 ice cream fan wafers
silver balls
jewel sweets

MATERIALS AND EQUIPMENT
30 cm/12 inch square cake board
wooden cocktail sticks

1 ▲ Split the cakes and fill with a little butter icing. Sandwich one on top of the other and place on the board. Shape the top cake into a dome. Brush with apricot jam and cover with a layer of marzipan. On a work surface dusted with icing sugar, roll out three-quarters of the sugarpaste icing and use to cover the cake.

2 ▲ Colour the remaining sugarpaste icing red and use to cover the dome of the cake. Trim away the excess with a knife.

3 ▲ Spoon rough mounds of royal icing around the base of the cake and stick a black jelly sweet on each mound.

4 ▲ Cut the ice cream wafers in half with a sharp knife.

5 ▲ Spread both sides of the wafers with royal icing and stick to the cake, smoothing the icing level with the sides of the cake. Use cocktail sticks to support until dry. Put a silver ball on top of each point and jewel sweets around the sides of the crown, sticking in place with a little royal icing.

Monsters on the Moon

A great cake for little monsters!
This cake is best eaten on the day of making.

INGREDIENTS
Serves 12–15
1 quantity Quick-Mix Sponge
Cake mix
115 g/4 oz/¹⁄3 quantity Sugarpaste
Icing
edible silver glitter powder
(optional)

For the Icing
375 g/12 oz/1¾ cups plus 2 tbsp
caster sugar
2 size 3 egg whites
4 tbsp water

MATERIALS AND EQUIPMENT
ovenproof wok
various sizes of plain round cutters
30 cm/12 inch round cake board
several small monster toys

1 ▲ Preheat the oven to 180°C/350°F/ Gas 4. Grease the wok, line the base with greaseproof paper and grease the paper. Spoon in the cake mixture and smooth the surface. Bake in the centre of the oven for 35–40 minutes or until a skewer inserted into the centre of the cake comes out clean. Leave the cake in the wok for about 5 minutes, then turn out on to a wire rack, peel off the lining paper and leave to cool completely.

2 ▲ With the cake dome side up, use the round cutters to cut out craters. Press in a cutter about 2.5 cm/1 inch deep, then remove and use a knife to cut out the cake to make a crater.

3 ▲ Pull off small pieces of the sugarpaste icing and press them into uneven strips which can be moulded around the edges of the craters. Make one of the craters especially deep by adding an extra-wide sugarpaste strip to make the edges higher.

4 Place the cake on the cake board. To make the icing, place all the ingredients in a heatproof bowl, then sit the bowl over a saucepan of simmering water. Beat until thick and peaky. Spoon the icing over the cake, swirling it into the craters and peaking it unevenly. Sprinkle over the silver glitter powder, if using, then position the monsters on the cake.

Tip

To cover the cake board, roll out 450 g/1 lb of black sugarpaste icing. Trim the edges. Using various sizes of star-shaped cutters, stamp out stars from the black icing. Roll out 285 g/8 oz of yellow marzipan thinly and use the star-shaped cutters to stamp out replacement stars. Dust with a little extra silver powder.

Rosette Cake

This lovely cake is actually very quick to decorate. If the icing becomes too soft, put it in the fridge to firm up. If you make a mistake, then you can always try again until you get a good finish.

INGREDIENTS
Serves 10
1½ x quantity Quick-mix Sponge
Cake baked in a 20 cm/8 inch
square cake tin
350 g/12 oz/1 quantity Butter Icing
45 ml/3 tbsp apricot jam, warmed
and sieved
mulberry red food colouring
crystallized violets

MATERIALS AND EQUIPMENT
25 cm/10 inch square cake board
cake comb
piping bag
No 8 star nozzle
candles

2 ▲ Using the cake comb, hold it against the cake and move it from side to side across the top to create the impression of waves.

3 ▲ Put the rest of the butter icing into a piping bag fitted with a star nozzle. Mark a 15 cm/6 inch circle on the top of the cake and pipe stars around it and around the base of the cake. Place the candles and flowers in the corners.

1 ▲ Split the cake and fill with a little butter icing. Place in the centre of the cake board and brush with apricot jam. Colour the remaining butter icing dark pink. Spread the top and sides with butter icing. Hold the comb against the side of the cake, resting the flat edge on the board and draw along to give straight ridges down each side.

Index

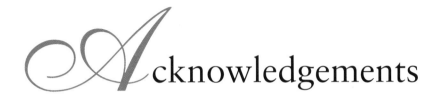

Acknowledgements

The publisher and authors would like to thank the following for supplying props and equipment for photography: Scenics Cakes Boards, Colours Direct, the Cloth Store, Cake Fayre, Jean Ainger, Braun and Kenwood. Thanks also to Stork Cookery Service for the Rich Fruit Cake chart, and Jackie Mason, Mavis Giles and Teresa Goldfinch for their help.